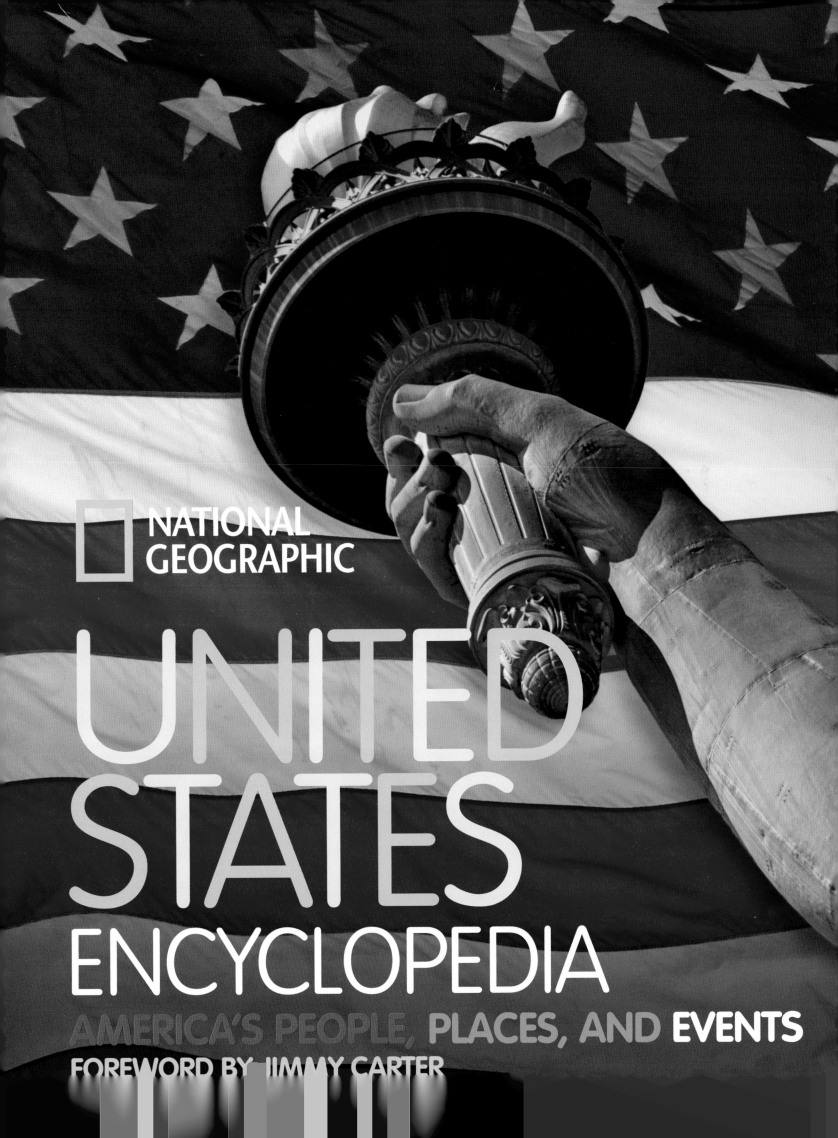

NATIONAL
GEOGRAPHIC

UNITED STATES

ENCYCLOPEDIA

AMERICA'S PEOPLE, PLACES, AND EVENTS

FOREWORD BY JIMMY CARTER

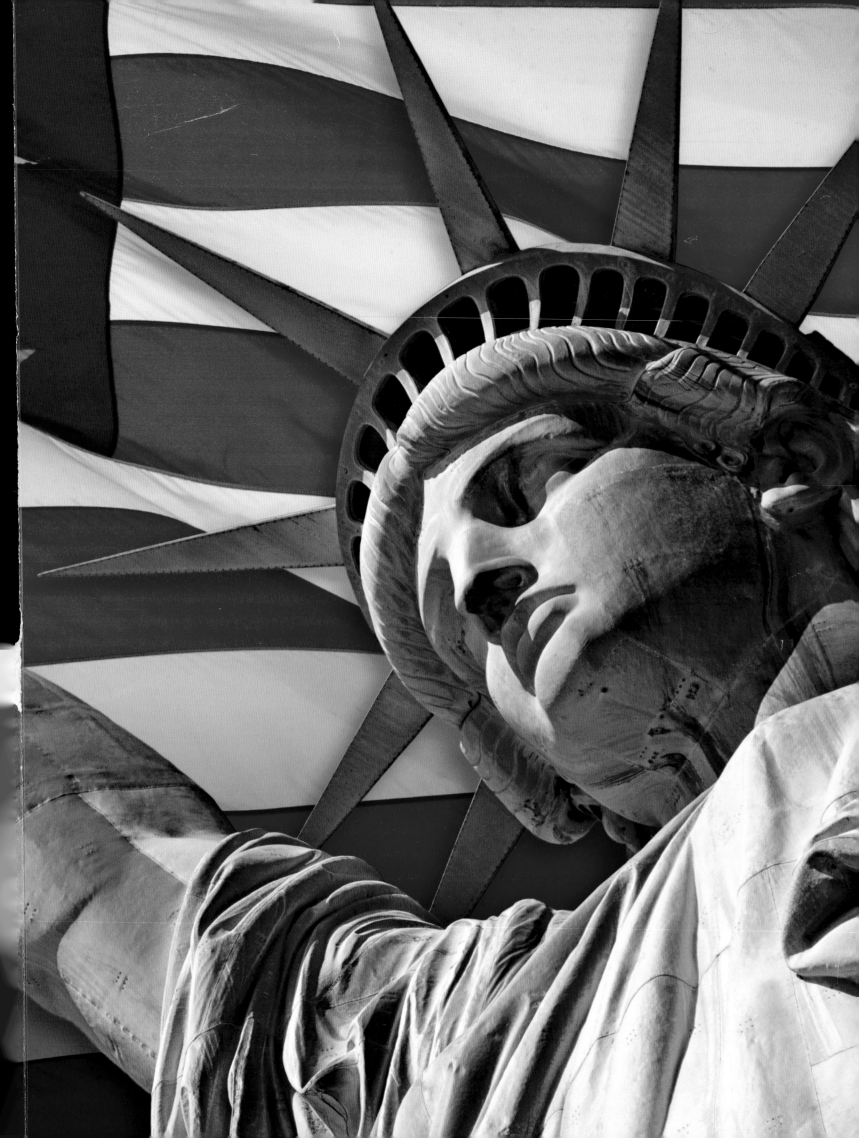

CONTENTS

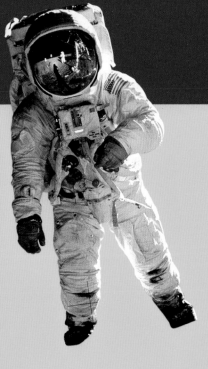

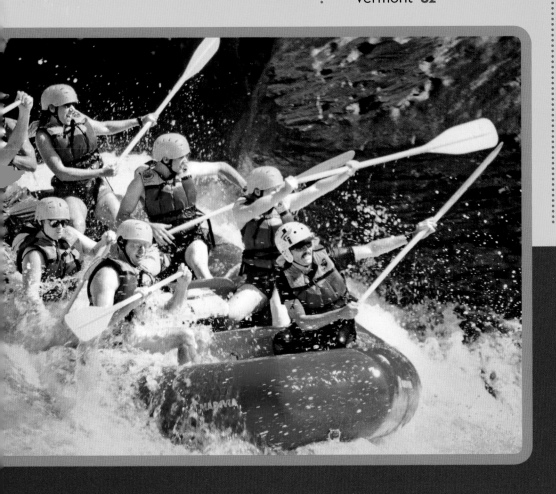

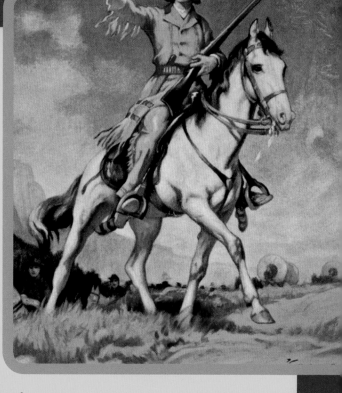

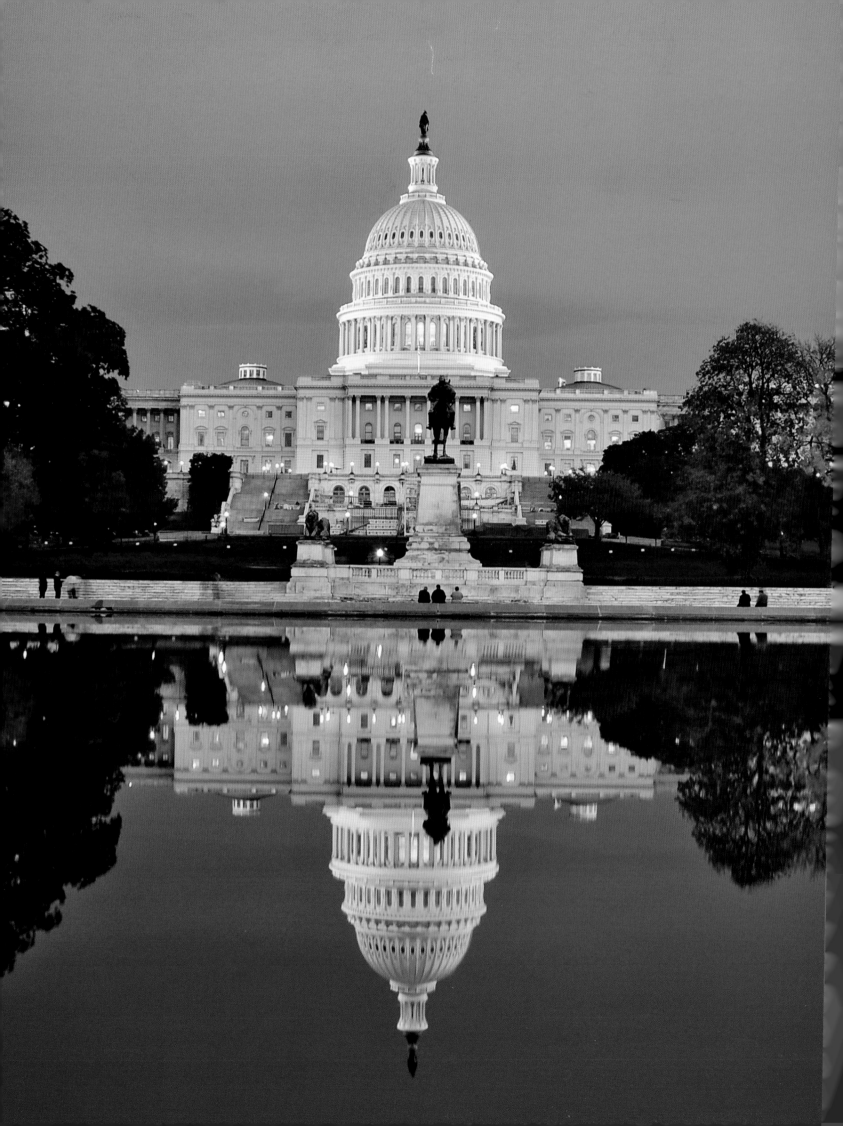

FOREWORD

BY JIMMY CARTER

am sure that every American can name a favorite place that brings spiritual comfort, a fresh outlook, peaceful and refreshing repose. I have found many such sanctuaries throughout our 50 states, in many different corners of this great country.

Growing up on a farm in southwest Georgia, I first fell in love with this part of America, and have many boyhood memories, such as hunting for arrowheads as I worked in the fields and fishing with a cane pole in a wooded creek near our home, eyes always open for snakes and an occasional otter. Much later, I recall lying on my back on the lawn of the Governor's Mansion in Atlanta watching a horde of monarch butterflies as they migrated south.

There were times during my presidency when our family would climb to the roof of the White House to watch the Canada geese fly overhead, their faint, haunting calls just audible above the noise of the capital city at night. I have fond memories with my wife, Rosalynn, and our children of quiet moments at Camp David on a mountaintop in northern Maryland, cross-country skiing on pristine trails, and heading to Pennsylvania streams to cast for trout.

On the wild Alaska lands I was privileged to help protect, we witnessed timber wolves, musk oxen, polar bears, and a herd of caribou—100,000 strong—migrating across the land in stately grandeur.

But America's greatness comes not just from a collection of beloved corners like these but from its diverse and vibrant whole. The richness of this land in a myriad of special places has shaped the character of our people and our history. We citizens love our country, and it is our duty and our pleasure to know it well—from "amber waves of grain" to "alabaster cities."

This book puts geographic knowledge about our country at your fingertips. Enjoy your special places, and then discover new ones. From this process, you will know even better the beauty that is America.

Jimmy Carter

Jimmy Carter is the 39th president of the United States, a recipient of the Nobel Peace Prize, and the Co-Chair, along with his wife, Rosalynn, of the Carter Center in Atlanta, Georgia.

Cape Flattery

Seattle
Olympia ⊛ Tacoma
Spokane
W A S H I N G T O N
Yakima
Columbia
Lewiston

Portland
Salem ⊛
Eugene
O R E G O N

Medford
Klamath Falls

Eureka
Redding

Sacramento ⊛
San Francisco
Oakland
San Jose
Salinas
Fresno
Bakersfield

Point Conception

Los Angeles
Long Beach
Riverside

San Diego
Yuma

Columbia

C A S C A D E   R A N G E

I D A H O
Boise
Idaho Falls
Pocatello
Snake

Great Falls
M O N T A N A
Helena ⊛
Butte
Billings
Missouri

Minot
Grand Forks
N O R T H   D A K O T A
Bismarck ⊛
Aberdeen
S O U T H   D A K O T A
Pierre ⊛
Rapid City
Missouri

Yellowstone L.
Cody
W Y O M I N G
Casper
Cheyenne
Laramie
N. Platte

G R E A T

Grand Island
N E B R A S K A
Platte
S. Platte

Reno
Carson City ⊛
Lake Tahoe
G R E A T   B A S I N
N E V A D A

Great Salt Lake
Ogden
Salt Lake City ⊛
Provo
U T A H

Mt. Whitney
14,494 ft
4,418 m

Death Valley
-282 ft
-86 m

Las Vegas

M O J A V E   D E S E R T

Lake Mead

St. George
Lake Powell
Colorado

Grand Junction

Grand Canyon

Fort Collins
Boulder
Mt. Elbert
14,433 ft
4,399 m
Denver ⊛
C O L O R A D O
Colorado Springs
Pueblo

Dodge City
K A N S A S
Arkansas
Wichita

Salton Sea
Colorado

Flagstaff
A R I Z O N A
Phoenix ⊛ Mesa

Tucson

Santa Fe ⊛
Albuquerque
N E W   M E X I C O
Rio Grande
Roswell
Las Cruces
El Paso

S A N G R E   D E   C R I S T O

O K L A H O M A
Amarillo
Oklahoma City ⊛
Lawton
Lubbock
Wichita Falls
Red
Abilene
Midland
Odessa
Fort Worth
Waco
T E X A S
Austin ⊛
San Antonio
Rio Grande
Corpus Christi
Laredo
Brownsville

North Slope
Brooks Range
A L A S K A
Yukon
Alaska Range
Mt. McKinley (Denali)
20,320 ft
6,194 m
Anchorage
Juneau

Alaska Peninsula
A L E U T I A N   I S L A N D S

0   400 miles
0   400 kilometers

Kauai
Niihau
Oahu
Honolulu ⊛
Molokai
Lanai
Maui
H A W A I'I
Kahoolawe
Hawaii
Hilo

0   150 mi
0   150 km

8

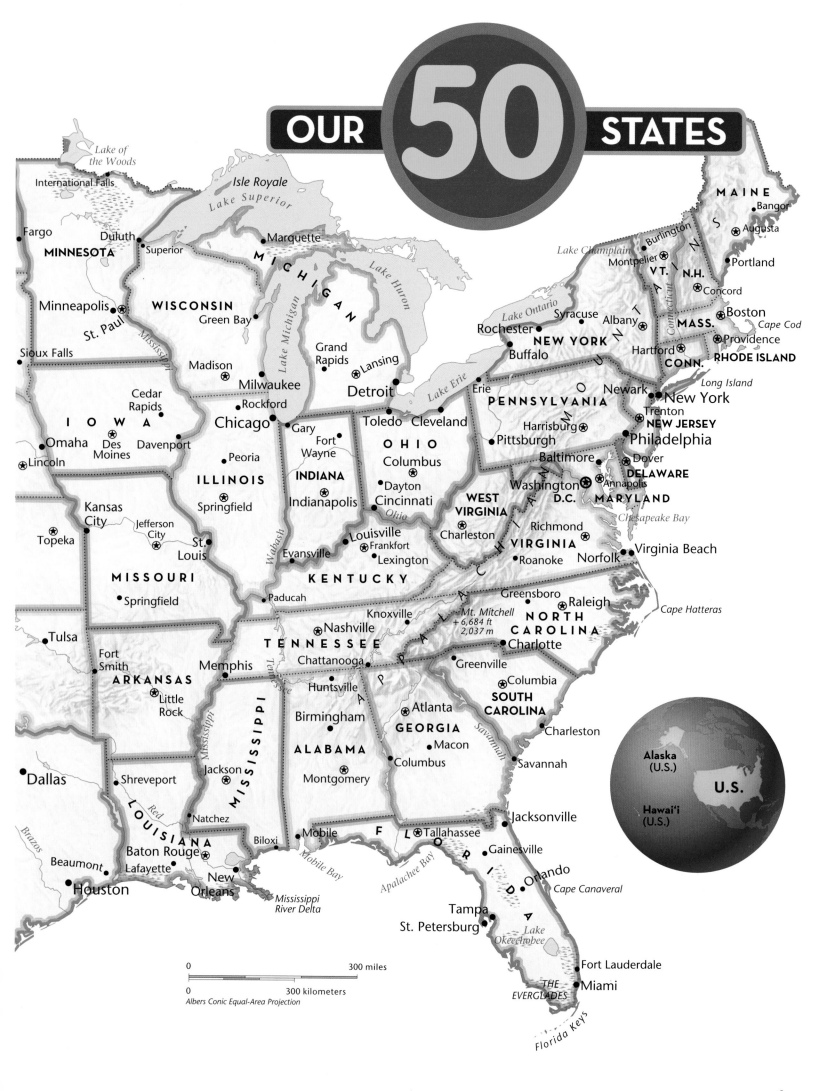

OUR 50 STATES

Lake of the Woods

International Falls

Isle Royale

Lake Superior

Fargo

Duluth

Marquette

MINNESOTA

Superior

MICHIGAN

Lake Huron

MAINE

Bangor

Augusta

Burlington

Lake Champlain

Montpelier

VT.

Portland

N.H.

Concord

Minneapolis

WISCONSIN

Green Bay

Lake Michigan

Lake Ontario

Syracuse

Albany

Boston

Cape Cod

St. Paul

Rochester

NEW YORK

MASS.

Sioux Falls

Madison

Milwaukee

Grand Rapids

Lansing

Detroit

Buffalo

Hartford

Providence

RHODE ISLAND

CONN.

Long Island

Cedar Rapids

Rockford

Chicago

Gary

Lake Erie

Erie

Newark

New York

I O W A

PENNSYLVANIA

Trenton

NEW JERSEY

Omaha

Des Moines

Davenport

Peoria

Fort Wayne

Toledo

Cleveland

Pittsburgh

Harrisburg

Philadelphia

Lincoln

ILLINOIS

Springfield

INDIANA

Indianapolis

OHIO

Columbus

Dayton

Cincinnati

Baltimore

Dover

DELAWARE

Washington D.C.

Annapolis

MARYLAND

Chesapeake Bay

Kansas City

Jefferson City

St. Louis

Evansville

Louisville

Frankfort

Lexington

WEST VIRGINIA

Charleston

Richmond

VIRGINIA

Topeka

MISSOURI

KENTUCKY

Roanoke

Norfolk

Virginia Beach

Springfield

Paducah

Knoxville

Greensboro

Raleigh

Cape Hatteras

Tulsa

Nashville

Mt. Mitchell
+ 6,684 ft
2,037 m

NORTH CAROLINA

Charlotte

T E N N E S S E E

Chattanooga

Fort Smith

Memphis

Huntsville

Greenville

ARKANSAS

Little Rock

Birmingham

Columbia

SOUTH CAROLINA

Atlanta

MISSISSIPPI

ALABAMA

GEORGIA

Macon

Charleston

Dallas

Shreveport

Jackson

Columbus

Savannah

Montgomery

LOUISIANA

Natchez

Mobile

Biloxi

Jacksonville

Beaumont

Baton Rouge

Lafayette

New Orleans

Mobile Bay

Apalachee Bay

Tallahassee

Gainesville

Orlando

Cape Canaveral

Houston

Mississippi River Delta

F L O R I D A

Tampa

St. Petersburg

Lake Okeechobee

Fort Lauderdale

THE EVERGLADES

Miami

Florida Keys

Brazos

Red

Mississippi

Ohio

Wabash

Tennessee

Savannah

Alaska (U.S.)

U.S.

Hawai'i (U.S.)

0   300 miles

0   300 kilometers

Albers Conic Equal-Area Projection

9

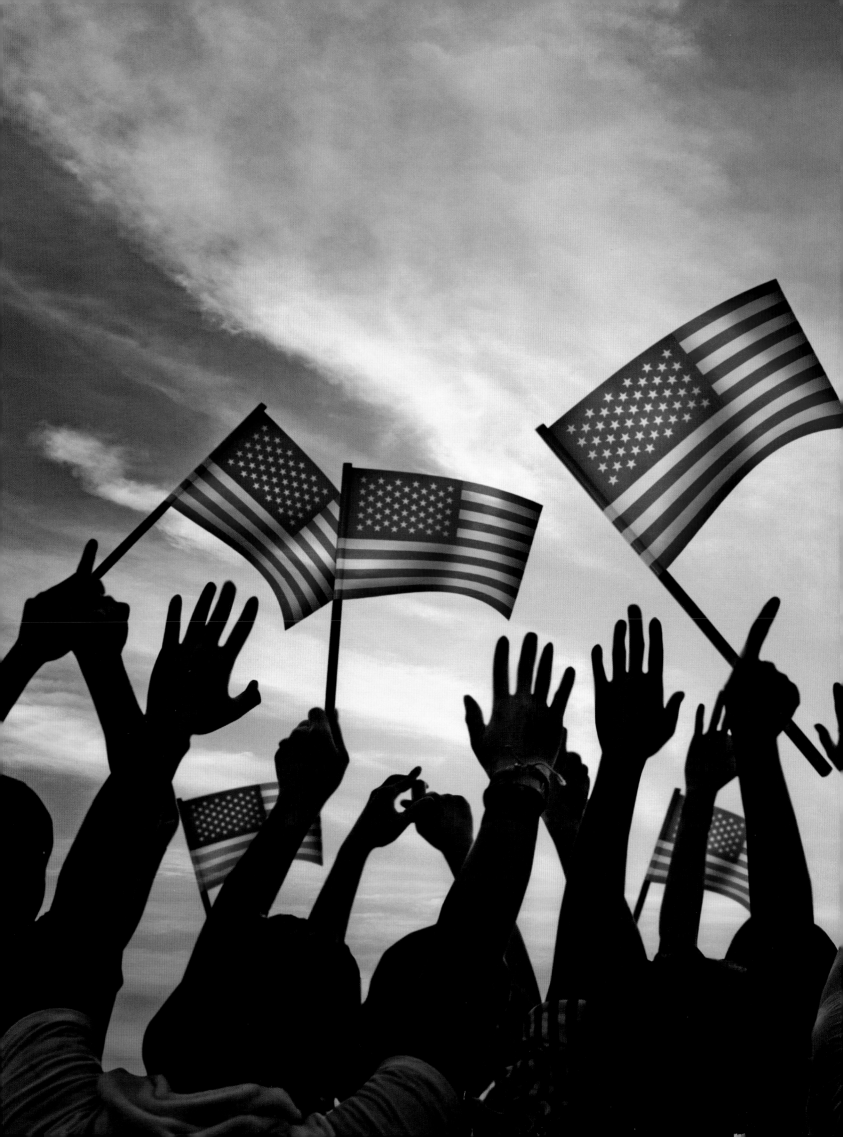

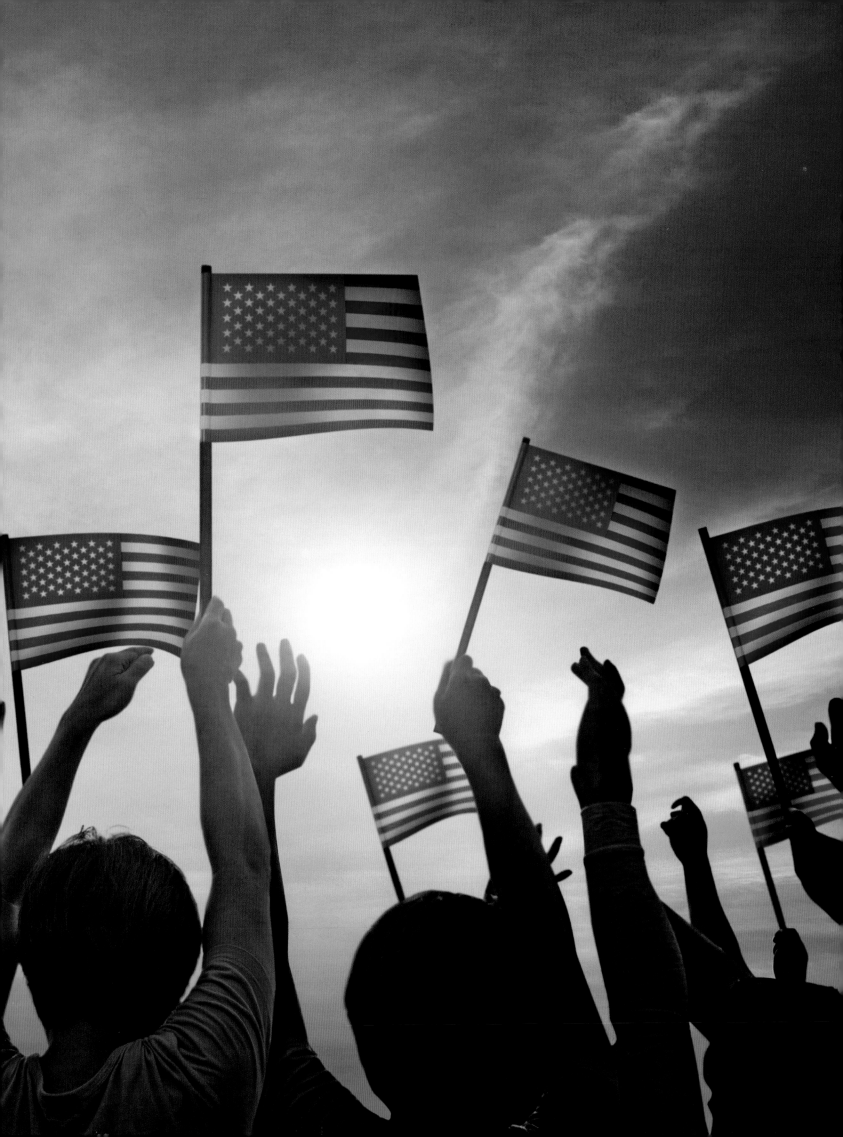

THE AMERICAS UP TO 1700

How did the first Americans arrive? Scientists believe they traveled across the Bering land bridge between today's Russia and Alaska as early as 30,000 years ago. Some settled in northern lands; others moved south. When Christopher Columbus arrived in 1492, rich and diverse cultures thrived throughout the Americas. European settlers introduced new diseases, and violent conflict took a toll on native peoples. By 1700 Spanish influence was strong in western North America. Great Britain, France, Sweden, and the Netherlands also had spheres of influence, ranging from the eastern seaboard to the Great Lakes and St. Lawrence River. New settlers struggled to build strong working communities, while their homeland governments struggled for control in the New World.

THE ENGLISH ARRIVE IN NORTH AMERICA

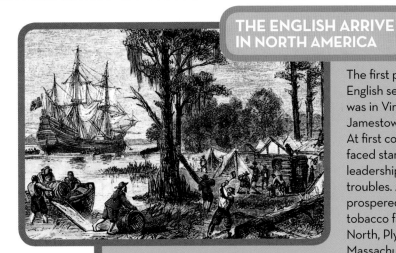

The first permanent English settlement was in Virginia, at Jamestown, in 1607. At first colonists faced starvation, poor leadership, and Indian troubles. At last they prospered through tobacco farming. In the North, Plymouth and Massachusetts Bay were settled in the 1620s by Puritans who had come to America for religious freedom. Early labor was provided by indentured servants: In exchange for passage they worked for five to seven years for a master. By the late 1600s settlers imported slaves from Africa, to work for a lifetime—against their will. By the time of the American Revolution, 20 percent of the population was enslaved.

WITCH TRIALS

When a Puritan girl in Salem, Massachusetts, started behaving strangely, a doctor suggested it was witchcraft. Soon many people were accused of being witches. Resulting trials put 20 people to death and many more in prison before the hysteria ended.

THE VIEWPOINT OF THE ORIGINAL SETTLERS

The Bering land bridge crossed by early settlers from Asia to America was an ancient glacier surrounded by lower sea levels. Today it's underwater. The settlers moved south, creating hundreds of languages. Some of these groups moved often, following the seasons for wild game, fish, and plants. Others built thriving cities and stayed in place. As European settlers arrived, some native peoples helped them and formed alliances; others resisted their control and fought against the "intruders." Settlers often did not consider that the lands were ancestral territories of the first peoples.

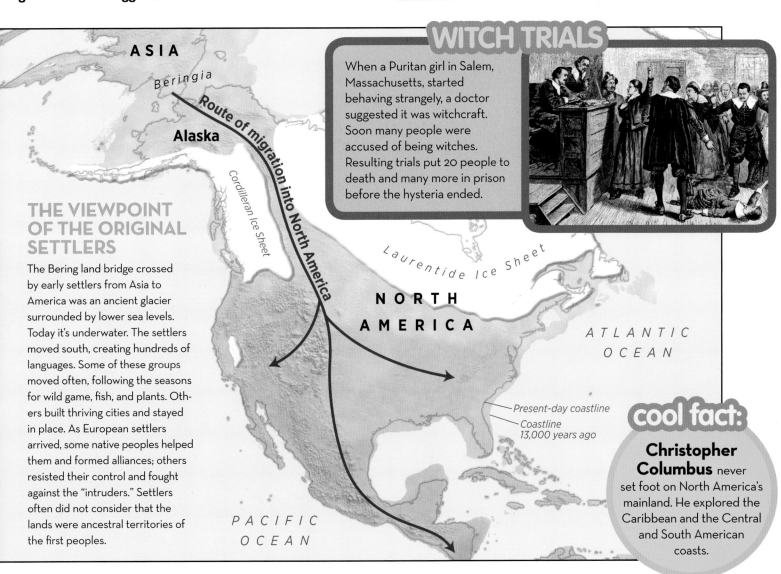

ASIA

Beringia

Alaska

Route of migration into North America

Cordilleran Ice Sheet

Laurentide Ice Sheet

NORTH AMERICA

ATLANTIC OCEAN

Present-day coastline

Coastline 13,000 years ago

PACIFIC OCEAN

cool fact:

Christopher Columbus never set foot on North America's mainland. He explored the Caribbean and the Central and South American coasts.

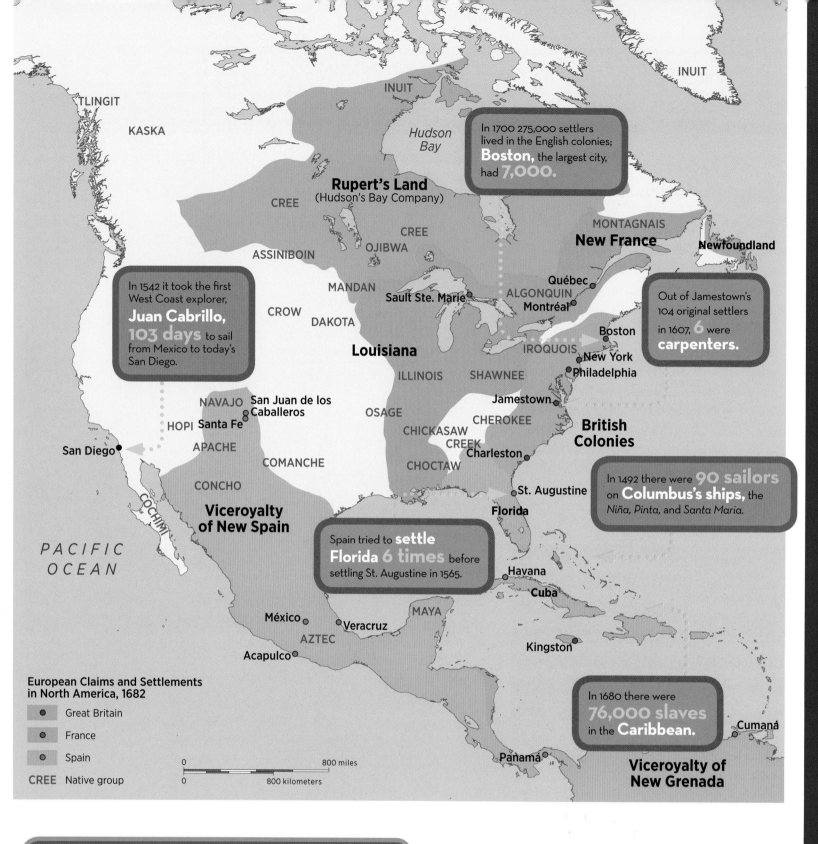

TLINGIT

KASKA

INUIT

INUIT

Hudson Bay

In 1700 275,000 settlers lived in the English colonies; **Boston,** the largest city, had **7,000.**

Rupert's Land
(Hudson's Bay Company)

CREE

CREE

OJIBWA

MONTAGNAIS

New France

Newfoundland

ASSINIBOIN

In 1542 it took the first West Coast explorer, **Juan Cabrillo, 103 days** to sail from Mexico to today's San Diego.

MANDAN

CROW

DAKOTA

Sault Ste. Marie

Québec

ALGONQUIN

Montréal

Boston

Out of Jamestown's 104 original settlers in 1607, **6** were **carpenters.**

Louisiana

ILLINOIS

SHAWNEE

IROQUOIS

New York

Philadelphia

NAVAJO

San Juan de los Caballeros

OSAGE

Jamestown

HOPI

Santa Fe

CHEROKEE

British Colonies

San Diego

APACHE

CHICKASAW

CREEK

Charleston

COMANCHE

CHOCTAW

In 1492 there were **90 sailors** on **Columbus's ships,** the *Niña, Pinta,* and *Santa Maria.*

CONCHO

St. Augustine

Viceroyalty of New Spain

Spain tried to **settle Florida 6 times** before settling St. Augustine in 1565.

Florida

COCHIMI

PACIFIC OCEAN

Havana

Cuba

MAYA

México

Veracruz

AZTEC

Acapulco

Kingston

European Claims and Settlements in North America, 1682

- Great Britain
- France
- Spain

CREE   Native group

0   800 miles

0   800 kilometers

In 1680 there were **76,000 slaves** in the **Caribbean.**

Cumaná

Panamá

Viceroyalty of New Grenada

TIME LINE OF U.S. SETTLEMENT

1675–76: The **King Philip's War** between the colonists and Indians in New England takes place.

Oct. 12, 1492: A sailor on **Christopher Columbus's** boat, the *Pinta,* sees land in the Bahamas.

May 14, 1607: The Virginia Company starts the first permanent English settlement at **Jamestown.**

Nov. 1620: Pilgrims land at Cape Cod, in what is today Massachusetts; the Mayflower Compact is the basis for laws in the New World.

1689: The **King William's War** between Great Britain and France begins in New England and Canada.

| 1000 | 1492 | 1565 | 1598 | 1607 | 1620 | 1625 | 1675 | 1689 | 1692 |

circa 1000: Norseman **Leif Eriksson** starts North America's first European settlement in today's Newfoundland, Canada.

1565: The Spanish create the **first European settlement** in the future United States: St. Augustine, Florida.

July 11, 1598: San Juan de los Caballeros is established as the **first Spanish capital of New Mexico.**

1625: Thirty Dutch families settle in today's **Manhattan.**

May–Oct. 1692: Fears of **witchcraft** in Salem, Massachusetts, end with 20 people being put to death.

THE AMERICAN REVOLUTION

1770–1781

By the mid-1700s Great Britain's colonies in North America were growing and thriving far from their homeland. In 1763 Britain began enforcing old taxes and added a new one, the Stamp Act. Tensions grew until the Revolutionary War broke out in April 1775. Despite lack of money, poor supplies, disorganization, and many colonists who remained loyal to Britain, the patriots scored important victories, partly with help from France. In October 1781 the British suffered a final defeat, and the independent colonies were recognized through the Treaty of Paris in 1783. Great Britain and the United States fought again in the War of 1812, a controversial war that saw no loss in territory.

THE BRITISH

KING GEORGE III
1738–1820

Who: King of Great Britain and Ireland, 1760–1820; England's longest ruling monarch before Queen Victoria

Known for: Losing the American Colonies. He set the foundations for Great Britain's global empire, including the West Indies, India, Canada, and Australia.

GEN. WILLIAM HOWE
1729–1814

Who: Commander in Chief of the British Army in North America, Oct. 1775–April 1778

Known for: Brilliant military leadership during the Seven Years' War against France, 1754–1763. After Revolutionary War losses, he resigned in 1778.

THE COLONIES

GEORGE WASHINGTON
1732–1799

Who: Commander in Chief of the Continental Armies; first president of the United States, 1789–1797

Known for: Superb leadership on and off the field of battle. Elected leader of the Continental Army in 1775.

NATHANAEL GREENE
1742–1786

Who: Commander of the Southern Department of the Continental Army in 1780

Known for: Being a key general in the Revolutionary War. He first won acclaim at the Battle of Kings Mountain, South Carolina, in 1780.

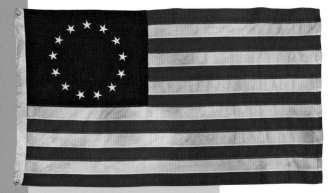

OLD GLORY: THE AMERICAN FLAG

Imagine seeing a flag raised outside Gen. George Washington's headquarters in July 1776, a new flag representing the American Colonies instead of Great Britain! It was an exciting new symbol for the Colonies, but the new flag had to wait until June 1777 to become official. That's when the new colonial government, the Continental Congress, met and adopted it. The first flag had 13 stars arranged in a circle, very different from the design we know today with 50 stars for 50 states. In fact, the flag has had 27 versions since its debut. But this remains the same: 13 stripes for the original 13 Colonies.

THE 13 COLONIES: HOW THEY'VE GROWN

From Virginia's Jamestown settlement in 1607 to Massachusetts' Plymouth Bay Colony in 1620, the eastern seaboard grew into 13 flourishing states by 1790. Today some states support millions of people.

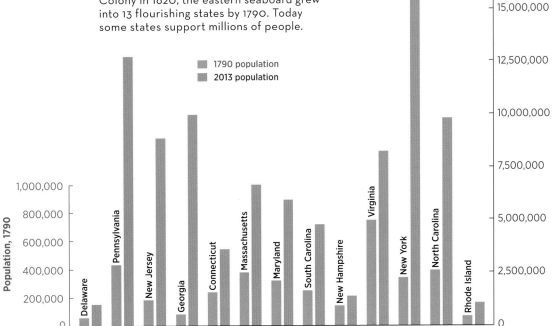

Population, 1790

Population, 2013

■ 1790 population
■ 2013 population

Delaware, Pennsylvania, New Jersey, Georgia, Connecticut, Massachusetts, Maryland, South Carolina, New Hampshire, Virginia, New York, North Carolina, Rhode Island

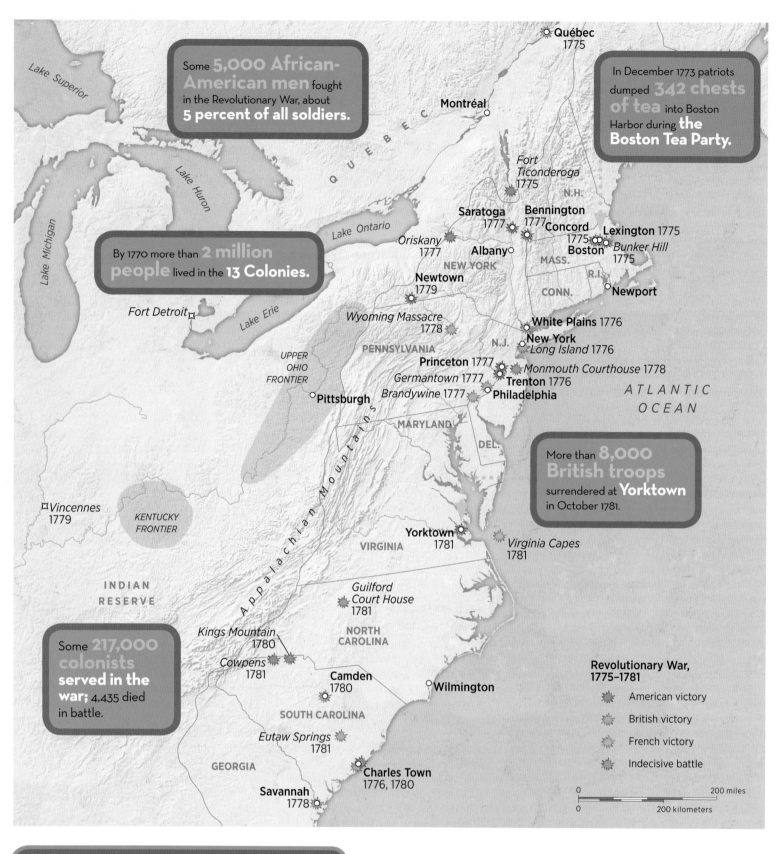

Some **5,000 African-American men** fought in the Revolutionary War, about **5 percent of all soldiers.**

In December 1773 patriots dumped **342 chests of tea** into Boston Harbor during **the Boston Tea Party.**

By 1770 more than **2 million people** lived in the **13 Colonies.**

More than **8,000 British troops** surrendered at **Yorktown** in October 1781.

Some **217,000 colonists served in the war;** 4,435 died in battle.

Lake Superior
Lake Michigan
Lake Huron
Lake Ontario
Lake Erie

Québec 1775
Montréal
QUEBEC
Fort Ticonderoga 1775
N.H.
Saratoga 1777
Bennington 1777
Concord 1775
Lexington 1775
Oriskany 1777
Albany
Boston
Bunker Hill 1775
NEW YORK
MASS.
R.I.
Newtown 1779
CONN.
Newport
Fort Detroit
Wyoming Massacre 1778
White Plains 1776
New York
Long Island 1776
PENNSYLVANIA
N.J.
Princeton 1777
Monmouth Courthouse 1778
Germantown 1777
Trenton 1776
Brandywine 1777
Pittsburgh
Philadelphia
ATLANTIC OCEAN
UPPER OHIO FRONTIER
MARYLAND
DEL.
Vincennes 1779
KENTUCKY FRONTIER
Yorktown 1781
Virginia Capes 1781
VIRGINIA
INDIAN RESERVE
Guilford Court House 1781
Kings Mountain 1780
NORTH CAROLINA
Cowpens 1781
Camden 1780
Wilmington
SOUTH CAROLINA
Eutaw Springs 1781
Charles Town 1776, 1780
GEORGIA
Savannah 1778
Appalachian Mountains

Revolutionary War, 1775–1781
- American victory
- British victory
- French victory
- Indecisive battle

0   200 miles
0   200 kilometers

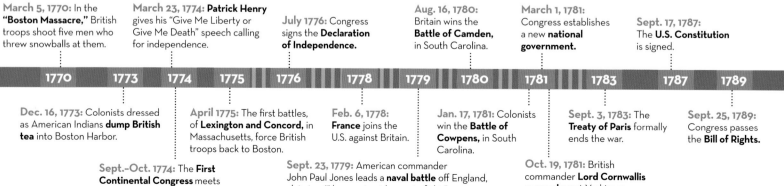

TIME LINE OF WAR EVENTS

March 5, 1770: In the **"Boston Massacre,"** British troops shoot five men who threw snowballs at them.

March 23, 1774: Patrick Henry gives his "Give Me Liberty or Give Me Death" speech calling for independence.

July 1776: Congress signs the **Declaration of Independence.**

Aug. 16, 1780: Britain wins the **Battle of Camden,** in South Carolina.

March 1, 1781: Congress establishes a new **national government.**

Sept. 17, 1787: The **U.S. Constitution** is signed.

| 1770 | 1773 | 1774 | 1775 | 1776 | 1778 | 1779 | 1780 | 1781 | 1783 | 1787 | 1789 |

Dec. 16, 1773: Colonists dressed as American Indians **dump British tea** into Boston Harbor.

April 1775: The first battles, of **Lexington and Concord,** in Massachusetts, force British troops back to Boston.

Feb. 6, 1778: France joins the U.S. against Britain.

Jan. 17, 1781: Colonists win the **Battle of Cowpens,** in South Carolina.

Sept. 3, 1783: The **Treaty of Paris** formally ends the war.

Sept. 25, 1789: Congress passes the **Bill of Rights.**

Sept.–Oct. 1774: The **First Continental Congress** meets in Philadelphia.

Sept. 23, 1779: American commander John Paul Jones leads a **naval battle** off England, claiming, "I have not yet begun to fight."

Oct. 19, 1781: British commander **Lord Cornwallis surrenders** at Yorktown.

WESTWARD EXPANSION

1800–1900

At the turn of the 19th century the newly independent citizens of the United States were on the move. Leaving the established East, many migrated in search of financial opportunity. They established farms west of the Appalachians and poured into what is now considered the Midwest states. Settlers, starting in Independence, Missouri, rode the Oregon Trail to the Willamette Valley. Between 1849 and 1853, after word that there was gold in California had spread like wildfire, migrants moved quickly to seek their fortune. By the 1870s all but the cattle-grazing lands of the Great Plains were settled; by 1900 that land flourished as farmland, and westward expansion in the continental U.S. was complete.

THE CONESTOGA WAGON

The Conestoga wagon was the semitrailer truck of its day. Made for hauling large loads over bumpy trails, it could hold up to 6 tons (5,443 kg)—that's the weight of five small cars! The floor was curved, which kept cargo from sliding around, and it had a white top made of sturdy canvas for protection from wind, rain, and snow. Measuring some 26 feet (8 m) long—the length of two small cars (and about twice as tall, at 11 feet/3.5 m)—Conestoga wagons were pulled by four to six horses. Starting in the late 1700s, the vehicles were the most reliable way to transport manufactured goods to the West, and raw goods, like tobacco in the 1850s.

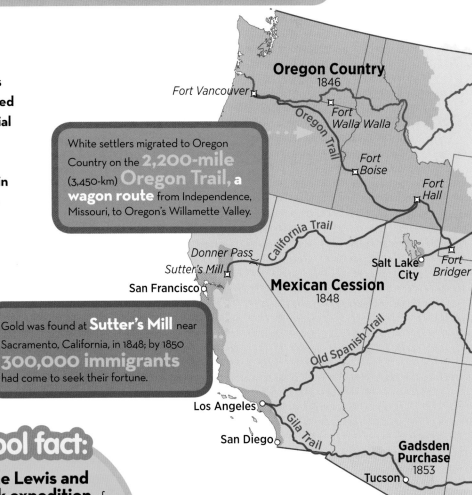

White settlers migrated to Oregon Country on the **2,200-mile** (3,450-km) **Oregon Trail, a wagon route** from Independence, Missouri, to Oregon's Willamette Valley.

Gold was found at **Sutter's Mill** near Sacramento, California, in 1848; by 1850 **300,000 immigrants** had come to seek their fortune.

cool fact:

The Lewis and Clark expedition of 1804-06—an exploration of 8,000 miles (12,870 km) of the Louisiana Purchase and the West ordered by President Thomas Jefferson—cost $39,000. That's 15 times more than the amount they had budgeted.

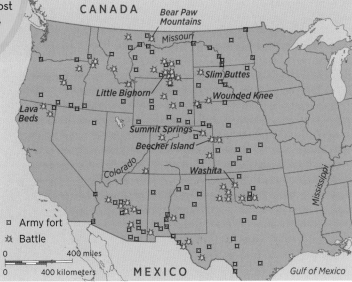

NATIVE AMERICAN CONFLICT

After the Civil War, westbound settlers overtook Native Americans' land and threatened their way of life. Tribes fought back, often battling the U.S. Army. The 1876 Battle of Little Bighorn, at the height of Indian power, was the Army's greatest loss: When Lt. Col. George Custer and his troops tried to force Lakota Indians onto a reservation, the Army forces were killed. A barrage of U.S. troops forced the Lakota to surrender.

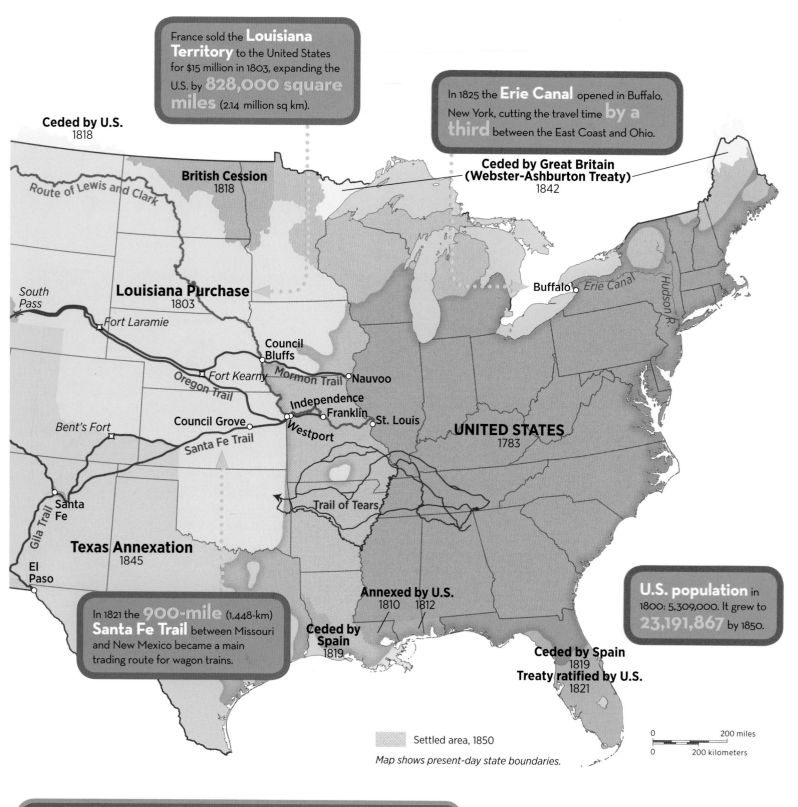

France sold the **Louisiana Territory** to the United States for $15 million in 1803, expanding the U.S. by **828,000 square miles** (2.14 million sq km).

In 1825 the **Erie Canal** opened in Buffalo, New York, cutting the travel time **by a third** between the East Coast and Ohio.

Ceded by U.S.
1818

British Cession
1818

Route of Lewis and Clark

South Pass

Louisiana Purchase
1803

Fort Laramie

Ceded by Great Britain (Webster-Ashburton Treaty)
1842

Buffalo · Erie Canal

Hudson R.

Council Bluffs

Fort Kearny
Mormon Trail · Nauvoo

Oregon Trail

Bent's Fort

Council Grove
Independence
Franklin
Westport
St. Louis

UNITED STATES
1783

Santa Fe Trail

Gila Trail

Santa Fe

Texas Annexation
1845

El Paso

Trail of Tears

Annexed by U.S.
1810   1812

In 1821 the **900-mile** (1,448-km) **Santa Fe Trail** between Missouri and New Mexico became a main trading route for wagon trains.

Ceded by Spain
1819

Ceded by Spain
1819
Treaty ratified by U.S.
1821

U.S. population in 1800: 5,309,000. It grew to **23,191,867** by 1850.

Settled area, 1850

0   200 miles
0   200 kilometers

Map shows present-day state boundaries.

TIME LINE OF WESTERN EXPANSION

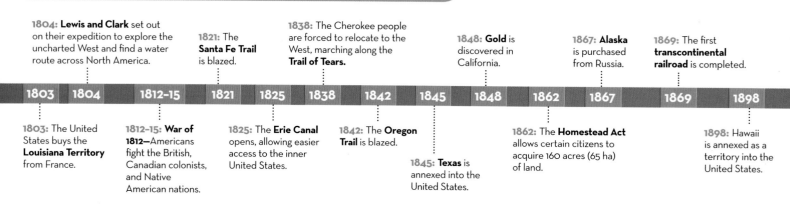

1804: Lewis and Clark set out on their expedition to explore the uncharted West and find a water route across North America.

1821: The **Santa Fe Trail** is blazed.

1838: The Cherokee people are forced to relocate to the West, marching along the **Trail of Tears.**

1848: Gold is discovered in California.

1867: Alaska is purchased from Russia.

1869: The first **transcontinental railroad** is completed.

| 1803 | 1804 | 1812–15 | 1821 | 1825 | 1838 | 1842 | 1845 | 1848 | 1862 | 1867 | 1869 | 1898 |

1803: The United States buys the **Louisiana Territory** from France.

1812–15: War of 1812—Americans fight the British, Canadian colonists, and Native American nations.

1825: The **Erie Canal** opens, allowing easier access to the inner United States.

1842: The **Oregon Trail** is blazed.

1845: Texas is annexed into the United States.

1862: The **Homestead Act** allows certain citizens to acquire 160 acres (65 ha) of land.

1898: Hawaii is annexed as a territory into the United States.

THE CIVIL WAR

1861-65

The American Civil War, fought between 1861 and 1865, threatened to tear the young United States apart. The war's underlying cause was slavery—the treatment of people as property—in the South. Political differences and a growing division between an industrial North and an agricultural South made matters worse. Although the Confederacy was led by the brilliant Gen. Robert E. Lee, the Union's wealth and military might won out. The Confederates surrendered in 1865. Twelve years of Reconstruction helped stitch the country back together, but it did not establish the rights of newly freed slaves.

LEADERS OF THE NORTH AND SOUTH

THE NORTH

PRESIDENT ABRAHAM LINCOLN
1809–1865

Who: 16th president of the United States, 1861–65

Known for: Rising from humble origins. He led the nation to abolish slavery and win the Civil War.

GEN. ULYSSES S. GRANT
1822–1885

Who: Commander of the Union Army, 1864–65

Known for: Leading the Union Army to victory after failed attempts by other generals. Writing fair surrender terms for the South. Facing the challenges of Reconstruction during his presidency.

THE SOUTH

PRESIDENT JEFFERSON DAVIS
1808–1889

Who: President of the Confederate States of America, 1861–65

Known for: Winning key battles during the Mexican War, and then reluctantly serving as president of the Confederacy. After the war, he was imprisoned for two years at Fort Monroe, Virginia.

GEN. ROBERT E. LEE
1807–1870

Who: Commander of the Army of Northern Virginia, 1862–65

Known for: Turning down President Lincoln's offer to command Union forces, and then serving as the brilliant, decisive commander of the Confederate armies. After the war, he was president of today's Washington and Lee University, in Lexington, Virginia.

A SOLDIER'S LIFE

More than 3 million Union and Confederate soldiers fought in the war—some as young as 12. Long marches, poor food rations, and scarce medical treatment made life hard. But friendships were strong. In camp, men sang, played cards, and waited for letters from home.

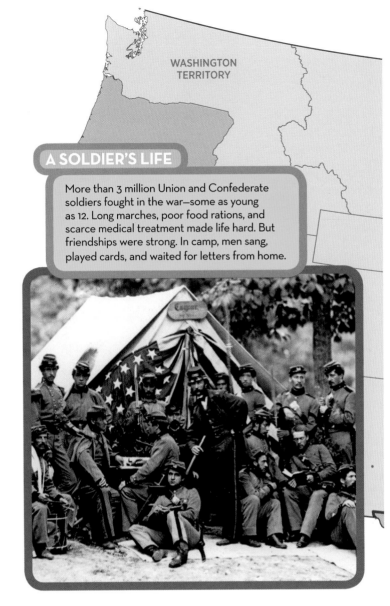

WASHINGTON TERRITORY

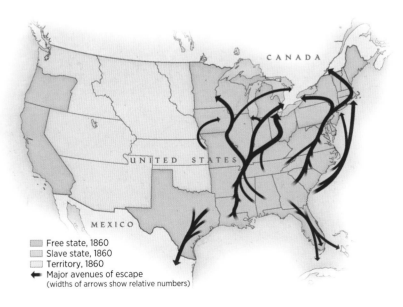

CANADA

UNITED STATES

MEXICO

- ▨ Free state, 1860
- ▨ Slave state, 1860
- ▨ Territory, 1860
- ← Major avenues of escape
  (widths of arrows show relative numbers)

UNDERGROUND RAILROAD

The Underground Railroad wasn't actually a railroad but a network of safe houses that ranged from the South to the free North, where people hid slaves and guided them north. Free blacks, ex-slaves, and antislavery activists all helped. Former slave Harriet Tubman, nicknamed "Moses" for leading her people to freedom, helped 70 slaves escape over 11 years. In 1850 the Fugitive Slave Law allowed slaves to be caught as far north as New England. Canada became the only safe destination.

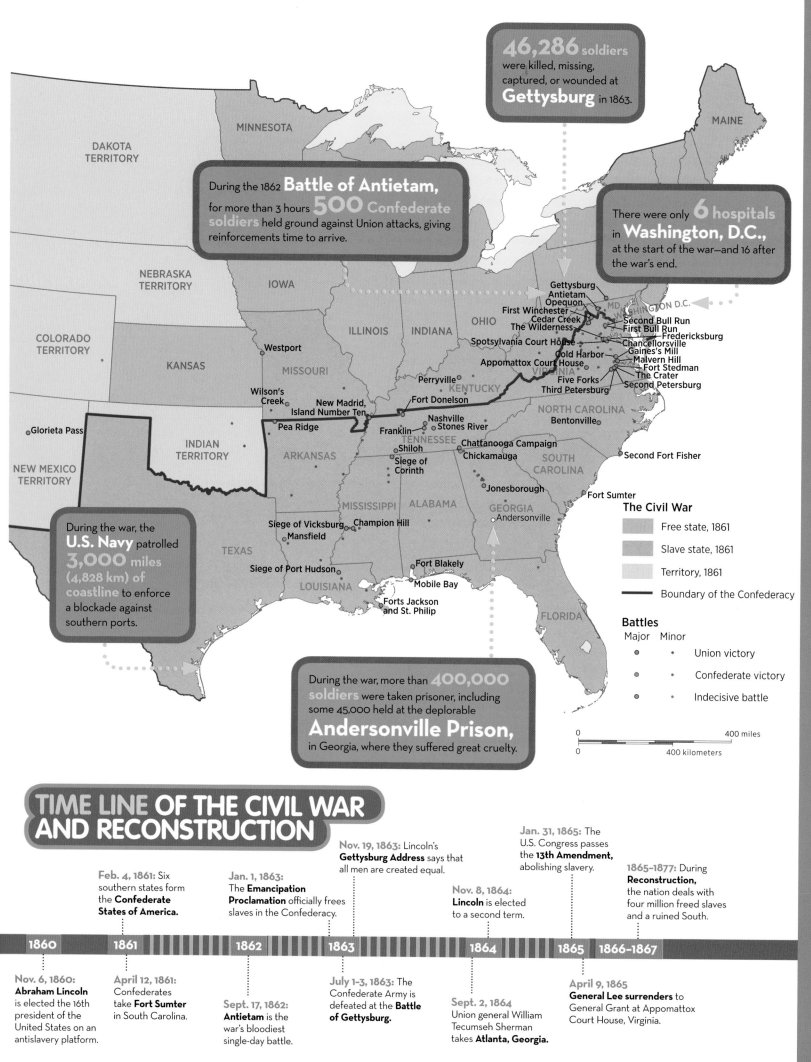

46,286 soldiers were killed, missing, captured, or wounded at **Gettysburg** in 1863.

During the 1862 **Battle of Antietam,** for more than 3 hours **500** Confederate soldiers held ground against Union attacks, giving reinforcements time to arrive.

There were only **6** hospitals in **Washington, D.C.,** at the start of the war—and 16 after the war's end.

During the war, the **U.S. Navy** patrolled **3,000** miles (4,828 km) of coastline to enforce a blockade against southern ports.

During the war, more than **400,000** soldiers were taken prisoner, including some 45,000 held at the deplorable **Andersonville Prison,** in Georgia, where they suffered great cruelty.

DAKOTA TERRITORY

MINNESOTA

MAINE

NEBRASKA TERRITORY

IOWA

COLORADO TERRITORY

KANSAS

MISSOURI

ILLINOIS

INDIANA

OHIO

Westport

Gettysburg
Antietam
Opequon
First Winchester
Cedar Creek
The Wilderness
Spotsylvania Court House
Cold Harbor
Appomattox Court House
VIRGINIA
Five Forks
Third Petersburg

MD.
WASHINGTON D.C.
Second Bull Run
First Bull Run
Fredericksburg
Chancellorsville
Gaines's Mill
Malvern Hill
Fort Stedman
The Crater
Second Petersburg

NEW MEXICO TERRITORY

Glorieta Pass

INDIAN TERRITORY

Wilson's Creek
New Madrid, Island Number Ten
Pea Ridge

Fort Donelson
KENTUCKY
Perryville
Franklin
Nashville
Stones River
TENNESSEE
Shiloh
Siege of Corinth

NORTH CAROLINA
Bentonville

Chattanooga Campaign
Chickamauga

SOUTH CAROLINA

Second Fort Fisher

ARKANSAS

MISSISSIPPI

ALABAMA

GEORGIA
Andersonville

Jonesborough

Fort Sumter

Siege of Vicksburg
Champion Hill
Mansfield

TEXAS

Siege of Port Hudson
LOUISIANA

Fort Blakely
Mobile Bay

Forts Jackson and St. Philip

FLORIDA

The Civil War

Free state, 1861
Slave state, 1861
Territory, 1861
Boundary of the Confederacy

Battles
Major   Minor
   Union victory
   Confederate victory
   Indecisive battle

0   400 miles
0   400 kilometers

TIME LINE OF THE CIVIL WAR AND RECONSTRUCTION

Feb. 4, 1861: Six southern states form the **Confederate States of America.**

Jan. 1, 1863: The **Emancipation Proclamation** officially frees slaves in the Confederacy.

Nov. 19, 1863: Lincoln's **Gettysburg Address** says that all men are created equal.

Jan. 31, 1865: The U.S. Congress passes the **13th Amendment,** abolishing slavery.

Nov. 8, 1864: **Lincoln** is elected to a second term.

1865–1877: During **Reconstruction,** the nation deals with four million freed slaves and a ruined South.

| 1860 | 1861 | 1862 | 1863 | 1864 | 1865 | 1866–1867 |

Nov. 6, 1860: **Abraham Lincoln** is elected the 16th president of the United States on an antislavery platform.

April 12, 1861: Confederates take **Fort Sumter** in South Carolina.

Sept. 17, 1862: **Antietam** is the war's bloodiest single-day battle.

July 1–3, 1863: The Confederate Army is defeated at the **Battle of Gettysburg.**

Sept. 2, 1864 Union general William Tecumseh Sherman takes **Atlanta, Georgia.**

April 9, 1865 **General Lee surrenders** to General Grant at Appomattox Court House, Virginia.

INDUSTRY TAKES OFF

1865–1908

America's industrial revolution began in its smallest state—Rhode Island—where the first successful water-powered, cotton-spinning factory went into operation in Pawtucket in the 1790s; steam power followed in 1809, and traditional farming life was replaced by factory work. Mills required large numbers of workers, and European immigrants flocked to them. Later, factories were run on the steam engine, an invention that also changed transportation. Steam locomotives moved massive amounts of goods quickly and over great distances. By 1869 a transcontinental railroad spanned the entire continent. The efficient railroad system, plus advancements in oil production, steelmaking, mining, and manufacturing, turned the United States into a major industrialized nation by the early 20th century.

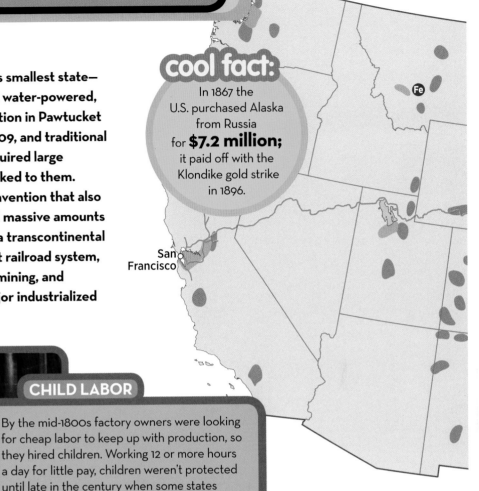

cool fact:
In 1867 the U.S. purchased Alaska from Russia for **$7.2 million;** it paid off with the Klondike gold strike in 1896.

San Francisco

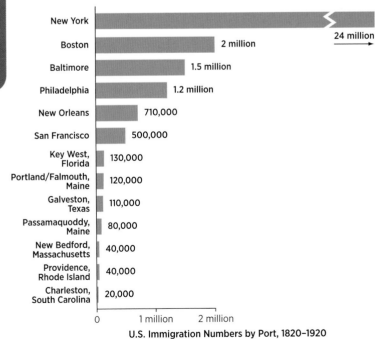

CHILD LABOR

By the mid-1800s factory owners were looking for cheap labor to keep up with production, so they hired children. Working 12 or more hours a day for little pay, children weren't protected until late in the century when some states started to pass laws to regulate child labor.

CAPTAINS OF INDUSTRY

ANDREW CARNEGIE
1835–1919

Known for: Working his way up from a cotton mill worker as a boy. Carnegie invested in oil, and then became a tycoon in the steel industry and one of the most wealthy industrialists of the day.

JOHN D. ROCKEFELLER
1839–1937

Known for: Being the founder of Standard Oil, the most dominant oil company in the country. The company's practices lead to antimonopoly laws, but only after Rockefeller became one of the richest men in the world.

Port	Immigrants
New York	24 million
Boston	2 million
Baltimore	1.5 million
Philadelphia	1.2 million
New Orleans	710,000
San Francisco	500,000
Key West, Florida	130,000
Portland/Falmouth, Maine	120,000
Galveston, Texas	110,000
Passamaquoddy, Maine	80,000
New Bedford, Massachusetts	40,000
Providence, Rhode Island	40,000
Charleston, South Carolina	20,000

0   1 million   2 million

U.S. Immigration Numbers by Port, 1820–1920

IMMIGRATION, 1820–1920

By 1895 immigrants from other nations were arriving at ports around the United States. New York's Ellis Island—the main port of entry from abroad—was a hopping place. It was by far the most popular immigration station, but there were many other places where people entered the land of opportunity.

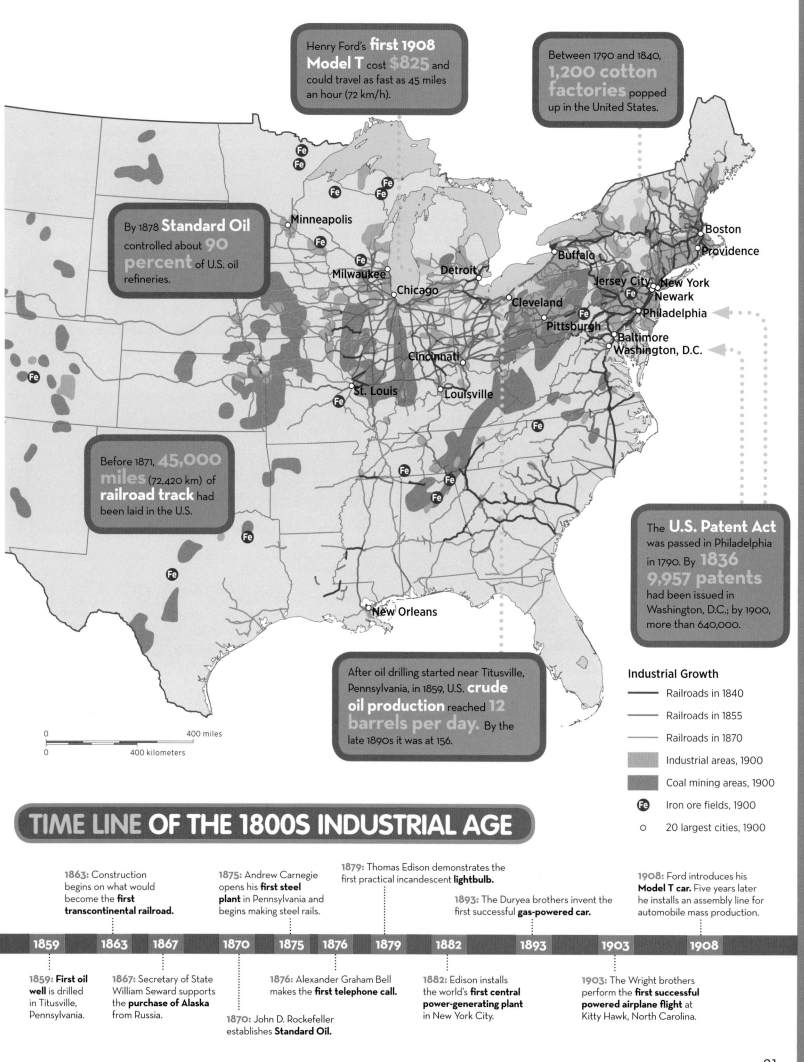

Henry Ford's **first 1908 Model T** cost **$825** and could travel as fast as 45 miles an hour (72 km/h).

Between 1790 and 1840, **1,200 cotton factories** popped up in the United States.

By 1878 **Standard Oil** controlled about **90 percent** of U.S. oil refineries.

Before 1871, **45,000 miles** (72,420 km) of **railroad track** had been laid in the U.S.

The **U.S. Patent Act** was passed in Philadelphia in 1790. By **1836 9,957 patents** had been issued in Washington, D.C.; by 1900, more than 640,000.

After oil drilling started near Titusville, Pennsylvania, in 1859, U.S. **crude oil production** reached **12 barrels per day.** By the late 1890s it was at 156.

Minneapolis
Milwaukee
Chicago
Detroit
Cleveland
Pittsburgh
Buffalo
Jersey City
New York
Newark
Philadelphia
Baltimore
Washington, D.C.
Boston
Providence
Cincinnati
St. Louis
Louisville
New Orleans

0   400 miles
0   400 kilometers

Industrial Growth

—— Railroads in 1840
—— Railroads in 1855
—— Railroads in 1870
■ Industrial areas, 1900
■ Coal mining areas, 1900
Fe Iron ore fields, 1900
○ 20 largest cities, 1900

TIME LINE OF THE 1800S INDUSTRIAL AGE

1863: Construction begins on what would become the **first transcontinental railroad.**

1875: Andrew Carnegie opens his **first steel plant** in Pennsylvania and begins making steel rails.

1879: Thomas Edison demonstrates the first practical incandescent **lightbulb.**

1893: The Duryea brothers invent the first successful **gas-powered car.**

1908: Ford introduces his **Model T car.** Five years later he installs an assembly line for automobile mass production.

| 1859 | 1863 | 1867 | 1870 | 1875 | 1876 | 1879 | 1882 | 1893 | 1903 | 1908 |

1859: First oil well is drilled in Titusville, Pennsylvania.

1867: Secretary of State William Seward supports the **purchase of Alaska** from Russia.

1870: John D. Rockefeller establishes **Standard Oil.**

1876: Alexander Graham Bell makes the **first telephone call.**

1882: Edison installs the world's **first central power-generating plant** in New York City.

1903: The Wright brothers perform the **first successful powered airplane flight** at Kitty Hawk, North Carolina.

U.S. RISE TO GLOBAL POWER

1898-1945

A decade after the Civil War, the United States began to strengthen its Navy, to help with international trade. Meanwhile, tensions rose between the U.S. and Spain over the independence of the island of Cuba, near the U.S. In 1898 a massive explosion sank a U.S. battleship in a Cuban harbor; Spain appeared to be the culprit. The Spanish-American War broke out, and Spain ultimately lost control of Cuba and nearby islands. Barely two decades later, in 1914, World War I erupted in Europe, caused by military tensions and alliances among the economic powers of Europe, Russia, parts of the Middle East, and the East. World War II, which began in 1939, was in many ways a continuation of unresolved issues from the First World War. Lasting until 1945, the war ended with power shifting away from Europe and toward the U.S. and the Soviet Union.

DOUGHBOYS OF WORLD WAR I

It doesn't sound like a tough-guy name, but American infantrymen during **World War I** were nicknamed doughboys. It's unclear where the term came from, but it may have started during the Mexican-American War of 1846-48, when marching soldiers became covered in white adobe dust. Their nickname, "adobes," may have turned into "doughboys."

GIS OF WORLD WAR II

By World War II the term "doughboy" was replaced by "GI." Originally the initials stood for "galvanized iron," but then turned into "general issue," or "government issue." Soldiers were also called "GI Joe."

THE SPANISH-AMERICAN WAR

In the second half of the 19th century the United States looked beyond its immediate states to broaden its reach. It purchased Alaska from Russia and claimed several Pacific islands, some because they had rich deposits of guano—waste from birds used as fertilizer—and others to pursue economic interests in Asia. At the end of the Spanish-American War, Spain was forced to hand over Guam and Puerto Rico to the U.S. The nation also sold America the Philippines. These acquisitions gave the U.S. newfound status as an imperial power.

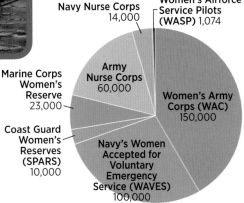

Navy Nurse Corps 14,000
Women's Airforce Service Pilots (WASP) 1,074
Army Nurse Corps 60,000
Marine Corps Women's Reserve 23,000
Women's Army Corps (WAC) 150,000
Coast Guard Women's Reserves (SPARS) 10,000
Navy's Women Accepted for Voluntary Emergency Service (WAVES) 100,000

WOMEN IN WORLD WAR II

While American women first began serving in the military overseas during World War I, their role vastly expanded during World War II, with more than 350,000 serving in positions ranging from nurses to truck drivers to radio operators to test pilots. And with so many men fighting abroad, women at home worked in factories turning out food rations, uniforms, aircraft, and even weapons to supply the Allied troops. Some 3.5 million women volunteered for the American Red Cross.

TIME LINE OF THE U.S. RISE TO POWER

July 28, 1914: After its heir to the throne is assassinated, **Austria-Hungary declares war on Serbia.** Russia aligns with Serbia.

April 1917: The U.S. declares war on Germany (and on Austria-Hungary in December).

Nov. 1918: Austria-Hungary signs a **peace treaty** with Italy.

1898 **1914** **1917** **1918** **1919**

April 25, 1898: The U.S. declares war on Spain; it gains Guam, Puerto Rico, and the Philippines.

Aug. 1-4, 1914: Germany and Austria-Hungary declare war on Russia. Germany declares war on France and Belgium. Britain declares war on Germany. Western Front trenches are quickly dug.

Dec. 1917: The fledgling Soviet Union signs a **truce** with Germany and allies.

June 1919: Germany signs a **peace treaty** with the Allies, ending World War I.

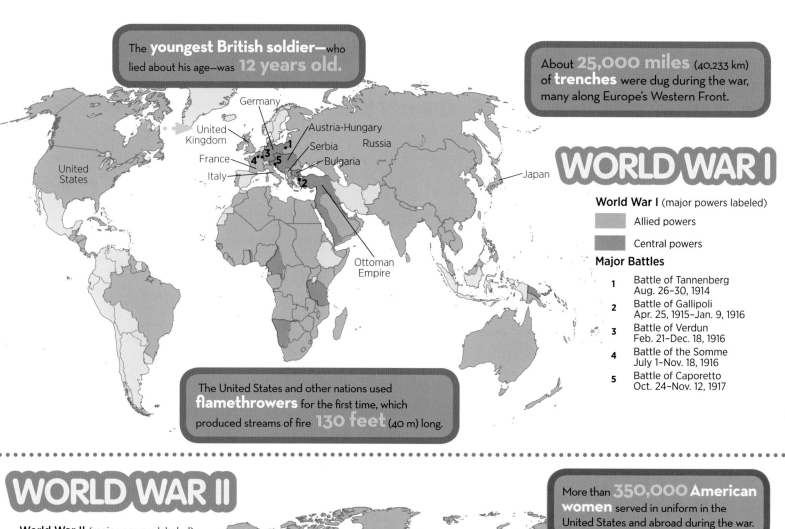

The **youngest British soldier**—who lied about his age—was **12 years old.**

About **25,000 miles** (40,233 km) of **trenches** were dug during the war, many along Europe's Western Front.

Germany
United Kingdom
Austria-Hungary
Serbia
Russia
France
Bulgaria
Italy
Japan
United States
Ottoman Empire

WORLD WAR I

World War I (major powers labeled)

Allied powers

Central powers

Major Battles

1 Battle of Tannenberg
Aug. 26–30, 1914
2 Battle of Gallipoli
Apr. 25, 1915–Jan. 9, 1916
3 Battle of Verdun
Feb. 21–Dec. 18, 1916
4 Battle of the Somme
July 1–Nov. 18, 1916
5 Battle of Caporetto
Oct. 24–Nov. 12, 1917

The United States and other nations used **flamethrowers** for the first time, which produced streams of fire **130 feet** (40 m) long.

WORLD WAR II

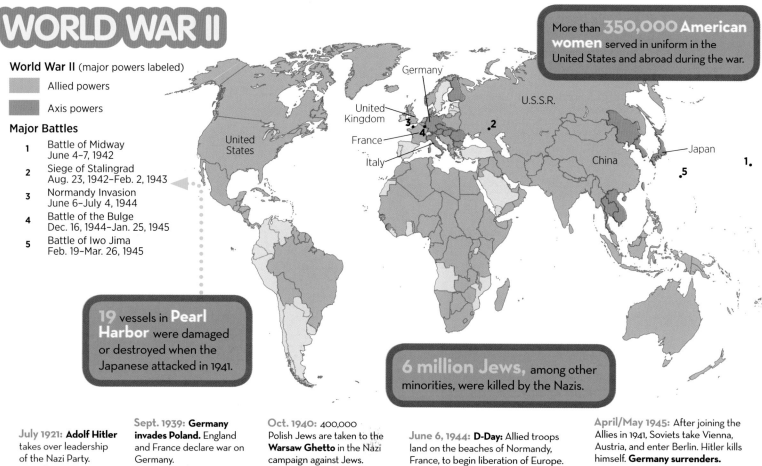

More than **350,000 American women** served in uniform in the United States and abroad during the war.

World War II (major powers labeled)

Allied powers

Axis powers

Major Battles

1 Battle of Midway
June 4–7, 1942
2 Siege of Stalingrad
Aug. 23, 1942–Feb. 2, 1943
3 Normandy Invasion
June 6–July 4, 1944
4 Battle of the Bulge
Dec. 16, 1944–Jan. 25, 1945
5 Battle of Iwo Jima
Feb. 19–Mar. 26, 1945

Germany
United Kingdom
France
Italy
U.S.S.R.
United States
China
Japan

19 vessels in **Pearl Harbor** were damaged or destroyed when the Japanese attacked in 1941.

6 million Jews, among other minorities, were killed by the Nazis.

July 1921: Adolf Hitler takes over leadership of the Nazi Party.

Sept. 1939: Germany invades Poland. England and France declare war on Germany.

Oct. 1940: 400,000 Polish Jews are taken to the **Warsaw Ghetto** in the Nazi campaign against Jews.

June 6, 1944: D-Day: Allied troops land on the beaches of Normandy, France, to begin liberation of Europe.

April/May 1945: After joining the Allies in 1941, Soviets take Vienna, Austria, and enter Berlin. Hitler kills himself. **Germany surrenders.**

| 1921 | 1931 | 1939 | 1940 | 1942 | 1944 | 1945 |

Sept. 18, 1931: To expand its empire and gather resources, **Japan invades Manchuria.**

1940: Japan occupies Indochina; it signs a pact with Germany and Italy to establish "a new order of things."

Dec. 1940: Japan attacks Hawaii's **Pearl Harbor.** Battles begin in the Pacific.

June 4–7, 1942: U.S. code breakers alert the army to a Japanese invasion of **Midway,** a base that guards Hawaii in the Pacific. Four Japanese carriers are destroyed.

Aug. 1945: The U.S. drops the **atomic bomb** on Hiroshima and then Nagasaki. Japan surrenders and World War II ends.

23

THE CIVIL RIGHTS MOVEMENT

1954–1968

The modern civil rights movement—a period centered around the struggle for African-American equality—emerged after World War II. In many places in the South, African Americans couldn't share water fountains, restaurants, or schools with whites. Activists used protests—sometimes violent—such as marches, boycotts, and sit-ins to change these racist laws and customs. Their movement inspired others, including Native Americans, Asian Americans, Latinos, gays and lesbians—and women—to demand their constitutional rights.

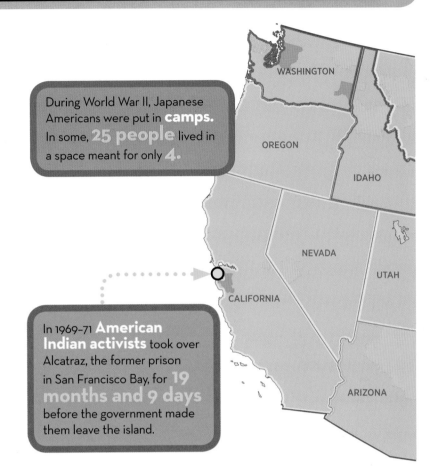

During World War II, Japanese Americans were put in **camps.** In some, **25 people** lived in a space meant for only **4.**

In 1969–71 **American Indian activists** took over Alcatraz, the former prison in San Francisco Bay, for **19 months and 9 days** before the government made them leave the island.

CIVIL RIGHTS LEADERS

THURGOOD MARSHALL
1908–1993

Who: First African-American member of the U.S. Supreme Court

Known for: Working as a lawyer for the NAACP on the *Brown v. Board of Education* case in 1950, which desegregated schools

MARTIN LUTHER KING
1929–1968

Who: Baptist minister and national face of the civil rights cause

Known for: Leading nonviolent protests against racial inequality; his "I Have a Dream" speech given on the National Mall in Washington, D.C., in 1963

JOHN F. KENNEDY
1917–1963

Who: 35th president of the United States

Known for: Leading the early charge to advance civil rights; he was assassinated in November 1963.

LYNDON B. JOHNSON
1908–1973

Who: 36th U.S. president, who took office after President Kennedy was assassinated

Known for: The "Great Society" program of legislation that included the 1964 Civil Rights Act and 1965 Voting Rights Act, and a push to end poverty and inequality

VOICES OF THE PEOPLE

"Our mistreatment was just not right, and I was tired of it."
—ROSA PARKS, chapter secretary of the Montgomery National Association for the Advancement of Colored People (NAACP) in the 1940s and 1950s. She was arrested when she refused to give up her bus seat to a white passenger on December 1, 1955, further catalyzing the civil rights movement.

"I won't have it made until the most underprivileged Negro in Mississippi can live in equal dignity with anyone else in America."
—JACKIE ROBINSON, the first African American to play major league baseball in the 20th century and member of the Baseball Hall of Fame. He spoke out strongly for black civil rights.

"The artist must elect to fight for Freedom or for Slavery. I have made my choice. I had no alternative."
—PAUL ROBESON, actor, singer, and lawyer. He spoke strongly for civil rights and against racism. The U.S. government persecuted him in the 1940s and 1950s for his communist beliefs.

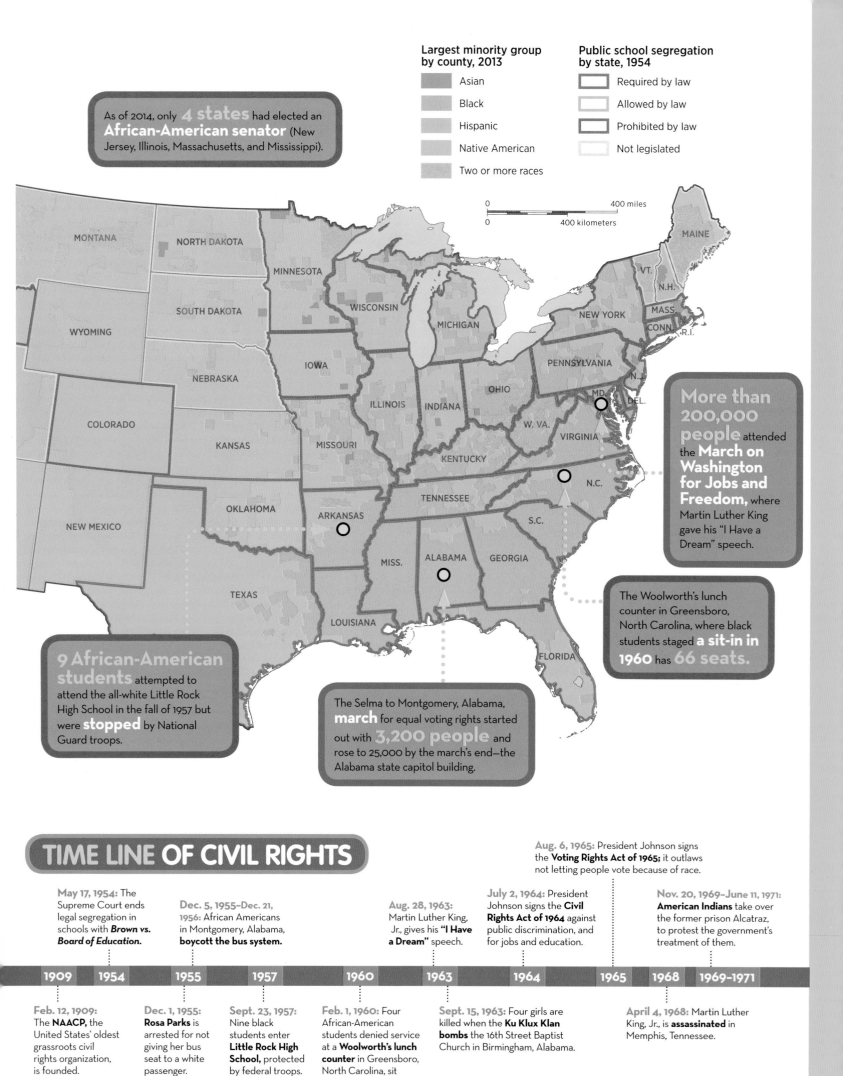

As of 2014, only **4 states** had elected an **African-American senator** (New Jersey, Illinois, Massachusetts, and Mississippi).

Largest minority group by county, 2013
- Asian
- Black
- Hispanic
- Native American
- Two or more races

Public school segregation by state, 1954
- Required by law
- Allowed by law
- Prohibited by law
- Not legislated

0   400 miles
0   400 kilometers

More than **200,000 people** attended the **March on Washington for Jobs and Freedom**, where Martin Luther King gave his "I Have a Dream" speech.

The Woolworth's lunch counter in Greensboro, North Carolina, where black students staged **a sit-in in 1960** has **66 seats.**

9 African-American students attempted to attend the all-white Little Rock High School in the fall of 1957 but were **stopped** by National Guard troops.

The Selma to Montgomery, Alabama, **march** for equal voting rights started out with **3,200 people** and rose to 25,000 by the march's end—the Alabama state capitol building.

MONTANA, NORTH DAKOTA, MINNESOTA, MAINE, VT., N.H., WISCONSIN, MICHIGAN, NEW YORK, MASS., CONN., R.I., SOUTH DAKOTA, WYOMING, IOWA, PENNSYLVANIA, N.J., NEBRASKA, OHIO, MD., DEL., ILLINOIS, INDIANA, W. VA., VIRGINIA, COLORADO, KANSAS, MISSOURI, KENTUCKY, N.C., NEW MEXICO, OKLAHOMA, ARKANSAS, TENNESSEE, S.C., TEXAS, MISS., ALABAMA, GEORGIA, LOUISIANA, FLORIDA

TIME LINE OF CIVIL RIGHTS

May 17, 1954: The Supreme Court ends legal segregation in schools with *Brown vs. Board of Education.*

Dec. 5, 1955–Dec. 21, 1956: African Americans in Montgomery, Alabama, **boycott the bus system.**

Aug. 28, 1963: Martin Luther King, Jr., gives his **"I Have a Dream"** speech.

July 2, 1964: President Johnson signs the **Civil Rights Act of 1964** against public discrimination, and for jobs and education.

Aug. 6, 1965: President Johnson signs the **Voting Rights Act of 1965;** it outlaws not letting people vote because of race.

Nov. 20, 1969–June 11, 1971: **American Indians** take over the former prison Alcatraz, to protest the government's treatment of them.

| 1909 | 1954 | 1955 | 1957 | 1960 | 1963 | 1964 | 1965 | 1968 | 1969–1971 |

Feb. 12, 1909: The **NAACP,** the United States' oldest grassroots civil rights organization, is founded.

Dec. 1, 1955: **Rosa Parks** is arrested for not giving her bus seat to a white passenger.

Sept. 23, 1957: Nine black students enter **Little Rock High School,** protected by federal troops.

Feb. 1, 1960: Four African-American students denied service at a **Woolworth's lunch counter** in Greensboro, North Carolina, sit there in protest.

Sept. 15, 1963: Four girls are killed when the **Ku Klux Klan bombs** the 16th Street Baptist Church in Birmingham, Alabama.

April 4, 1968: Martin Luther King, Jr., is **assassinated** in Memphis, Tennessee.

THE COLD WAR AND CHANGE

1945–1999

With the end of World War II, the United States entered a "Cold War" with the Soviet Union, spending trillions of dollars to counter what the U.S. perceived was a Soviet desire to conquer the world through a philosophy called communism—in which there are no social classes and all property is held in common. While the countries never met on the battlefield, the U.S. did fight communist threats in Korea and Vietnam. In 1991 the Soviet Union dissolved into 15 countries (including the largest, Russia), and the Cold War ended. By the end of the 20th century, the world could watch global events in real time—TVs and computers were standard in American homes and the Internet connected people globally.

NUCLEAR BOMB THREATS

During the Cold War, Americans worried that a nuclear attack could happen at any time. School-kids across the country engaged in "duck-and-cover" drills in their classrooms, where they would hide under their desks. Families built bomb shelters in their backyards. The threat gradually lessened, and today these drills are a thing of the past.

EAST GERMANY

Checkpoint

Wall

FRENCH SECTOR

West Berlin

BRITISH SECTOR

AMERICAN SECTOR

SOVIET SECTOR

East Berlin

Tempelhof Airport

EAST GERMANY

0   4 miles
0   4 kilometers

Historic boundaries are shown.

THE BERLIN WALL: A CITY DIVIDED

In 1961 the Berlin Wall was built in an effort to keep East Germans from crossing from communist East Berlin into democratic West Berlin. Thousands of people tried to escape by jumping over the wall, tunneling underneath it, hiding in secret compartments in cars to pass through checkpoints, or even walking a tightrope across to the West. While many were successful, many died in their daring attempts to reach freedom.

Orbital Space Launch Totals by Decade

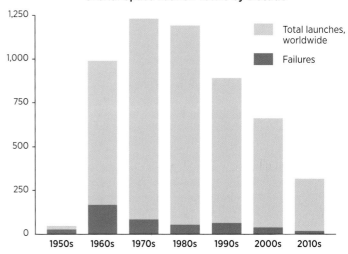

Total launches, worldwide

Failures

1,250 · 1,000 · 750 · 500 · 250 · 0

1950s · 1960s · 1970s · 1980s · 1990s · 2000s · 2010s

FROM TV TO INTERNET:

CONNECTING THE WORLD

In 1945 people read newspapers and listened to the radio for current news. By the end of the 1960s, some 95 percent of all American households owned a TV. By the 1990s another new technology—the Internet—was changing communication by connecting computers (and people) around the world.

THE SPACE RACE

When in 1957 the Soviet Union launched a satellite, Sputnik 1, into space, the "space race" between the United States and the Soviet Union had started. In 1961 President John F. Kennedy challenged the U.S. to put a man on the moon by the end of the 1960s. In July 1969 that promise became a reality when Neil Armstrong and then Buzz Aldrin stepped out onto the moon's surface. Soon other countries were spending money to join in the space race.

Worldwide, an estimated **528 million people** watched American astronauts **walk on the moon in 1969.**

At least **138 people** died trying to cross the **Berlin Wall** or were killed by accident.

In 1950 only **11 percent** of American households had a **TV;** by 1960 that number was 88 percent.

Soviet Union (U.S.S.R.)

United States

During the **Vietnam War, 58,220 U.S. soldiers** died.

The **Cuban Missile Crisis—** when the Soviet Union started to move nuclear missiles to Cuba—lasted for **13 days** in October 1962.

About **40 percent** of all American households had a **personal computer** in 1997. Only a third of those could connect to the Internet.

The Cold War, 1945–1991

United States and allies

American influence

Allied colonies

Soviet Union and allies

Soviet influence

Map shows boundaries of 1962.

TIME LINE OF THE COLD WAR

June 30, 1950: President Truman orders U.S. troops to fight communist forces in **Korea.** A truce is declared in 1953.

Sept. 26, 1960: A **televised presidential debate** between John F. Kennedy and Richard Nixon helps elect Kennedy.

Aug. 13, 1961: The **Berlin Wall** encircles East Berlin, Germany.

July 20, 1969: The Apollo 11 lunar module, the Eagle, and its crew **land on the moon.**

Nov. 22, 1963: President Kennedy is **assassinated** in Dallas, Texas.

April 30, 1975: South Vietnam falls to communist troops, ending the Vietnam War.

Nov. 9, 1989: The **Berlin Wall comes down** and the Soviet Union starts to collapse.

| 1947 | 1953 | 1957 | 1960 | 1961 | 1962 | 1963 | 1964 | 1969 | 1974 | 1975 | 1981 | 1989 |

March 12, 1947: President Harry Truman says the United States will help countries fight communist forces. The **Cold War** begins.

Oct. 4, 1957: The Soviet Union launches **Sputnik 1,** the first satellite in space. The American-Soviet "space race" begins.

April 12, 1961: Soviet cosmonaut Yuri Gagarin becomes the **first person in space.**

Oct. 1962: The Soviet Union and the U.S. agree to **remove their nuclear weapons** from Cuba and Turkey.

Aug. 7, 1964: Congress supports defending Southeast Asia against communism. The **Vietnam War** builds.

Aug. 9, 1974: President Nixon resigns after the **Watergate scandal** exposes presidential wrongdoing.

Jan. 20, 1981: President Ronald Reagan takes office. His **"Reagan Revolution"** reduces the role of government.

THE NEW MILLENNIUM

2000-PLUS

Phones on our wrists and computers on our sunglasses. Robotic hands and artificial hearts. Self-driving cars and an expedition to Mars. What was once the stuff of science fiction is becoming reality in the first two decades of the 21st century. Smartphones have been imagined and continuously reinvented during this century. Medical advancements are leading to longer, more productive lives. Scientists are combating climate change with cleaner forms of energy. And plans are in the works to send civilians into space—and some day to colonize Mars!

9/11/2001
TRAGEDY AND WORLD CHANGE

On the morning of September 11, 2001, an Islamist extremist group called al Qaeda coordinated terrorist attacks that killed nearly 3,000 people. Four commercial airplanes were hijacked: Two crashed into the twin towers of New York City's World Trade Center, causing their collapse; a third plane crashed into the Pentagon in Arlington, Virginia; a fourth crashed in a field in Pennsylvania after passengers fought the terrorists. Those events led to the United States launching a "War on Terror" and invading Afghanistan to take down al Qaeda. Also, security was increased at airports and borders. Today, the 9/11 Memorial replaces the twin towers. Two reflecting pools feature 30-foot (9-m) waterfalls—the largest man-made waterfalls in North America.

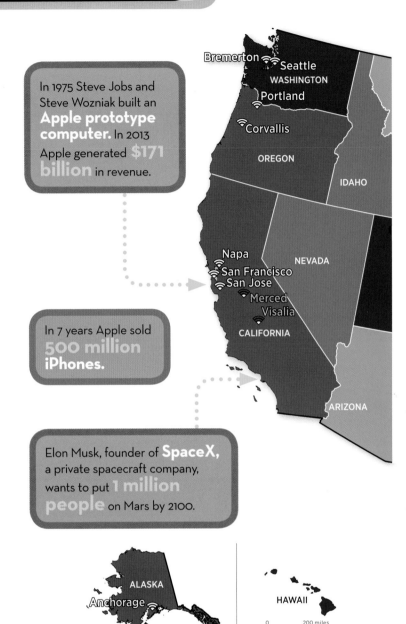

In 1975 Steve Jobs and Steve Wozniak built an **Apple prototype computer.** In 2013 Apple generated **$171 billion** in revenue.

In 7 years Apple sold **500 million iPhones.**

Elon Musk, founder of **SpaceX,** a private spacecraft company, wants to put **1 million people** on Mars by 2100.

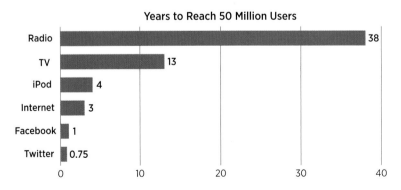

Years to Reach 50 Million Users

Medium	Years
Radio	38
TV	13
iPod	4
Internet	3
Facebook	1
Twitter	0.75

SUPER CONNECTORS

Radio and TV were key communications tools in the 20th century. Today, getting news and staying in touch is super speedy thanks to new tools. Some 98 percent of Americans use the Internet—through computers, phones, even watches. Compare how long it took mediums from radio to Twitter to reach 50 million users.

28

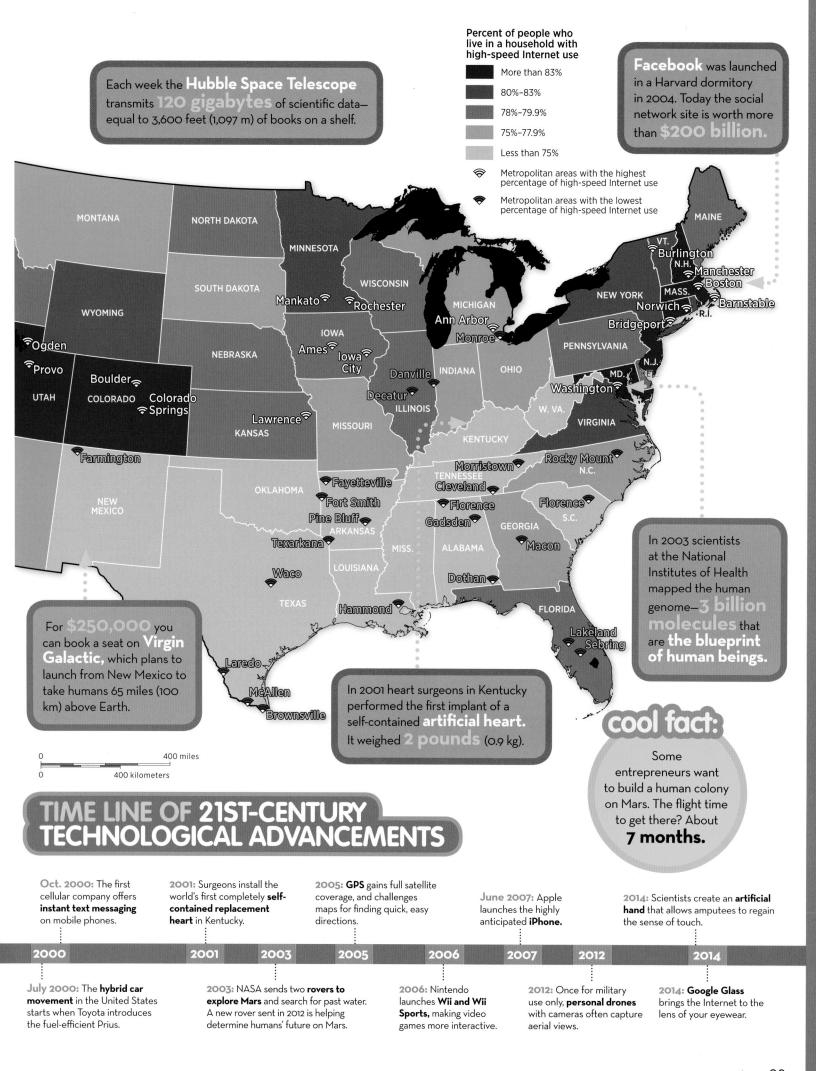

Each week the **Hubble Space Telescope** transmits **120 gigabytes** of scientific data—equal to 3,600 feet (1,097 m) of books on a shelf.

Facebook was launched in a Harvard dormitory in 2004. Today the social network site is worth more than **$200 billion.**

Percent of people who live in a household with high-speed Internet use
- More than 83%
- 80%–83%
- 78%–79.9%
- 75%–77.9%
- Less than 75%

Metropolitan areas with the highest percentage of high-speed Internet use
Metropolitan areas with the lowest percentage of high-speed Internet use

In 2003 scientists at the National Institutes of Health mapped the human genome—**3 billion molecules** that are **the blueprint of human beings.**

For **$250,000** you can book a seat on **Virgin Galactic,** which plans to launch from New Mexico to take humans 65 miles (100 km) above Earth.

In 2001 heart surgeons in Kentucky performed the first implant of a self-contained **artificial heart.** It weighed **2 pounds** (0.9 kg).

cool fact:
Some entrepreneurs want to build a human colony on Mars. The flight time to get there? About **7 months.**

0   400 miles
0   400 kilometers

TIME LINE OF 21ST-CENTURY TECHNOLOGICAL ADVANCEMENTS

Oct. 2000: The first cellular company offers **instant text messaging** on mobile phones.

2001: Surgeons install the world's first completely **self-contained replacement heart** in Kentucky.

2005: GPS gains full satellite coverage, and challenges maps for finding quick, easy directions.

June 2007: Apple launches the highly anticipated **iPhone.**

2014: Scientists create an **artificial hand** that allows amputees to regain the sense of touch.

| 2000 | 2001 | 2003 | 2005 | 2006 | 2007 | 2012 | 2014 |

July 2000: The **hybrid car movement** in the United States starts when Toyota introduces the fuel-efficient Prius.

2003: NASA sends two **rovers to explore Mars** and search for past water. A new rover sent in 2012 is helping determine humans' future on Mars.

2006: Nintendo launches **Wii and Wii Sports,** making video games more interactive.

2012: Once for military use only, **personal drones** with cameras often capture aerial views.

2014: Google Glass brings the Internet to the lens of your eyewear.

POPULATION

IT'S RISING FAST!

The population of the United States topped 300 million in 2006, and it continues to grow by more than 600,000 people each year. New York City alone has at least 8.1 million. The map shows the number of people per square mile for each county in every state. Populations are most dense in the East and along the West Coast, especially around major cities. The most rapid growth is in the South and West.

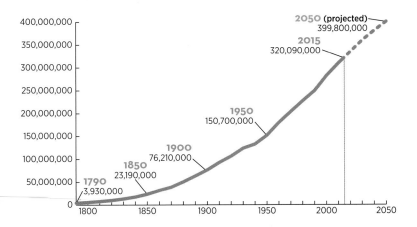

- 2050 (projected) 399,800,000
- 2015 320,090,000
- 1950 150,700,000
- 1900 76,210,000
- 1850 23,190,000
- 1790 3,930,000

THE FIRST UNITED STATES CENSUS was taken in 1790 after the passage of the U.S. Constitution, under Secretary of State Thomas Jefferson. This official count of all people living in U.S. homes has taken place every decade since—a total of 22! People counted include citizens, noncitizen legal residents, noncitizen long-term visitors, and illegal immigrants.

19.6 percent of Alaska's population is **American Indian, or Alaska native.**

56 percent of the population of Hawaii is Asian.

ALASKA

400 miles
400 kilometers

HAWAII

150 miles
150 kilometers

WASHINGTON
Seattle
Portland
OREGON
IDAHO
Sacramento   NEVADA   UTAH
San Francisco Oakland
San Jose
Fresno
CALIFORNIA
Las Vegas
Los Angeles
Long Beach   ARIZONA
San Diego   Phoenix
Mesa
Tucson

Los Angeles ranks as the city with the worst traffic in the United States. The average commuter there spends **90 hours a year** stuck in traffic.

14.5 million people in California are Hispanic, the largest Hispanic population of any state.

RUSH HOUR!

In **Los Angeles,** known to have some of the worst traffic in the country, cars flood the streets and freeways during rush hour. With more than three-quarters of the U.S. population living in urban areas, commuter transportation poses a major challenge to U.S. cities. In Los Angeles County, with a population of nearly 10 million people, morning backups can begin before 5 A.M.

Most Populous Countries, 2015

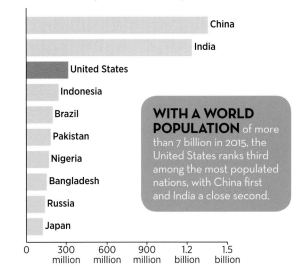

China
India
United States
Indonesia
Brazil
Pakistan
Nigeria
Bangladesh
Russia
Japan

0 | 300 million | 600 million | 900 million | 1.2 billion | 1.5 billion

WITH A WORLD POPULATION of more than 7 billion in 2015, the United States ranks third among the most populated nations, with China first and India a close second.

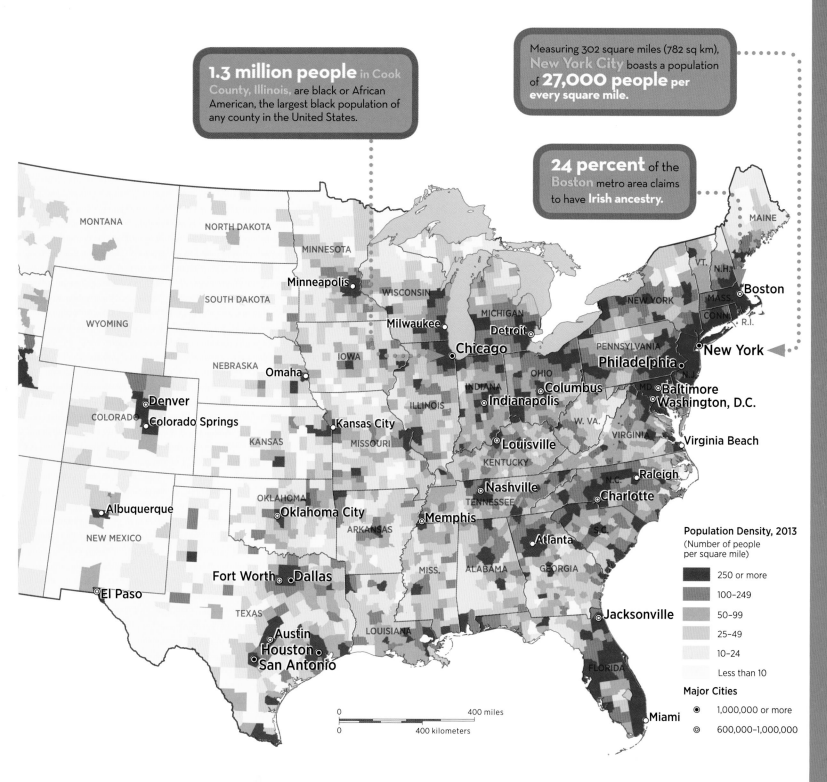

1.3 million people in Cook County, Illinois, are black or African American, the largest black population of any county in the United States.

Measuring 302 square miles (782 sq km), **New York City** boasts a population of **27,000 people** per every square mile.

24 percent of the **Boston** metro area claims to have **Irish ancestry.**

MONTANA

NORTH DAKOTA

MINNESOTA

MAINE

WISCONSIN

SOUTH DAKOTA

Minneapolis

MICHIGAN

VT.

N.H.

WYOMING

Milwaukee

Detroit

NEW YORK

MASS.

Boston

NEBRASKA

IOWA

Chicago

CONN.

R.I.

Omaha

PENNSYLVANIA

New York

ILLINOIS

INDIANA

OHIO

Columbus

Philadelphia

N.J.

Denver

Indianapolis

MD.

Baltimore

COLORADO

Colorado Springs

Washington, D.C.

KANSAS

MISSOURI

Kansas City

Louisville

W. VA.

Virginia Beach

KENTUCKY

VIRGINIA

Albuquerque

OKLAHOMA

Nashville

N.C.

Raleigh

NEW MEXICO

Oklahoma City

TENNESSEE

Charlotte

ARKANSAS

Memphis

S.C.

El Paso

Atlanta

MISS.

ALABAMA

GEORGIA

Fort Worth

Dallas

TEXAS

LOUISIANA

Austin

Houston

Jacksonville

San Antonio

FLORIDA

Miami

Population Density, 2013
(Number of people per square mile)

- 250 or more
- 100–249
- 50–99
- 25–49
- 10–24
- Less than 10

Major Cities

- 1,000,000 or more
- 600,000–1,000,000

0   400 miles
0   400 kilometers

HOW OLD ARE WE?

A group of people who share common characteristics or experiences is called a cohort. Today's population falls into five main cohorts, with birth dates from 1925 to the present day:

- **SILENT GENERATION: Born 1925–1942.** Second smallest generation born in the United States, probably due to the Great Depression

- **BABY BOOMERS: Born 1946–1964.** One of America's largest generations, born after WWII

- **GENERATION X: Born 1965–1981.** Often called "Baby Bust" because of the lower number of births after the "boom"

- **GENERATION Y: Born 1980s to early 2000s.** Also called "Millennials" and "Echo Boom," their large numbers are the result of many baby boomers having children.

- **GENERATION Z: Born mid-2000s to today.** Also called the "Homeland Generation" or "digital natives" for their birth into the digital world

OUR LAND AND RESOURCES

Wild Lands, Wild Weather

From vast deserts to temperate rain forests to rocky coasts to mangrove swamps, America's land is one of the most varied in the world. It's also rich in natural resources—including timber, natural gas, iron, and the world's largest coal reserves. In 1916 the National Park Service was established to conserve the scenery, natural and historic objects, and wildlife in places set aside as U.S. parks and monuments. Today the National Park Service has more than 400 properties.

cool fact:

The U.S. has the highest rate of **tornadoes** of any country—an average of more than 1,000 per year.

Timber harvest has reduced the number of old-growth coast redwood forests to only **120,000 acres** (48,562 ha). That's 5 percent of the original size.

Death Valley National Park had the hottest temperature ever recorded in the U.S. at **134°F** (56°C).

The trans-Alaska pipeline— which transports crude oil from Alaska's North Slope to Prince William Sound in the south, is **800 miles** (1,287 km) long and 4 feet (1.2 m) in diameter.

WASHINGTON
OREGON
NEVADA
CALIFORNIA
ALASKA

0   400 miles
0   400 kilometers

HAWAII

0   150 miles
0   150 kilometers

ENDANGERED ANIMALS

KEMP'S RIDLEY SEA TURTLE

The Kemp's ridley sea turtle, which lives primarily in the Gulf of Mexico, is the most endangered sea turtle. Weighing about 100 pounds (45 kg), the turtle's population has been devastated by overharvesting of eggs and by juveniles and adults getting caught in fishing nets. Only about 1,000 breeding females exist worldwide.

MOST ENDANGERED

GRAY WOLF

Gray wolves, once widespread throughout North America, were hunted to near-extinction in the lower 48 states by the early 20th century—mostly by settlers in the West who blamed the wolves for killing their livestock. In the 1970s gray wolves gained protective status, and in the 1990s they were reintroduced into the greater Yellowstone ecosystem. Today some 6,000 gray wolves roam Yellowstone's northern Rockies and beyond—to the western Great Lakes regions—a conservation success story.

BIGGEST COMEBACK

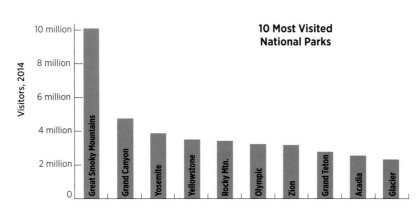

10 Most Visited National Parks

Visitors, 2014

- 10 million — Great Smoky Mountains
- 8 million
- 6 million
- 4 million — Grand Canyon
- 2 million — Yosemite, Yellowstone, Rocky Mtn., Olympic, Zion, Grand Teton, Acadia, Glacier
- 0

TOP 10 MOST VISITED U.S. NATIONAL PARKS

In 1872 Yellowstone was established as America's first national park "for the benefit and enjoyment of the people." Today the government and private companies work together to keep lands protected and accessible for the 275 million visitors who come from around the world to visit U.S. national parks every year.

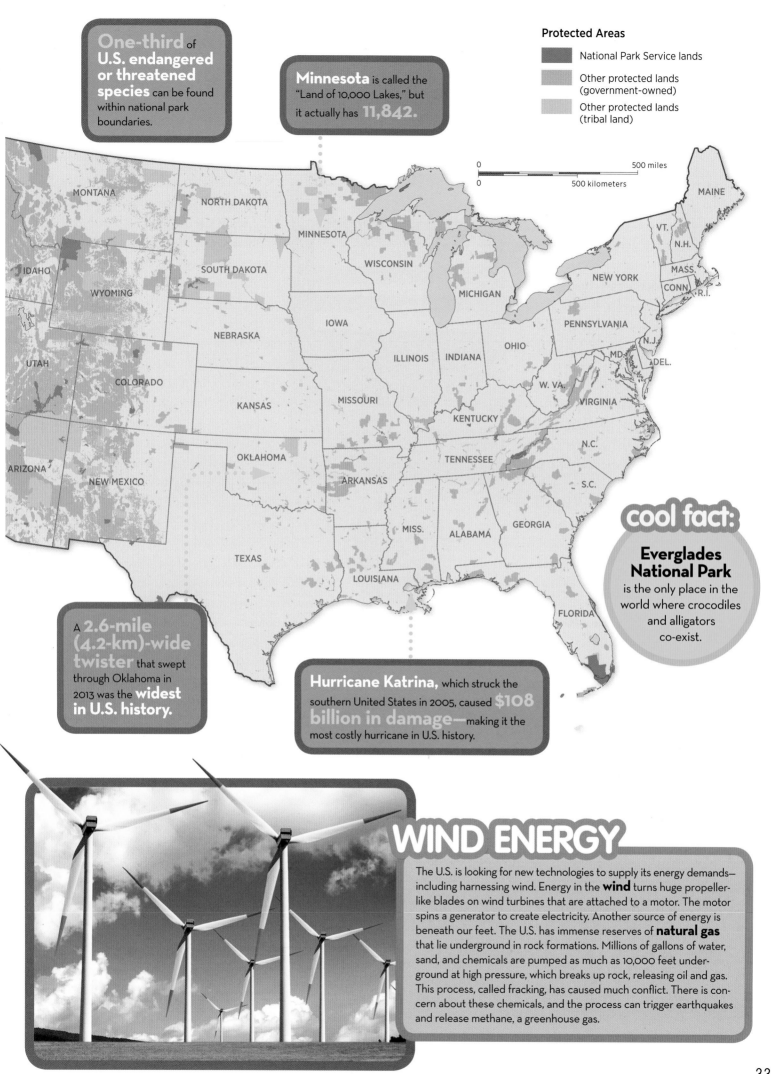

One-third of **U.S. endangered or threatened species** can be found within national park boundaries.

Minnesota is called the "Land of 10,000 Lakes," but it actually has **11,842**.

Protected Areas

- National Park Service lands
- Other protected lands (government-owned)
- Other protected lands (tribal land)

0   500 miles
0   500 kilometers

MONTANA

NORTH DAKOTA

MINNESOTA

MAINE

IDAHO

SOUTH DAKOTA

WISCONSIN

VT.

N.H.

WYOMING

MICHIGAN

NEW YORK

MASS.

CONN.

R.I.

UTAH

NEBRASKA

IOWA

PENNSYLVANIA

N.J.

COLORADO

ILLINOIS

INDIANA

OHIO

MD.

DEL.

ARIZONA

KANSAS

MISSOURI

W. VA.

VIRGINIA

NEW MEXICO

OKLAHOMA

KENTUCKY

N.C.

TENNESSEE

S.C.

ARKANSAS

GEORGIA

MISS.

ALABAMA

TEXAS

LOUISIANA

FLORIDA

cool fact:

Everglades National Park is the only place in the world where crocodiles and alligators co-exist.

A **2.6-mile (4.2-km)-wide twister** that swept through Oklahoma in 2013 was the **widest in U.S. history.**

Hurricane Katrina, which struck the southern United States in 2005, caused **$108 billion in damage**—making it the most costly hurricane in U.S. history.

WIND ENERGY

The U.S. is looking for new technologies to supply its energy demands—including harnessing wind. Energy in the **wind** turns huge propeller-like blades on wind turbines that are attached to a motor. The motor spins a generator to create electricity. Another source of energy is beneath our feet. The U.S. has immense reserves of **natural gas** that lie underground in rock formations. Millions of gallons of water, sand, and chemicals are pumped as much as 10,000 feet underground at high pressure, which breaks up rock, releasing oil and gas. This process, called fracking, has caused much conflict. There is concern about these chemicals, and the process can trigger earthquakes and release methane, a greenhouse gas.

WASHINGTON, D.C.

THE NATION'S CAPITAL

The nation's capital. To the people of the United States, it is a place of symbol and power like no other. It is the seat of the U.S. government, where decisions are made that affect not only the country but the world. It is a magnet for tourists, who come to see its splendid monuments and museums, and home to more than 600,000 ordinary citizens.

In 1790 northern and southern leaders agreed on a capital location somewhere along the Potomac River. A compromise was made between Alexander Hamilton, who represented the northern states' wish for a new government to take over debts from the Revolutionary War, and Thomas Jefferson, who voiced the southern states' desire for a capital close to the agricultural South and friendly to slaveholders.

It was President Washington who chose the exact spot the following year. He also selected French architect Pierre L'Enfant to design a grand city of massive boulevards and spaces for ceremony, like his home city of Paris, France. A self-taught African-American mathematical genius, Benjamin Banneker, aided L'Enfant by making the calculations for surveying and planning the city. The new city grew up on land originally donated by Maryland and Virginia. Congress used Maryland's share but gave back Virginia's land in 1846.

The young city had its share of growing pains: It was burned by the British during the War of 1812; today's National Mall housed an encampment of Union soldiers during the Civil War; and streets remained little more than dirt paths until the Northwest quadrant was paved in 1871.

OFFICIAL FLAG

The first flag design in 1924 had two horizontal red stripes and three blue five-pointed stars, based on George Washington's personal coat of arms.

OFFICIAL FLOWER
American Beauty Rose

OFFICIAL BIRD
Wood Thrush

One hundred years after its founding, for its centennial, Washington's role as a monumental city was at last realized with the development of the National Mall and many of the monuments visitors enjoy today.

Washington has come to rank among the world's great capital cities. It has been home to more than 40 presidents. It houses more than 160 embassies, with representatives from around the world. And it welcomes millions of visitors each year to its National Mall with the Capitol, the Washington Monument, the Smithsonian Institution, and other museums and federal buildings. Its theaters and art centers, including the John F. Kennedy Center for the Performing Arts, welcome performers from New York to Japan and around the world.

The greater Washington metropolitan area has one of the most affluent, diverse, and educated populations in the United States. Most Washingtonians don't work for the government. Many settled here for opportunities in technology, education, international affairs, and journalism. A large core of native Washingtonians, particularly African-American families, moved here from the South generations ago when jobs in the federal government offered one of the few avenues of advancement for blacks. Now about 50 percent of the city's population is black.

City leaders look to find ways to improve life for all residents. A heavy influx of young people to Washington in recent years was reflected in a recent survey that tied the city with Seattle as the country's number one "youth magnet." A city honoring the father of our country and a district named for Columbus, Washington, D.C., remains a source of pride for all Americans.

IT'S A FACT:

D.C. residents pay more than $2 billion a year in federal taxes, yet they lack a voting representative in Congress. In 2000 a resident came up with a popular license plate motto: "Taxation Without Representation."

A TIME LINE OF THE NATION'S CAPITAL

1791
George Washington selected **Pierre L'Enfant** to design the city on land by the Potomac River.

1814
The city of Washington and the **White House** were burned by the British in the War of 1812.

1865
President Abraham Lincoln was assassinated at **Ford's Theatre** by actor John Wilkes Booth.

1912
1,800 cherry trees, a gift from Japan, were planted around the Tidal Basin at the **Jefferson Memorial.**

1986
The **Friendship Archway** over H Street in Chinatown was built to celebrate the friendship between Washington and her sister city, Beijing, China.

Present

The **Legacy Plan,** started in 1999, revitalizes the city, including redesign, renovation, and additions to the downtown, the Mall, and beyond.

ON THE MAP

MARYLAND

Potomac River

DISTRICT OF COLUMBIA

Area Enlarged

VIRGINIA

Anacostia River

0   5 mi
0   5 km

LOCATION, LOCATION

Located in the mid-Atlantic region 90 miles (145 km) inland from the Atlantic Ocean, Washington, D.C., shares a border to the north with Maryland and a southern border, the Potomac River, with Virginia. Its small plot of land—61 square miles (158 sq km)—was originally part of Maryland.

BLAIR HOUSE:
Across the street from the White House, this home was made famous by Francis Preston Blair, a key member of President Andrew Jackson's Cabinet. Today it is the guesthouse for heads of state from around the world who are visiting the president. After the White House was burned in the War of 1812, it served as the temporary residence for the president.

C & O CANAL:
Running 184.5 miles (297 km) along the Potomac River, from Georgetown to Cumberland, Maryland, the Chesapeake and Ohio Canal was vital for commerce. Barges with coal, lumber, and food were hauled by mules led along a sandy towpath.

LINCOLN MEMORIAL:
Among the most visited monuments in Washington, the Lincoln Memorial features a 19-foot (5.8-m)-high seated statue of President Abraham Lincoln, America's 16th president. He gazes across a reflecting pool toward the Washington Monument. Here, in 1963 Martin Luther King, Jr., gave his famous "I Have a Dream" speech for equality.

WHITE HOUSE:
With its site chosen by George Washington in 1791 and the unfinished house first occupied in 1800 by fourth president John Adams, the White House has been home to more than 40 presidents—including the first African-American one—and their families.

Map labels

WASHINGTON CIRCLE
K STREET
FARRAGUT SQUARE
McPHERSON SQUARE
FRANKLIN PARK
24TH STREET
I (EYE) STREET
FOGGY
St. John's Church
Department of Veterans Affairs
14TH STREET
NEW HAMPSHIRE AVENUE
PENNSYLVANIA AVENUE
17TH STREET
H STREET
NEW YORK AVENUE
22ND STREET
H STREET
Renwick Gallery
LAFAYETTE PARK
BOTTOM
George Washington University
World Bank
Blair House
ROCK CREEK AND POTOMAC PARKWAY
Watergate Complex
21ST STREET
20TH STREET
19TH STREET
G STREET
15TH STREET
F STREET
The White House
Department of the Treasury
Pan American Health Organization
General Services Administration
National Theatre
John F. Kennedy Center for the Performing Arts
Office of Personnel Management
E STREET
E STREET
Corcoran Gallery of Art
Eisenhower Executive Office Building
PERSHING PARK
FREEDOM PLAZA
Georgetown Channel
18TH STREET
VIRGINIA AVENUE
Department of Commerce
Department of State
23RD STREET
Federal Reserve Board
Department of the Interior
DAR Constitution Hall
THE ELLIPSE
National Aquarium
Ronald Reagan Building
C STREET
National Academy of Sciences
CONSTITUTION AVENUE
Organization of American States
THEODORE ROOSEVELT MEMORIAL BRIDGE
Vietnam Veterans Memorial
Vietnam Women's Memorial
THE NATIONAL MALL AND MEMORIALS PARK
Lincoln Memorial
National World War II Memorial
National Museum of American History
Potomac
Reflecting Pool
Washington Monument
ARLINGTON MEMORIAL BRIDGE
WEST POTOMAC PARK
Korean War Veterans Memorial
Sylvan Theatre
14TH STREET
INDEPENDENCE AVENUE
KUTZ BRIDGE
U.S. Holocaust Memorial Museum
GEORGE WASHINGTON MEMORIAL PARKWAY
River
FRANKLIN DELANO ROOSEVELT MEMORIAL PARK
Tidal Basin
Bureau of Engraving and Printing
D STREET
LADY BIRD JOHNSON PARK
Franklin Delano Roosevelt Memorial
OUTLET BRIDGE
OHIO DRIVE
Jefferson Memorial

0   0.125   0.25 miles
0   0.125   0.25 kilometers

STATS & FACTS

FOUNDED: 1790

LAND AREA: 61 sq mi; 159 sq km

POPULATION: 658,893

POPULATION DENSITY: 10,801 people per sq mi

MAJOR RACIAL/ETHNIC GROUPS: 50.7% African American, 38.5% white, 3.5% Asian, 0.3% Native American, Hispanic (any race) 9.1%

INDUSTRY: government, services, tourism

AGRICULTURE: cattle, cotton, dairy products, sheep, greenhouse, wheat, hay, pecans, corn

The Washington Monument: Built between 1848 and 1884 as a tribute to President George Washington, this famous landmark weighs 81,120 tons (73,590 metric tons) and rises some 555 feet (169 m) above the city.

THE U.S. CAPITOL: It marks the city center. Atop its dome, the Statue of Freedom towers 288 feet (88 m) above the ground. Inside the dome is a painting of George Washington in the heavens as a god.

Washington is divided into quadrants centered on the U.S. Capitol. Streets are numbered and lettered the same in each quadrant. The designation NW, NE, SW, or SE distinguishes one location, such as Third and K Streets, from three others identically named.

Major point of interest
Government offices and other buildings
Park and open area

SMITHSONIAN INSTITUTION: The world's largest museum and research complex, with 19 museums, started in 1849 with a redbrick castle on the Mall. It was built with a gift from wealthy Englishman James Smithson.

LIBRARY OF CONGRESS: The nation's biggest library is a leader among world libraries, with more than 36 million books and other print material in 460 languages—and 838 miles (1,349 km) of bookshelves!

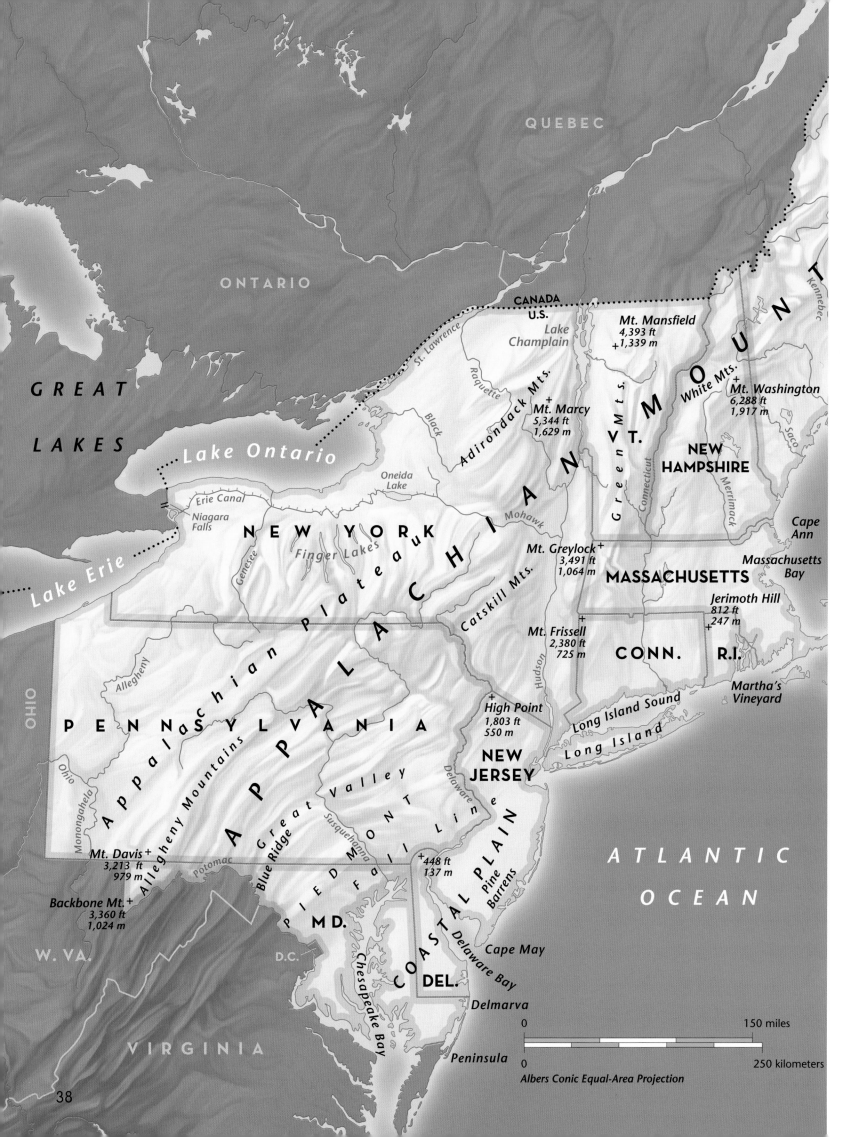

QUEBEC

ONTARIO

CANADA
U.S.

G R E A T

L A K E S

Lake Ontario

St. Lawrence

Raquette

Black

Adirondack Mts.

Lake
Champlain

Mt. Mansfield
4,393 ft
+1,339 m

White Mts.

+ Mt. Washington
6,288 ft
1,917 m

Kennebec

Saco

Mt. Marcy
+
5,344 ft
1,629 m

Green Mts.

V T.

Connecticut

NEW
HAMPSHIRE

Merrimack

Erie Canal

Niagara
Falls

N E W   Y O R K

Oneida
Lake

Mohawk

Finger Lakes

Genesee

Cape
Ann

Lake Erie

Appalachian Plateau

Catskill Mts.

Mt. Greylock +
3,491 ft
1,064 m

MASSACHUSETTS

Massachusetts
Bay

Jerimoth Hill
812 ft
+247 m

OHIO

P E N N S Y L V A N I A

A P P A L A C H I A N

Allegheny

Mt. Frissell
2,380 ft
725 m

Hudson

CONN.

R.I.

A P P A L A

Allegheny Mountains

High Point
+
1,803 ft
550 m

Long Island Sound

Long Island

Martha's
Vineyard

Ohio

Monongahela

Great

Valley

Susquehanna

P I E D M O N T

Delaware

NEW
JERSEY

Mt. Davis +
3,213 ft
979 m

Blue Ridge

Fall Line

+ 448 ft
137 m

A T L A N T I C

Backbone Mt. +
3,360 ft
1,024 m

Potomac

Pine
Barrens

C O A S T A L   P L A I N

O C E A N

W. VA.

D.C.

M D.

Cape May

Delaware Bay

Chesapeake Bay

DEL.

V I R G I N I A

Delmarva

Peninsula

0   150 miles

0   250 kilometers

Albers Conic Equal-Area Projection

38

St. John
Allagash
N S
CANADA
U.S.
+Mt. Katahdin
5,268 ft
1,605 m
MAINE
St. Croix
Penobscot

NEW BRUNSWICK

P.E.I.

NOVA SCOTIA

Mt. Desert Island

Gulf of Maine

Cape Cod

Nantucket Island

THE NORTHEAST

Retreating glaciers helped shape this crumpled landscape. The forested mountains, fertile valleys, navigable rivers, and excellent harbors attracted settlers. Over time, the Northeast has become the country's most densely populated region. The ancient Appalachian Mountains, stretching from Maine to southwestern Maryland and beyond, form the geologic backbone. The chief ranges—the White Mountains and Green Mountains of New Hampshire and Vermont, the Catskills of New York, and the Alleghenies and Blue Ridge of Pennsylvania, Maryland, and Virginia—provide mineral wealth, timber resources, and recreational playgrounds. Croplands and towns fill the valleys. Rivers flowing east out of the mountains onto the flat Atlantic Coastal Plain have helped power the industry and commerce of some of the country's oldest and largest cities from Boston to Baltimore. Waterways flowing west link the region to the Great Lakes and the Mississippi Valley.

THE NORTHEAST

ANCIENT WILDERNESS MEETS MODERN MEGALOPOLIS

This compact landscape of rocky coastline, fertile valleys, and rolling mountains inspired local author Emily Dickinson to "Think New Englandy." The Northeast's rich history of self-governing began in the 1500s (and perhaps much earlier), when five Native American tribes agreed to mutual trade and peaceful treaties under the Iroquois Confederacy. The original Mohawk, Oneida, Onondaga, Cayuga, and Seneca tribes thrived by hunting, fishing, collecting berries, and trading these and other resources with nearby tribes.

In 1620 the region's first European colonists arrived and began gradually displacing the Indians. Employing "Yankee ingenuity" and a strong dose of Puritan work ethic, America's colonial economy literally sprang from the earth. Trees cut from the dense forests provided ample wood to craft into homes, barns, and ships. On this newly cleared land, settlers raised corn, wheat, and livestock. They also tapped maple trees for tasty syrup. From the mountains to the coastal plain, they harnessed water to drive mills—initially to grind flour and mill lumber and then, as the economy developed, to power textile factories. Although most people farmed, whalers, fishermen, shipbuilders, barrelmakers, blacksmiths, and shopkeepers all played important roles in this emerging economy.

For two centuries waves of immigrants helped propel the Northeast into the center of American manufacturing and trade. By the early 1800s cities and family farms dominated the region. An expanding network of post roads (built to deliver mail), canals, and railroads linked the growing population and their markets. Ports such as Philadelphia and Baltimore became key centers of international trade.

Throughout the 19th century the Northeast was a global industrial powerhouse. Coal, railroads, and labor powered vast iron- and steelworks and factories for manufactured goods. During the Civil War, the Northeast, with its rich resources and industrial might, was the core of the Union.

During the 20th century, the economy began to change. Rapidly expanding cities such as New York, Boston, and Hartford swallowed up farms, while many factories relocated to the South, and then abroad, where land and labor cost less. As manufacturing declined, the Northeast was reborn into a powerful center of international business. Today, suburbs link cities into a giant interconnected metropolitan area—called a megalopolis—that stretches from Boston to Washington, D.C., and that is home to one in five Americans. Tourism also provides new jobs, as people flock to some of America's largest parks and seashores.

CONNECTICUT
DELAWARE
MAINE
MARYLAND
MASSACHUSETTS
NEW HAMPSHIRE
NEW JERSEY
NEW YORK
PENNSYLVANIA
RHODE ISLAND
VERMONT

"I NEVER SAW AN AUTUMNAL LANDSCAPE SO BEAUTIFULLY PAINTED…IT WAS LIKE THE RICHEST RUG IMAGINABLE SPREAD OVER AN UNEVEN SURFACE."
—AUTHOR AND NATURALIST HENRY DAVID THOREAU

CONNECTICUT

THE CONSTITUTION STATE

Yankee quality is assured. The word "Yankee" probably started out as *Jankes (Yahn kes)*, a name the Dutch used to make fun of the tradespeople they competed with in the New World. By the American Revolution, people were happy to call themselves Yankees. With a long tradition of excellence and leadership in politics, seafaring, inventions, and insurance, Connecticut Yankees have plenty of reasons to be proud.

The Dutch were the first to scout the coast in 1614, but it was English colonists from Massachusetts, led by Thomas Hooker and others, who established a series of permanent settlements, including Hartford in 1635. The Pequot, the most powerful of several native groups, attacked settlements that they saw as a challenge to their regional power. In 1637 the Pequot threat was largely eliminated by soldiers who burned a native fort, killing hundreds of Indians. By the 1660s Connecticut was a colony chartered by the English king.

Critical ideas about a government "by the people" have roots in Connecticut. The early Hartford community's Fundamental Orders, based on a sermon by Thomas Hooker, became law in 1639, giving people the right to elect government officials. Nearly 150 years later, the Connecticut Compromise was adopted at the Constitutional Convention. By providing that each state would be represented by two senators, it ensured that states with small populations would be fairly represented in the new nation's Congress. Connecticut became the fifth state in early 1788, with Hartford as its capital.

The state has hummed with industry since colonial times, beginning with

STATE FLOWER
Mountain Laurel

STATE BIRD
Robin

clocks, tin pots and pans, and silverware by the 1740s. Fertile Connecticut River Valley farmlands grew plenty of corn, beans, and tobacco, and its coastal waters produced seafood. During the Revolution, cannon, cannonballs, and shot for muskets rolled from ironworks to American fighting ships and army units, starting a long tradition of military manufacturing and defense support. Connecticut inventors provided revolutionary ideas in industry. Eli Whitney came up with the idea of interchangeable parts, which made mass production possible. Samuel Colt invented the repeating pistol in 1836, and Charles Goodyear patented his method of vulcanizing, or strengthening, rubber in 1844.

Connecticut's trade and shipbuilding also flourished in the 1800s. At mid-century whaling was a huge enterprise, but it soon declined. Connecticut's ties to the sea have not. New London is home to the U.S. Coast Guard Academy; Groton is site of the U.S. Naval Submarine Base. Sea connections helped launch today's insurance industry. After the Revolution, state businessmen agreed to pay shipowners for lost cargo in return for a share of the profits if the voyage was successful. Thus was born the U.S. insurance business.

In the late 20th century many New York City–based insurance and other prominent businesses moved their headquarters to Connecticut. This brought many high-paying white collar jobs to the state, but it did little to help old industrial cities, which began to lose jobs by the 1970s. Efforts to revitalize cities, limit sprawl, and preserve the state's scenic rural areas are a focus of the state today, as Connecticut fights to keep its industrial jobs and attract more technology business. These are good Connecticut Yankee ideas likely to ensure success and keep the state a leader.

IT'S A FACT:
In 1901 Connecticut was the first state to pass a speed limit law for automobiles: 12 miles an hour (19 km/h) within cities.

A TIME LINE OF THE CONSTITUTION STATE

1635
Minister **Thomas Hooker** and a group of followers founded Hartford. He preached that government should be by the consent of the people.

1790s
Just as his **cotton gin** revolutionized the South, Eli Whitney's concept of mass production revolutionized industry in the North.

1839–1840
The ruling that freed the slaves of the *Amistad* was a landmark decision. It called attention to the right of all people to rebel against injustices.

1866
Dinosaurs died out 65 million years ago, but their fossilized skeletons still rule at the **Yale Peabody Museum of Natural History,** founded in 1866.

1949
Renowned architect Philip Johnson completed the unique **Glass House** to blend into the landscape at New Canaan.

Present
Groton, home to the **U.S. Naval Submarine Base,** is where the Virginia-class submarines, the country's newest nuclear attack subs, are being built.

ON THE MAP

LOCATION, LOCATION

Nestled between Massachusetts, New York, Rhode Island, and Long Island Sound, Connecticut's coastal location supports a long seafaring tradition. The Connecticut River flows through the center of the state, south to the sound. The name Connecticut comes from the Algonquian word for "long tidal river."

EAST GRANBY: Old New-Gate, in this city north of Hartford, was the first state prison in America. Originally a copper mine, it was used to house Loyalists to the King during the Revolutionary War.

HARTFORD: The capital, also called the "insurance capital of the world," is the birthplace of the Boys and Girls Clubs of America and home to the world's first FM radio station.

SIMSBURY: The first fully operational steel mill in the U.S. opened here in 1728.

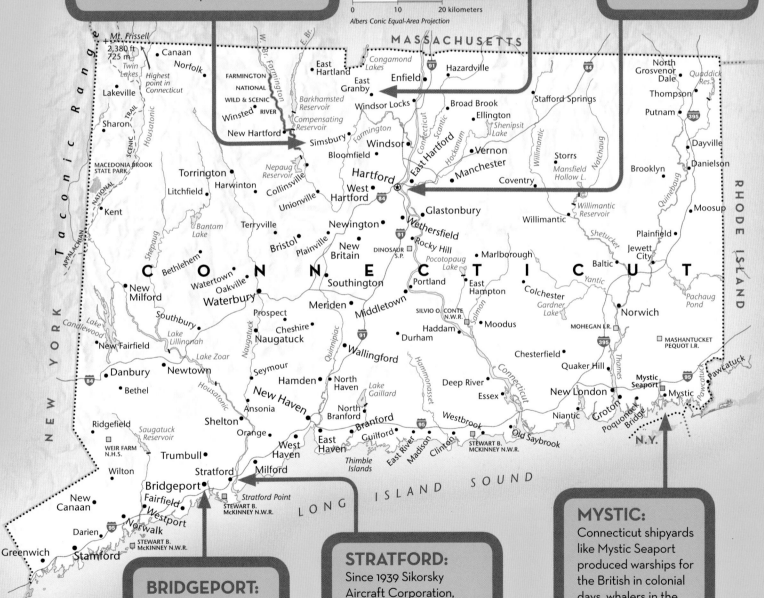

BRIDGEPORT: Connecticut's largest city (pop. 144,229), on the coast, is a 90-minute hop by train or car to New York City.

STRATFORD: Since 1939 Sikorsky Aircraft Corporation, based here, has made helicopters that contribute to the nation's military.

MYSTIC: Connecticut shipyards like Mystic Seaport produced warships for the British in colonial days, whalers in the 1800s, then clipper ships and steamers.

We the People

insure domestic Tranquility, provide for the common...
and our Posterity, do ordain and establish this Constitu...

STATS & FACTS

STATEHOOD: January 9, 1788; 5th state

CAPITAL: Hartford

TOTAL AREA: 5,543 sq mi; 14,357 sq km

LAND AREA: 4,845 sq mi; 12,548 sq km

POPULATION: 3,596,677

POPULATION DENSITY: 742 people per sq mi

MAJOR RACIAL/ETHNIC GROUPS: 77.6% white, 10.1% African American, 3.8% Asian, 0.3% Native American, Hispanic (any race) 13.4%

INDUSTRY: insurance, finance, real estate, manufacturing, service industries

AGRICULTURE: dairy products, eggs, seafood, tobacco, hay, corn, greenhouse

NATURAL FEATURES: Connecticut is home to **more than 1,000 lakes.**

HISTORY: Connecticut's 17th-century settlers governed under the "Fundamental Orders," a document that gave the people the right to elect government officials. This became a model for the **U.S. Constitution** nearly 150 years later—the basis for Connecticut's name: the Constitution State.

NATURAL FORCES: Connecticut's northwest hills average **50 inches (127 cm) of annual snowfall.**

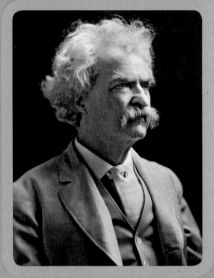

PEOPLE/ CULTURE: Nineteenth-century writer Samuel Langhorne Clemens, better known by his pen name **Mark Twain,** wrote his famous *Adventures of Huckleberry Finn* while living in Hartford.

ANIMALS: The **sperm whale,** Connecticut's state animal, has the largest brain of any creature known to have lived on Earth.

DELAWARE

THE FIRST STATE

A Jewel among states," said Thomas Jefferson about Delaware. Though Delaware is the second smallest state in area, its economic importance has long been huge. Favorable laws for starting and operating businesses have attracted a variety of enterprises. More than half of the country's largest companies call themselves Delaware corporations—even if their offices in the state are just on paper. Delaware's place in the nation's history is oversize, too. When the time came to approve the U.S. Constitution, Delaware was at the head of the line. The First State signed on December 7, 1787.

Barrier island beaches stretch for 28 miles (45 km) along Delaware's southeastern Atlantic coast. Spanning its southernmost border with Maryland is the Cypress Swamp, home of one of the northernmost stands of cypress trees in the country. Northward, the state's shoreline faces the Delaware Bay. Salt marshes here provide nesting sites for birds and breeding grounds for shellfish. In the south, farms grow soybeans and corn, which help feed the more than 200 billion broiler chickens produced annually. A wide variety of vegetables and fruits are grown for processing or transporting from "truck farms" to nearby cities. In the north, where the state narrows to less than 10 miles (16 km) in width, the Chesapeake and Delaware Canal links the two great bays. Approximately 60 percent of Delaware's population lives in this largely urban and industrial region.

When Henry Hudson sailed into Delaware Bay in 1609, Lenni-Lenape, Nanticoke, and Minqua peoples lived there. The next year, English ship captain Samuel Argall named a point of land Cape De La Warr, for the governor of Virginia. Later, the bay,

river, and state all took the name Delaware. Dutch, Swedish, and English interests competed for control of the region. New Sweden, a small colony of Swedes and Finns, was founded in 1638. A Dutch force from New Amsterdam took over in 1655, and the English finally secured the area in 1674. Eight years later, it was made part of Pennsylvania. Over time, Delaware began to operate like, then finally became, an independent colony. Its population was split between Loyalists and those wanting independence, but Delaware voted to break away.

A French immigrant, Éleuthère Irénée du Pont de Nemours, opened a gunpowder factory on Brandywine Creek in 1802, bringing industry to northern Delaware. Water powered Wilmington-area mills that made flour, paper, and cloth. Though some landowners in its southern counties used slaves, Delaware stayed in the Union. But pro-southern feelings grew during the Civil War, and Delaware did not approve the U.S. amendments securing racial equality until 1901. In the mid-1900s integration of schools and housing was hard.

Delaware continued its industrial growth in the 20th century, building oil refineries, shipyards, automaking plants, and metalworking factories during the two World Wars and after. The creek-side gunpowder mill grew into one of the world's top chemical companies, DuPont. Among its many products was the first human-made fiber—nylon—in 1935. Today Delaware enjoys better economic conditions than many states and has added roughly 17,000 jobs in the past several years. But two centuries of industrial pollution have made environmental cleanup a priority. Also under way are attempts to save remaining natural areas from development.

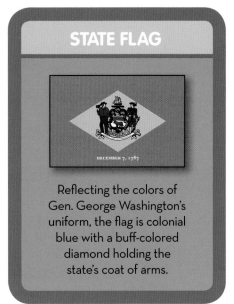

STATE FLAG

Reflecting the colors of Gen. George Washington's uniform, the flag is colonial blue with a buff-colored diamond holding the state's coat of arms.

STATE FLOWER
Peach Blossom

STATE BIRD
Blue Hen Chicken

IT'S A FACT:
Thomas Jefferson once called Delaware the "Diamond State" because it was a jewel among states due to its position on the Atlantic coast.

A TIME LINE OF THE FIRST STATE

1638

The Swedish and Finnish pioneers who founded New Sweden were skilled woodsmen who built the **first log cabins** in the New World.

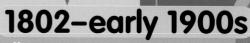

1802–early 1900s

The **E. I. du Pont mill,** which made gunpowder during the War of 1812, developed into Delaware's giant chemical industry.

1859

The foreboding island fortress called **Fort Delaware,** built in 1859, held imprisoned Confederate soldiers during the Civil War. Today it's a state park open to the public.

1951

The **Delaware Memorial Bridge** opened in 1951, providing a faster and more direct route to New Jersey and New York.

1971

Delaware took the lead in **coastal conservation** and passed laws protecting its beaches from polluting industries.

Present

As a research center for several major chemical companies, Wilmington holds the title **"chemical capital of the world."**

ON THE MAP

LOCATION, LOCATION

Bordered by Pennsylvania, New Jersey, and Maryland, Delaware enjoys an Atlantic coast lined with beautiful beaches. Its name comes from the Delaware River, named by European explorers after English governor Thomas West, the third Baron De La Warr.

WINTERTHUR:
Home of the du Pont family estate. For more than 200 years the family's wealth has supported schools, roads, and other public projects across the state.

WILMINGTON:
The largest city, with more than 71,525 people, has this motto: "A Place to Be Somebody." The area was settled by the Lenape Indians before English explorer Henry Hudson arrived in 1609.

BRANDYWINE CREEK STATE PARK:
This 1,000-acre (405-ha) home to two nature preserves includes a stand of 200-year-old tulip poplar trees.

DOVER:
The capital was named in 1683 by William Penn for Dover in Kent, England. It is home to Revolutionary War hero and Declaration of Independence signer Caesar Rodney.

KENT COUNTY:
Home of the blue hen chicken, the state bird, which symbolizes fighting spirit. One hard-fighting Revolutionary War regiment was called the Blue Hen's Chickens.

CAPE HENLOPEN STATE PARK:
Visitors can not only relax on sandy beaches and hike forest trails but also climb to the top of the WWII Observation Tower, which gives spectacular 360-degree views.

Map labels

PENNSYLVANIA

Highest point in Delaware
+ 448 ft
137 m

BRANDYWINE CREEK S.P.
Winterthur Museum, Garden & Library
Claymont
Elsmere
Marshallton
Newport
Wilmington
Newark
FIRST STATE NAT. MON.
Brookside
NEW JERSEY
Christina
Bear
Glasgow
New Castle
Delaware City
Pea Patch Island
Chesapeake and Delaware Canal
St. George
Port Penn
Reedy I.

D E L A W A R E

Odessa
Middletown
Noxontown Pond
Liston Pt.
Townsend

Smyrna
Clayton
BOMBAY HOOK NATIONAL WILDLIFE REFUGE
Goose Point
Leipsic
Deepwater Point
Cheswold
Dover International Speedway
St. Jones
Dover
Delaware Bay

Camden
Kitts Hummock
Marydel
KENT COUNTY
Bowers Beach
Felton
Frederica

D E L A W A R E

Harrington
Houston
Slaughter Beach
Milford
PRIME HOOK NATIONAL WILDLIFE REFUGE
Lincoln
Broadkill Beach
Greenwood
Ellendale
Cape Henlopen
Milton
CAPE HENLOPEN S.P.
Lewes
Lewes & Rehoboth Canal
ATLANTIC
Bridgeville
Harbeson
Rehoboth Beach
Midway
Dewey Beach
Georgetown
Rehoboth Bay
OCEAN
Seaford
Oak Orchard
Indian River Bay
Blades
Millsboro
Indian River Inlet
Laurel
Dagsboro
Ocean View
Bethany Beach
Assawoman Canal
Cypress Swamp
Frankford
South Bethany
Delmar
Selbyville
Fenwick Island

P E N I N S U L A

M A R Y L A N D

Choptank
Marshyhope
Nanticoke
Creek

0   5   10 miles
0   5   10 kilometers
Albers Conic Equal-Area Projection

STATS & FACTS

STATEHOOD: December 7, 1787; 1st state

CAPITAL: Dover

TOTAL AREA: 2,489 sq mi; 6,447 sq km

LAND AREA: 1,954 sq mi; 5,060 sq km

POPULATION: 935,614

POPULATION DENSITY: 479 people per sq mi

MAJOR RACIAL/ETHNIC GROUPS: 68.9% white, 21.4% African American, 3.2% Asian, 0.5% Native American, Hispanic (any race) 8.2%

INDUSTRY: financial services, insurance, chemicals, manufacturing, food processing

AGRICULTURE: chickens, corn, soybeans, wheat, dairy products, barley

HISTORY: Delaware got its "First State" nickname because it was the **first state to ratify the U.S. Constitution.**

ANIMALS: During full and new moons and high tides in May and June, hundreds of thousands of **horseshoe crabs** gather at Delaware Bay to mate and lay eggs.

NATURAL FEATURES: Delaware and Pennsylvania are the only states that share **a border shaped like a partial circle.**

NATURAL FORCES: About 57 percent of Delaware's days are **sunny.**

PEOPLE/CULTURE: In 1921 Margaret Gorman, a high school junior, won the **first Miss America Pageant,** held in Rehoboth Beach. Her prize was the Golden Mermaid trophy.

MAINE

THE PINE TREE STATE

Coastline and pine. Maine is known especially for these, and both have helped make the state what it is today. Evergreen forests reach down to the Atlantic shore, along the rocky, bay-indented, 3,500-mile (5,600-km)-long ocean edge of the Pine Tree State.

Massive Ice Age glaciers left Maine's jagged coastline with perhaps 1,100 islands, big and small. Sculpted by the moving ice and then partly submerged by rising sea level as the huge sheets of ice melted, once onshore hilltops became offshore islands.

While Viking Leif Eriksson probably visited the coast here about A.D. 1000, the English and French definitely began scouting it in the 1500s. Maine is believed to have taken its name from English explorers who called the shore the "maine-land" to set it apart from the many islands. Several English communities were founded along the southern coast by 1623. After decades of ownership disputes, Massachusetts gained control of the territory of Maine by 1677. The French gave up all claims after the French and Indian War in 1763, but many French settlers stayed and played a key role in the economy's development. Treaties cost the Algonquian-speaking peoples most of their land.

Maine's people, like other Americans, hated what they saw as unfair British rule and taxes. Thousands of men joined the fight for freedom. After the American Revolution, Maine's population grew quickly. Eventually, people wanted to separate from Massachusetts, and in 1819 they voted to do just that. In a "package deal" known as the Missouri Compromise, made between antislavery and proslavery states, Maine entered the Union "slave free" as the 23rd state in 1820.

The same blue as the U.S. flag, the Maine flag features the state coat of arms with the North Star and the state motto, "I Lead."

STATE FLOWER
White Pine Cone

STATE BIRD
Chickadee

(Missouri entered as a slave state the next year.)

Logging, shipping, and shipbuilding in Maine grew from the 1600s onward. The tallest, straightest white pines were perfect for the masts of sailing ships. When two centuries of cutting took most of these giants, loggers turned to woods such as oak and maple to make other products. Using river power, textile and shoe-making industries grew in the mid-1800s—though many mills moved south in the early 1900s. By then, Maine's rivers were harnessed for hydroelectric power, especially for paper and pulp mills. Shipbuilding cities like Bath and Portland, using first wood and then steel, launched thousands of vessels for military and merchant use and for fishing and lobstering, too.

Largest of the six New England states in area, Maine has the lowest population density of any state east of the Mississippi River. Most "Mainers" live near the coast in a string of communities that arc from the New Hampshire border to Bangor. The state's northern two-thirds are, in Henry David Thoreau's words, "all mossy and moosey" and much less populated. The cool, moist climate and shallow soils make much of the state's lands unsuitable for crops. Areas in the Aroostook River Valley have some of the best soils, and they make Maine a big potato producer. Food processing has grown in importance, as has tourism.

Like other New England states, Maine has lost industrial jobs, such as in paper mills. Even so, Maine remains a big producer of paper and wood products, while working to preserve its forests. As a pioneer in restoring free-flowing waterways, Maine removed the 160-year-old Edwards Dam in Augusta to allow salmon and other fish to ascend the Kennebec River. The state works hard to build "new economy" businesses, such as the making of computer components. Residents see that sustaining the state's environment will bring future growth.

IT'S A FACT:
Forests cover nearly 90 percent of Maine.

A TIME LINE OF THE PINE TREE STATE

1498

John Cabot probably reached the Maine coast in 1498, claiming it for England. Conflicting claims with the French ended in 1763.

1775

British Navy vessels raid the town of Falmouth—which is now the city of Portland—one of the opening actions of the Revolutionary War.

1809–1891

A strong voice in support of freedom for slaves, Maine native **Hannibal Hamlin** was Abraham Lincoln's first vice president.

1942–45

During World War II, Maine shipyards **built 236 Liberty ships** to haul grain, ore, munitions, and troops to our Allies in Europe.

2012

91.1 million pounds (41.3 million kg) of **wild blueberries** are harvested (no state harvests more!) for jellies, jams, syrups, and fillings.

Present

Lobsters are the heart of Maine's seafood industry. The state supplies more than half of the nation's total harvest.

ON THE MAP

LOCATION, LOCATION

This northeasternmost state is known for the pounding surf and strong tides along its coast, where lighthouses have long guided sailors. Maine's rocky soil and short growing season allow for only a few kinds of vegetables and fruits: Potatoes and blueberries are favorites!

BORDER OF MAINE AND NEW BRUNSWICK, CANADA: Potatoes thrive in this area's soil.

BAXTER STATE PARK:
Between 1931 and 1962 Governor Percival Baxter donated the land that makes up this state park, declaring that it must "remain in the Natural Wild State."

WEST QUODDY HEAD: It's the easternmost point of land on the mainland of the United States!

BANGOR:
You'll find the home of horror writer Stephen King here. It's surrounded by a spooky wrought-iron fence with figures of bats and spiderwebs!

PORTLAND HEAD: Keepers in the lighthouse, built in 1791, long alerted sailors to dangerous rocky shores and pounding surf. Today the lighthouse is electronically controlled.

STATS & FACTS

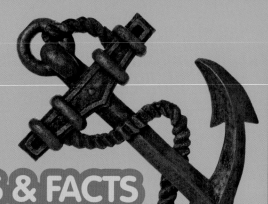

STATEHOOD: March 15, 1820; 23rd state

CAPITAL: Augusta

TOTAL AREA: 35,385 sq mi; 91,646 sq km

LAND AREA: 30,862 sq mi; 79,931 sq km

POPULATION: 1,330,089

POPULATION DENSITY: 43 people per sq mi

MAJOR RACIAL/ETHNIC GROUPS: 95.2% white, 1.2% African American, 1.0% Asian, 0.6% Native American, Hispanic (any race) 1.3%

INDUSTRY: manufacturing, paper and wood products, food processing, tourism, transportation equipment

AGRICULTURE: potatoes, dairy products, eggs, wild blueberries, seafood, hay, oats, barley

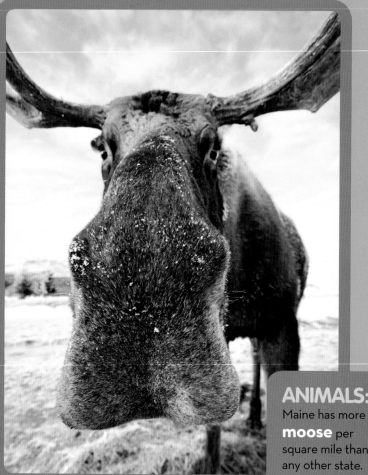

ANIMALS: Maine has more **moose** per square mile than any other state.

HISTORY: Leif Eriksson may have explored Maine's coastline 500 years before Columbus sailed across the Atlantic in 1492. He was likely sent by the King of Norway to Greenland to spread Christianity, and his ship sailed off course.

NATURAL FEATURES: Acadia is the only national park in New England. The park's **Cadillac Mountain** is the highest point along the Atlantic coast of North America.

PEOPLE/CULTURE: The French colony of **Acadia, settled in 1604**—three years before the first British colony at Jamestown—included part of what is now Maine. Almost a quarter of the state's population is of French descent, and 6 percent are French speaking.

NATURAL FORCES: Maine's average annual precipitation is **41 inches** (104 cm).

53

MARYLAND

THE OLD LINE STATE

"Save the Bay!" Heard across Maryland and beyond, this slogan reminds people to care for their beautiful Chesapeake Bay. This estuary, largest in the country, is the state's greatest economic and environmental resource. Both Maryland's history and its future are tied to this vast yet vulnerable arm of the Atlantic Ocean.

Splitting Maryland almost in half, the Chesapeake separates most of the Atlantic Coastal Plain from the state's strip of Piedmont and oddly shaped Appalachian panhandle. Fed by the Susquehanna and other rivers, the bay is home to the state's main seaports, Baltimore and Annapolis. Watermen have long made their living from the bay's rich populations of oysters, blue crabs, and fish.

In 1608 John Smith became the first European to chart the bay. George Calvert, whose title was Lord Baltimore, received a grant from King Charles I for the northern part of the Virginia Colony. His son settled Maryland in 1634, naming the area in honor of the English king's wife, Henrietta Maria. Planters in some Tidewater areas used slaves to farm tobacco. Such labor was not needed on small, mixed-crop and wheat farms to the east, north, and west. When the Revolution came, most Marylanders supported it. The Treaty of Paris, which ended the war, was ratified in 1784 in the statehouse in Annapolis. The building was used as the new nation's capitol for a nine-month period beginning the previous year. Maryland became the seventh state in 1788. Three years later it donated land for the building of a federal city in the District of Columbia.

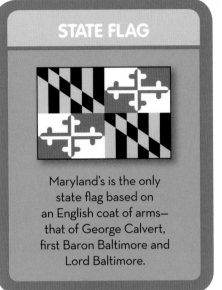

STATE FLAG

Maryland's is the only state flag based on an English coat of arms—that of George Calvert, first Baron Baltimore and Lord Baltimore.

STATE FLOWER
Black-Eyed Susan

STATE BIRD
Northern (Baltimore) Oriole

Maryland grew quickly in the 19th century. A fine harbor and many waterfalls to power industry resulted in Baltimore's rise as a major East Coast port. Key road and canal routes linked it to the state's far-western reaches and beyond, and the Baltimore & Ohio Railroad began service in 1830. As the Civil War loomed, Maryland was divided on the issue of slavery. It stayed in the Union as a Border State, seeing many skirmishes and some major battles.

In the postwar period Maryland became a bustling rail and ship transport center reconnecting North and South. Steelmaking, shipbuilding, and aircraft manufacturing attracted more workers during the two World Wars. Nearly 90 percent of all Marylanders now live in the 35-mile (56-km)-long corridor between D.C. and Baltimore, which has become a huge swath of suburban homes, shopping centers, and office parks. The state boasts more than 50 major federal research facilities and has become a magnet for high-tech businesses. Though more than a third of the state is still forested, and agriculture—led by poultry raising—remains important, more and more land is being shifted to urban uses.

Tourists and residents alike sail, fish, swim, bird-watch, and simply soak up the sun and sea breezes on the bay. But the mighty Chesapeake is in danger. Runoff drains billions of gallons of pollutants into the estuary. Oysters, which serve as natural filters to clean the bay's waters, have declined dramatically. Between 1885 and 2003 the annual oyster harvest fell from 15 million bushels to 15 thousand bushels. Amazingly, the bay still supports a wide array of wildlife. Millions of migrating birds feed here, and the state harvests more blue crabs than any other. Efforts now focus on reducing runoff, upgrading sewage treatment plants, and slowing suburban sprawl. Work to rebuild oyster populations has yielded success. If all goes well, Maryland's people will one day be able to say, "We saved the bay!"

IT'S A FACT:
The first successful passenger balloon flight in the United States took place in Baltimore on June 24, 1784. The only person on board was a 13-year-old boy!

A TIME LINE OF THE OLD LINE STATE

1634
Maryland's first settlement, St. Marys City, near the Potomac's confluence with the Chesapeake Bay, was founded by **Leonard Calvert.**

1814
Watching Fort McHenry defend Baltimore in the War of 1812 inspired Francis Scott Key to write **"The Star-Spangled Banner."**

1862
The **Battle of Antietam,** on September 17, 1862, was the costliest day of the Civil War in terms of lives lost.

1942
Established as "Shangri-La" and renamed **Camp David** in 1953, the presidential retreat in rural northern Maryland has been both a vacation spot and the site of high-level conferences.

1996
The **National Museum of Dentistry in Baltimore** opened, featuring George Washington's false choppers made of hippopotamus ivory, whopping whale teeth, and more.

Present
Harborplace, which opened in 1980 as a tourist, cultural, and business center, is bringing new life to the port of Baltimore.

ON THE MAP

LOCATION, LOCATION

Maryland has many faces. With its sprawling Chesapeake Bay, a large harbor in Baltimore, and more navigable rivers than any other state, it loves its water! Because of landscapes from mountains to waterways, it's been called "America in miniature."

BALTIMORE: This largest city has a population of 622,104. It's the center for commerce, the arts, education, and sports—as well as home to Fort McHenry, where the Star-Spangled Banner flew.

CUMBERLAND: This historic city lies at the end of the Chesapeake and Ohio Canal that runs 184.5 miles (297 km) from Washington, D.C. In the 1700s it was a frontier outpost for Col. George Washington during the French and Indian War.

ST. MICHAELS: Here, the Chesapeake Bay Maritime Museum preserves symbols of bay life, including the Hooper Strait Lighthouse.

HOYE-CREST: This summit on Backbone Mountain in western Maryland is the highest point in the state, at 3,360 feet (1,020 m).

ANTIETAM: During this Civil War battle, some 22,717 were killed, wounded, or lost. It was America's bloodiest one-day battle ever.

ANNAPOLIS: Home of the U.S. Naval Academy, it is also the capital city, whose Maryland State House is the oldest state capitol building in continuous use for meetings of the state legislature.

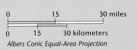

0   15   30 miles
0   15   30 kilometers
Albers Conic Equal-Area Projection

STATS & FACTS

STATEHOOD: April 28, 1788; 7th state

CAPITAL: Annapolis

TOTAL AREA: 12,407 sq mi; 32,133 sq km

LAND AREA: 9,774 sq mi; 25,314 sq km

POPULATION: 5,976,407

POPULATION DENSITY: 611 people per sq mi

MAJOR RACIAL/ETHNIC GROUPS: 58.2% white, 29.4% African American, 5.5% Asian, 0.4% Native American, Hispanic (any race) 8.2%

INDUSTRY: shipping, tourism, biotechnology, information technology, insurance, finance, real estate, manufacturing

AGRICULTURE: broiler chickens, greenhouse, corn, dairy products, soybeans, wheat, barley, hay

ANIMALS: From spring through autumn along Maryland's Eastern Shore, check out the **orange-billed oystercatcher.** You can't miss its shrill *wheep!* Its favorite food is—you guessed it!—oysters from Chesapeake Bay, which it slits open with its blade-like bill.

HISTORY: Maryland's nickname—the Old Line State—stems from the praise of its **"troops of the line"** earned from George Washington during the Revolutionary War.

NATURAL FORCES: **Thunderstorms** in July and August average one every five days.

PEOPLE/CULTURE: Explorer **Matthew Henson** was the co-discoverer of the North Pole with Robert Peary in 1909. Born in Charles County, Henson ran away from home at age 11. His adventures included living with people of the Arctic and learning their language.

NATURAL FEATURES: The average depth of the **Chesapeake Bay** and its tributaries is only 21 feet (6.5 m).

MASSACHUSETTS

THE BAY STATE

New life, new ideas. That's what the Pilgrims wanted when they crossed the Atlantic in 1620. Landing first near the tip of Cape Cod, and then across the bay on a mainland spot they named Plymouth, these settlers eventually found a better life. New ideas arose when they set down rules to govern themselves—the Mayflower Compact. Ever since, Massachusetts ideas have had a huge influence on American life—in government, education, business, and culture.

The Bay State's best known feature is Cape Cod, curling like an arm around its large bay. This and many landscapes were shaped as gigantic glaciers pushed south more than 10,000 years ago. The Connecticut River Valley was scooped out and then later filled in with fertile soils. Thin soils elsewhere limit farming. Ice sheets piled up sandy ridges, which remain today as Cape Cod and the famous islands Nantucket and Martha's Vineyard. West of the coastal plain rise rolling mountains, including the Berkshires.

The Pilgrims' new home became known as Massachusetts, after one of the groups of Algonquian-speaking peoples who lived there. Other immigrants settled nearby in Naumkeag (Salem) and Shawmut (Boston), which became part of the Massachusetts Bay Colony. Here, political freedoms and representative government were begun, though everyone still had to be a Puritan.

Conflict had a role in colonial history here, too. Relations between settlers and native peoples began on friendly terms but grew hostile over time. King Philip, chief of the Wampanoag people, declared war on the colonists in 1675. Hundreds died on both sides until, eventually, the colonists won. The English combined Plymouth and Massachusetts Bay in 1691. Later, the colonists helped the British win the French and Indian War, which ended in 1763. Shipping became a huge business, including the trading of slaves. Colonists up and down the Atlantic coast grew frustrated over the control of trade and other rights by faraway England. In April 1775 British troops and colonists fought the opening battles of the American Revolution at Lexington and Concord. Great leaders such as early patriots John and Samuel Adams made lasting impacts on the new nation. Massachusetts became the sixth state in 1788, with Boston as its capital.

Hardships caused by a law halting trade with European countries and then the War of 1812 brought huge changes for the state. Textile mills sprouted in areas along rivers, beginning with Lowell in 1814. Shipping flourished in ports like Boston and Salem. Whalers sailed from New Bedford and Nantucket for decades until about 1900. The state contributed nearly 150,000 men and many ships to the Union effort in the Civil War. Industrialization increased for the rest of the century. By 1900 the state produced half the shoes made in America, as well as woolens and other clothing. The 20th century brought difficulties with labor strife and jobs leaving the state. World War II sparked shipbuilding and other war-materials business, but by the 1960s the shift from old industries to high-tech research and products was under way. Thousands of new jobs have recently been created.

Though there are many positives, Massachusetts's more than 6.5 million people face challenges, too. Boston is choked with the sprawl of modern urban life. There is a shortage of affordable housing and a surplus of traffic. Whatever the problems, it seems certain Massachusetts will seek—and most likely find—new ideas to solve them.

STATE FLAG

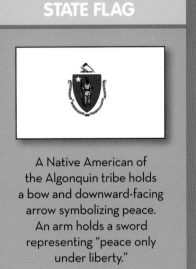

A Native American of the Algonquin tribe holds a bow and downward-facing arrow symbolizing peace. An arm holds a sword representing "peace only under liberty."

STATE FLOWER
Mayflower

STATE BIRD
Chickadee

IT'S A FACT:
The U.S.S. *Constitution* (Old Ironsides)—the oldest fully commissioned ship in the U.S. Navy—is permanently docked at Charlestown Navy Yard.

A TIME LINE OF THE BAY STATE

1620

The men aboard the *Mayflower* signed the **Mayflower Compact,** agreeing to write and obey "just and equal laws" in the new land.

1713

The **Old State House,** built in 1713, was a center of political life in 18th-century Boston. The lion and unicorn on either side of its clock tower are symbols of British authority.

1775

The first battles of the American Revolution were fought in **Lexington and Concord,** where 95 Americans and 273 British died.

1800s

The state became a center of the **textile, woolen, and tanning industries,** which often hired women and immigrants at low pay.

1900s

Federal and state regulations are put into place to protect **great white sharks** off Massachusetts and other North Atlantic states after fishing drastically reduced the population.

Present

First known as "America's Marathon" when it began in 1897, the 26.2-mile (42-km) **Boston Marathon** draws thousands of runners and spectators from around the world every April.

ON THE MAP

LOCATION, LOCATION

With the entire eastern state border open to the Atlantic Ocean, Massachusetts was home to the whaling trade, which peaked in the 1800s. Today whale-watching, not catching, is a major industry. Inside the state, massive flooded fields, or bogs, yield tons of cranberries—a major agricultural product.

SALEM: At the Salem Witch Museum, talking figures tell the grizzly story of the 1692 witch trials, when 20 accused "witches" were put to death. Discover centuries of beliefs about witchcraft, too.

BOSTON: This bustling capital with a population of 645,966 has a rich Revolutionary War history. The home of Samuel Adams, John Adams, and Paul Revere, its "Freedom Trail" takes visitors to key sites.

LOWELL: The country's first planned industrial community—mainly of textile mills—was built here about 1822. By the 1840s the city led textile manufacturing in America.

PLYMOUTH: Explore the cramped quarters of a reproduction of the *Mayflower*. It carried 102 Pilgrims across the Atlantic in 1620.

NEW BEDFORD: Called "the whaling city," it was one of the world's major whaling ports in the 19th century. This thriving African-American community was also home to abolitionist Frederick Douglass.

PROVINCETOWN: Visit the Whydah Museum, to see treasures and artifacts pulled from the deep after the namesake pirate ship sank in a storm nearby in 1717.

Map labels

VERMONT
NEW HAMPSHIRE
NEW YORK
MASSACHUSETTS
PIONEER VALLEY
CONNECTICUT
RHODE ISLAND
ATLANTIC OCEAN

Highest point in Massachusetts
Mt. Greylock 3,491 ft 1,064 m
North Adams
Adams
Shelburne Falls
Greenfield
Deerfield
Pittsfield
Dalton
Cheshire Res.
Lenox
Lee
Stockbridge
Great Barrington
Westfield National Wild & Scenic River
Silvio O. Conte N.W.R.
Easthampton
Northampton
Amherst
Ware
Chicopee
Holyoke
Ludlow
Westfield
Springfield
Springfield Armory N.H.S.
Agawam
Winchendon
Orange
Athol
Gardner
Fitchburg
Leominster
Chelmsford
Westford
Oxbow N.W.R.
Dracut
Lowell
Lowell N.H.P.
Sudbury Assabet & Concord Nat. W.&S.R.
Concord
Marlborough
Shrewsbury
Worcester
Spencer
Wachusett Res.
Quabbin Reservoir
Sturbridge
Old Sturbridge Village
Southbridge
Webster
Oxford
Auburn
Milford
Franklin
Bellingham
Webster
Wellesley
Framingham
Great Meadows N.W.R.
Lexington
Woburn
Medford
Cambridge
Boston
Brookline
Milton
Quincy
Norwood
Stoughton
Randolph
Rockland
Whitman
Brockton
Bridgewater
North Attleboro
Attleboro
Taunton
Seekonk
Somerset
Fall River
New Bedford Whaling N.H.P.
Fairhaven
Woods Hole
East Falmouth
Falmouth
Mashpee N.W.R.
Amesbury
Haverhill
Methuen
Lawrence
Wilmington
Danvers
Peabody
Salem
Beverly
Marblehead
Lynn
Malden
Newburyport
Parker River N.W.R.
Ipswich
Gloucester
Cape Ann
Massachusetts Bay
Stellwagen Bank National Marine Sanctuary
Boston Harbor Islands N.R.A.
Weymouth
Silver Lake
Plymouth
Massasoit N.W.R.
Middleboro
Assawompset Pond
Great Quittacus Pond
Long Pond
Sandwich
Buzzards Bay
Barnstable
Cape Cod Canal
Cape Cod Bay
Provincetown
Truro
Wellfleet
Orleans
Dennis
Chatham
South Yarmouth
Hyannis
Monomoy Island
Monomoy N.W.R.
Cape Cod National Seashore
CAPE COD
Nantucket Sound
Nantucket Island
Vineyard Haven
Oak Bluffs
Edgartown
Chappaquiddick Island
Martha's Vineyard
Gay Head Wampanoag I.R.
Nomans Land Island N.W.R.
Nomans Land
Elizabeth Islands
Vineyard Sound
Buzzards Bay
Rhode Island Sound

0 10 20 miles
0 10 20 kilometers
Albers Conic Equal-Area Projection

STATS & FACTS

STATEHOOD: February 6, 1788; 6th state

CAPITAL: Boston

TOTAL AREA: 10,555 sq mi; 27,336 sq km

LAND AREA: 7,840 sq mi; 102,896 sq km

POPULATION: 6,745,408

POPULATION DENSITY: 860 people per sq mi

MAJOR RACIAL/ETHNIC GROUPS: 80.4% white, 6.6% African American, 5.3% Asian, 0.3% Native American, Hispanic (any race) 9.6%

INDUSTRY: manufacturing, tourism, high-tech research and development, finance, trade, biotechnology

AGRICULTURE: greenhouse, cranberries, dairy products, apples, corn, seafood, hay, potatoes

HISTORY: Massachusetts is home to the country's first institute of higher learning **(Harvard, 1636)**, its first printing press (Cambridge, 1638), its first post office (Richard Fairbank's tavern, Boston, 1639), and its first ironworks (Lynn, 1643).

NATURAL FORCES: Blue Hill, Massachusetts, is the second windiest weather station in the lower 48 states, recording an **average annual wind speed of 15.2 miles an hour** (24.5 km/h).

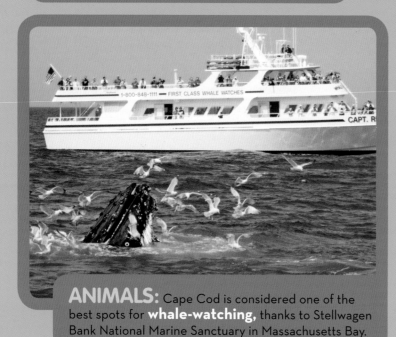

ANIMALS: Cape Cod is considered one of the best spots for **whale-watching,** thanks to Stellwagen Bank National Marine Sanctuary in Massachusetts Bay.

NATURAL FEATURES: Lake Webster's Algonquian name is Lake **Chargoggagoggmanchaugg- gagoggchaubunagungamaugg**—the longest place-name in the country. It has been translated as: "You fish on your side; I fish on my side; nobody fish in the middle."

PEOPLE/CULTURE: Massachusetts is the birthplace of several famous inventors, including Eli Whitney (the cotton gin), **Samuel Morse (the telegraph),** and Benjamin Franklin (the lightning rod—and much more!).

NEW HAMPSHIRE

THE GRANITE STATE

The Granite State. Though named for hard rock formations under the state, the nickname also reflects New Hampshire's strong feelings about liberty. As the first of the British colonies to become self-governing, it's no surprise that New Hampshire's state motto, written by Revolutionary War hero John Stark, declares "Live Free or Die."

The Appalachians form New Hampshire's backbone. Highest of the Northeast's peaks is 6,288-foot (1,917-m) Mount Washington, in the Presidential Range of the White Mountains, which is famed for fearsome winter storms. A weather station atop the mountain once recorded winds of 231 miles an hour (372 km/h)! The Connecticut River flows out of the mountains to form most of the state's boundary with Vermont. More than four-fifths of the state is forested with spruce, fir, maple, oak, beech, and other trees. White-tailed deer abound, as do black bears and moose. A short but important 18-mile (29-km) coastline stretches between Maine and Massachusetts.

To this shore came the English, founding their first settlements in 1623 along the Piscataqua River near present-day Portsmouth and Dover. Nearby communities Hampton and Exeter were soon established, and New Hampshire was made a royal colony in 1679. Long-running boundary disputes were settled with Massachusetts in the 1740s, with New York in the 1790s, and with Canada in 1842. Settlers and Abenaki peoples got along at first, but greater numbers of newcomers caused increased conflicts over hunting grounds and fishing rights. Native resistance ended by the close of the French and Indian War in 1763.

New Hampshire's patriotic colors showed early. A key event—which some consider the first strike in the fight for independence—was

STATE FLAG

It features one of America's first 13 warships, the frigate *Raleigh*, built in Portsmouth, New Hampshire, in 1776. The wreath traditionally symbolizes fame, honor, and victory.

STATE FLOWER
Purple Lilac

STATE BIRD
Purple Finch

the taking of gunpowder from an English fort at Portsmouth by a band of the colony's men in late 1774. Six months before the Declaration of Independence, New Hampshire declared its freedom from England on January 5, 1776. The state was the ninth and deciding state to approve the U.S. Constitution in mid-1788. New Hampshire was strongly against slavery. During the Civil War, it supported the Union with troops and supplies.

Industrialization started up early. The textile and woolen industries threaded their way through the Merrimack River Valley. Manchester's massive Amoskeag Mills stretched along the river and canals below its original power source, Amoskeag Falls. By 1915 this single company employed 17,000 workers—many from Canada, Ireland, Greece, and Poland—in 30 mills and turned out 50 miles (80 km) of finished cloth per hour! Change came starting in 1922, when many mills slowed or closed due to major labor strikes and competition from lower-cost mills in southern states. World War II helped the state rebound from the Great Depression. New businesses replaced old industries by the 1980s. Portsmouth, Nashua, and other cities benefit from their closeness to Boston, attracting high-technology companies that take advantage of an educated, skilled workforce. Some traditional state work is still strong. The Portsmouth Naval Shipyard repairs nuclear submarines; maple trees are still tapped for syrup; and forests still supply wood products and pulp to mills.

Natural resources have long been important to the state's economy. Conservation measures protecting river headwaters and large tracts of woodland have been in place since the early 1900s, and four-season tourism has begun to play a larger role in the state. Today residents understand that natural resources sustained can be even more valuable than those removed.

IT'S A FACT:
The first potato grown in the United States was planted in New Hampshire in 1719.

A TIME LINE OF THE GRANITE STATE

1777

Native son **Gen. John Stark's** victory at the Battle of Bennington, in Vermont, was a turning point in the Revolution.

1850s

Mills producing lumber, paper, textiles, and woolens industrialized the state. It became a leader in **child labor laws.**

1944

World attention focused on the state when President Franklin Roosevelt hosted a **global economic conference** at Bretton Woods.

1961

Alan Shepard of East Derry manned a Mercury spacecraft and became the first American in space.

1964

New Hampshire became the first U.S. state to revive use of a **legal lottery** in the 20th century. Since then, it's raised more than $1.5 billion to aid education.

Present

Every four years, New Hampshire's tradition of holding the **first presidential primary election** draws national attention.

CHANGE
WE CAN BELIEVE IN
BarackObama.com

ON THE MAP

LOCATION, LOCATION

Bounded by Maine, Vermont, and Massachusetts, it has the shortest coastline of the eastern states—just 18 miles (29 km) long! For some 200 years its many rivers have provided industrial power and rich fishing. Its northern climate makes for spectacular fall colors, too.

MOUNT WASHINGTON: In the Presidential Range of the White Mountains, it is famed for its winds recorded up to 231 miles an hour (372 km/h).

CONCORD: The world-famous Concord stagecoach was built here by the Abbot-Downing Company in 1827. When the owners failed to turn it into a horseless carriage in the early 1900s, the company closed down. Some may return to the streets as displays.

LAKE WINNIPESAUKEE: It's New Hampshire's largest lake, covering 71 square miles (184 sq km) in the east-central part of the state.

EXETER: Here, on January 5, 1776, the New Hampshire Congress declared independence from England before any other colony.

MANCHESTER: New Hampshire's largest city, it has a population of 110,378.

PETERBOROUGH: In 1833 the town founded the world's first tax-supported public library.

Map labels

QUEBEC

Pittsburg
CANADA
U.S.
Third L.
Second Lake
First Connecticut Lake
Lake Francis

Colebrook
Blue Mt. 3,723 ft +1,135 m
LAKE UMBAGOG N.W.R.
Umbagog L.

North Stratford

Groveton
WHITE MTN. NAT. FOREST
Mt. Cabot 4,160 ft 1,268 m +
Lancaster
Berlin
Gorham

VERMONT

Moore Reservoir

Littleton
Franconia
Mt. Washington 6,288 ft 1,917 m +
Highest point in New Hampshire
Pinkham Notch
Presidential Range
Mts.
WILDCAT BROOK NATIONAL WILD & SCENIC RIVER

Bath-Haverhill Bridge
Oldest covered bridge in New Hampshire (1829)
FRANCONIA NOTCH S.P.
Mt. Lafayette 5,249 ft 1,600 m +
CRAWFORD NOTCH S.P.
WHITE

Woodsville
Haverhill
White MOUNTAINS
Lincoln
North Conway
Conway
Conway Lake

Warren
Orford
TRAIL
NAT. FOREST
NEW
MAINE

APPALACHIAN NATIONAL SCENIC
MOUNTAINS
HAMPSHIRE
Ossipee
Center Ossipee
Lake Wentworth

Squam Lake
Bearcamp
Center Sandwich

Hanover
Canaan
Ashland
Meredith
Lake Winnipesaukee

Lebanon
Enfield
Newfound Lake
APPALACHIAN
Mascoma Lake
Bristol
Sanbornville
Merrymeeting Lake

SAINT-GAUDENS N.H.S.
Grafton
Winnisquam Lake
Laconia
Milton

Sunapee Lake
New London
Franklin
Tilton
Alton Bay
Crystal Lake
Farmington

Claremont
MT. SUNAPEE S.P.
Mt. Sunapee 2,743 ft 836 m
JOHN HAY N.W.R.
Northfield
Suncook Lakes
Rochester
Somersworth

Charlestown
Contoocook
Canterbury
Pittsfield

North Walpole
President Pierce's birthplace
Concord
Suncook
Dover
Durham

Walpole
Highland Lake
Hillsborough
GREAT BAY N.W.R.
Newmarket
Great Bay
Portsmouth

Antrim
Nubanusit Lake
Raymond
Massabesic Lake
Exeter
Rye
Isles of Shoals

Keene
Monadnock Mt. 3,165 ft 965 m
Peterborough
WAPACK N.W.R.
Manchester
Kingston
East Derry
Hampton
ATLANTIC OCEAN

PISGAH S.P.
Troy
Jaffrey
Merrimack
Derry
Londonderry
Plaistow

Hinsdale
Souhegan
Milford
Greenville
New Ipswich
Nashua
Salem

MASSACHUSETTS

Connecticut
Ammonoosuc
Androscoggin
Saco
Pemigewasset
Baker
Merrimack
Contoocook
Ashuelot
Cocheco
Salmon Falls
Piscataqua
Lamprey

0   10   20 miles
0   10   20 kilometers
Albers Conic Equal-Area Projection

STATS & FACTS

STATEHOOD: June 21, 1788; 9th state

CAPITAL: Concord

TOTAL AREA: 9,350 sq mi; 24,216 sq km

LAND AREA: 8,968 sq mi; 23,227 sq km

POPULATION: 1,326,813

POPULATION DENSITY: 148 people per sq mi

MAJOR RACIAL/ETHNIC GROUPS: 93.9% white, 2.2% Asian, 1.1% African American, 0.2% Native American, Hispanic (any race) 2.8%

INDUSTRY: timber, technology, tourism, manufacturing, machinery, metals and plastics

AGRICULTURE: dairy products, apples, eggs, corn, hay, greenhouse

NATURAL FEATURES: The famous naturally carved granite profile known as the **"Old Man of the Mountain"** in the White Mountains was destroyed by a rock slide in 2003. It can still be seen on the U.S. Mint's quarter for the state.

NATURAL FORCES: The world record for highest ground wind speed of 231 miles an hour (372 km/h) was set on **Mount Washington** in 1934.

HISTORY: New Hampshire was named by **Capt. John Mason** after his home county of Hampshire, in England.

PEOPLE/CULTURE: The **first strike organized by women workers** in the United States occurred in New Hampshire in December 1828. Several hundred workers walked out of the Dover Cotton Factory to protest new management policies that banned talking on the job, reduced wages from 58 cents a day to 53 cents, and docked them a fourth of a day's wage if they arrived after the morning bell stopped ringing.

ANIMALS: New Hampshire gardeners may meet the **star-nosed mole.** It can't see well, but it feels its way with a multifingered snout that has 250,000 tiny sensors.

NEW JERSEY

THE GARDEN STATE

Crossroads of the East. New Jersey's location has placed it squarely in the middle of Atlantic coast action for four centuries. Benjamin Franklin called it a "barrel tapped at both ends," referring both to its abundant farm production and to its position between New York City and Philadelphia.

The Dutch set up their first trading post here near present-day Jersey City in 1618 as part of New Netherland. They surrendered the land to England in 1664, and it was renamed New Jersey after the English Channel Isle of Jersey. Following decades of legal tug-of-war between leaders from New York City and Philadelphia, New Jersey became its own royal colony in 1738. It was in the thick of things during the American Revolution, with more than 90 battles fought here, including important victories at Trenton, Princeton, and Monmouth. New Jersey was the third state to ratify the Constitution in late 1787, and Trenton was made its capital three years later.

By the 19th century the state was in the middle of the industrial revolution. There was still farming, but factories produced textiles, shoes, bricks, and more. Roads were built, canals dug, and rail lines laid down. New Jersey gave soldiers, supplies, and monetary support to the Union during the Civil War. The war fueled industries and attracted thousands of European immigrants. Most factory workers crowded into Newark and other northern cities, often living in poverty. Manufacturing eventually declined—as did the health of New Jersey's urban neighborhoods. Riots broke out in Newark in 1967, calling attention to the need for change.

New Jersey's economy has turned increasingly to a wide range of service and trade businesses. The state has long been a top research center. Manufacturing has not died, though: New Jersey still has thousands of firms producing a vast array of products.

New Jersey boasts a wide range of landscapes. Its northern third, covered by glaciers 20,000 years ago, is hilly, rocky, and spotted with lakes and wetlands. The ancient Kittatinny Mountains stretch along its northwestern border. From Sandy Hook to Cape May, the Jersey Shore sports some of the Atlantic coast's best beaches. Most of southern New Jersey is low coastal plain that supports a people-light, wildlife-heavy region called the Pine Barrens. Called "barren" only because it wasn't good for farming, its forests, bogs, and swamps are home to more than a thousand plant and animal species. In 1978 Congress set aside 1.1 million acres (450,000 ha) as the first national reserve. This wilderness survives in the country's most densely populated state. Despite the state's overall urban and industrial character, dozens of different kinds of fruits and vegetables are grown on more than 10,000 farms that give it the nickname Garden State. New Jersey ranks in the top five states in output of cranberries, spinach, peaches, bell peppers, and blueberries. Produce is either trucked fresh to regional cities or processed in factories.

All ten of New Jersey's largest cities are within 30 miles (48 km) of New York City or Philadelphia. In New Jersey, as across the United States, people have chosen for decades to leave cities and build suburbs. The state's Smart Growth Plan and other strategies have made it a national leader in efforts to slow this sprawl and protect farmlands. As of January 2013 there were more than 200,000 acres (80,940 ha) of preserved farmland. By working to balance the needs of its cities, countryside, and connections to its neighbors, New Jersey seeks a lasting and vital middle ground.

STATE FLAG

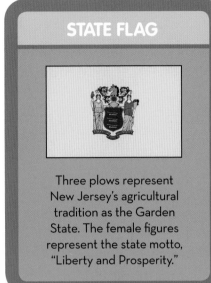

Three plows represent New Jersey's agricultural tradition as the Garden State. The female figures represent the state motto, "Liberty and Prosperity."

STATE FLOWER
Violet

STATE BIRD
American Goldfinch

IT'S A FACT:
Early settlers mined the bogs of the Pine Barrens for iron to make kettles and cannonballs.

A TIME LINE OF THE GARDEN STATE

1524–early 1600s

The **Lenni-Lenape,** a peaceful farming people, greeted a succession of Europeans who came ashore in what is now New Jersey.

1778

George Washington honored **Mary Ludwig Hays McCauly** (Molly Pitcher) for her bravery at the Battle of Monmouth.

1858

The **first dinosaur skeleton** found in North America was excavated at Haddonfield. It was named *Hadrosaurus* in honor of its discovery site.

1869

The Joseph A. Campbell Preserve Company, now the **Campbell Soup Company,** began selling canned soups from its Camden plant in 1869.

2012

New Jersey was the first state hit by **Hurricane Sandy,** a storm that would eventually cause more than $70 billion in damage to the Northeast coast.

Present

The manufacture of medicine is a growing New Jersey industry and has earned the state the nickname **"the medicine chest of the world."**

ON THE MAP

LOCATION, LOCATION
Named for Jersey, the largest of England's Channel Islands, New Jersey is known for its Jersey Shore beaches, including Asbury Park, with its mile (1.6-km)-long boardwalk. New York forms its north and eastern borders; Pennsylvania lies to the west and Delaware to the south.

NEWARK: Just 8 miles (13 km) from New York City, Newark is New Jersey's largest city, with a population of 278,427.

FAIR LAWN: Herds of animal crackers stampede out of the Nabisco bakery. Since 1898 the National Biscuit Company has produced crackers, cookies, and snacks in this city.

MONMOUTH BATTLEFIELD STATE PARK: The major Revolutionary War battle of 1778 is reenacted every year on these grounds.

JOHNSON'S FERRY: George Washington landed here after crossing the icy Delaware River with 2,400 troops on Christmas night of 1776. The next morning he surprise-attacked German soldiers fighting for the British.

CAMDEN: The poet Walt Whitman, also a journalist who cared for wounded soldiers during the Civil War, lived here in his last years. Campbell Soup is here, too!

TOMS RIVER: The city's Insectropolis is New Jersey's bug museum, dedicated to insects and creepy-crawlies. Besides checking out exhibits, the Mud Tube, and the Hive Airport, kids can attend a Buguniversity.

ATLANTIC CITY: Tourists first came to this resort city by train in 1854. In 2012, Hurricane Sandy damaged it, but its famous boardwalk was mostly protected by a dune restoration project.

Map labels

Highest point in New Jersey
High Point 1,803 ft / 550 m
APPALACHIAN NATIONAL SCENIC TRAIL
DELAWARE WATER GAP N.R.A.
WALLKILL RIVER N.W.R.
Kittatinny Mountains
NEW YORK
Highland Lakes
West Milford
Franklin
Ringwood
Ramsey
Newton
Sparta
Wanaque
Wanaque Reservoir
Ridgewood
Fair Lawn
Paramus
Lake Hopatcong
Hopatcong
Wayne
Paterson
PATERSON GREAT FALLS N.H.P.
Hackensack
Fort Lee
Budd Lake
Dover
Parsippany
Lambert Castle Museum
Clifton
Passaic
Hackettstown
Morristown
MORRISTOWN N.H.P.
EDISON N.H.S.
Union City
Jersey City
Washington
Bernardsville
GREAT SWAMP N.W.R.
Irvington
Newark
Bayonne
Ellis Island
Phillipsburg
High Bridge
Berkeley Heights
Elizabeth
Round Valley Res.
Electric light invented by Thomas Edison, 1879
Plainfield
Somerville
Menlo Park
Rahway
Flemington
Piscataway
Edison
Perth Amboy
Sandy Hook
Hillsborough
New Brunswick
GATEWAY N.R.A.
Sayreville
Keansburg
Lambertville
Kendall Park
East Brunswick
Cheesequake
Red Bank
Princeton
WASHINGTON CROSSING STATE PARK
Hightstown
Eatontown
Long Branch
Ewing
Trenton
Mercerville
MONMOUTH BATTLEFIELD S.P.
Freehold
White Horse
Neptune
Asbury Park
Belmar
Manasquan
PENNSYLVANIA
NEW JERSEY
Lakewood
Point Pleasant
Burlington
Willingboro
Cinnaminson
Browns Mills
Lakehurst
Gilford Park
Seaside Heights
Pennsauken
Camden
Cherry Hill
Mount Holly
Crestwood Village
Toms River
Haddonfield
First dinosaur skeleton discovered in North America, 1858
Paulsboro
Woodbury
Lindenwold
Pine Hill
PINE BARRENS
Penns Grove
Glassboro
Williamstown
Hammonton
Long Beach Island
Surf City
Ship Bottom
Salem
Woodstown
GREAT EGG HARBOR NAT. WILD & SCENIC RIVER
Egg Harbor City
E. B. FORSYTHE N.W.R.
Beach Haven
Pennsville
SUPAWNA MEADOWS N.W.R.
Mystic Island
Great Bay
Little Egg Harbor
Bridgeton
Vineland
Absecon
Pleasantville
Brigantine
MAURICE NAT. WILD & SCENIC RIVER
Millville
Mays Landing
Atlantic City
Ventnor City
Margate City
DELAWARE
Somers Point
Ocean City
Woodbine
ATLANTIC OCEAN
Cohansey
Delaware Bay
Sea Isle City
CAPE MAY N.W.R.
Cape May Court House
CAPE MAY
North Wildwood
Wildwood
Cape May Canal
Cape May

0   10   20 miles
0   10   20 kilometers
Albers Conic Equal-Area Projection

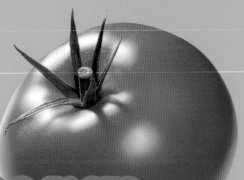

STATS & FACTS

STATEHOOD: December 18, 1787; 3rd state

CAPITAL: Trenton

TOTAL AREA: 8,721 sq mi; 22,588 sq km

LAND AREA: 7,417 sq mi; 19,211 sq km

POPULATION: 8,938,175

POPULATION DENSITY: 1,205 people per sq mi

MAJOR RACIAL/ETHNIC GROUPS: 68.6% white, 13.7% African American, 8.3% Asian, 0.3% Native American, Hispanic (any race) 17.7%

INDUSTRY: pharmaceuticals, tourism, telecommunications, machinery, electronics

AGRICULTURE: greenhouse, blueberries, cranberries, peaches, corn, dairy products, seafood

HISTORY: **Cape May** became the nation's first seaside resort in 1761. It was named for the Dutch sea captain Cornelius Jacobsen May, who explored the region in the 1620s.

PEOPLE/CULTURE: Famed inventor **Thomas A. Edison** filed more than 400 patents from his laboratory in Menlo Park. During the seven years he worked there, his achievements included perfecting the lightbulb and the telephone and inventing the phonograph and the multiplex telegraph.

NATURAL FEATURES: Beneath the **Pine Barrens** lie aquifers that hold 17 trillion gallons (64.35 trillion L) of freshwater.

NATURAL FORCES: The chances of **a direct hit by a hurricane** along the New Jersey coastline is 1 in 200.

ANIMALS: New Jersey is home to 26 known nesting pairs of **peregrine falcons,** the fastest animal on Earth.

NEW YORK

THE EMPIRE STATE

Gateway to a nation. New York has long been America's front door, welcoming millions of people from all over the world to new homes. Now the largest Northeast state in area and fourth in population and long the nation's chief commercial center, New York fits the Empire State nickname, traceable to George Washington.

The Appalachians and Adirondacks arc across the state's eastern half, while the Alleghenies rise in the west. Glaciers scooped out Lakes Ontario and Erie as well as the narrow Finger Lakes. Long Island is a great ridge of sand and rock left behind by retreating ice. Western lowlands and broad valleys carved by the Mohawk and Hudson Rivers offer fertile croplands.

Long before Europeans walked its lands, the powerful Iroquois Confederacy and Algonquian-speaking peoples lived here. In 1609 French explorer Samuel de Champlain explored the lake that today bears his name, and Englishman Henry Hudson explored the river now named for him. Acting on Hudson's reports, a Dutch company set up the New Netherland colony, including a settlement near present-day Albany and another on the island of Manhattan. The colony was taken over by the English in 1664 and renamed for the Duke of York. New York was the site of many conflicts in the French and Indian War. Split loyalties among the Iroquois then and during the American Revolution cost them dearly. They had lost most of their land by the time New York became the 11th state in 1788.

New York City has been the nation's most populous city ever since the first U.S. Census in 1790. The key factor in its 19th-century growth was the digging of the Erie Canal, which by 1825 connected it—via the Hudson River—with Lake Erie and western lands beyond. Vast waves of immigrants flowed to and through New York City. Many newcomers stayed on, making the city a "melting pot" of peoples and cultures. African Americans moved to the city from the South in the decades after the Civil War, and the Harlem neighborhood grew into a focal point for black cultural life. Already the nation's leading trade center, New York City soon sewed up the top spot in the country's garment (clothing) industry, too. Printing and publishing boomed, and Wall Street in Manhattan became the country's financial hub. The 20th century saw New York City grow into an international stage for theater, television, film, advertising, and music recording. And the United Nations has been headquartered in the city since 1946.

New Yorkers call almost all of the state north of New York City "Upstate," and it's a different world from "The City." A quarter of state lands are devoted to agriculture, including dairy farming, fruits, and vegetables. Only Vermont taps more sugar maples for syrup. Industrial cities include Buffalo, Schenectady, Syracuse, and Utica. Rochester is known for photographic and optical equipment. Tourism is huge in the state, too, with both urban and natural areas drawing visitors year-round.

Today, the state of New York ranks third in population, with the New York City metropolitan area one of the biggest on Earth, with approximately 8.1 million people. Now standing proudly in Lower Manhattan is the 1,776-foot (541-m) Freedom Tower, America's tallest building and a testament to New York's resilience after the 9/11 terrorist attack. While New York's role as a commerce capital remains, its old industries face long-term decline. The state works to attract new industry and to clean up its natural environments, such as the long-polluted Hudson River. In New York City's harbor, the Statue of Liberty stands as a beacon of freedom and an invitation to people everywhere.

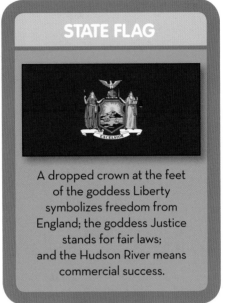

STATE FLAG

A dropped crown at the feet of the goddess Liberty symbolizes freedom from England; the goddess Justice stands for fair laws; and the Hudson River means commercial success.

STATE FLOWER
Rose

STATE BIRD
Eastern Bluebird

IT'S A FACT:
With more than twice the population of the next largest U.S. city, New York City is the country's largest city.

A TIME LINE OF THE EMPIRE STATE

1626

Peter Minuit, Governor-General of New Amsterdam, **bought Manhattan Island** for goods worth about 60 Dutch guilders ($24).

1825

The opening of the **Erie Canal** linked the Atlantic and the Great Lakes, bringing prosperity to New York cities along its route.

1931

Standing 1,250 feet (381 m) tall, the **Empire State Building** has been a towering symbol of New York City since it was completed in this year. From the tower's 86th-floor observation deck, visitors can see four neighboring states!

1936

The **National Baseball Hall of Fame** opened in Cooperstown. Some 300,000 people visit it each year. The Hall and its museum honor more than 300 members—and all of baseball!

2001

The 9/11 attack on the **World Trade Center** destroyed it and killed almost 2,800 people, and changed forever everyday life in America.

Present

The **New York Stock Exchange**, located on Wall Street, is the world's largest stock exchange, with billions of dollars of trades made five days a week.

ON THE MAP

LOCATION, LOCATION

This third most populous state borders five other states, with Canada to the north. Its New York City is a global seaport and center for finance, culture, and diplomacy. "Upstate," as New Yorkers call the north, is a lush land of farms, forests, mountains, and lakes.

ADIRONDACK PARK: It's the largest park in the lower 48 states—almost as big as Yellowstone, Yosemite, Grand Canyon, and Olympic National Parks combined.

NIAGARA RIVER: Its magnificent Niagara Falls include American, Bridal Veil, and Horseshoe Falls. Each minute, the falls send some 40 million gallons (150 million L) of water thundering 175 feet (53 m) over the ledges.

ALBANY: The state capital since 1797, it is one of New York's oldest settlements. In the 20th century it opened America's first municipal airport, one of the world's first.

HUDSON RIVER: It was sailed by English explorer Henry Hudson in 1609 and is key to New York City commerce today. Its beauty inspired the Hudson River school of landscape painting in the 1800s.

FINGER LAKES: This group of glacially carved lakes bears the names of various Native American tribes, including the Seneca, Cayuga, and Canandaigua.

NEW YORK CITY: It's the state's largest city, with some 8.1 million people. It is home to the United Nations and to Liberty Island—home to the Statue of Liberty.

0   50   100 miles
0   50   100 kilometers
Albers Conic Equal-Area Projection

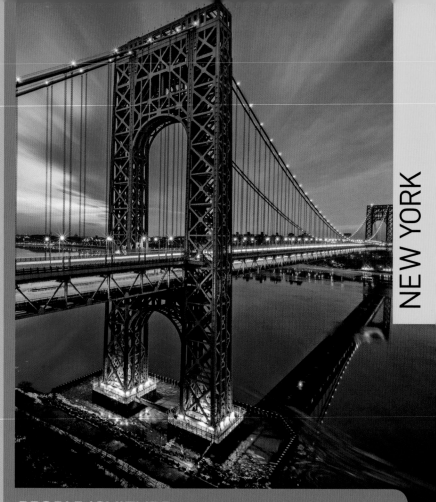

STATS & FACTS

STATEHOOD: July 26, 1788; 11th state

CAPITAL: Albany

TOTAL AREA: 54,556 sq mi; 141,299 sq km

LAND AREA: 47,214 sq mi; 122,283 sq km

POPULATION: 19,746,227

POPULATION DENSITY: 418 people per sq mi

MAJOR RACIAL/ETHNIC GROUPS: 65.7% white, 15.9% African American, 7.3% Asian, 0.6% Native American, Hispanic (any race) 17.6%

INDUSTRY: printing and publishing, advertising, tourism, finance, manufacturing, entertainment, business services

AGRICULTURE: dairy products, corn, oats, apples, cattle, maple syrup, greenhouse, vegetables, hay, wheat, soybeans, potatoes, dry edible beans, barley, fruit

PEOPLE/CULTURE: Many men of the Mohawk tribe have a seeming lack of fear of heights that makes them especially suited to working as riveters on steel bridges and skyscrapers, such as the Empire State Building and the **George Washington Bridge.**

NATURAL FEATURES: New York is the only state that borders **both the Atlantic Ocean and the Great Lakes.**

NATURAL FORCES: In 1900 **49 inches (125 cm) of snow fell in 24 hours** in Watertown. The state averages just 25 inches (63.5 cm) a year.

HISTORY: First settled by the Dutch in 1658, the New York City neighborhood of **Harlem** is known as the "black mecca" of the world, a center for African-American culture and arts.

ANIMALS: New York City's **Central Park** is home to 10 species of mammals—including bats and raccoons—and 50 species of birds.

PENNSYLVANIA

THE KEYSTONE STATE

The Keystone State. To a builder, the keystone is at the center of an arch, the stone that binds the others together. Pennsylvania was key to the nation's successful start, and a major force in holding the Union together during its toughest time.

William Penn's heavily forested colony was named for his father, Adm. William Penn. (*Sylvania* is a Latin word meaning "woodlands.") In October 1682 the younger William brought 360 settlers who believed in religious freedom and a fair government to form this 12th of the 13 English colonies. Penn treated Native Americans with respect, signing a fair treaty with Delaware chiefs. In 1701 the colony's Charter of Privilege gave its elected assembly greater power than any other in the English world. Though Penn was a Quaker, people of other religions were welcome. The colony expanded farther west, too. There, settlers met resistance from native peoples and the French. These conflicts did not end until 1763, after the French and Indian War.

Pennsylvania's lands were packed with resources. Beech and maple uplands plus lowlands of oak and hickory made up "Penn's woods." Fertile valley soils, especially in the southeast, proved perfect for grain and dairy farming. Coal, iron, limestone, and oil supplied the minerals for industry. The many rivers and streams—and later a link to Lake Erie—offered water power and transportation.

Wealthy, populous Pennsylvania took center stage in the move to gain independence. Representatives from the 13 Colonies met in Philadelphia to adopt the Declaration of Independence, which local resident Benjamin Franklin helped draft.

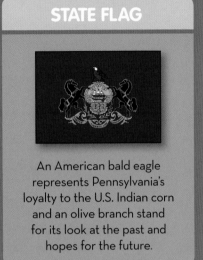

STATE FLOWER
Mountain Laurel

STATE BIRD
Ruffled Grouse

Pennsylvania became the second state in 1787. In the next century the stately merchant city of Philadelphia became a brawny industrial giant. It launched steamships, rolled out locomotives, and milled textiles, clothing, paper, and more. Immigrants came from Ireland, Germany, and elsewhere. Located at the junction of three rivers, Pittsburgh used in-state coal and Great Lakes iron ore to make iron and later steel. Other cities boomed, too, making a thousand different products. The state contributed huge volumes of material and tens of thousands of soldiers to the Civil War.

After the war, the industrial boom continued, and waves of immigrants poured in from Europe; others came from the rural South to work in the state's mines and factories. Owners became wealthy, but life was tough and often dangerous for workers. To gain safer working conditions and better pay, labor unions were formed, leading to violent strikes in the late 1800s and early 1900s. Though industrial success continued through the two World Wars, the steel industry began to decline in the 1980s. Less coal was needed as the steel business moved overseas, where it could be made more cheaply.

Today Pittsburgh's mills are gone, but the city still has advanced manufacturing—plus world-class medical and life sciences research. Philadelphia is becoming a center for information technology and financial services. But Pennsylvania remains a mining and industrial force, ranking fourth in coal production and fifth in steel output. It's an agricultural state, too, with more than 63,000 farms producing dairy products, fresh vegetables, and eggs. Tourists increasingly find the state's rural landscapes, plentiful wild spaces, and key historic sites to be unbeatable destinations. Though Pennsylvania is different now from when Penn and Franklin walked its cobblestones, the Keystone State still has a key place in the workings of the nation.

IT'S A FACT:
During the American Revolution, the Liberty Bell was moved from Philadelphia to Allentown. It was returned after the British evacuated Philadelphia.

A TIME LINE OF THE KEYSTONE STATE

1682
William Penn founded his colony in 1682 on land west of the Delaware River granted to him by King Charles II in a charter.

1752
Philadelphia inventor and statesman **Benjamin Franklin** experimented with a kite to determine that lightning is a form of electricity.

1863
At Gettysburg, the Union withstood **"Pickett's Charge,"** stopping the South's advance. This was the turning point in the Civil War.

1870–1970s
Pittsburgh grew to be a steel powerhouse. By 1900 the city's mill workers turned out two-thirds of the country's steel.

1979
The near disaster at the **Three Mile Island** nuclear power plant near Harrisburg stopped U.S. development of nuclear plants for 30 years.

Present
Lancaster County generates thousands of tourist dollars from people coming to visit the settlements of the **Amish**—people who came to Pennsylvania in the early 1700s from Switzerland and Germany and still live in traditional farming communities, shunning modern technology.

ON THE MAP

LOCATION, LOCATION

Pennsylvania borders six states, including New York to the north and Maryland to the south. The southern border is the Mason-Dixon Line, created over a period of 21 years—from 1763 to 1784—to officially divide the North United States from the South.

SUSQUEHANNA RIVER: Along its winding route through Pennsylvania, the river provides as much as 446 million gallons (1,688 million L) of water to millions of Pennsylvanians every day, for uses ranging from drinking to farming.

EASTON: The Crayola crayon factory opened here in 1969. It became company headquarters in 1976.

TITUSVILLE: Edwin Drake launched the petroleum industry when he drilled the first oil well in 1859.

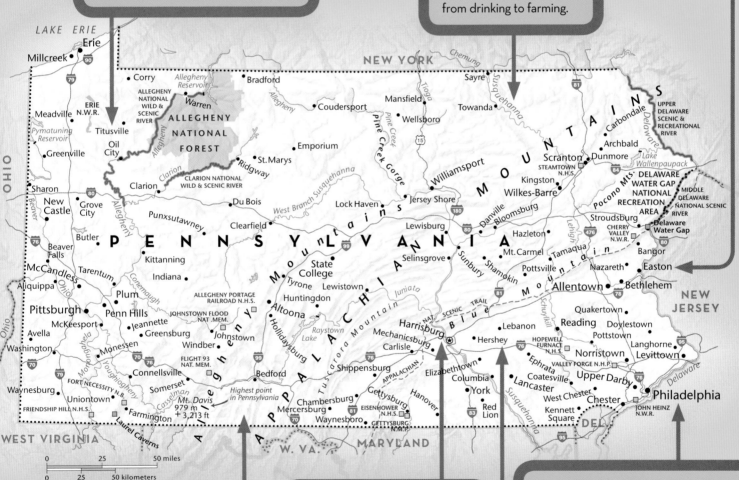

PENN'S WOODS: This wildlife-rich area boasts one of America's largest deer populations and thousands of black bears. Elk, once endangered, have made a comeback.

HARRISBURG: President Theodore Roosevelt called the Harrisburg capitol building "the handsomest building I ever saw."

PHILADELPHIA: The largest city, with 1,553,000 people, is called the City of Brotherly Love. Here, the 1776 Continental Congress wrote the Declaration of Independence from England.

HERSHEY: Home of the candy company, the town calls itself "the sweetest place on earth." Each year enough Hershey's Kisses are produced to form a line more than 300,000 miles (482,800 km) long.

STATS & FACTS

STATEHOOD: December 12, 1787; 2nd state

CAPITAL: Harrisburg

TOTAL AREA: 46,055 sq mi; 119,283 sq km

LAND AREA: 44,817 sq mi; 116,075 sq km

POPULATION: 12,787,209

POPULATION DENSITY: 285 people per sq mi

MAJOR RACIAL/ETHNIC GROUPS: 81.9% white, 10.8% African American, 2.7% Asian, 0.2% Native American, Hispanic (any race) 5.7%

INDUSTRY: manufacturing, machinery, metals, tourism, chemicals, coal production, natural gas production, biotechnology

AGRICULTURE: dairy products, cattle, eggs, corn, oats, soybeans, wheat, hay, barley, fruit, potatoes, dry edible beans

ANIMALS: All year-round you can visit **Punxsutawney Phil,** the groundhog that predicts whether or not there will be six more weeks of winter weather on Groundhog Day, at the Punxsutawney Zoo.

NATURAL FEATURES: **Balanced Rock,** located in Trough Creek State Park, is a huge boulder perched on a cliff. Erosion makes it appear like it could tip at any moment.

PEOPLE/CULTURE: Considered the father of the American steel industry, **Andrew Carnegie** was born in Scotland but built his empire in Pennsylvania, opening his first mill in Braddock in 1874.

HISTORY: Philadelphia was chosen as the first site of the **U.S. Mint** in 1792, when it was the nation's capital. It was believed that some of the silver used in making the first silver coins was donated by President George Washington.

NATURAL FORCES: When a dam failed near **Johnstown during massive rains in 1889,** 20 million gallons (76 million L) of water flooded the city. Some 2,000 people died.

RHODE ISLAND

THE OCEAN STATE

Small space. Special place. Rhode Island is the smallest state in area—tinier than some counties in other states—but it's founded on freedoms still revered across the nation. There's much that makes Rhode Island special.

The Dutch explored the coastline in 1614—possibly giving it the name Roodt Eylandt (Red Island)—but it was Roger Williams who began white settlement there in 1636. Forced to leave Massachusetts because he disagreed with its Puritan leaders, Williams wanted to create a place of religious freedom. He obtained land along a large bay from the Narragansett people, naming his community Providence. Other like-minded people later established Newport, Portsmouth, and Warwick. The settlements joined together for protection. Over time, relations with the Indians worsened. King Philip's War ended native resistance to white settlement in 1676.

Rhode Island steered an independent course as a colony, avoiding outside affairs. But the people soon realized that such connections were needed and began trading their harvests and catches for goods from other colonies and countries. In the 1700s Newport emerged as the leading port in the very profitable "triangle trade," in which ships carrying lumber to the West Indies returned with molasses for making rum. Rum was then sent to Africa in exchange for slaves. In the 1780s a state law banned the slave trade and provided for the gradual emancipation of children of slaves.

In the first years of the United States, Rhode Island's independent attitude kept it from signing the Constitution. It pressed for greater freedom of worship and other rights, for slavery to be abolished, for changes in trade rules and in taxes, and for a method of representation in Congress that was not based on population alone. With the addition of the Bill of Rights and the provision that each state would have two senators in Congress plus a number of representatives based on state population, Rhode Island finally signed the Constitution in 1790 and became the 13th state.

Rhode Island had what was needed to be a leader in the new U.S. economy: wealth from trade, power from its rivers, and cheap labor. Dozens of textile mill towns prospered, attracting immigrants first from Ireland, England, and Scotland and later from Italy and Portugal. Providence, linked by sea and rail, became Rhode Island's biggest commercial center. Newport developed as a vacation spot for the wealthy. In spite of its cotton-trade ties to the South, the state's antislavery stand made it a Union supporter in the Civil War.

Textiles began a gradual decline that continued into the 20th century. Labor strikes caused by a gap between wealthy business owners and poor workers developed in the 1920s. Tough times continued during the Depression. World War II helped the state's economy, but it suffered later when military bases were closed in the 1970s.

In recent years Rhode Island has seen economic improvement. It has a thriving jewelry and silverware industry and manufactures electronics, scientific instruments, machines, and some textiles. Like other old industrial states, Rhode Island is switching to a more service-based economy. Biotechnology is growing, and the state is working to preserve the environment of Narragansett Bay, source of much of its wealth. The Ocean State also looks to expand tourism, drawing visitors with its rich history and a variety of water sports. No place in this small state is more than a half-hour drive from the ocean or bay—something special that no big state can match.

STATE FLAG

The gold anchor and the state motto, "Hope," may have been inspired by the biblical verse from Hebrews 6:18-19: "Hope we have as an anchor of the soul."

STATE FLOWER
Violet

STATE BIRD
Rhode Island Red

IT'S A FACT:
In 1708 the colony's first census was taken. Its population was only 7,181.

A TIME LINE OF THE OCEAN STATE

1636
Roger Williams founded Rhode Island and Providence Plantations and also wrote America's first document separating church and state.

1793
Samuel Slater's use of water to power a cotton mill started the **industrial revolution** in the U.S. and New England's textile empire.

1870–1970s
The Breakers was one of several "cottages" built in Newport by wealthy business barons from New York in the 1890s. It actually has 70 rooms and was modeled after a 16th-century palace.

1930
Newport began hosting the world-famous **America's Cup** yacht races.

1954
The **Tennis Hall of Fame** was founded by James Van Alen at the Newport Casino, also site of the first U.S. National Championships in 1881.

Present
Nearly 100 bonfires called **WaterFire**—sculpture installation art—illuminate Providence's three downtown rivers and draw tourists in the evenings from May through October.

ON THE MAP

LOCATION, LOCATION

Bordering the Atlantic, this smallest state is flat: Its highest point is Jerimoth Hill, just 812 feet (247 m) above sea level. The state is only 37 miles (60 km) wide and 48 miles (77 km) long, but its 384-mile (618-km)-long coast of bays and inlets is a sailing paradise.

PAWTUCKET: Samuel Slater built the first water-powered cotton spinning mill in 1790, launching the U.S. industrial revolution.

PROVIDENCE: The state capital and largest city with 177,994 people, it's the birthplace of George M. Cohan, who wrote "I'm a Yankee Doodle Dandy."

LITTLE COMPTON: The first girl born to colonists in New England—to pilgrims John and Priscilla Alden—is buried here.

QUONSET POINT: The Quonset hut takes its name from this point, home of the Naval Air Station where the rounded and ridged steel structure was first built.

NEWPORT: This key port in the colonial Triangle Trade of slaves, molasses, and rum is the historical home of the America's Cup yacht races and a favorite sailing destination.

FORT ADAMS: Built in the 1800s to protect Narragansett Bay, it's the largest coastal fortification in America, with tunnels you can explore.

WATCH HILL: It's the home of the Flying Horse Carousel, with beautiful carved wooden horses—the nation's oldest of its kind.

Map labels

Wallum Lake, Slatersville, Woonsocket, Pawtucket Reservoir, Glendale, Union Village, Cumberland Hill, Harrisville, Manville, Ashton, Pascoag Lake, Pascoag, Blackstone, Valley Falls, Woonasquatucket Reservoir, Lonsdale, Central Falls, Chepachet, Saylesville, Esmond, Pawtucket, Harmony, Greenville, North Providence, North Scituate, Providence, Johnston, East Providence, ROGER WILLIAMS NAT. MEM., Foster Center, Cranston, Scituate Reservoir, Barrington, Warren, R H O D E, Hope, Harris, Bristol, Coventry Center, Anthony, West Warwick, Warwick, Rice City, Flat River Reservoir, Tiogue L., East Greenwich, Stafford Pond, I S L A N D, Tiverton, Island Park, Prudence Island, Portsmouth, Nonquit Pond, Austin, Quonset Point, Exeter, Wickford, Rhode Island, Adamsville, Hamilton, Conanicut Island, Allenton, Saunderstown, Middletown, Little Compton, Hope Valley, Wyoming, Newport, SACHUEST POINT N.W.R., West Kingston, Kingston, Jamestown, FORT ADAMS STATE PARK, TOURO SYNAGOGUE N.H.S., Sakonnet Point, Carolina, Wakefield, JOHN H. CHAFEE N.W.R., Shannock, Narragansett Pier, Ashaway, Worden Pond, NARRAGANSETT INDIAN RES., Point Judith Pond, Bradford, Watchaug Pond, Jerusalem, Galilee, Westerly, Ninigret Pond, Charlestown, TRUSTOM POND N.W.R., Point Judith, Quonochontaug Pond, NINIGRET N.W.R., Quonochontaug, Watch Hill, Napatree Point

CONNECTICUT

MASSACHUSETTS

Highest point in Rhode Island
Jerimoth Hill
812 ft 247 m

Ponaganset Res.
Ponaganset
Moosup
Wood
Queen
Pawcatuck
Pawcatuck
Narragansett Bay
Mount Hope Bay
Sakonnet River
Palmer
Providence
Pawtuxet

N.Y.

Rhode Island Sound

Block Island Sound

BLOCK ISLAND N.W.R.
Sandy Point
Block Island
Block Island

ATLANTIC OCEAN

0   5   10 miles
0   5   10 kilometers
Albers Conic Equal-Area Projection

STATS & FACTS

STATEHOOD: May 29, 1790; 13th state

CAPITAL: Providence

TOTAL AREA: 1,545 sq mi; 4,002 sq km

LAND AREA: 1,045 sq mi; 2,706 sq km

POPULATION: 1,055,173

POPULATION DENSITY: 1,009 people per sq mi

MAJOR RACIAL/ETHNIC GROUPS: 81.4% white, 5.7% African American, 2.9% Asian, 0.6% Native American, Hispanic (any race) 12.4%

INDUSTRY: business services, trade (retail and wholesale), finance, jewelry, metal products, tourism

AGRICULTURE: greenhouse, dairy products, apples, seafood, corn, hay, potatoes

NATURAL FORCES: Because it is the meeting place of storm tracks, Rhode Island can be hit with **gales, hurricanes, and severe blizzards.**

HISTORY: The rights guaranteed to all Americans in the First Amendment to the Constitution, including freedom of religion, speech, and assembly, were among the rights promised much earlier to settlers in Rhode Island by **Roger Williams,** the colony's founder.

NATURAL FEATURES: As the **smallest U.S. state** in area, Rhode Island would fit almost 425 times into the giant landmass of Alaska.

ANIMALS: The **Rhode Island Red** was one of the first chicken breeds developed to increase quality and quantity of egg and meat production.

PEOPLE/ CULTURE:

Pawtucket is one of several communities in Rhode Island that have become home to a growing number of **people from Cape Verde.** Drought has forced people from this African country to find a new place to live.

VERMONT

THE GREEN MOUNTAIN STATE

Green mountain majesty. When the French explorer Samuel de Champlain viewed a ridge of a long, forest-cloaked dividing range, he called it *vert mont*—green mountain. Ever since, these granite and green slopes of the northern Appalachians have defined the region. Still four-fifths wooded and split north to south by rugged lines of peaks, Vermont proudly wears its nickname: Green Mountain State.

The only New England state without direct access to the Atlantic, Vermont has a freshwater sea instead: Lake Champlain. Shared with New York and Quebec, the glacially carved, 120-mile (193-km)-long lake is the sixth largest inland water body in the country. Vermont has plentiful water elsewhere, too. Among its many rivers, the Connecticut forms the state's long eastern boundary. Vermont's northern location and high ridges bring heavy snows during cold winters. Cool, short summers and poor, rocky soils limit most agriculture to lake and river lowlands.

The French traded in the area and built their first settlement in 1666, but it did not last. In 1724 the English founded Fort Dummer near present-day Brattleboro. The two empires fought over Vermont, with the French retreating to Canada at the close of the French and Indian War in 1763. Shaped like a rocky wedge between New York and New Hampshire, Vermont once divided those colonies. Each wanted the territory, and they actually fought over Vermont. Among the battlers was fiercely proud Ethan Allen, who at first led efforts to join these lands to New Hampshire. But once the American Revolution began, he and his Green Mountain Boys switched to fight the British. Allen's daring capture of Fort Ticonderoga sparked early war efforts by patriots all across New England and beyond.

Vermonters' independent attitudes caused them to declare freedom not just from British rule in 1777 but from all their neighbors, too. After some talk of joining with Canada, Vermont joined the United States as the 14th state in 1791. Montpelier became its capital in 1805. Stability brought more immigrants to Vermont, and sheep farming and woolen mills proved successful for the first half of the 19th century. Railroads arrived in 1849 to help transport Vermont resources.

Vermont's geology plays a key role in its economy. The world's largest granite quarry and the largest underground marble quarry produce building stone. Aboveground, Vermont's green treasures include hardwoods for furniture and softwoods for pulp and paper. Milk and cheese are produced from dairy herds grazed on mountain pastures. For years tourists have enjoyed the state's country roads, hiking trails, water activities, and winter sports. In recent decades computer and other high-tech companies have found Burlington and other Vermont cities fine spots to locate operations.

Vermonters have traditionally blazed their own path in politics, and ideas born here have often led the country. Vermont's 1777 constitution banned slavery and gave the vote to all men even if they did not own land—two ideas that were way ahead of their time. By 1970 Vermont was a national leader in environmental legislation. Today the state struggles to balance environmental protection and economic growth. Recent problems include the loss of dairy farms, pollution, and an increase in part-time residents who bring money to the state but reduce its rural nature. Success in preserving Vermont's natural resources will safeguard opportunities for future generations of Green Mountain boys and girls.

STATE FLAG

The Green Mountains, a pine tree, and a deer head indicate natural wealth. The motto, "Freedom and Unity," represents individual freedom and the welfare of all.

STATE FLOWER
Red Clover

STATE BIRD
Hermit Thrush

IT'S A FACT:
Vermont produces 1.3 million gallons (4.9 million L) of maple syrup a year, more than any other state.

A TIME LINE OF THE GREEN MOUNTAIN STATE

1609

Samuel de Champlain, with the aid of Huron people, was the first European to explore the region, claiming it for France.

1775

Ethan Allen and his Green Mountain Boys won fame by capturing New York's Fort Ticonderoga, on Lake Champlain, from the British.

1811–1850s

Wool from **merino sheep** imported from Spain supplied wool mills and made the breed the state's chief livestock animal until the 1850s.

1978

After taking a $5 correspondence course on ice-cream making, **Ben and Jerry** started their world-famous ice-cream shop in a renovated garage in Burlington.

Present

Tourism is now a top state business. Skiers and snowboarders flock to the slopes, which are considered some of the best on the East Coast.

ON THE MAP

LOCATION, LOCATION

The only New England state not on the Atlantic Ocean, Vermont is a lush area with forests, mountains, and lakes. It shares Lake Champlain with its western neighbor, New York. Its Green Mountain National Forest is famed for its fall foliage—a tourist favorite.

JAY PEAK: Just a few miles from the Canadian border, its powdery mountains are a favorite for extreme skiers and snowboarders.

BURLINGTON: Vermont's largest city has a population of 42,417. Here, you can see a statue of Champ, Lake Champlain's version of the Loch Ness Monster.

SHELBURNE: One of Vermont's oldest cities, it has one of the nation's finest collections of folk art and artifacts from early America.

RUTLAND: This home of the New England Maple Museum shows how Native Americans first turned maple tree sap into syrup, and how syrup is an American staple today.

MONTPELIER: It's the only U.S. state capital that doesn't have a McDonald's fast-food restaurant.

PUTNEY: The home of U.S. senator George Aiken, once described as the "essence of Vermont." From 1931 to 1975, Aiken served as state representative, governor, then U.S. senator. He played a key role in the passage of the Civil Rights Act in 1964.

BENNINGTON: Americans won a major Revolutionary War battle here on August 16, 1777, against the British. This turning point is celebrated as a legal holiday.

STATS & FACTS

STATEHOOD: March 4, 1791; 14th state

CAPITAL: Montpelier

TOTAL AREA: 9,614 sq mi; 24,901 sq km

LAND AREA: 9,250 sq mi; 23,956 sq km

POPULATION: 626,562

POPULATION DENSITY: 68 people per sq mi

MAJOR RACIAL/ETHNIC GROUPS: 95.3% white, 1.3% Asian, 1.0% African American, 0.4% Native American, Hispanic (any race) 1.5%

INDUSTRY: minerals, computer components, food products, pulp and paper, tourism

AGRICULTURE: dairy products, cattle, greenhouse, maple syrup, hay, corn

NATURAL FORCES: Sunny days and freezing nights of early spring make sap flow in Vermont's **maple trees,** and syrup makers get busy: It takes 40 buckets of sap to produce one bucket of maple syrup.

ANIMALS: Morgan horses, an American breed known for its stamina, vigor, and all-purpose usefulness, have been raised on farms throughout Vermont since just after the Revolution. The First Vermont Cavalry rode Morgans in the Civil War, and Confederate general Stonewall Jackson's horse "Little Sorrel" was a Morgan.

PEOPLE/ CULTURE: Vermont has never been heavily **populated.** Today only Wyoming has fewer residents.

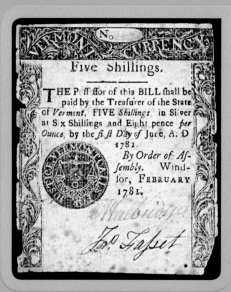

HISTORY: From 1777 until it became a state in 1791, Vermont had its own **postal and monetary systems.**

NATURAL FEATURES: The Long Trail is a 265-mile (426-km)-long recreational trail that runs along the ridges of the **Green Mountains** for the entire length of the state.

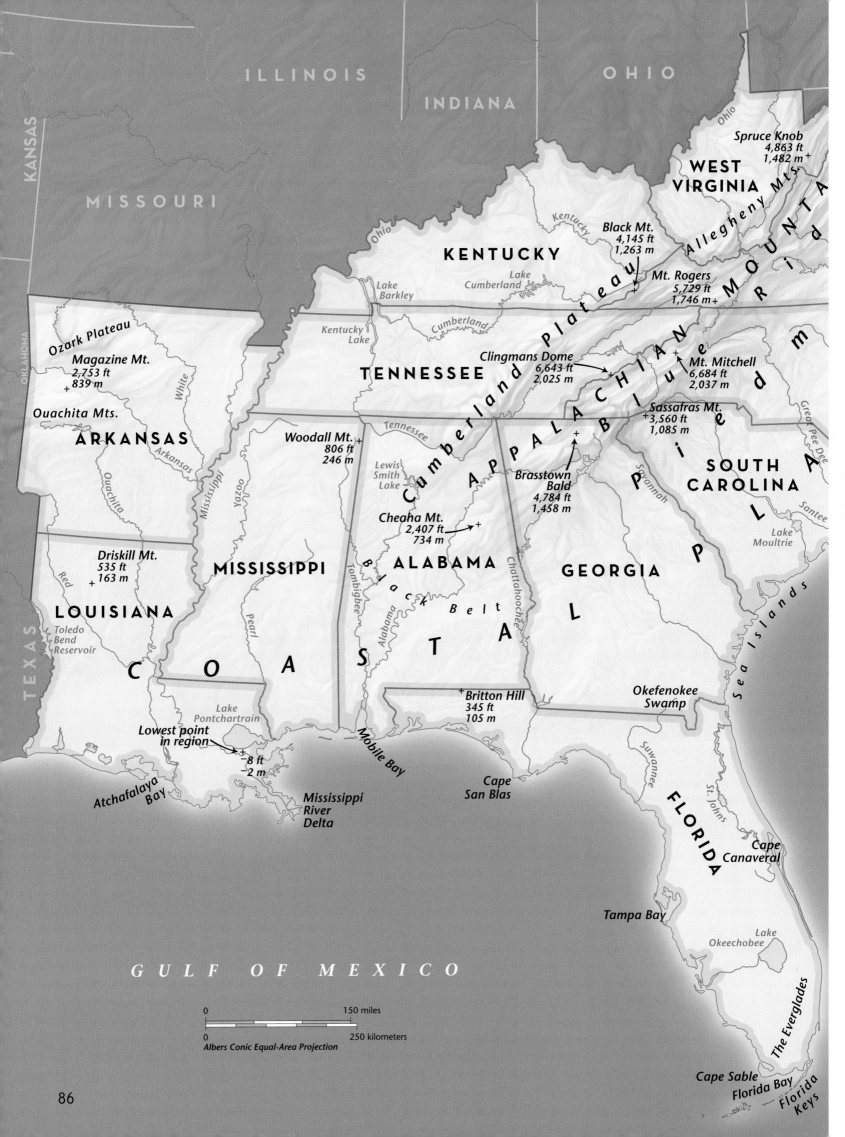

KANSAS

MISSOURI

ILLINOIS

INDIANA

OHIO

OKLAHOMA

TEXAS

WEST VIRGINIA

Spruce Knob
4,863 ft
1,482 m +

Ohio

Allegheny Mts.

KENTUCKY

Kentucky

Black Mt.
4,145 ft
1,263 m

Mt. Rogers
5,729 ft
1,746 m +

Lake
Cumberland

Ohio

Lake
Barkley

Cumberland

Kentucky
Lake

Ozark Plateau

Magazine Mt.
2,753 ft
+ 839 m

White

Ouachita Mts.

ARKANSAS

Arkansas

Ouachita

Driskill Mt.
535 ft
+ 163 m

Red

LOUISIANA

Toledo
Bend
Reservoir

TENNESSEE

Tennessee

Cumberland Plateau

Clingmans Dome
6,643 ft
2,025 m

Mt. Mitchell
6,684 ft
2,037 m

APPALACHIAN

Blue Ridge

Piedmont

Sassafras Mt.
+ 3,560 ft
1,085 m

SOUTH CAROLINA

Lake
Moultrie

Great Pee Dee

Santee

Woodall Mt.
806 ft
246 m

Lewis
Smith
Lake

Cheaha Mt.
2,407 ft
734 m +

Brasstown
Bald
4,784 ft
1,458 m

Savannah

MISSISSIPPI

Yazoo

Mississippi

ALABAMA

Black

Belt

GEORGIA

Chattahoochee

Sea Islands

Tombigbee

Alabama

Pearl

C O A S T A L

P L A I N

Okefenokee
Swamp

Lake
Pontchartrain

Britton Hill
345 ft
105 m +

Lowest point
in region

−8 ft
−2 m

*Mississippi
River
Delta*

Mobile Bay

Cape
San Blas

Suwannee

St. Johns

Atchafalaya
Bay

FLORIDA

Cape
Canaveral

G U L F   O F   M E X I C O

Tampa Bay

Lake
Okeechobee

0   150 miles

0   250 kilometers

Albers Conic Equal-Area Projection

The Everglades

Cape Sable
Florida Bay
Florida
Keys

SOUTHEAST

PENNSYLVANIA

N.J.

MD.

D.C.

DEL.

Potomac

Chesapeake Bay

*Delmarva
Peninsula*

VIRGINIA

James

Great *Dismal
Swamp*

*Albemarle
Sound*

Roanoke

NORTH
CAROLINA

*Pamlico
Sound*

Outer Banks

*Cape
Hatteras*

Cape Fear

Cape Lookout

*Cape
Fear*

*ATLANTIC
OCEAN*

STRAITS OF
FLORIDA

R ounded mountains, big rivers, and fertile plains characterize the Southeast. Southern ranges of the Appalachians— the Allegheny, Blue Ridge, and Cumberland Plateau—form a divide through the region. Streams flowing west of this divide join and enlarge the mighty Mississippi. Those draining east cross the Piedmont to a coastal plain that wraps around the southern tip of the Appalachians to Louisiana's Gulf Coast—a watery world of meandering rivers, deltas, swamps, and barrier islands.

West of the Mississippi the Ouachita Mountains and Ozark Plateau overlook Arkansas. The Florida peninsula is built on a limestone foundation punctuated by numerous lakes, sinkholes, islands, and America's most famous swamp—the Everglades. Throughout the Southeast needleleaf, broadleaf, and mixed forests thrive in a mostly mild climate where rainfall occurs in every month.

THE
SOUTHEAST

TRADITION AND CHANGE BETWEEN TWO COASTS

Abundant natural resources have always influenced how people live in this well-watered land. Native Cherokee, Choctaw, Creek, and Seminole tribes thrived by hunting in the forest, fishing, and gathering fruits, nuts, and berries that appear to grow everywhere. Many tribes also planted the "three sisters"—corn, squash, and beans.

Spain's Juan Ponce de León reached Florida in 1513. By 1565 the Spanish had founded the first permanent colony in the Americas at St. Augustine, Florida—55 years before the Pilgrims landed in Massachusetts. In 1673 two Frenchmen, missionary Jacques Marquette and explorer Louis Joliet, paddled down the Mississippi River to the mouth of the Arkansas River. France soon claimed the entire area drained by the Mississippi. The English colonized Virginia in the early 1600s and slowly extended settlements south to Georgia by the 1730s.

The colonists took advantage of the natural resources, planting tobacco, mining coal and iron ore in the Appalachians, and turning marshlands into rice fields. The rivers plus Atlantic and Gulf waters were chock-full of fish, while the broadleaf and pine forests yielded plenty of game and timber.

After frontiersman Daniel Boone blazed the Wilderness Road across the Appalachians in 1775, American farmers migrated into the Kentucky, Ohio, and Tennessee River Valleys. Elsewhere the rise of wheat and cotton in addition to tobacco created a plantation economy dependent upon slave labor. To open lands for settlers in the 1830s, the government forced thousands of Native Americans westward along what became known as the Trail of Tears.

By 1861 tensions over slavery between northern and southern states erupted in the Civil War. All the states in this region except Kentucky and West Virginia seceded from the Union to form the Confederacy. The Union victory after four years of war left most of the region broken but soon moving toward new agricultural and city growth. But racial inequality continued.

By the 1930s two events changed the Southeast: A 1920s plague of boll weevils devastated cotton crops and forced farmers to diversify, and the Tennessee Valley Authority built dams to control flooding and provide power. Abundant electricity and nonunion labor attracted northern-based companies and people.

Today crops like Georgia peaches, Louisiana rice, and Florida oranges are known worldwide. Arkansas chickens, Kentucky racehorses, and Gulf Coast oil are key products. Cities such as Atlanta, Charlotte, and Miami are leaders in business, research, and tourism. Development brings challenges, but it is also a sign that the Southeast is thriving.

ALABAMA
ARKANSAS
FLORIDA
GEORGIA
KENTUCKY
LOUISIANA
MISSISSIPPI
NORTH CAROLINA
SOUTH CAROLINA
TENNESSEE
VIRGINIA
WEST VIRGINIA

" … LOUISIANA BAYOUS, … SUN, COTTON FIELDS,
LONESOME ROADS, TRAIN WHISTLES IN THE NIGHT … "
—POET AND ACTIVIST LANGSTON HUGHES,
FROM "MUSIC AT YEAR'S END,"
CHICAGO DEFENDER, JANUARY 9, 1943

ALABAMA

THE HEART OF DIXIE

O h, I wish I was in the land of cotton, old times there are not forgotten!" So begins the famous song "Dixie," a favorite of Confederate troops as they battled to maintain their way of life. Today, Alabama's nickname is Heart of Dixie, which fits as well in today's South as when the state anchored the Confederate States.

The Spanish explored the region in the 1500s, but the French established the first permanent European settlement along Mobile Bay in 1702. They named the region for Indians who called themselves "Alibamu." The British won control of the land after the French and Indian War, but lost it after the Revolutionary War. Andrew Jackson's defeat of Creek warriors in the War of 1812 and the rising demand for cotton spurred immigration from Tennessee and Georgia. The Territory of Alabama was formed in 1817 and became a state two years later. Native Americans were forced to relocate to Oklahoma during the 1830s.

Alabamans settled a state of mostly low, rolling plains. The rugged southern reaches of the Cumberland Plateau and the Appalachian Mountains stretch into the northeast. Except for the Tennessee River, which arcs through Alabama's northern districts, most rivers flow from northeast to southwest, emptying into Mobile Bay. Spanning the middle is the black belt, a band of rich, dark soil that made cotton Alabama's chief crop. Wealthy landowners, using slaves for labor, established big plantations in fertile bottomlands. They led the state to secession from the Union in 1861.

The Confederacy's government was formed in Montgomery, which acted as its capital for a time. Selma was a center of ammunition manufacture, and Mobile was a critical port.

STATE FLAG

The cross of St. Andrew on a field of white is called a saltire. It is said that St. Andrew was martyred on this kind of cross.

STATE FLOWER
Camellia

STATE BIRD
Northern Flicker

The Civil War cost 15,000 Alabama soldiers their lives. Postwar Reconstruction governments struggled with rebuilding economies and the persistence of racial inequalities and injustices. The years after Reconstruction saw the rise of Birmingham as the "Pittsburgh of the South" as railroads carried Alabama coal, iron ore, and limestone to the city's steel mills. But it took a tiny insect to spark a transformation in the economy.

In the 1920s the boll weevil destroyed the cotton harvest. Together with declining soil fertility caused by planting cotton year after year, the weevil infestation forced farmers to finally break away from a single crop. Cotton is still important, but so are peanuts, sweet potatoes, pecans, chickens, and pond-raised catfish. Vast stands of oak and pine support a giant forest-products industry. Beginning in 1933, the Tennessee Valley Authority's dam at Muscle Shoals provided plentiful and cheap electricity. The opening of the Tennessee-Tombigbee Waterway in 1985 dramatically increased barge traffic by linking the Tennessee River and Mobile Bay. Huntsville has attracted space-related and high-tech businesses since NASA's Marshall Space Flight Center opened in 1960.

Alabama's 4.8 million people have not forgotten their state's past. More than one-fourth of the population is African American, and those who are old enough remember terrible days of violence and racial injustice. But in the 1950s and 1960s gains in voting and other civil rights were achieved across the country.

The economy continues to diversify. All three automakers with assembly operations in the state set production records in 2012. Alabama hosts a diverse array of aerospace industry and defense companies, including Lockheed Martin and Boeing. While learning from its "old times," Alabama is marching toward new and better ones.

IT'S A FACT:
The Tennessee-Tombigbee Waterway, which extends into Alabama, is five times longer than the Panama Canal.

A TIME LINE OF THE HEART OF DIXIE

1813–14

Defeated after the massacre of settlers at Fort Mims, the **Creek people** were forced to give up their lands to the U.S. government.

1833

A massive nine-hour Leonids meteor shower causes the night of November 12–13 to be known as **"the night stars fell on Alabama."**

1880

Alabama's iron and steel industry was launched with the opening of Birmingham's **first blast furnace,** Alice No. 1.

1936

Alabama native Jesse Owens wins four Olympic gold medals in Berlin, Germany.

1955

When **Rosa Parks** refused to give up her bus seat to a white man in Montgomery, her arrest was a key event in the civil rights movement.

Present

Space Camp, in Huntsville, is one of several NASA programs that provide jobs and revenue for the state.

ON THE MAP

LOCATION, LOCATION

The Heart of Dixie is the appropriate term for this state nestled among four other southern states. With only a few mountains in the north, its flat lowlands, rich soil, and steamy climate combine for the growth of cash crops like pecans and peanuts.

BRIDGEPORT: Nearby Russell Cave was home to prehistoric peoples for more than 10,000 years. Today visitors can tour the caves and see the kinds of weapons and tools they used.

HUNTSVILLE: The U.S. Space and Rocket Center here hosts Space Camp, and NASA's Marshall Space Flight Center built the earliest rockets that took us to the moon.

DESOTO FALLS: Cave-dwelling peoples lived some 10–12,000 years ago in this rugged region named for Spanish gold seeker Hernando de Soto, who trekked through in 1540.

BIRMINGHAM: The state's largest city has a population of 212,113. It is the birthplace of Condoleezza Rice, the first African-American woman to serve as U.S. secretary of state.

TALLADEGA NATIONAL FOREST: Here, in the foothills of the Appalachian range, rises Cheaha Mountain, Alabama's tallest peak.

MONTGOMERY: The capital is the site of the Civil Rights Memorial inspired by Dr. Martin Luther King, Jr., and the civil rights movement. The names of 40 victims of civil rights violence are etched in black granite.

TUSKEGEE: This birthplace of Rosa Parks, "mother of the modern civil rights movement," is also home to the historically black Tuskegee Institute (now University) and its Tuskegee Airmen of World War II.

TENNESSEE

Tennessee Parkway · Natchez Trace Parkway · Florence · Wilson Lake · Athens · Madison · Huntsville · Scottsboro · Bridgeport · RUSSELL CAVE NAT. MON. · Pickwick Lake · KEY CAVE N.W.R. · Muscle Shoals · Wheeler Lake · Guntersville Lake · Desoto Falls · LITTLE RIVER CANYON NAT. PRESERVE · Red Bay · Russellville · Decatur · Hartselle · WHEELER N.W.R. · Fort Payne · Bear Cr. · SIPSEY FORK N.W.&S.R. · WILLIAM B. BANKHEAD NATIONAL FOREST · Guntersville · Albertville · Weiss L. · Hamilton · Cullman · Boaz · APPALACHIAN MOUNTAINS · Cumberland Plateau · Tennessee · GEORGIA · Winfield · Lewis Smith Lake · Jasper · Warrior · Gadsden · Piedmont · Jacksonville · Fayette · Mulberry Fork · Locust Fork · Coosa · TALLADEGA · Center Point · Anniston · NATIONAL · Birmingham · Pell City · Cheaha Mt. 2,407 ft 734 m · Hueytown · Homewood · Talladega · FOREST · Highest point in Alabama · Bessemer · Hoover · Tuscaloosa · Alabaster · Roanoke · West Point Lake · Aliceville · Montevallo · Sylacauga · HORSESHOE BEND N.M.P. · Lanett · Sipsey · CAHABA RIVER N.W.R. · Alexander City · Lake Martin · Valley · TALLADEGA NATIONAL FOREST · Clanton · A L A B A M A · Black Warrior · Livingston · Marion · Cahaba · Auburn · Opelika · Demopolis · POARCH CREEK IND. RES. · Tallassee · TUSKEGEE NAT. FOR. · Phenix City · York · Selma · Prattville · Millbrook · Tuskegee · TUSKEGEE INSTITUTE N.H.S. · Tallapoosa · Montgomery · Alabama · Chattahoochee · Tombigbee · William "Bill" Dannelly Reservoir · Union Springs · EUFAULA N.W.R. · Thomasville · B l a c k · B e l t · Eufaula · CHOCTAW N.W.R. · Greenville · Troy · Walter F. George Reservoir · Jackson · Monroeville · Abbeville · Pea · Fort Rucker · Ozark · Evergreen · Enterprise · Andalusia · Opp · Daleville · Dothan · Citronelle · POARCH CREEK INDIAN RESERVATION · Conecuh · Geneva · Choctawhatchee · Atmore · Brewton · CONECUH NATIONAL FOREST · Saraland · Bay Minette · FLORIDA · Prichard · Tensaw · Mobile · Daphne · GRAND BAY N.W.R. · Fairhope · Foley · Intracoastal Waterway · Bayou La Batre · Mobile Bay · Perdido · Mississippi Sound · Dauphin Island · Gulf Shores · BON SECOUR N.W.R.

GULF OF MEXICO

MISSISSIPPI

0 20 40 miles
0 20 40 kilometers
Albers Conic Equal-Area Projection

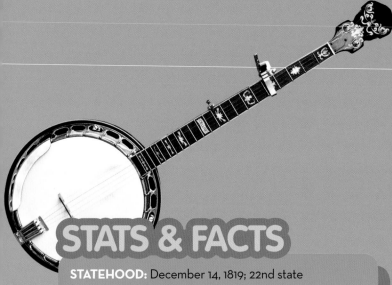

STATS & FACTS

STATEHOOD: December 14, 1819; 22nd state

CAPITAL: Montgomery

TOTAL AREA: 52,419 sq mi; 135,765 sq km

LAND AREA: 50,744 sq mi; 131,426 sq km

POPULATION: 4,849,377

POPULATION DENSITY: 96 people per sq mi

MAJOR RACIAL/ETHNIC GROUPS: 68.5% white, 26.2% African American, 1.1% Asian, 0.6% Native American, Hispanic (any race) 3.9%

INDUSTRY: manufacturing, automotive, aerospace, electronics, finance, construction, pulp and paper products

AGRICULTURE: broiler chickens, cattle, eggs, cotton, peanuts, greenhouse/nursery, wheat

ANIMALS: **Bobcats**—medium-size cats with a bobbed tail—are found throughout Alabama.

NATURAL FORCES: Of the **17 hurricanes** that have battered the Alabama coast since 1900, Ivan in 2004 was one of the worst, with winds at landfall of up to 130 miles an hour (209 km/h).

HISTORY: In 1955 Alabama became the first state to have **a state-owned television station.**

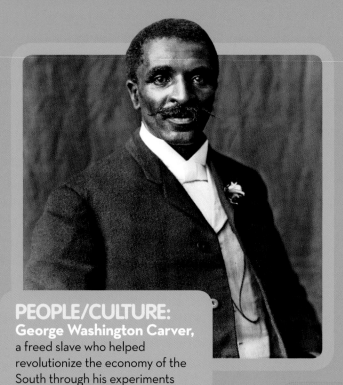

PEOPLE/CULTURE: **George Washington Carver,** a freed slave who helped revolutionize the economy of the South through his experiments with peanuts, soybeans, alternatives for cotton, and sweet potatoes, was the director of agricultural research at the Tuskegee Institute.

NATURAL FEATURES: Dismals Canyon, a few miles south of Russellville, has natural bridges, waterfalls, and one of the few stands of virgin forest east of the Mississippi River.

93

ARKANSAS

THE NATURAL STATE

Diverse landscapes and outdoor activities aplenty earn Arkansas its nickname, the Natural State. On its north and west rise the rugged Ouachita Mountains and the Ozark Plateau. Between them flows the Arkansas River, south and east across the state to the Gulf Coastal Plain. There it joins the Mississippi River, along Arkansas's eastern border.

Spaniard Hernando de Soto ventured into the region in 1541, and French explorers scouted its resources in the 1670s. The French learned of a native group named for the south wind. The Algonquian called them the Oo-ka-na-sa, and French missionary Jacques Marquette wrote "Arkansas" (pronounced ARK-an-saw). The French, Spanish, and British each controlled the land for periods of time, but Arkansas became part of the United States with the Louisiana Purchase in 1803. The Arkansas Territory was formed in 1819, and settlement increased with the forced departure of most Choctaw and Cherokee peoples. Slaveholding planters arrived to grow cotton in the Mississippi bottomlands. The wide valley of the Arkansas River provided fine farmlands, too. Poorer settlers from the southern Appalachians began moving into the Ozarks and Ouachitas, bringing their traditions of music and crafts.

As for the territory's largest city and future state capital, French traders crossed the Arkansas River at a spot where a *"petite roche"* offered a good landmark. Little Rock was on the map—founded in 1821. Improved river transport was key to early territorial expansion. A steamboat first chugged 300 miles (480 km) up the snag-filled Arkansas River in 1822.

Arkansas entered the Union as the 25th state in 1836. Difficult times followed after the state joined the Confederacy in 1861. The Union Army occupied the northern part of the state by early 1863. After the war, the state, like other southern states, was not readmitted to the Union until African Americans were given the right to vote. This happened in 1868. Southern blacks lost that right again, beginning in the late 1800s. Some left for northern industrial cities in the early 20th century; others migrated west during the Great Depression.

The past few decades have brought better days to Arkansas. The state population is now nearing three million, with nearly one in six residents of African-American heritage. Agriculture is thriving. Soggy Mississippi River lowlands provide fine rice-growing conditions. The flooded rice fields are also used to farm fish, with nutrients from fish waste providing fertilizer for the next rice crop. The state is in the top five for cotton, turkeys, and catfish production and is a leader in raising and processing chickens for sale. Arkansas continues to be the nation's leader in bauxite production. It is still first in bromine.

Arkansas's economic success is tied to sustainable use of its varied natural resources. Visitors flock to the scenic wooded trails and whitewater routes of the Ozarks and Ouachitas, where forests are managed for recreation, wildlife habitat, and a variety of wood products. The Arkansas Heritage Program maintains a biodiversity database on the state's natural communities and on almost 900 rare species of animals and plants, tracking their location and status. This data can be used for land management planning, biodiversity assessment, and environmental information-sharing. Wise water management is also critical to the state's economy, since both surface and underground sources provide for drinking, industry, and irrigation. Continued growth—both urban and rural—depends upon adequate and clean water supplies. People of the Natural State know they need to care for the natural environment that nurtures them.

STATE FLAG

The 25 stars stand for the 25th state to join the union. The diamond represents Arkansas as the nation's first diamond-producing state.

STATE FLOWER
Apple Blossom

STATE BIRD
Mockingbird

IT'S A FACT:
The average temperature of the waters in the 47 springs that flow out of Hot Springs Mountain is 143°F (62°C).

A TIME LINE OF THE NATURAL STATE

1686

Fur trader **Henri de Tonty,** the father of Arkansas, founded the first permanent European settlement on the Arkansas River.

1862

After their victory at **Pea Ridge,** the largest Civil War battle west of the Mississippi, the Union Army went on to capture Little Rock.

1957

Amid violent protests, this girl and eight other African Americans began attending formerly all-white **Little Rock Central High School.**

2004

President Bill Clinton's presidential library, located in Little Rock, opened. Clinton was born in Hope, Arkansas.

2007

A 13-year-old girl from Missouri found a **2.93-carat diamond** in Crater of Diamonds State Park.

Present

Arkansas-based **Walmart,** the world's largest retailer, attracts many suppliers and other businesses to the state.

ON THE MAP

LOCATION, LOCATION

The rugged Ouachita Mountains and the Ozark Plateau rise in the north and west. From them flows the Arkansas River south and east across the state to the Gulf Coastal Plain to join the Mississippi River—a protected wildlife area and migratory bird route.

MOUNTAIN VIEW: In the Ozarks, the Blanchard Springs Cavern has towering underground columns named the Titans.

BENTONVILLE: This is home to the superstore Walmart, with more than 4,400 stores and 643 Sam's Clubs across the U.S., and 6,154 stores worldwide.

LITTLE ROCK: The capital and largest city has a population of 197,357.

EL DORADO: A walking tour takes visitors by the mansions of wealthy oil barons who struck it rich in the 1920s at wells just west of town. The city sign reads "Arkansas' Original Boomtown."

TEXARKANA: This city spans the Arkansas-Texas border, so it has two governments—one for each state.

FORT SMITH: In this Wild West outpost on the banks of the Arkansas River, former slave Bass Reeves became one of the first black lawmen west of the Mississippi River. Visit the 25-foot (7.5-m)-tall statue in his honor.

HOT SPRINGS NATIONAL PARK: Visitors can slip into a soothing, spring-fed thermal bath in one of the country's oldest national parks.

WHITE RIVER NATIONAL WILDLIFE REFUGE: This bird-watchers' heaven, established in 1935 where the White River meets the Mississippi, is a protected habitat for migratory birds.

Map labels

0   25   50 miles
0   25   50 kilometers
Albers Conic Equal-Area Projection

MISSOURI

TENNESSEE

MISSISSIPPI

LOUISIANA

TEXAS

OKLAHOMA

ARKANSAS

OZARK PLATEAU

Boston Mountains

Ouachita Mountains

OUACHITA NATIONAL FOREST

Table Rock Lake, Bull Shoals Lake, Norfork Lake, Beaver Lake, White, Buffalo, Black, Spring, St. Francis, Mississippi, Crowleys Ridge, L'Anguille, Cache, Red, Little, Arkansas, Little Missouri, Cossatot, Saline, Ouachita, Bayou Bartholomew, White Oak Lake, Millwood Lake, Lake Erling, Lake Jack Lee, Lake Greeson, De Gray Lake, Lake Ouachita, Lake Dardanelle, Big Piney, Mulberry, White

Pea Ridge N.M.P., Eureka Springs, Lead Hill, Mammoth Spring S.P., Cherokee Village, Corning, Bentonville, Rogers, Berryville, Pocahontas, Siloam Springs, Springdale, Harrison, Mountain Home, Horseshoe Bend, Paragould, Walnut Ridge, Big Lake N.W.R., Ozark N.F., Fayetteville, Buffalo Nat. River, North Sylamore Creek N.W.&S.R., Jonesboro, Manila, Blytheville, Hurricane Creek N.W.&S.R., Richland Creek N.W.&S.R., Mountain View, Tuckerman, Trumann, Osceola, Mulberry N.W.&S.R., Fairfield Bay, Batesville, Newport, Marked Tree, Fort Smith N.H.S., Van Buren, Clarksville, Clinton, Heber Springs, Wapanocca N.W.R., Fort Smith, Ozark, Russellville, Greers Ferry Lake, Bald Knob, Searcy, Wynne, Earle, West Memphis, Paris, Dardanelle, Morrilton, Greenbrier, Bald Knob N.W.R., Forrest City, Magazine Mt. 2,753 ft 839 m, Highest point in Arkansas, Booneville, Holla Bend N.W.R., Conway, Cabot, Beebe, Brinkley, Marianna, Greenwood, Waldron, Maumelle, Jacksonville, North Little Rock, St. Francis Nat. For., Little Rock, Little Rock Central High School N.H.S., White River Nat. Wildl. Refuge, Mena, Bryant, Benton, England, Stuttgart, West Helena, Helena, Cossatot N.W.&S.R., Little Missouri N.W.&S.R., Hot Springs Nat. Park, Hot Springs, Malvern, Sheridan, De Witt, Pine Bluff, Murfreesboro, Arkadelphia, Arkansas Post Nat. Mem., De Queen, Crater of Diamonds S.P., Pond Creek N.W.R., Nashville, Prescott, Gurdon, Fordyce, Monticello, Dumas, McGehee, Ashdown, Hope, Camden, Warren, Dermott, Lake Village, President William Jefferson Clinton Birthplace Home N.H.S., Texarkana, Stamps, Smackover, El Dorado, Felsenthal N.W.R., Hamburg, Crossett, Eudora, Magnolia, Overflow N.W.R.

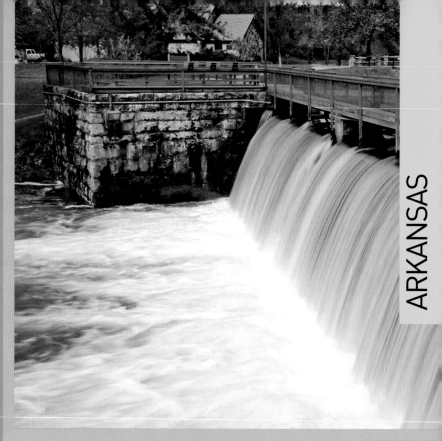

STATS & FACTS

STATEHOOD: June 15, 1836; 25th state

CAPITAL: Little Rock

TOTAL AREA: 53,179 sq mi; 137,732 sq km

LAND AREA: 52,068 sq mi; 134,856 sq km

POPULATION: 2,966,369

POPULATION DENSITY: 57 people per sq mi

MAJOR RACIAL/ETHNIC GROUPS: 77.0% white, 15.4% African American, 1.2% Asian, 0.8% Native American, Hispanic (any race) 6.4%

INDUSTRY: natural gas production, food products, lumber and paper goods, machinery, chemicals, minerals

AGRICULTURE: broiler chickens, rice, soybeans, cotton, cattle, sorghum grain, oats

NATURAL FEATURES: Nine million gallons (34.07 million L) of water flow from **Mammoth Spring** each hour, making it the second largest spring in the Ozarks.

NATURAL FORCES: The highest temperature ever recorded in Arkansas was **120°F (49°C)**.

ANIMALS: With the state's duck population at a record high of 49.2 million in 2014, contestants continue flocking to the annual **World Championship Duck Calling Contest** at Stuttgart—a happening since 1936.

HISTORY: In 1924 Arkansas's **Crater of Diamonds State Park** yielded the largest natural diamond ever found in the United States. At 40.23 carats, it was named "Uncle Sam."

PEOPLE/ CULTURE: In 1932 Arkansas elected **Hattie Caraway** to become the first woman in the U.S. Senate.

FLORIDA

THE SUNSHINE STATE

Coast to coast—to coast! Florida boasts three distinct shores. A long strand of hard-packed sand stretches along 400 miles (640 km) of Atlantic beachfront. Across the giant peninsula are softer, seashell-rich beaches, lining the Gulf of Mexico. To the northwest people play on panhandle beaches with the color and feel of white sugar. Once a limestone seafloor, the low-relief platform that makes up the state was uncovered as sea level dropped. Florida is the lowest and flattest state.

The Spanish founded St. Augustine in 1565, making it the continent's oldest permanent European settlement. Spain lost the territory to Britain in 1763 but regained it 20 years later. Farmland attracted American settlers in the early 1800s, and a treaty with Spain allowed the United States to obtain the territory in 1821. Native Seminoles fought to keep their lands, but most were forced west. When Florida became the 27th state in 1845, Tallahassee was made its capital city.

Florida joined the Confederacy and seceded from the Union just 16 years after statehood. It was readmitted in 1868. Florida's modernization followed the railroads built along its Atlantic and Gulf coasts in the 1890s. Land sales boomed, orange groves were planted, and tourists began to visit from the chilly north. Beachfront hotels and resorts sprang up along the train routes. The Spanish-American War of 1898 and the two World Wars boosted Florida's growth, with an ever greater need for military bases and agricultural products. The state soon became a retirement haven for senior citizens, as well as a refuge for immigrants after the Cuban Revolution in 1959. Miami grew to become the nation's major gateway to the Caribbean and much of Latin America.

STATE FLAG

In 1985 the seal in the flag's center was corrected to show a Seminole Indian woman from Florida instead of an Indian from the U.S. western plains.

STATE FLOWER
Orange Blossom

STATE BIRD
Mockingbird

Since 1950 Florida's population has blossomed from about 3 million people to more than 19 million. This more than sixfold increase has made Florida the nation's fourth largest state in population. More than one in five Floridians is Hispanic, many of them Cuban, and more than one in six is African American. Vacationers arrive year-round, but especially in the winter and spring seasons. Spectacular theme parks in Orlando entertain millions annually. Tourists ooh and aah watching space launches from NASA's Kennedy Space Center. The Everglades, a unique ecosystem of marsh and swamp fed by waterways linked to Lake Okeechobee, is another major attraction. Alligators and crocodiles live here, as do hundreds of bird species and the endangered Florida panther.

Fertile soils and a warm, wet subtropical climate in the Sunshine State provide farming riches, too. Florida tops the nation in sugarcane and citrus fruit and ranks second in output of tomatoes, strawberries, and greenhouse and nursery products. There are huge harvests of dozens of other fruits and vegetables as well as thousands of beef-cattle operations, especially in the panhandle. Military bases plus related defense and research companies play a large role in the state's economy and have helped Florida lead the country in job growth.

Though Florida continues to prosper, both natural and human-caused difficulties confront the state. Droughts have been damaging to the state, as have storms such as 1992's Category 5 Hurricane Andrew. For decades, abundant water resources have been directed away from the Everglades and other natural needs to those of expanding farms and cities. Efforts are under way to restore this life-giving flow of water. Florida's fast population growth strains all resources. The challenge will be to grow without sacrificing the state's natural treasures.

IT'S A FACT:
Florida has been called the lightning capital of the United States. Central Florida has an average of 100 days a year of lightning storms.

A TIME LINE OF THE SUNSHINE STATE

1513

Juan Ponce de León, seeker of the fabled **Fountain of Youth,** claimed Florida for Spain, naming it Pascua Florida ("flowery Easter").

1835

Although the **Seminole Wars** cost these native people most of their lands, some found refuge and new homes in the Everglades.

1896–1912

By building the **Florida East Coast Railway** to Miami and then Key West, Henry M. Flagler opened the state to development.

1967

Orange juice was named the state's official drink. After scientists invented frozen concentrate during World War II, **orange juice** became a multibillion-dollar industry.

1971

Orlando, once an agricultural area, became home to **Disney's Magic Kingdom,** with some 18.6 million visitors annually.

Present

Cape Canaveral, site of NASA's Kennedy Space Center, is a hub for space-age technology as well as a major tourist attraction.

ON THE MAP

LOCATION, LOCATION

Of its 1,200 miles of sand beaches, Florida boasts three distinct shores: the Atlantic, the Gulf of Mexico, and the northwest panhandle. The year-round warm climate has made the state a tourist haven. Nearly 90 million visitors came in 2012.

TALLAHASSEE: The name of the state capital comes from the Apalachee Indian word for "the old fields" that it once encompassed.

JACKSONVILLE: This most populated city, with more than 842,583 residents, was named for Andrew Jackson, Florida's first military governor. It is home to the Jaguars NFL team.

ST. AUGUSTINE: Juan Ponce de León likely landed here in 1513 and claimed Florida for Spain. Spaniards built the first permanent European settlement here in 1565.

BRITTON HILL: Florida's highest point is only 345 feet (105 m) above sea level.

LAKE OKEECHOBEE: It's the state's largest lake at 730 square miles (1,890 sq km), and the third largest freshwater lake wholly in the U.S.

EVERGLADES: The duckweed-filled waters of this national park and World Heritage site support alligators, crocodiles, and manatees. The Florida panther roams here, too.

KEY WEST: After moving here in 1928, Ernest Hemingway wrote his award-winning novel about World War I: *A Farewell to Arms*. Today six-toed tomcats roam the grounds of his home; they may be descendants of Hemingway's own cat.

MIAMI: Vibrant and diverse, Miami and neighbor Fort Lauderdale form the most populated metro area. Many residents have South American, African, Cuban, or Caribbean roots.

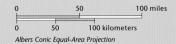

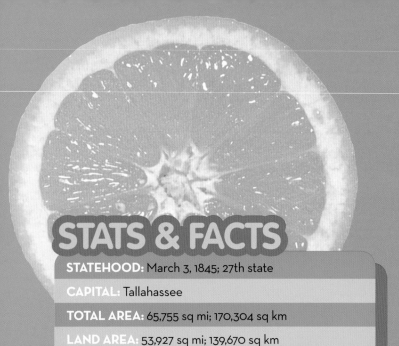

STATS & FACTS

STATEHOOD: March 3, 1845; 27th state

CAPITAL: Tallahassee

TOTAL AREA: 65,755 sq mi; 170,304 sq km

LAND AREA: 53,927 sq mi; 139,670 sq km

POPULATION: 19,893,297

POPULATION DENSITY: 369 people per sq mi

MAJOR RACIAL/ETHNIC GROUPS: 75.0% white, 16.0% African American, 2.4% Asian, 0.4% Native American, Hispanic (any race) 22.5%

INDUSTRY: tourism, defense and scientific research, electrical and electronic equipment, business services, biotechnology, banking

AGRICULTURE: greenhouse, oranges, tomatoes, dairy products, cane for sugar, peanuts, vegetables, fruit

ANIMALS: Everglades National Park is home to rare and endangered species such as the American crocodile, Florida panther, and **West Indian manatee.**

NATURAL FEATURES: Counting bays and barrier islands along its Atlantic and Gulf coasts, Florida has **8,500 miles of shoreline.** Alaska is the only state with more.

PEOPLE/ CULTURE: Sidney Poitier, a Miami native, is the first African-American actor to win an Oscar—for the movie *Lilies of the Fields,* in 1964.

NATURAL FORCES: Hurricane Andrew, which struck the Homestead area of South Florida in August 1992, was one of the most expensive natural disasters in U.S. history.

HISTORY: In 1937 **Amelia Earhart** and her navigator took off from Miami with the goal of making an around-the-world flight. Near the end of their journey, her plane disappeared over the Pacific and they were never seen again.

GEORGIA

THE EMPIRE STATE OF THE SOUTH

"Empire State of the South." A regal-sounding nickname for a U.S. state may seem odd, but it fits Georgia. From majestic, forested highlands to a grand seaport on a palm-fringed coast, Georgia is as landscape-rich as any state. Last established of the 13 British colonies, it's even named for royalty: King George II.

Scouted by one empire and settled by another, the territory was of interest to the Spanish as early as the 1500s but under English control from 1733. While begun as a place for poor English people to start life anew after serving time in debtors' prisons, Georgia soon was like other southern colonies, exporting products such as rice, cotton, lumber, and deerskins to England—with slave labor. After the American Revolution, it ratified the Constitution in 1788, the fourth state to do so. At the time, Augusta was the capital city. Georgia's plantation economy, with its large slave labor force, boomed after the invention of the cotton gin in 1793. Gold discovered in its northern region in 1828 further speeded settlement and signaled the end of Creek and Cherokee success in resisting the newcomers. These Native Americans were among those forced to walk the Trail of Tears in the 1830s.

Georgia tilts southeastward, from Appalachian heights to a coastline dotted with wildlife refuges that are a bird-watcher's paradise. Spanning the Florida border, the Okefenokee National Wildlife Refuge harbors alligators, river otters, and black bears in 700 square miles (1,820 sq km) of untamed swamps, bogs, and marshes. Between its low coastal plain and northern wooded heights lies a broad area of rolling forested hills and farmlands—the Piedmont.

It was on the Piedmont, at the foot of the Blue Ridge mountains,

STATE FLAG

From 2001 to 2003 Georgia redesigned its flag three times, to move it away from its Confederate origins. Thirteen white stars represent the 13 Colonies.

STATE FLOWER
Cherokee Rose

STATE BIRD
Brown Thrasher

that a settlement named Terminus was founded in 1837 at the endpoint of the promising new rail line. Within a decade the prospering city took a name invented from the Georgia and Atlantic Railroad: Atlanta. The city and the state supplied food and other resources for the Confederate war effort. Atlanta and Georgia became Civil War targets by 1864. Union forces streamed through the state in the fall of that year, seizing food, ransacking homes, and frightening residents. Sherman's army destroyed the people's spirit but did not burn everything in its path on its legendary march to the sea.

Georgia suffered through decades of post–Civil War poverty. Sharecropping, soil erosion, and the boll weevil invasion of the early 20th century hurt farming. Savannah declined in importance, but Atlanta was quickly rebuilt and developed into the transportation, trade, and financial hub of the South.

Though still a leader in cotton production, Georgia's agriculture has diversified. It leads in broiler chicken and egg production and is known for peanuts, pecans, peaches, and Vidalia onions. Vast pine forests help make it a leader in forest products and paper production. From northeastern quarries, Georgia produces the Greene County granite used to form the plaza of the National World War II Memorial on the Mall in Washington, D.C.

Georgia has ten million residents. Three in ten Georgians have African-American heritage. In 1967 racial violence erupted in Atlanta, which had became a center of the civil rights movement, especially due to Martin Luther King, Jr.'s leadership. Georgia native Jimmy Carter, who was governor before becoming president in 1976, pushed strongly for equal opportunity. Rapid population gains have caused resource strains on education, health care, and highways.

IT'S A FACT:
More than 90 million passengers went through Atlanta's Hartsfield-Jackson International Airport in 2013, making it the world's busiest passenger airport.

A TIME LINE OF THE EMPIRE STATE OF THE SOUTH

1733

James Oglethorpe founded Savannah as part of a slave-free colony but soon discovered that slave labor brought greater profits.

1794

Eli Whitney helped make cotton king by inventing a gin that could separate cottonseeds from fiber faster than could be done by hand.

1864

After burning Atlanta, the Union's **Gen. William T. Sherman** began his march to the sea, destroying property and railroads as he went.

1886

Coca-Cola was invented in Atlanta by Dr. John Pemberton and was first sold at a local pharmacy soda fountain. First-year sales: $50. Its secret recipe is in a vault, on display at the World of Coca-Cola museum.

2012

In 2012 the state grew about 45 percent of the nation's **peanut harvest.** Peanuts have been grown here since colonial times.

Present

For the past decade Atlanta has been a center of **hip-hop music;** the city is also known for its R&B and soul artists.

ON THE MAP

LOCATION, LOCATION

From the Appalachian Mountains to a coastline dotted with wildlife refuges that are a bird-watcher's paradise, Georgia is a state of untamed beauty. Spanning the Georgia-Florida border, the Okefenokee National Wildlife Refuge harbors alligators, river otters, and bears in its swamps, bogs, and marshes.

STONE MOUNTAIN: Depictions of Confederate leaders Robert E. Lee, Thomas "Stonewall" Jackson, and Jefferson Davis carved into granite Stone Mountain make up the world's largest high-relief sculpture—1,700 feet (518 m) tall!

ATLANTA: It's been called the "economic capital of the Southeast." The city alone has 447,841 residents, with a metro area population of 4.2 million!

SAVANNAH: It was the first of five capital cities in the state from 1775 to 1785. The others: Augusta, Louisville, Milledgeville, and today's Atlanta.

PLAINS: Jimmy Carter, elected 39th president in 1976, was born here. Today's Jimmy Carter National Historic Site has an archive and museum to the president.

ASHBURN: This home of the world's largest peanut monument also has the world's largest peanut-shelling plant—with tours!

JEKYLL ISLAND: This exclusive island resort is the site where, in 1858, one of the last groups of slaves was smuggled onto American shores, aboard a ship called *The Wanderer*. Today a memorial honors those slaves.

SEA ISLANDS: These coastal barrier islands are home to the Gullah and Geechee people, who have retained their ethnic traditions from West Africa since the mid-1700s.

Map labels

TENNESSEE
NORTH CAROLINA
SOUTH CAROLINA
ALABAMA
FLORIDA
GEORGIA

Highest point in Georgia
CHICKAMAUGA AND CHATTANOOGA N.M.P.
CHATTAHOOCHEE NATIONAL FOR.
Brasstown Bald 4,784 ft 1,458 m
Springer Mt. 3,782 ft 1,153 m
AMICALOLA FALLS STATE PARK
CHATTOOGA NATIONAL WILD & SCENIC RIVER
APPALACHIAN NAT. SCENIC TRAIL
Blue Ridge
Appalachian Mts.
LaFayette
Dalton
Calhoun
Dahlonega
Toccoa
Hartwell L.
Lake Sidney Lanier
Gainesville
Hartwell
Richard B. Russell Lake
Elberton
Athens
Rome
Allatoona Lake
KENNESAW MOUNTAIN N.B.P.
Roswell
CHATTAHOOCHEE RIVER N.R.A.
Marietta
Sandy Springs
Smyrna
Atlanta
Stone Mountain Park
East Point
MARTIN LUTHER KING, JR. N.H.S.
Monroe
OCONEE
Washington
Evans
Carrollton
Covington
Thomson
Augusta
Peachtree City
Newnan
NATIONAL FOREST
Eatonton
Lake Oconee
Waynesboro
Griffin
Milledgeville
Sandersville
Millen
West Point Lake
PIEDMONT N.W.R.
Lake Sinclair
La Grange
Thomaston
OCMULGEE NATIONAL MONUMENT
Macon
BOND SWAMP N.W.R.
Warner Robins
Swainsboro
Statesboro
Perry
Dublin
SAVANNAH N.W.R.
Columbus
ANDERSONVILLE N.H.S.
Eastman
Vidalia
Savannah
Plains
Americus
JIMMY CARTER N.H.S.
Cordele
Hazlehurst
Hinesville
FORT PULASKI NAT. MONUMENT
Tybee Island
EUFAULA N.W.R.
Dawson
Fitzgerald
Ashburn
Jesup
WASSAW N.W.R.
Ossabaw Island
Albany
Walter F. George Reservoir
HARRIS NECK N.W.R.
St. Catherines Island
Tifton
Douglas
BLACKBEARD ISLAND N.W.R.
Sapelo Island
Blakely
Camilla
Moultrie
Adel
Waycross
FORT FREDERICA NAT. MONUMENT
GRAY'S REEF N.M.S.
Little St. Simon Island
Sea Island
Brunswick
St. Simons Island
Jekyll Island
Bainbridge
BANKS LAKE N.W.R.
OKEFENOKEE NATIONAL WILDLIFE REFUGE
St. Marys
Kingsland
St. Andrew Sound
Cumberland Island
CUMBERLAND ISLAND NATIONAL SEASHORE
Cairo
Thomasville
Quitman
Valdosta
Okefenokee Swamp
Lake Seminole
J. Strom Thurmond Reservoir

Rivers: Tennessee, Chattooga, Savannah, Chattahoochee, Coosa, Oostanaula, Etowah, Broad, Oconee, Ocmulgee, Flint, Ohoopee, Canoochee, Altamaha, Withlacoochee, Alapaha, Ocmulgee, Satilla, Ochlockonee, Suwanee, St. Marys, Walter F. George Reservoir, Lake Harding, Lake Oliver

SEA ISLANDS
ATLANTIC OCEAN

0   25   40 miles
0   25   40 kilometers
Albers Conic Equal-Area Projection

STATS & FACTS

STATEHOOD: January 2, 1788; 4th state

CAPITAL: Atlanta

TOTAL AREA: 59,425 sq mi; 153,909 sq km

LAND AREA: 57,906 sq mi; 149,976 sq km

POPULATION: 10,097,343

POPULATION DENSITY: 174 people per sq mi

MAJOR RACIAL/ETHNIC GROUPS: 59.7% white, 30.5% African American, 3.2% Asian, 0.3% Native American, Hispanic (any race) 8.8%

INDUSTRY: tourism, textiles, transportation equipment and automotive, foods, paper products, chemicals

AGRICULTURE: broiler chickens, eggs, cotton, peanuts, pecans, peaches, blueberries, vegetables

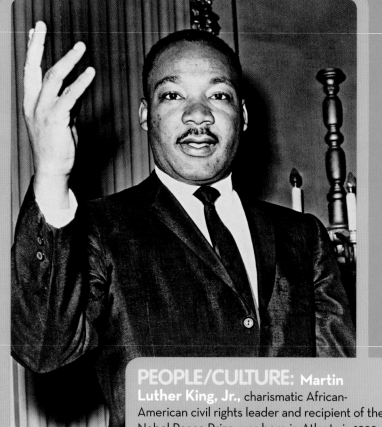

PEOPLE/CULTURE: Martin Luther King, Jr., charismatic African-American civil rights leader and recipient of the Nobel Peace Prize, was born in Atlanta in 1929.

NATURAL FORCES: Georgia's warm weather and long growing season help its farmers produce about half of the country's **peanuts.**

HISTORY: The **first U.S. gold rush** happened in 1828 near Dahlonega, which means "yellow money" in Cherokee.

ANIMALS: Bottlenose dolphins live year-round in Georgia's estuaries and nearshore ocean waters.

NATURAL FEATURES: The **Okefenokee Swamp,** the largest swamp in North America, is home to many meat-eating plants, which capture animals for food.

KENTUCKY

THE BLUEGRASS STATE

Bluegrass State. Whether one hears the nickname or the refrain from the state song "My Old Kentucky Home," pleasant rural images come to mind. Though Kentucky contains plenty of southern hospitality, it's also a mining and manufacturing state like industrial states to the north.

In the local Native American language, *kentake* meant "prairie," for the open, grassy spaces among its hardwood forests. Kentucky has more than 1,000 miles (1,600 km) of navigable waterways, including the Tennessee, Cumberland, Green, Kentucky, and Licking Rivers, which all flow into the Ohio. This broad, deep river forms the state's northern border, joining the Mississippi at Kentucky's southwestern tip. High ridges and deep, narrow valleys of the Appalachians and adjoining Cumberland Plateau make up most of eastern Kentucky. Rivers have carved twisting gorges called gaps through the mountains.

Through these passages pioneers reached central and western Kentucky. When a treaty with the Cherokee opened the region to easterners in 1775, the legendary but real-life Daniel Boone was quick to travel through the Cumberland Gap. He brought his family and others to build Boonesborough. When the American Revolution ended, streams of settlers flowed into what was then a huge, western "county" of Virginia. Kentucky became the 15th state in 1792, with the town of Frankfort as its capital.

After the last Native American claims to Kentucky lands were resolved in 1818, the state developed a booming tobacco-based economy. A proslavery/antislavery split developed, dividing the state between plantation owners and small-scale farmers and crafts people. Neutral at the outbreak of the Civil War, Kentucky eventually sided with the Union, but about a third of its soldiers fought for the Confederacy.

Eastern Kentucky's enormous deposits of soft bituminous coal have been mined in great quantities for more than 150 years. This resource provided wealth, fueled labor movements, and caused disastrous environmental problems. Deep-shaft mines and dangerous hand labor were the rule for decades. Eventually, machines did much of the work. Later, shallower western Kentucky coal reserves were strip-mined by huge power shovels and bulldozers. Since the 1970s federal laws have required that stripped lands be restored to their original condition, but many older mines leave scars on the land.

Kentucky's central Bluegrass region provided green alternatives to the coal economy. A long, warm growing season and calcium-rich soils here yield excellent tobacco and winning horses. At its heart is Lexington. Louisville, home to the famous Kentucky Derby horse race, is a major Ohio River port and highway and air-transport center.

Long a victim of a boom-and-bust mining economy, eastern Kentucky is still the state's poorest region, but it is culturally rich. Its Scotch-Irish heritage is preserved in its distinctive crafts and music. Its forests of oak, walnut, and hickory help make Kentucky a leader among hardwood-producing states. Tourism is increasing in this region of pioneer history, state parks, and federal recreation lands.

Kentuckians retain old customs and activities as they blaze new trails, with most now living in metropolitan areas. Still a major coal producer, the state explores clean-burning coal technology. Manufacturing remains a force, too, with the state rating highly for its automotive manufacturing strength. Kentucky seeks to better its standard of living by improving education, by making technology part of everyday life, and by developing strong ties to the national and global economy. People want to share their ideas and culture with the world as they build their "new" Kentucky home.

STATE FLAG

The state flower blooms beneath the state seal of two men embracing—one a frontiersman and one a gentleman, representing country and city residents.

STATE FLOWER
Goldenrod

STATE BIRD
Cardinal

IT'S A FACT:
"Happy Birthday to You," one of the most popular songs in the English language, was the creation of two Louisville sisters in 1893.

A TIME LINE OF THE BLUEGRASS STATE

1775

Daniel Boone opened up the Northwest Territory by leading settlers through the Cumberland Gap from Virginia to Kentucky.

1852

A Kentucky slave auction inspired Harriet Beecher Stowe to write her powerful antislavery novel, *Uncle Tom's Cabin.*

1930s

The attempt by labor unions to secure better wages and working conditions for **coal miners** led to violent strikes in Harlan County.

1939

Musician Bill Monroe started his band, **The Blue Grass Boys.** Their music, which they called "bluegrass," has roots in the tunes of Scotch-Irish immigrants to the Appalachians and in the music of African-American slaves.

Present

Approximately 1.8 million **Louisville Sluggers,** the official bat of Major League Baseball, are produced in Kentucky each year.

ON THE MAP

LOCATION, LOCATION

Through Kentucky's open, grassy spaces and hardwood forests run the Kentucky and Tennessee Rivers, which flow into the Ohio River, Kentucky's natural northern border. To the east, America's early pioneers passed through gaps in the Appalachian Mountains on their journey west.

FRANKFORT: The capital city was founded on one of the great buffalo trails that early settlers used as highways. The first statehouse opened in 1794.

LEXINGTON: Lexington is the bustling hub of the state's horse-raising operations. The top-notch racers, Kentucky Thoroughbreds, are a breed originally from England.

LOUISVILLE: With a metro population of 741,096, this home of the Kentucky Derby features a renowned park system designed by Frederick Law Olmsted, who designed New York City's Central Park.

OWENSBORO: At the International Bluegrass Music Museum you can listen to the music of Kentucky's bluegrass plains and learn its history.

UNION COUNTY: In 2012 this county replaced Pike County, once called "America's energy capital," as Kentucky's leading producer of coal.

FAIRVIEW: Jefferson Davis, who became president of the Confederacy, was born here in 1808.

SINKING SPRING FARM: Southeast of Elizabethtown, it was the birthplace in 1809 of the United States' 16th president, Abraham Lincoln.

NATURAL BRIDGE STATE RESORT PARK: In Daniel Boone National Forest you can find hundreds of spectacular sandstone formations.

Map labels

OHIO

INDIANA

ILLINOIS

MISSOURI

TENNESSEE

WEST VIRGINIA

VIRGINIA

Newport
Florence • Covington
Ohio
BIG BONE LICK S.P.
Licking
Williamstown
North Fork
Maysville
Vanceburg
Flatwoods
Ashland
Ohio
La Grange
Cynthiana
Morehead
Little Sandy
Levisa Fork
Tug Fork
Big Sandy
Louisville
Shelbyville • Frankfort
Georgetown • Paris
Lexington
Pleasure Ridge Park
Jeffersontown
Lawrenceburg
Versailles
Winchester
Mt. Sterling
Cave Run Lake
DANIEL
Brandenburg
Salt
Fort Knox
Radcliff
Bardstown
BLUE GRASS PARKWAY
BOONESBOROUGH S.P.
RED N.W.&S.R.
NATURAL BRIDGE STATE RESORT PARK
Prestonsburg
Henderson
Morganfield
Owensboro
Hardinsburg
Elizabethtown
ABRAHAM LINCOLN BIRTHPLACE N.H.P. (SINKING SPRING FARM)
Harrodsburg
Richmond
Berea
BOONE
Jackson
Pikeville
UNION COUNTY
Green
Madisonville
Rough River Lake
Leitchfield
Rolling Fork
Lebanon
Danville
NATIONAL
Hazard
Marion
Tradewater
Pond
KENTUCKY
Brownsville
Nolin River Lake
Green
Campbellsville
Mount Vernon
FOREST
VIRGINIA
Calvert City
Princeton
WESTERN
NATCHER PKWY.
MAMMOTH CAVE NAT. PARK
Cave City
Green River Lake
Somerset
London
Corbin
JEFFERSON
Black Mt. 4,145 ft 1,263 m
Highest point in Kentucky
Paducah
Mayfield
LAND BETWEEN THE LAKES NATIONAL REC. AREA
Hopkinsville
Bowling Green
Glasgow
Barren River Lake
LOUIE B. NUNN PKWY.
Cumberland
Lake Cumberland
Williamsburg
Cumberland Gap
CUMBERLAND GAP N.H.P.
CLARKS RIVER N.W.R.
Fairview
Russellville
Franklin
Date Hollow Lake
Albany
BIG SOUTH FORK NAT. RIVER & REC. AREA
Middlesboro
APPALACHIAN MOUNTAINS
CUMBERLAND PLATEAU
REELFOOT N.W.R.
Mississippi
Kentucky Lake
Lake Barkley
Tennessee
Cumberland
Fulton

0 25 50 miles
0 25 50 kilometers
Albers Conic Equal-Area Projection

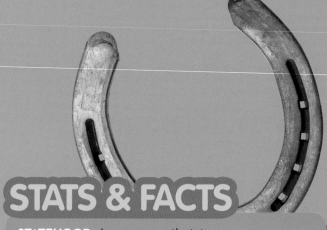

STATS & FACTS

STATEHOOD: June 1, 1792; 15th state

CAPITAL: Frankfort

TOTAL AREA: 40,409 sq mi; 104,659 sq km

LAND AREA: 39,728 sq mi; 102,896 sq km

POPULATION: 4,413,457

POPULATION DENSITY: 111 people per sq mi

MAJOR RACIAL/ETHNIC GROUPS: 87.8% white, 7.8% African American, 1.1% Asian, 0.2% Native American, Hispanic (any race) 3.1%

INDUSTRY: manufacturing, coal production, automotive, wood materials/lumber, machinery, tourism

AGRICULTURE: horses, tobacco, corn, cattle, soybeans, hay, broiler chickens

NATURAL FEATURES: Mammoth Cave, with its 360 miles (580 km) of mapped passageways, is the longest cave system in the world.

PEOPLE/CULTURE:
Abraham Lincoln and **Jefferson Davis,** respective presidents of the Union and the Confederacy during the Civil War, were both born in log houses in Kentucky.

NATURAL FORCES:
Kentucky's cool, humid weather is the ideal climate to grow **Kentucky bluegrass,** which gets its name from the bluish buds the grass produces in the spring and that make meadows look blue.

ANIMALS:
More than 75 percent of Kentucky Derby winners have been Kentucky-bred **Thoroughbreds.**

HISTORY: The **Kentucky Derby,** an annual horse race in Louisville, was established in 1875, although horse racing had been popular in the city since the late 18th century.

LOUISIANA

THE PELICAN STATE

The Bayou State or the Pelican State. Take your pick, both nicknames are about water. Looking like a boot on the Gulf of Mexico shore, Louisiana stands between Texas and Mississippi, with Arkansas to its north. Fresh, salty, or a mix of both called brackish, water is the source of the state's successes—and some of its troubles.

Water was the highway when French explorer La Salle sailed down the Mississippi River in 1682, claiming—and naming—the entire valley for his king, Louis XIV. "Louisiana" was a vast realm then, but the territory eventually was reduced to form the state of today, surrounding the lower reaches of the great river.

With the Louisiana Purchase in 1803, New Orleans, founded almost a century before on a strip of land along a sweeping bend of the Mississippi, was positioned to become the commercial focus for the sprawling river basin. Steamboats reached Louisiana at about the time it became the 18th state in 1812. The state capital was moved upriver to Baton Rouge in 1849. By that time, New Orleans had become not only a bustling port for cotton and other plantation products but also the biggest slave-trading market in the South. The state joined the Confederacy, but by 1862 it was in Union hands.

Louisiana's post–Civil War decades brought hard times, including a declining cotton economy and continued racial inequalities. Poor African-American farmers struggled to survive in an unfair system. Oil and gas, discovered there in 1901, helped change the state's fortunes. Today Louisiana is a major producer of crude oil and natural gas, ranking third in total energy production. The state's offshore petroleum industry suffered a major blow when in 2005 Hurricanes Katrina and Rita

STATE FLAG

A brown pelican feeds her chicks with drops of blood from her own breast. Pelicans, great caregivers, don't actually hurt themselves to feed their chicks.

STATE FLOWER
Magnolia

STATE BIRD
Brown Pelican

damaged offshore oil platforms and impeded production for several months. In 2010 the Deepwater Horizon oil rig exploded and sank in the Gulf of Mexico, a disaster causing nearly five million barrels of oil to leak into the Gulf.

Louisiana owes its existence to upstream erosion. Borne by the Mississippi and other rivers, sediment has built up the river's lower reaches and shifting delta for millions of years. Well-watered Louisiana lies low, averaging just 100 feet (30 m) above sea level. From hills near Shreveport, the land descends to marshes, swamps, and slow-moving streams called bayous along its Gulf Coast. Here, live Cajuns, whose ancestors—the Acadians—were forced from French Canada by the British in the 1700s. Many Cajuns still speak a dialect of French, and their spicy foods and toe-tapping music combine to make rural Louisiana culture unlike that of any other state.

Louisiana lands the nation's second biggest commercial fish catch, including shrimp and oysters, and ranks in the top five in the production of sweet potatoes, sugarcane, and rice. Fields are flooded to raise catfish and crayfish. One of the world's busiest ports for river and oceangoing traffic, New Orleans is also a famous tourist destination.

While the lives and livelihoods of Louisiana's 4.6 million people are rooted in water, threats from water keep them on guard. Levees designed to protect them were breached by 2005's Hurricane Katrina. At one point at least 80 percent of New Orleans was under floodwater largely due to levee failures. The state has wetlands rich in wildlife, including alligators, muskrats, and waterfowl. Both urban and rural activities threaten this water-land paradise, as do agricultural and urban pollutants from half the country that wash down the Mississippi. Recovery from the 2010 oil spill is ongoing on Louisiana's coastline, and the impact on the state's economy and ecosystem is still being analyzed.

IT'S A FACT:
New Orleans' cemeteries with aboveground tombs are known as Cities of the Dead because the rows of tombs resemble city streets.

A TIME LINE OF THE PELICAN STATE

1803

The raising of the American flag in New Orleans celebrated the **Louisiana Purchase,** which doubled the size of the United States.

1862

Confederate sharpshooters failed to keep the Union from **capturing New Orleans** and gaining control of the mouth of the Mississippi River.

1930s

Huey Long, a strong advocate of education, the poor, and states' rights, was the most influential politician in Louisiana history.

1970

Legendary gospel singer Mahalia Jackson and musician Duke Ellington helped kick off the first **New Orleans Jazz & Heritage Fest,** now an annual celebration of this birthplace of jazz.

2005

Hurricane Katrina, with 140-mile-an-hour (225-km/h) winds, killed some 2,000 people in New Orleans and surrounding cities and states, displaced hundreds of thousands, and affected some 90,000 square miles (233,100 sq km) of the United States.

Present

Massive **oil and natural gas rigs** in the Gulf of Mexico help make the state one of the top U.S. producers of these energy sources.

ON THE MAP

LOCATION, LOCATION

Nestled between Texas, Mississippi, and Arkansas, Louisiana juts into the Gulf of Mexico like a boot. The Gulf is the state's main source of industry, including fishing, shipping, and offshore drilling for oil and gas. From here, boats on the Mississippi can reach ten states.

MISSISSIPPI RIVER: River-churning "tows" navigate the mighty Mississippi and the Intracoastal Waterway in Louisiana, with cargoes such as coal, cement, and grain. A typical load: 1,500 tons (1,361 metric T).

BATON ROUGE: The capital city, established by French explorers in 1699, was called "red stick," for the reddened poles the local Indians used in spiritual ceremonies.

LAKE PONTCHARTRAIN: Its 24-mile (39-km)-long causeway is the world's longest continuous bridge over water.

SHREVEPORT: The city's American Rose Society Gardens is the nation's biggest park dedicated to roses. Stroll among 20,000 rose bushes between April and October.

ATCHAFALAYA: Now a national park and cultural center, it was once the hangout of the infamous pirate Jean Lafitte—of Cajun origin.

THIBODAUX: Like other towns along the coast, it's part of the Louisiana bayou. This coastal area is also home of the Cajuns—people whose ancestors came from Acadia—and is legendary for its spicy food and fun-loving people.

NEW ORLEANS: This largest city in Louisiana and the U.S. center for jazz is nicknamed the Big Easy, some say because it's easy for jazz musicians to play here. Founded by French settlers, today its food, arts, and customs are a rich mix of European, Caribbean, and African cultures.

STATS & FACTS

STATEHOOD: April 30, 1812; 18th state

CAPITAL: Baton Rouge

TOTAL AREA: 51,840 sq mi; 134,264 sq km

LAND AREA: 43,562 sq mi; 112,825 sq km

POPULATION: 4,649,676

POPULATION DENSITY: 108 people per sq mi

MAJOR RACIAL/ETHNIC GROUPS: 62.6% white, 32.0% African American, 1.5% Asian, 0.7% Native American, Hispanic (any race) 4.2%

INDUSTRY: natural gas production, crude oil production, manufacturing, tourism, wood materials/lumber, food production

AGRICULTURE: seafood, cane for sugar, rice, broiler chickens, soybeans, cattle, sorghum grain

ANIMALS: The **brown pelican,** the Louisiana state bird, was placed on the endangered species list in 1970. The species has made a remarkable recovery and is no longer on the list.

NATURAL FEATURES: Louisiana's coastal areas are some of the most wetland-rich regions in the world. Marshes and swamps are home to **American alligators** and black bears.

NATURAL FORCES: Late summer coastal hurricanes bring massive winds and rains. Before 2005's devastating Katrina, **Hurricane Andrew** struck in 1992, with 8-foot (2.4-m) tidal surges and inland tornadoes.

PEOPLE/CULTURE: Louisiana's **Creole society** is made up of descendants of people of Spanish or French heritage mixed with that of African slaves who gained their freedom before the Civil War.

HISTORY: Since the 1830s New Orleans' streets fill with a parade of people in colorful costumes celebrating the day before Lent, a Christian period of fasting. **Mardi Gras,** or Fat Tuesday, was a day of feasting in medieval France.

MISSISSIPPI

THE MAGNOLIA STATE

Stop changing channels! Apparently no one told the loopy Mississippi River that. It has meandered along for ages to form the scalloped western boundary of its namesake state. When the river curls far enough back on itself, it can cut across the narrow neck of land to form what's called an oxbow lake. Dozens of these water bodies lie along the lower reaches of the Mississippi.

Hernando de Soto scouted the Mississippi for Spain in 1540. The territory was later claimed by the French, who founded their first settlement in 1699 on the Gulf Coast near present-day Ocean Springs. Britain controlled the region after the French and Indian War until it passed to the United States in 1783. But Spain did not give up its coastal claims. Spanish West Florida, including Mississippi's present shoreline, was officially transferred to the United States in 1819.

Three major native groups were living here when Europeans arrived: the Natchez, remembered for "tracing" a trail from their lowland home to hunting grounds in present-day Tennessee; the Chickasaw, great warriors who later helped the British battle the French; and the Choctaw, skilled farmers and the dominant group. Nearly all eventually were forced off their lands, and many trekked the Trail of Tears to Oklahoma in the 1830s—or died along the way. The Mississippi Territory was created in 1798, and it included for a time present-day Alabama. Mississippi entered the Union as the 20th state in 1817, with Jackson becoming state capital in 1821.

For more than a century, the state's economy and society were dominated by the growing, processing, and selling of "King Cotton." For much of this time, wealthy white plantation owners lived like royalty while African Americans were enslaved. Poor white, non-slaveholding farmers lived free but like peasants. Mississippi joined the Confederacy and paid dearly for it. Some 770 Civil War battles and skirmishes were fought here, Jackson was burned three times, and at least 25,000 Mississippi soldiers died.

Though slavery was officially abolished after the war, the economic and the social realities did not change much. Both white and black sharecroppers were supplied with land to farm, seeds to plant, and tools to use in exchange for a heavy share of the harvest going to the wealthy landowner. Most African-American civil rights were withheld until the protests, violence, and legislation of the 1950s and 1960s finally achieved integration and began to build equal rights. Not all of Mississippi's problems are solved, and the state still works to correct the impacts of a painful past.

For the more than half of a century since the civil rights era, Mississippi has worked both to broaden its farm economy and to balance it with other activities. Long, hot summers, annual rainfall averaging more than 50 inches (127 cm), and rich soils allow diverse agriculture—cotton (a national leader), rice, soybeans, sorghum, and other crops. Mississippi is the country's largest supplier of pond-raised catfish and a major chicken producer, too.

The state's southern yellow pine forests yield lumber and other forest products. On the Gulf Coast, residents catch and process seafood, pump and refine oil and gas, and build ships. Today the coast attracts increasing numbers of tourists. Mississippi is also home to a number of key military facilities.

The state strives to improve the lives of all its citizens by pressing for improved education and for more and higher-paying jobs.

STATE FLAG

Some say the 13 stars represent the first 13 states; others say they represent the number of Confederate states at the end of the Civil War.

STATE FLOWER
Magnolia

STATE BIRD
Mockingbird

IT'S A FACT:
Blues music traces its roots to Mississippi's cotton fields and the sorrows of West Africans traveling on slave ships to the Americas.

A TIME LINE OF THE MAGNOLIA STATE

1806

Using seeds imported from Mexico, planters developed **a new variety of cotton** that helped make Mississippi a major cotton producer.

1863

The capture of Vicksburg after a 47-day siege gave the Union control of the Mississippi River and hastened the end of the Civil War.

1870

Sharecroppers were paid pennies per pound picked; today **mechanized cotton harvesters** cost hundreds of thousands of dollars each.

1963

Medgar Evers was killed for trying to end the segregation of African Americans. In 1969 his brother was elected mayor of Fayette.

1969

Sesame Street made its debut on national TV with the creations of **Greenville's Jim Henson:** the Muppets, including Big Bird, Kermit, and Oscar the Grouch.

Present

The **annual shrimp harvest** is an important part of Mississippi's seafood industry, along with oysters and red snappers.

ON THE MAP

LOCATION, LOCATION

Bordered by four states and with the Mississippi River to the west, Mississippi's short southern coastline faces the Gulf of Mexico. The state is made up of low plains and hills, with rich soil along the Mississippi River and fertile bottomland along the Gulf Coast.

BELZONI: Most of the nation's farm-raised catfish comes from Belzoni. Mississippi is the nation's biggest supplier of catfish.

JACKSON: The capital is also the state's largest city, with 172,638 residents. Built in 1821 on a "high, handsome bluff," it was burned three times by Union troops in the Civil War.

PORT GIBSON: Nearby Windsor Ruins is simply 23 huge columns that made up the state's largest mansion before and during the Civil War. Fire destroyed it in 1890.

NATCHEZ: Regular steamboat service for passengers and freight operated between Natchez and New Orleans in the 1800s.

MISSISSIPPI PETRIFIED FOREST: A forest 100 feet (30 m) tall once stood here. More than a million years ago the trees were felled by a flood and turned to stone.

HANCOCK COUNTY: The John C. Stennis Space Center, America's leading rocket engine test complex, is located here.

GULF ISLANDS: Explore Civil War forts on these barrier Islands off the coast.

Map labels

TENNESSEE
ARKANSAS
LOUISIANA
ALABAMA
MISSISSIPPI

Southaven, Horn Lake, Holly Springs, HOLLY SPRINGS, Corinth, Iuka, Pickwick Lake, Tennessee, Arkabutla Lake, Ripley, Booneville, Woodall Mt. 806 ft 246 m, Highest point in Mississippi, Senatobia, NATIONAL FOREST, New Albany, Baldwyn, BRICES CROSS ROADS N.B.S., Coldwater, Little Tallahatchie, Sardis Lake, Clarksdale, Oxford, Pontotoc, Tupelo, TUPELO N.B., Fulton, Batesville, Enid Lake, Yocona, Water Valley, Tennessee-Tombigbee Waterway, TALLAHATCHIE NATIONAL WILDLIFE REFUGE, HOLLY SPRINGS NAT. FOR., TOMBIGBEE NAT. FOR., Okolona, Amory, Shelby, Big Sunflower, Grenada Lake, Houston, Cleveland, DAHOMEY N.W.R., Ruleville, Grenada, Yalobusha, Aberdeen, Indianola, Greenwood, Winona, West Point, Columbus, Leland, MATHEWS BRAKE N.W.R., Starkville, Greenville, MORGAN BRAKE N.W.R., Big Black, Koscuisko, TOMBIGBEE NATIONAL FOREST, NOXUBEE N.W.R., Louisville, Noxubee, Hollandale, HOLT COLLIER N.W.R., Belzoni, YAZOO N.W.R., Deer Creek, DELTA NAT. FOREST, PANTHER SWAMP N.W.R., Yazoo, Vaughan, Carthage, Philadelphia, MISSISSIPPI CHOCTAW I.R., Okatibbee Lake, Yazoo City, Canton, Pearl, Flora, VICKSBURG N.M.P., Mississippi Petrified Forest, Ridgeland, BIENVILLE, Meridian, Vicksburg, Clinton, Ross Barnett Reservoir, Forest, NATIONAL FOREST, Newton, Jackson, Pearl, Brandon, Quitman, Port Gibson, NATCHEZ TRACE PARKWAY, Crystal Springs, Strong, Leaf, Natchez, Hazlehurst, Magee, Laurel, Waynesboro, HOMOCHITTO, Brookhaven, Collins, Ellisville, Tallahala Cr., ST. CATHERINE CREEK N.W.R., NATIONAL FOREST, Homochitto, McComb, Columbia, Hattiesburg, Petal, DE SOTO, Chickasawhay, Centreville, Bogue Chitto, Pearl, NATIONAL, BLACK CREEK NATIONAL WILD & SCENIC RIVER, Lucedale, Poplarville, Wiggins, Black Creek, FOREST, Pascagoula, BOGUE CHITTO N.W.R., Picayune, Ocean Springs, Gulfport, Biloxi, MISSISSIPPI SANDHILL CRANE N.W.R., GRAND BAY N.W.R., Stennis Space Center, HANCOCK COUNTY, Long Beach, Moss Point, Pascagoula, Bay St. Louis, Mississippi Sound, GULF ISLANDS NATIONAL SEASHORE, GULF OF MEXICO

0   25   50 miles
0   25   50 kilometers
Albers Conic Equal-Area Projection

STATS & FACTS

STATEHOOD: December 10, 1817; 20th state

CAPITAL: Jackson

TOTAL AREA: 48,430 sq mi; 125,434 sq km

LAND AREA: 46,907 sq mi; 121,489 sq km

POPULATION: 2,994,079

POPULATION DENSITY: 64 people per sq mi

MAJOR RACIAL/ETHNIC GROUPS: 59.1% white, 37.0% African American, 0.9% Asian, 0.5% Native American, Hispanic (any race) 2.7%

INDUSTRY: oil and natural gas, chemicals, plastics, forest products, foods

AGRICULTURE: broiler chickens, soybeans, cotton, seafood, corn, rice, wheat, hay

NATURAL FEATURES: At 2,350 miles (3,781 km) from its source in Minnesota to the Gulf of Mexico, the **Mississippi River** is the third longest river in North America. Along it, boats and barges carry some 500 million tons (454 million metric T) of goods each year.

PEOPLE/CULTURE: In 1902, while on a hunting expedition in Mississippi, President Theodore (Teddy) Roosevelt refused to shoot a captured bear. When the story got out, the **world-famous teddy bear** was created.

HISTORY: The famous crash of the *Cannonball Express*, which killed folk-song hero Jonathan Luther "Casey" Jones, occurred in Vaughan on April 30, 1900.

NATURAL FORCES: Mississippi's flat land and coastal location make it a prime target for both **tornadoes and hurricanes.**

ANIMALS: The little **Mississippi gopher frog** is an endangered species, with about 100 frogs remaining in the wild. Living only in three small ponds in Harrison County, they're carefully watched by scientists.

NORTH CAROLINA

THE TAR HEEL STATE

From the mountains to the sea, across a broad, hilly piedmont to its wave-dashed Atlantic coastline, North Carolina holds rich and varied landscapes. Its Mount Mitchell—the highest point east of the Mississippi River—tops out at 6,684 feet (2,037 m) above sea level in the Blue Ridge mountains.

A French expedition sailed along the coast in 1524. Sixty-one years later Sir Walter Raleigh sent a colonizing expedition from England, but the settlers returned after a year. In 1587 more than a hundred people settled on and later vanished from Roanoke Island. In 1629 King Charles I split off a portion of the Virginia Colony and named it after himself (Carolus is Latin for Charles). In the 1650s most Indians were forced out when conflicts erupted between settlers and the Creek, Cherokee, and Algonquian. In 1729 the royal colonies of North and South Carolina were formed. The economy centered on naval stores, such as pitch, tar, and turpentine. Soon, tobacco and cotton were grown in the English-settled eastern lowlands, while Scots, Irish, and Germans moved to lands farther west. Opposition to English taxes made North Carolina eager to join the Revolutionary War, and a victory near Wilmington helped win the region for the Americans.

Capes Hatteras, Lookout, and Fear poke seaward from the arc of barrier islands that protect species-rich sounds and bays along the coast. Battered by high winds, Outer Banks waters are hazardous: More than 600 ships have sunk here. Big rivers run swiftly southeast from the uplands, changing to wider, slower waterways the closer they get to the ocean.

STATE FLOWER
Flowering Dogwood

STATE BIRD
Cardinal

North Carolina joined the Union as the 12th state in 1789 and maintained a mostly agricultural economy, which included the use of slaves on cotton and tobacco plantations. Though its citizens were split on the issue of slavery, the state joined the Confederacy in 1861. North Carolina struggled after the war with rural poverty and racial inequalities that persisted well into the 20th century. In 1971 Charlotte was the site of the first major school-busing program to eliminate school segregation.

The tobacco business boomed after the invention of the cigarette-making machine in the 1880s. Textile mills found power in numerous rivers. By the 1920s oak and maple forests supplied a huge furniture-making industry, which is still going strong. Rich fisheries and numerous mineral resources were developed, too. Military spending began during World War II and is still strong.

Now, high-tech industries prosper in the Research Triangle between Chapel Hill, Durham, and the state capital, Raleigh. Charlotte has grown into one of the top banking cities in the country. Tourists flock to the seashores of the Outer Banks, while Great Smoky Mountains National Park and the Appalachian Trail draw vacationers to the wild western highlands. The state's diverse agriculture leads the nation in tobacco production and in pounds of turkey produced, and is among the top hog-raising states.

Both highs and lows seem likely in North Carolina's future. Some businesses, like technology and finance, should continue to shine. But state manufacturing doesn't look so bright. The U.S. has lost many thousands of textile and apparel jobs in the past decade as a result of both buying from factories abroad and advances in automation, and projections are for continued job loss in the industry. State leaders are working to solve these problems.

IT'S A FACT:
Cape Hatteras Lighthouse, the tallest brick lighthouse in the United States, is 198 feet (60 m) tall and made of more than 1,250,000 bricks.

A TIME LINE OF THE TAR HEEL STATE

1591

The word "Croatoan" was the only evidence found of colonists who disappeared from England's first settlement on **Roanoke Island**.

Early 1900s

Textile mills became the state's chief employer, as farmers left their fields to work in mills, where children often provided cheap labor.

1914

Baseball legend **Babe Ruth** hit his first professional home run in Fayetteville.

1960

A sit-in at an all-white **lunch counter** in Greensboro was one of many protests that led to laws banning segregation in public places.

Present

Fort Bragg and Camp Lejeune are among the military bases that give the armed forces a large presence in North Carolina.

119

ON THE MAP

LOCATION, LOCATION

North Carolina is a state of contrasts, from the spectacular Appalachian Mountains, where you can take a curvy ride along the Blue Ridge Parkway, to the wave-rippled coastline, home of the East Coast's tallest natural sand dune system (the Wright brothers first flew from here!).

PEA ISLAND NATIONAL WILDLIFE REFUGE:
On these 5,834 acres (2,360 ha) of protected land and 25,700 acres (11,128 ha) of boundary waters, discover pelicans, loggerhead sea turtles, and otters among more than 365 species of mammals, birds, and amphibians.

WHITEWATER FALLS:
It's the highest waterfall on the East Coast and one of more than 200 in the state!

MOUNT MITCHELL:
It's the tallest peak east of the Mississippi at 6,684 feet (2,037 m).

GREAT DISMAL SWAMP:
On the North Carolina–Virginia border, the Great Dismal Swamp boasts one of the oldest canals in the nation, built under George Washington in 1793. In the 1800s escaping slaves followed it along the Underground Railroad route.

ASHEVILLE:
The city's Biltmore estate, owned by the descendants of the great businessman Cornelius Vanderbilt, is one of the largest private residences in the U.S. It was built to resemble a French château.

CHARLOTTE:
This largest city has a population of 731,424. It's named after the wife of King George III, who was Britain's king when the colonies separated.

CHAPEL HILL:
The University of North Carolina at Chapel Hill, which opened in 1795, is the oldest state university in the U.S.

CAPE LOOKOUT NATIONAL SEASHORE:
Climb the 207 steps of the lighthouse at this point which once was a lookout for pirates. Back on the mainland, check out the North Carolina Maritime Museum to discover the story of Calico Jack, William Kidd, and other pirates who haunted the coast.

0   50   100 miles
0   50   100 kilometers
Albers Conic Equal-Area Projection

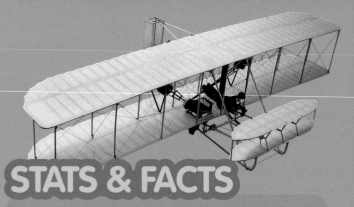

STATS & FACTS

STATEHOOD: November 21, 1789; 12th state

CAPITAL: Raleigh

TOTAL AREA: 53,819 sq mi; 139,389 sq km

LAND AREA: 48,711 sq mi; 126,161 sq km

POPULATION: 9,943,964

POPULATION DENSITY: 204 people per sq mi

MAJOR RACIAL/ETHNIC GROUPS: 68.5% white, 21.5% African American, 2.2% Asian, 1.3% Native American, Hispanic (any race) 8.4%

INDUSTRY: textiles, furniture, automotive, information technology, chemicals, manufacturing, biotechnology

AGRICULTURE: broiler chickens, hogs, greenhouse, tobacco, turkeys, soybeans, hay, cotton, peanuts, corn, wheat, hay, potatoes

NATURAL FEATURES: The **Outer Banks** are a series of barrier islands off the coast of North Carolina. The pirate Edward Teach, better known as Blackbeard, used Ocracoke Island as a hideout.

HISTORY: How did the state nickname "Tar Heels" originate? Some say that North Carolina soldiers refused to turn and run during the Civil War, as if their heels were glued to the ground with tar. Confederate general Robert E. Lee proudly called them **"Tar Heel boys."**

NATURAL FORCES: Parts of North Carolina received a record 36 inches (91.5 cm) of snowfall in 24 hours during the **"storm of the century"** in March 1993.

ANIMALS: The nocturnal **northern flying squirrel** can be found gliding in the canopies of North Carolina's forests.

PEOPLE/CULTURE: In 1903 the **Wright brothers** made the first successful human-powered flight at Kill Devil Hill near Kitty Hawk on the Outer Banks.

121

SOUTH CAROLINA

THE PALMETTO STATE

Shaped like a wedge or a spreading fan, triangular South Carolina points to the Blue Ridge and waves at the Atlantic. On its ocean edge, warm sea breezes rustle coastal grasses and stately palmetto trees. From the time a Revolutionary War fort built from these tough trees withstood a British attack, South Carolina has been known as the Palmetto State. While smaller than its neighbors, South Carolina has played a major role in the nation's history.

South Carolinians usually divide their state into two broad regions. A small slice of Appalachian highlands and a larger piece of rolling piedmont form the northwestern third of the state called the Up Country. Here, swift streams and rivers roll from the highlands.

The southeastern two-thirds of the state are the Low Country, a South Carolina name for the broad Atlantic Coastal Plain. Here, rivers slow and flow across fine lowland soil and swampy lands. Mild winters and long, hot summers dominate, always with a threat of big storms. Hurricane Hugo tore through Charleston with winds of 135 miles an hour (217 kp/h) in 1989.

After Spanish and French attempts to colonize the coast failed, the English succeeded at Charles Towne—later renamed Charleston—in 1670. Located a few miles inland on a point between the Ashley and Cooper Rivers, the port prospered as slave-based plantation agriculture took root. Early farming here produced cotton, indigo, and tobacco, but rice soon became the biggest export crop. North and South Carolina were made separate royal colonies in 1729. The ragged shoreline of bays and islands harbored pirates, who raided Carolina shipping and settlements. South Carolina became the eighth state in 1788, and

Revolutionary War patriots wore this silver crescent on their hats. The palmetto tree symbolizes the patriot victory from a palmetto-log fort on Sullivan's Island.

STATE FLOWER
Yellow Jessamine

STATE BIRD
Carolina Wren

the capital was moved from Charleston to more centrally located Columbia in 1790.

The invention of the cotton gin in 1793 greatly increased production of the fiber crop. Low Country plantation owners, fearing loss of their wealth if slavery were abolished, led the fateful drive to withdraw from the Union in late 1860. By then 60 percent of the state's population was African American, almost all slaves. The Civil War's first shot was fired on the Union's Fort Sumter in Charleston's harbor on April 12, 1861.

South Carolina's economy suffered through hard times for decades after the war. Small-scale farmers toiled in poverty, and some migrated to Northern cities for work. Soil erosion damaged state farmlands, and cotton output was ruined by the boll weevil in the 1920s. Tobacco then increased in importance and is still a leading state crop. The soybean is also now one of South Carolina's chief crops, and the state is second only to California in overall peach production.

First railroads then freeways stitched South Carolina into the nation's industrial fabric along the textile belt between Greenville and Spartanburg. Longleaf and loblolly pine forests support a thriving pulp and paper industry. High-tech businesses, nuclear plants, and military bases also contribute to the economy.

Travelers make South Carolina a top stop. Seaside resorts like Myrtle Beach on the "Grand Strand of Sand" and Hilton Head in the Sea Islands attract millions of visitors annually. Charleston's historic mansions display the lives of South Carolina's early "rich and famous," while the Old Slave Mart Museum shows the awful conditions of the slave trade. Today South Carolina works to provide better education, jobs, and quality of life for all its citizens. With its abundant resources and diverse economy, the Palmetto State can look forward to a strong future.

IT'S A FACT:
Home to some 50 miniature golf courses, Myrtle Beach is called the "miniature golf capital of the world."

A TIME LINE OF THE PALMETTO STATE

1700s

Slaves, shown here loading rice barges, taught their English masters **how to grow rice,** which flourished as a plantation crop.

1776

After a nine-hour battle against the American fort on **Sullivan's Island,** the British gave up. The fort's walls of spongy Palmetto logs caused the cannonballs to bounce off!

1838

Legend says that actor Junius Booth—father of John Wilkes Booth, who later assassinated President Lincoln—tried to kill his manager in **Charleston's Dock Street Theater—** one of America's most haunted buildings.

1861

The Civil War began with a Confederate attack on the Union's **Fort Sumter,** which guarded Charleston's harbor.

1920s

The damage done to cotton by the **boll weevil** forced South Carolina and other southern states to plant other crops.

Present

With its warm waters and sandy beaches, **Myrtle Beach** draws more than 15 million visitors a year.

ON THE MAP

LOCATION, LOCATION

Featuring a coastline of beaches for residents and tourists alike, South Carolina's southeastern two-thirds are called the Low Country, with a coastal plain where rivers flow across rich soil and swamplands. To the northwest, the piedmont and Appalachian highlands create the Up Country.

LANCASTER COUNTY: Fifty-six pillars of Kershaw granite from quarries here make up the National World War II Memorial, in Washington, D.C. The stone was chosen because it "shone like a diamond."

CONGAREE NATIONAL PARK: In this flooded forest you can go for an evening "owl prowl" led by park rangers—and hear the haunting hoots of barred owls.

COLUMBIA: The capital and largest city has 133,358 people. Its granite City Hall is in the National Register of Historic Places. In 1908 the city streets were paved with wooden blocks that floated away in heavy rains!

PARRIS ISLAND: The first French settlement in South Carolina was founded in 1562. Today it is a major military base.

KIAWAH ISLAND: Bobcats—wild cats about twice the size of a house cat—thrive in this resort community and keep the deer population under control.

CHARLESTON: Its historic downtown is considered a living museum of early southern life. Though damaged by Hurricane Hugo in 1989, its grand 18th- and 19th-century homes retain charm and grace.

MOUNT PLEASANT: For 300 years the community has made sweetgrass baskets, a traditional art form originating in Africa. Slaves first used the baskets for planting and processing rice.

124

STATS & FACTS

STATEHOOD: May 23, 1788; 8th state

CAPITAL: Columbia

TOTAL AREA: 32,020 sq mi; 82,932 sq km

LAND AREA: 30,110 sq mi; 77,983 sq km

POPULATION: 4,832,482

POPULATION DENSITY 160 people per sq mi

MAJOR RACIAL/ETHNIC GROUPS: 66.2% white, 27.9% African American, 1.3% Asian, 0.4% Native American, Hispanic (any race) 5.1%

INDUSTRY: textiles, forest products, tourism, chemicals, machinery, automotive, biotechnology

AGRICULTURE: broiler chickens, turkeys, tobacco, soybeans, cotton, corn, cattle, eggs, wheat, peanuts, hay

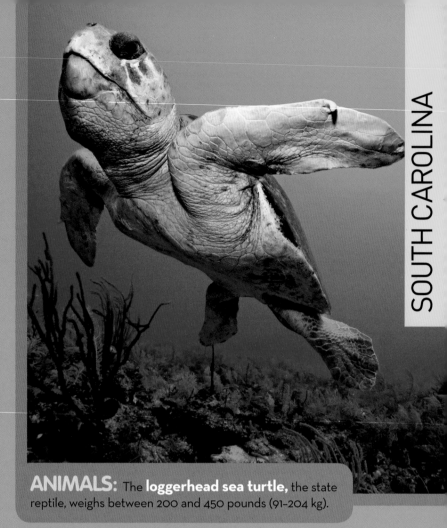

ANIMALS: The **loggerhead sea turtle,** the state reptile, weighs between 200 and 450 pounds (91–204 kg).

NATURAL FEATURES: Sand hills along the western edge of the coastal plain are the remains of beaches from an ancient sea that once covered the area.

NATURAL FORCES: Floods are vital to Congaree National Park's old-growth bottomland hardwood forest. The floodplains carry nutrients and sediments to support the trees.

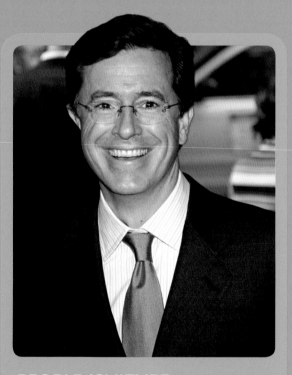

PEOPLE/CULTURE: Famed comedian of *The Colbert Report,* **Stephen Colbert** grew up in South Carolina's James Island. As a boy he loved role-playing games; he studied theater at Northwestern University before starting a comedy career on stage and television.

HISTORY: Sullivan's Island, off the coast of Charleston, is known as the Ellis Island of slavery. Some 200,000 to 360,000 men, women, and children who were brought to the United States from West Africa first set foot on American soil at Sullivan's Island.

125

TENNESSEE

THE VOLUNTEER STATE

I f you think Tennessee, think "three." Three stars on its flag represent the three physical regions of the state: East, Middle, and West. They may also symbolize that it was the third state to join the Union after the original 13.

East Tennessee is row after row of ridges, topped by the Great Smoky Mountains. Named for the combination of mist and plant vapors that hover in the steep-walled valleys, the Smokies are home to an amazing diversity of plants and animals. This region also includes the deeply eroded Cumberland Plateau. These eastern highlands give way to the gently rolling lands of Middle Tennessee, which boasts rich agricultural lands perfect for livestock grazing and crop raising—especially tobacco and corn. West Tennessee is in the flatter Mississippi River Valley; its fertile lands grow cotton.

The state's principal river is the Tennessee, which flows from near Knoxville southwest into northern Alabama. But then it loops back into the state, flowing north into Kentucky where it joins the Ohio River. The Mississippi River forms the state's western border. During massive earthquakes in 1811–12, the land sank and the Mississippi's water filled the depression, forming Reelfoot Lake—Tennessee's only large natural lake.

Cherokee people living along rivers of East Tennessee called one of their towns Tanasie, and the region took this name. The French scouted and traded on the rivers by the late 1600s. When Britain gained control after the French and Indian War, Virginians began to migrate to green Tennessee valleys. In 1780 Fort Nashborough was founded on the Cumberland River and later became Nashville, the state capital. Tennessee entered the Union in 1796. The

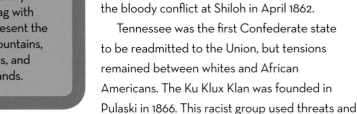

STATE FLAG

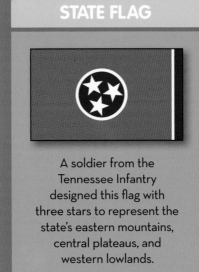

A soldier from the Tennessee Infantry designed this flag with three stars to represent the state's eastern mountains, central plateaus, and western lowlands.

STATE FLOWER
Iris

STATE BIRD
Mockingbird

Chickasaw were forced from their lands in western Tennessee by 1818. After Tennessee native Andrew Jackson became president, he removed remaining natives from the state in the 1830s.

Immigrants set up small farms in the valleys of East Tennessee, while southern cotton planters moved into western areas. The Civil War found the state deeply divided. Though Tennessee joined the Confederacy, thousands of residents fought for the Union. Some 24,000 men died in the bloody conflict at Shiloh in April 1862.

Tennessee was the first Confederate state to be readmitted to the Union, but tensions remained between whites and African Americans. The Ku Klux Klan was founded in Pulaski in 1866. This racist group used threats and violence to keep freed slaves from enjoying the same rights as whites. While the state attempted to rebuild its agricultural economy after the war, many small farmers suffered. Cholera epidemics hit Nashville, and yellow fever killed thousands in Memphis in 1878.

During the Great Depression, the federal government's Tennessee Valley Authority—or TVA—built dozens of dams along the Tennessee River and its tributaries for flood control, navigation, and electric power. With this new hydropower the state produced aluminum, steel, weapons, chemicals, and textiles. During World War II, the U.S. government built a secret research facility at Oak Ridge where scientists contributed to the development of the atomic bomb.

Tennessee's future looks promising. Great Smoky Mountains National Park attracts some nine million visitors annually. Middle Tennessee is a manufacturing hub, with auto assembly plants whose success depends on a strong national economy. The music industry—country in Nashville and blues in Memphis—continues to thrive.

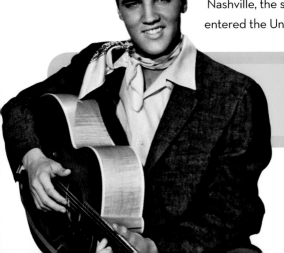

IT'S A FACT:
Attracting some 18 million visitors over 30 years, Graceland, Elvis Presley's mansion in Memphis, is one of the most visited houses in the United States.

A TIME LINE OF THE VOLUNTEER STATE

1812

Andrew Jackson, a founder of Tennessee, became known as a fierce Indian fighter in the War of 1812 and worked for the removal of all Native Americans.

1863

During the Civil War, Union forces captured **Chattanooga,** which gave them control of an important rail center.

1925

The **Grand Ole Opry** started as a radio show called *Barn Dance*. It became the world's largest broadcasting studio—a theater with 4,400 seats.

1934

Norris Dam was the first dam built under the Tennessee Valley Authority, which controlled flooding and provided electricity to rural areas.

1968

Civil rights leader **Martin Luther King, Jr., was assassinated** at Memphis's Lorraine Motel. Today it is the National Civil Rights Museum.

Present

Nashville—aka Music City—is known for its country music and also its recording studios and record labels.

ON THE MAP

LOCATION, LOCATION

East Tennessee is home to the Great Smoky Mountains, named for the mist that rises from its valleys. An amazing diversity of plants and animals thrives here. To the west, rolling bluegrass lands boast horse farms, and rich Mississippi River soil grows cotton.

KNOXVILLE: In this pioneering city, visit the James White Fort, home of one of the first settlers in the 1780s. Then stop by the 1792 Blount Mansion, a national historic landmark. Senator Blount was a signer of the U.S. Constitution, and he helped draft the Tennessee State Constitution, too.

NASHVILLE: The state capital, called Music City, is home to the Country Music Hall of Fame. Hundreds of thousands of people a year visit the Grand Ole Opry and other venues.

OAK RIDGE: This factory town was built almost overnight in 1942 for the Manhattan Project, which created the atomic bomb. Some 75,000 people worked and lived there.

LIMESTONE: Frontier hero Davy Crockett was born near Limestone in the 1700s. A song says "he killed a bear when he was only three." Is it true? Visitors can find out.

MEMPHIS: This largest city of 646,889 is the home of the National Civil Rights Museum and also the renowned Beale Street, running nearly 2 miles (3 km) to the Mississippi River and famous for its blues music. During the 1920s, it had a carnival atmosphere.

CHATTANOOGA: As visitors take a steep train ride up Lookout Mountain outside this city, they can see panoramic views of seven states. Now that's a Chattanooga Choo-choo!

GREAT SMOKY MOUNTAINS NATIONAL PARK: Crested by Clingmans Dome, the park stretches along the Tennessee–North Carolina border.

GATLINBURG: This Smoky Mountain family vacation destination features hiking, white-water rafting, horseback riding, and miniature golfing. There's even an aquarium, amusement park, and wax museum.

STATS & FACTS

STATEHOOD: June 1, 1796; 16th state

CAPITAL: Nashville

TOTAL AREA: 42,143 sq mi; 109,151 sq km

LAND AREA: 41,217 sq mi; 106,752 sq km

POPULATION: 6,549,352

POPULATION DENSITY 159 people per sq mi

MAJOR RACIAL/ETHNIC GROUPS: 77.6% white, 16.7% African American, 1.4% Asian, 0.3% Native American, Hispanic (any race) 4.6%

INDUSTRY: automotive, tourism, minerals, chemicals, foods, machinery

AGRICULTURE: cattle, broiler chickens, soybeans, corn, greenhouse, tobacco, cotton, hay, wheat

PEOPLE/CULTURE:
Davy Crockett, a pioneer and legendary figure, was born near Limestone and fought for the right of people to keep the land they had settled on in the new frontier.

ANIMALS:
Twenty-seven species of salamanders live in Great Smoky Mountains National Park, earning it the nickname "salamander capital of the world."

NATURAL FORCES:
Tennessee has a **varying landscape and climate.** Its year-round warm coastal plain has more than 220 days of growing season, while its mountain winter temperatures can plunge to minus 32°F (-36°C).

HISTORY:
Tennessee earned its nickname for its enthusiastic response to **President James Madison's call for volunteers** during the War of 1812. The state sent 1,500 men to fight at New Orleans.

NATURAL FEATURES:
Straddling the Tennessee–North Carolina border is a 200-million-year-old mountain range that forms **Great Smoky Mountains National Park.** The abundant rainfall and humidity create the "smoky" fog that gives the range its name.

VIRGINIA

THE OLD DOMINION

A state of beginnings—and endings. That's Virginia. Jamestown's founding in 1607 marked the first successful English settlement in America. The American Revolution ended at Yorktown in 1781. Eighty-four years later the Civil War ended at Appomattox Court House. Of the first five presidents, four were Virginians.

From ocean-side Virginia Beach, it's more than a 440-mile (708-km) hike to reach the Cumberland Gap at the state's southwestern tip. The low, sandy plain that extends out from the Chesapeake Bay is known as the Tidewater region, because its inlets and rivers feel the pull of ocean tides. Next inland is the Piedmont, which reaches west to the base of the scenic Blue Ridge mountains. Beyond lie the rich farmlands of the Shenandoah Valley and the rugged Appalachian terrain. A small section of Virginia forms the southern tip of the Delmarva Peninsula, east of the Chesapeake Bay.

In the early 17th century much of the continent not controlled by the Spanish or French was claimed by England and called Virginia (after Elizabeth I, who was known as the Virgin Queen). In 1607 an expedition sponsored by a merchant group named the Virginia Company established Jamestown along the James River. An attack led by Powhatan in 1622 killed not only a third of the colony's people but also the company, which lost its charter, or legal contract, for the land. Native American resistance was soon put down, and the territory was made a royal colony in 1624—the first in English history.

A plantation society eventually thrived in the Tidewater region, with fields of tobacco tended by thousands of African slaves. Small-scale farmers could not compete, and many moved west and south to pioneer new areas. By the 1760s Virginians were bitter about increasing British control and taxes. Many leaders in the movement for independence, including George Washington and Thomas Jefferson, were Virginians. The British were defeated in 1781. Virginia became the tenth state in 1788, with Richmond as its capital.

The debate over the continued use of slavery divided the country. Richmond was made capital of the Confederacy in 1861, and Virginia was a major battleground in the Civil War. At first, most conflicts fought on state soil were won by the South, but the tide turned by mid-1863. Richmond fell on April 3, 1865, and the South surrendered one week later.

The war left much of the state in ruins, and the end of slavery finished Virginia's plantation system. Virginia agriculture began to diversify. Tobacco was still the chief crop, but dairy farming expanded as did fruit and vegetable growing. The state industrialized, primarily in textiles, food processing, and shipbuilding. The deep-water harbor of the Hampton Roads area has long been a center of shipyards and naval bases. Virginia is also a major site for military training.

Today Virginia's population is one of the most diverse in the nation. Proximity to Washington, D.C., and increased federal spending have boosted the state's economy and help keep employment up. Northern Virginia attracts defense and other high-tech research activities. Traffic and other growth-related issues abound, with new housing even springing up near historic battlefields. Although the state is known as the Old Dominion, Virginia is really in a constant state of new beginnings.

STATE FLAG

The flag's seal dates to 1776, when the colonies declared independence from England. A goddess stands over a defeated opponent. The motto below reads "Thus Always to Tyrants."

STATE FLOWER
Flowering Dogwood

STATE BIRD
Cardinal

IT'S A FACT:
The Pentagon—headquarters of the U.S. Department of Defense—has three times the floor space as the Empire State Building.

A TIME LINE OF THE OLD DOMINION

1607

Pocahontas, by saving the life of John Smith, helped ensure the survival of Jamestown, the first permanent English colony in America.

1781

The British surrender to George Washington at **Yorktown** led to the end of the Revolutionary War and to independence for America.

1862

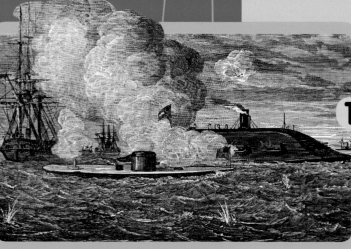

The **first battle between ironclad ships** was fought between the North's *Monitor* and the South's *Virginia* at Hampton Roads.

1989

Virginia voters elected the country's first African-American governor, **Douglas Wilder.**

Present

The National Air and Space Museum's **Udvar-Hazy Center** in Chantilly features the latest in flight, from spy planes and spacecraft to the chance to meet astronauts and turn somersaults in jet simulators.

ON THE MAP

LOCATION, LOCATION

In the 1600s English settlers found Virginia's lands and climate along the Chesapeake Bay ideal for tobacco farming. To the west, between the Blue Ridge and the Appalachians, are the fertile lands of the Shenandoah Valley, once called the "breadbasket of the Confederacy."

ARLINGTON: On green hillsides overlooking Washington, D.C., Arlington National Cemetery is the resting place for more than 250,000 men and women who served in the military or government. Once the property of Confederate general Robert E. Lee, the land was taken by the Union during the Civil War for a place to honor the dead.

MOUNT VERNON: The mansion and 500-acre (202-ha) farm of George Washington have been restored to their condition during his presidency in 1789.

CHARLOTTESVILLE: Nestled above the city, Monticello, which means "little mountain," was the home of the third president, Thomas Jefferson, who wrote the Declaration of Independence. It's filled with his unique inventions.

LEXINGTON: The famous Civil War Confederate general Thomas "Stonewall" Jackson lived and taught here at the Virginia Military Institute before becoming Gen. Robert E. Lee's right-hand officer in the fight against the Union Army.

RICHMOND: Today's capital was also the Confederate capital from 1861 to 1865. Confederate president Jefferson Davis lived here. Factories such as Tredegar Ironworks created arms for southern troops.

COLONIAL WILLIAMSBURG: The city has been restored as a living museum that gives visitors a glimpse of everyday life in Virginia's colonial capital city, from wigmaking to courtroom trials.

VIRGINIA BEACH: Virginia's largest city has 448,479 people. The *Guinness Book of World Records* says it has the longest pleasure beach in the world. Next door is Norfolk, the world's largest naval complex.

Map labels

WEST VIRGINIA

Winchester
Front Royal
Luray
Warrenton
Leesburg
McLean
Reston
Arlington
D.C.
Alexandria
MOUNT VERNON
Manassas
Dale City
Woodbridge
Colonial Beach
MARYLAND
SHENANDOAH
Bealeton
Harrisonburg
Culpeper
Bridgewater
NATIONAL PARK
Orange
Fredericksburg
GEO. WASHINGTON BIRTHPLACE N.M.
WASHINGTON
Staunton
Waynesboro
Charlottesville
RAPPAHANNOCK RIVER VALLEY N.W.R.
DELMARVA PENINSULA
ASSATEAGUE ISLAND NAT. SEASHORE
Stuarts Draft
MONTICELLO
Tangier
CHINCOTEAGUE N.W.R.
Chincoteague
Clifton Forge
Covington
Buena Vista
VIRGINIA
Onancock
ATLANTIC OCEAN
EASTERN SHORE OF VIRGINIA N.W.R.
Lexington
APPOMATTOX COURT HOUSE N.H.P.
Mechanicsville
West Point
Cape Charles
JEFFERSON
Lynchburg
Richmond
Colonial Williamsburg
COLONIAL N.H.P.
Yorktown
Poquoson
KENTUCKY
Bluefield
Bedford
Roanoke
Appomattox
Chester
Hopewell
Williamsburg
Jamestown
Newport News
Hampton
Tazewell
Radford
Salem
Timberlake
Farmville
Petersburg
Smithfield
Norfolk
Norton
Richlands
Marion
Wytheville
Christiansburg
Rocky Mount
Altavista
Blackstone
Portsmouth
Chesapeake
Virginia Beach
Big Stone Gap
Lebanon
JEFFERSON NATIONAL FOR.
Pulaski
Highest point in Virginia
South Boston
South Hill
Emporia
Suffolk
BACK BAY N.W.R.
CUMBERLAND GAP N.H.P.
Abingdon
Galax
Collinsville
Martinsville
Danville
Franklin
Lake Gaston
GREAT DISMAL SWAMP N.W.R.
MACKAY ISLAND N.W.R.
TENNESSEE
Bristol
Mt. Rogers 5,729 ft. 1,746 m
MT. ROGERS NAT. REC. AREA
BLUE RIDGE PKWY
NORTH CAROLINA
Great Dismal Swamp

APPALACHIAN MOUNTAINS
SHENANDOAH MOUNTAIN
BLUE RIDGE MOUNTAINS
Allegheny Mountains
Clinch Mtn.
Potomac River
Shenandoah River
James River
Appomattox
Roanoke (Staunton)
Smith Mountain Lake
John H. Kerr Res.
Meherrin
Nottoway
Chesapeake Bay

0 40 80 miles
0 40 80 kilometers
Albers Conic Equal-Area Projection

STATS & FACTS

STATEHOOD: June 25, 1788; 10th state

CAPITAL: Richmond

TOTAL AREA: 42,774 sq mi; 110,785 sq km

LAND AREA: 39,594 sq mi; 102,548 sq km

POPULATION: 8,326,289

POPULATION DENSITY: 210 people per sq mi

MAJOR RACIAL/ETHNIC GROUPS: 68.6% white, 19.4% African American, 5.5% Asian, 0.4% Native American, Hispanic (any race) 7.9%

INDUSTRY: information technology, chemicals, foods, textiles, communications, tourism, shipbuilding, transportation equipment

AGRICULTURE: broiler chickens, cattle, dairy products, tobacco, greenhouse/nursery, seafood, peanuts, hay, soybeans, wheat

NATURAL FEATURES: In Rockbridge County, Cedar Creek carved out **a natural bridge** from the limestone mountain. The bridge is a sacred site of the Monacan Indians, whose legend says it suddenly appeared when the tribe needed to escape from advancing enemies. Today it's a national historic landmark.

ANIMALS: **Wild ponies** have lived on Assateague Island for centuries. The ponies that live on the Virginia end of the island are owned by the Chincoteague Volunteer Fire Company. Each year in a roundup, young ponies swim to Chincoteague where they are auctioned off as a fund-raising event.

NATURAL FORCES: A **2011 earthquake** based in Virginia was felt by a third of the U.S. population, more than any other earthquake in history—although it was not as powerful as others.

PEOPLE/ CULTURE: Virginia is the birthplace of eight U.S. presidents—more than any other state. They include: George Washington, **Thomas Jefferson,** James Madison, James Monroe, William Harrison, John Tyler, Zachary Taylor, and Woodrow Wilson.

HISTORY: King James had high hopes that **Jamestown** would be suitable for the production of silk. But the imported silkworms and mulberry seedlings did not thrive. Tobacco, not silk, saved the colony from financial ruin.

WEST VIRGINIA

THE MOUNTAIN STATE

The Mountain State is a rough-and-tumble landscape of steep ridges and deep valleys that is sometimes called the Colorado of the East. Enclosed within crooked boundaries that mostly follow winding rivers and uneven mountaintops, West Virginia's rugged isolation has helped shape the state's history and its people.

The thickly forested Appalachians acted as a barrier, keeping people from the east away. Many early German and Scotch-Irish settlers came from Pennsylvania, following long north-south valleys. In 1727 New Mecklenburg (now Shepherdstown) became the first permanent community. Native Americans defended their hunting grounds against the newcomers, but they gave up claims to the region after a 1774 defeat.

Having little in common with wealthy, slaveholding Virginia planters who held political power over the region, people looked west to the Kanawha and Ohio Rivers for trade. Most held no slaves and did not want slavery in their region. They voted against secession from the Union in 1861. Outvoted, they decided to secede from Virginia instead. Two years later, West Virginia became the 35th state. Charleston was made its permanent capital in 1885.

The Mountain State's economy has had its highs and lows. Vast forests aboveground and abundant minerals below offered opportunities. Forests cover approximately three-quarters of the state's acreage, and it has long produced lumber for the nation. Salt began being mined in the Kanawha Valley in the early 1800s. Natural gas deposits made the state a leader in gas and oil production in the early 20th century.

But it was "Old King Coal" that really heated up state industrial growth. First discovered in the 1740s, vast deposits of soft bituminous coal lie beneath half the state. Coal provided fuel for salt and chemical works, iron and steel mills, and glassworks. Steamboats and then trains powered by coal traveled waterways and railways and transported coal, lumber, and other resources to homes and businesses across the nation. Immigrants, including whites from the North, blacks from the South, and southern Europeans, found work in state mines and factories. The two World Wars were boom times for West Virginia's economy. The chemical industry expanded and coal production peaked in 1947 with 176 million tons (159.7 million metric T).

But coal mining brought darker times to the state. Thousands of miners suffered from black lung disease after years of breathing coal dust, and many more died in accidents. Pay was low, with workers too often mistreated and cheated by mining companies. Workers' attempts to get better wages and working conditions by unionizing often ended in violence. The Great Depression brought hard times but also U.S. laws allowing labor unions. By the 1950s boom times for the nation's steel industry were over, and the market for coal was reduced. Later, environmental laws favored cleaner-burning coal from western states. In 1983 unemployment reached a terrible 21 percent. Though West Virginia today trails only Wyoming as a coal producer, the fuel's importance as a job source is declining, and the state has much environmental damage to repair from more than 150 years of mining.

In recent years West Virginia has turned to different resources—especially to its natural beauty—in attempts to strengthen its economy. The state's mostly rural residents work increasingly in service industries. Tourists love to hike the state's mountain trails, raft its rushing rivers, and sample its country crafts and culture. Like state residents, they seek to stay connected to the outside world but find serenity in West Virginia.

STATE FLAG

A mountaineer and a miner stand by a boulder with the date of statehood, June 20, 1863, and the state motto, meaning "Mountaineers Are Always Free."

STATE FLOWER
Rhododendron

STATE BIRD
Cardinal

IT'S A FACT:
The FBI crime data center in Clarksburg has the largest collection of fingerprints in the world.

A TIME LINE OF THE MOUNTAIN STATE

1859

Fiery abolitionist **John Brown** failed in his attempt to start a slave revolt by raiding the federal arsenal at Harpers Ferry.

1863–1891

One of America's most legendary family feuds was between the **Hatfields,** who lived on the West Virginia side of the Tug Fork River, and the McCoys, who lived on the Kentucky side.

Early 1900s

As coal came to dominate the economy, **labor union efforts** to win better working conditions for men and boys led to mine wars.

1956

The **National Radio Astronomy Observatory** at Green Bank opened. Rebuilt in 2000, the 485-foot (148-m) telescope is the largest of its kind; it helps astronomers explore deep space.

Present

Outdoor recreation seekers, such as these on the **Gauley River,** help make tourism one of West Virginia's chief businesses.

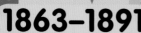

ON THE MAP

LOCATION, LOCATION

Once part of Virginia, this steep, rugged state with celebrated river gorges is sometimes called "the Colorado of the East." Winding rivers and thickly forested Appalachian Mountains form its boundaries. Rugged living makes for a small population of just 1.85 million, fewer than in Houston, Texas!

WEIRTON: Nestled between Ohio and Pennsylvania, it's the only city in the United States that sits in one state and has borders that touch two other states.

WELLSBURG: It's the home of the state's first plant for glassmaking, long a source of income and pride. Silica-rich sandstone provides the raw material for glass, and natural gas furnishes the heat to form it.

HARPERS FERRY: This town on the cliffs above the Potomac River has been restored to look as it did in 1859, when abolitionist John Brown robbed an arsenal in his battle against slavery.

MOUNDSVILLE: Located in the northern panhandle, this is one of the nation's oldest and largest Indian burial grounds.

CHARLESTON: The capital and largest city has a population of 50,821. The dome on the capitol building is 292 feet (89 m) high—higher than the nation's capitol dome in Washington, D.C.

FAYETTEVILLE: The New River Gorge Bridge is the longest steel-arch bridge in the United States. It stretches 1,815 feet (553 m) across the New River Canyon.

WHITE SULPHUR SPRINGS: In case of World War III, the Greenbrier Bunker was built here during the Cold War as a classified underground refuge for members of Congress. Today it's open to tourists.

Map labels

Ohio
Chester
Weirton
Follansbee
Wellsburg
Wheeling
Moundsville
Fish Creek
New Martinsville
Paden City
Mannington
Shinnston
Clarksburg
Salem
Williamstown
Vienna
Ohio
St. Marys
Parkersburg
Weston
Stonewall Jackson Lake
Ravenswood
Point Pleasant
Ripley
Spencer
Little Kanawha
OHIO
WEST VIRGINIA
Sutton Lake
Sissonville
Ohio Hurricane
Nitro Dunbar
St. Albans Charleston
South Charleston
Montgomery
Madison
New River Gorge Bridge
Fayetteville
Oak Hill
Logan
Beckley
Williamson
Mullens Hinton
Welch
Princeton
Bluefield
VIRGINIA
KENTUCKY
Big Sandy
Kenova
Tug Fork
Huntington
Big Coal
Guyandotte
Coal
Kanawha
Elk
Gauley
GAULEY RIVER N.R.A.
Summersville Lake
Summersville
Richwood
White Sulphur Springs
NEW RIVER GORGE NATIONAL RIVER
Lewisburg
BLUESTONE NATIONAL SCENIC RIVER
Bluestone Lake
Bluestone
New
PENNSYLVANIA
Morgantown
Kingwood
Fairmont
Grafton
Bridgeport
Philippi
Buckhannon
Elkins
Tygart Lake
MARYLAND
Monongahela
Cheat
North Branch
South Branch
Keyser
Romney
Petersburg
Moorefield
Cacapon
Martinsburg
HARPERS FERRY N.H.P.
Harpers Ferry
Charles Town
Shenandoah
Potomac
APPALACHIAN NAT. SCENIC TRAIL
MONONGAHELA
SPRUCE KNOB
Highest point in West Virginia
SENECA ROCKS
GEORGE WASHINGTON
Spruce Knob 4,863 ft 1,482 m
NAT. REC. AREA
NATIONAL FOREST
Cheat Mountain
Tygart Valley
Green Bank
Cass
NATIONAL FOREST
Greenbrier
APPALACHIAN
FOREST
JEFFERSON
NATIONAL FOREST
VIRGINIA

0   25   50 miles
0   25   50 kilometers
Albers Conic Equal-Area Projection

STATS & FACTS

STATEHOOD: June 20, 1863; 35th state

CAPITAL: Charleston

TOTAL AREA: 24,230 sq mi; 62,755 sq km

LAND AREA: 24,078 sq mi; 62,361 sq km

POPULATION: 1,850,326

POPULATION DENSITY: 77 people per sq mi

MAJOR RACIAL/ETHNIC GROUPS: 93.9% white, 3.4% African American, 0.7% Asian, 0.2% Native American, Hispanic (any race) 1.2%

INDUSTRY: coal production, natural gas production, tourism, forest products, minerals, metals, machinery

AGRICULTURE: broiler chickens, cattle, turkeys, dairy products, hay, soybeans, corn, wheat

NATURAL FEATURES: Nelson Rocks is a favorite spot for hang gliders because of the thermals—warm air currents that rise from below and lift up the glider wings.

HISTORY: The **first rural free mail delivery** in the United States started in Charles Town in 1896.

NATURAL FORCES: West Virginia's mean elevation of 1,500 feet (460 m) makes it the state with the highest average elevation east of the Mississippi. **Its record 24-hour snowfall is 35 inches** (89 cm).

PEOPLE/ CULTURE:
Legendary Confederate general **Thomas "Stonewall" Jackson** was born in Clarksburg. His childhood home became the first 4-H camp in the nation.

ANIMALS: In the 1950s a poll was conducted to pick a state animal symbol and the people chose the **black bear.**

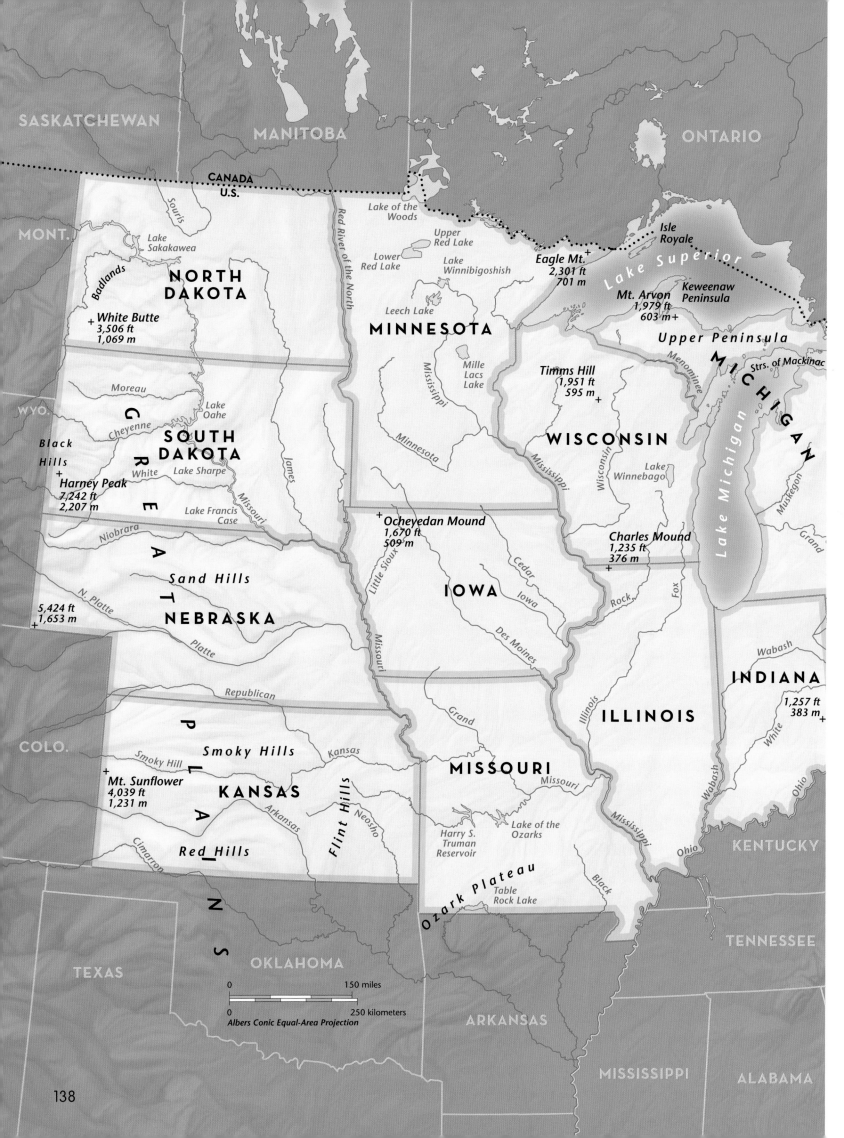

SASKATCHEWAN

MANITOBA

ONTARIO

CANADA
U.S.

MONT.

Souris

Lake
Sakakawea

Lake of the
Woods

Upper
Red Lake

Lower
Red Lake

Lake
Winnibigoshish

Eagle Mt.
2,301 ft
701 m

Isle
Royale

Lake Superior

Mt. Arvon
1,979 ft
603 m+

Keweenaw
Peninsula

Badlands

NORTH
DAKOTA

+ White Butte
3,506 ft
1,069 m

Leech Lake

MINNESOTA

Upper Peninsula

MICHIGAN

Strs. of Mackinac

WYO.

Moreau

Lake
Oahe

Cheyenne

Black
Hills
+
Harney Peak
7,242 ft
2,207 m

G
R
E
A
T

SOUTH
DAKOTA

White

Lake Sharpe

James

Lake Francis
Case

Mississippi

Mille
Lacs
Lake

Timms Hill
1,951 ft
595 m+

WISCONSIN

Mississippi

Wisconsin

Lake
Winnebago

Menominee

Lake
Michigan

Muskegon

Grand

Niobrara

5,424 ft
1,653 m

N. Platte

Sand Hills

NEBRASKA

Minnesota

Missouri

Little Sioux

+ Ocheyedan Mound
1,670 ft
509 m

IOWA

Cedar

Iowa

Des Moines

Charles Mound
1,235 ft
376 m

Rock

Fox

Platte

Republican

Smoky Hill

Smoky Hills

P
L
A

Mt. Sunflower
4,039 ft
1,231 m

+

KANSAS

Kansas

Flint Hills

Arkansas

Neosho

Red Hills

Grand

MISSOURI

Illinois

ILLINOIS

INDIANA

1,257 ft
383 m+

Wabash

White

Missouri

COLO.

I
N
S

Cimarron

Harry S.
Truman
Reservoir

Lake of the
Ozarks

Ozark Plateau

Table
Rock Lake

Mississippi

Black

Ohio

Wabash

Ohio

KENTUCKY

TEXAS

OKLAHOMA

TENNESSEE

0   150 miles

0   250 kilometers

Albers Conic Equal-Area Projection

ARKANSAS

MISSISSIPPI

ALABAMA

MAINE

V.T.

N.H.

Lake Huron

Georgian Bay

Saginaw Bay

Lower
Peninsula

Lake
St. Clair

Lake Erie

NEW YORK

MASS.

Maumee

Scioto

OHIO

Great Miami

Muskingum

Ohio

WEST
VIRGINIA

VA.

N.C.

SOUTH
CAROLINA

GEORGIA

THE MIDWEST

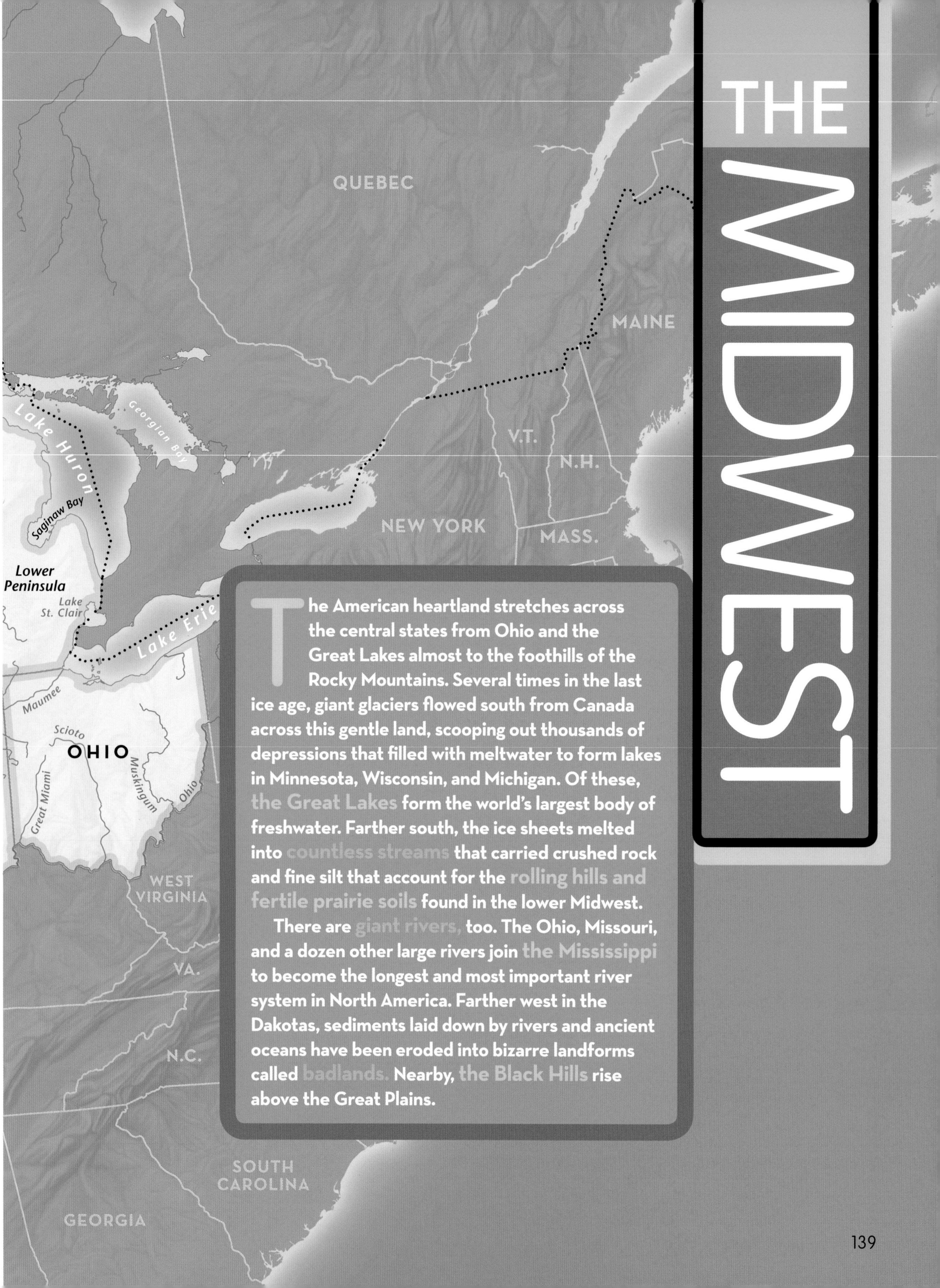

The American heartland stretches across the central states from Ohio and the Great Lakes almost to the foothills of the Rocky Mountains. Several times in the last ice age, giant glaciers flowed south from Canada across this gentle land, scooping out thousands of depressions that filled with meltwater to form lakes in Minnesota, Wisconsin, and Michigan. Of these, the Great Lakes form the world's largest body of freshwater. Farther south, the ice sheets melted into countless streams that carried crushed rock and fine silt that account for the rolling hills and fertile prairie soils found in the lower Midwest.

There are giant rivers, too. The Ohio, Missouri, and a dozen other large rivers join the Mississippi to become the longest and most important river system in North America. Farther west in the Dakotas, sediments laid down by rivers and ancient oceans have been eroded into bizarre landforms called badlands. Nearby, the Black Hills rise above the Great Plains.

THE MIDWEST

LAND OF PLENTY
UNDER THE PRAIRIE SKY

A vast landscape of great forests and endless prairies, this mid-continental heartland of rolling fields and farmlands adds a rural spirit to the United States. The bold mark of nature appears in sudden tornadoes, great floods, and thunderstorms that drop hailstones the size of baseballs. Winters can be long and very cold, especially in the far north along the border with Canada. Yet each one ultimately dissolves into humid spring warmth that nurtures new crops, wildflowers, and migrating birds.

For centuries eastern woodland Indians farmed and fished while seminomadic prairie tribes hunted bison, elk, coyotes, and other mammals on their grassy "American Serengeti." In the early 1600s French fur traders and missionaries arrived in the Great Lakes region and immediately became involved in long-standing Indian wars over territory and resources. In the 1760s France lost eastern portions of their Louisiana Territory to Britain after the French and Indian War and gave control of lands west of the Mississippi to Spain. These western lands were returned to France in 1800. America won the Northwest Territory—the area north of the Ohio River and west to the Mississippi—after the American Revolution and then purchased French Louisiana in 1803.

American settlers mainly from the Northeast moved first to Great Lakes areas. Later, railroads bridged the Mississippi to the West. The Homestead Act of 1862 made free land available to pioneers. The thickly matted roots of the rain-soaked fertile eastern prairie made the soil difficult to plow until the 1850s, when John Deere's steel-bladed plow came into widespread use. Farther west the climate was drier. Farmers used windmills to pull water from underground reservoirs called aquifers. Vast fields of wheat grew, and by 1900 the region had evolved into America's "breadbasket," growing wheat, corn, soybeans, and more.

By the end of the 19th century Chicago, St. Louis, Kansas City, and Omaha had become meatpacking centers. Today food processing is done in many rural towns. Rich deposits of iron ore and coal turned the Great Lakes region into a manufacturing empire. Steel mills and factories in Chicago, Gary, Detroit, and Cleveland employed a new wave of immigrants from Europe as well as African Americans migrating from the South. The watery highways that attracted Indians and settlers remain the principal routes for transporting grains and ores, while railroads and trucks carry manufactured goods to the rest of the country and beyond. Commerce still centers on Chicago, one of the busiest air, rail, and shipping crossroads on the continent.

ILLINOIS
INDIANA
IOWA
KANSAS
MICHIGAN
MINNESOTA
MISSOURI
NEBRASKA
NORTH DAKOTA
OHIO
SOUTH DAKOTA
WISCONSIN

"THERE WAS NOTHING BUT LAND...
THE MATERIAL OUT OF WHICH COUNTRIES ARE MADE."
—AUTHOR WILLA CATHER,
FROM *THE HOMESTEADER'S WORLD*

ILLINOIS

THE LAND OF LINCOLN

Pancake flat—that's what most of Illinois is except for some northwest uplands and a strip of southwest hills. Until less than two centuries ago it was covered by tall, waving prairie grasses. Thousands of years ago, invading ice sheets ended their southward campaign in Illinois, grinding down landforms on their advance and leaving rich, dark soils during their retreat. Hundreds of south-flowing rivers drain to the Wabash, Ohio, and Mississippi—rivers that form most of the state's boundaries.

When French missionary Jacques Marquette and explorer Louis Joliet canoed down the Mississippi in 1673, they met people who called themselves the "Illini"—an Algonquian word for "men" or "warriors." The European newcomers founded Cahokia along the big river as the first Illinois settlement in 1699. British military forces and traders followed, and for a time they lived in harmony with the French and various Native American groups. Peace turned to conflict with the French and Indian War. In 1763 the victorious British took over the Illinois region.

The United States gained control two decades later, following independence. Illinois formed part of the Northwest Territory of 1787, and settlers swarmed to the region. Illinois became the 21st state in 1818, with its capital first in Kaskaskia and then Vandalia—both in the south. Abraham Lincoln, then an Illinois legislator, worked hard to get the capital moved in 1839 to Springfield, a more central location. Today, that city celebrates the 16th president's many accomplishments, and Illinois is often called the Land of Lincoln.

Where nature once raised grasses, settlers planted wheat. At first, the gummy soils proved tough to plow with wooden or iron blades. But that was before 1838, when a blacksmith named John Deere perfected his steel plow. The prairie had finally met its match. Farm machinery is still a top Illinois export, and the state usually ranks second in both corn and soybean production.

Beginning in the 1860s, Illinois grew into an industrial as well as an agricultural giant—with Chicago leading the way. Its fiery steel mills boomed, with iron ore shipped in from the Lake Superior region and coal hauled in by rail from downstate deposits. Immigrants from all across Europe plus African Americans from southern states came to work in huge and often dangerous slaughterhouses, foundries, and other factories. Protests and strikes erupted between management and workers, and unions were eventually organized to improve working conditions.

Chicago is one of the world's great cities. With its 2.7 million people and a greater metro area population three and a half times that, it's bigger than any other city between New York City and Los Angeles. Located at the southern end of Lake Michigan, Chicago has long been the top transportation center in the country—by water, rail, truck, and air. Factories here still churn out everything from candy to machinery, but the industrial "city of the broad shoulders" increasingly processes ideas and information, too.

As they look forward, Illinois leaders tackle tough issues. The state suffered a 20 percent decline in manufacturing jobs from 2000 to 2010 alone, so keeping high-wage employment is a challenge. While more than four in five Illinois residents live in cities, roughly four of five state acres are farmed. But urban areas are sprawling out and taking over some of the world's best cropland. Some worry that Illinois should use that land to grow food. Some struggles will test the Illinois people as they face the future in the home they unofficially call the Prairie State.

STATE FLOWER
Violet

STATE BIRD
Cardinal

IT'S A FACT:
To celebrate St. Patrick's Day every year, green dye is dumped into the Chicago River, leaving the water a brilliant green for 6 to 12 hours.

A TIME LINE OF THE LAND OF LINCOLN

1673

French explorers **Father Jacques Marquette and Louis Joliet** were likely the first Europeans to enter the Illinois area.

1858

Views on slavery expressed by **Abraham Lincoln** in his debates with Stephen A. Douglas led to his election as president in 1860.

1908–1919

Rioting caused by racial tensions between blacks and whites in Chicago and other cities forced some people to move to safer places.

1967

The **Fermi National Accelerator Laboratory**—one of the world's leading centers for the study of the atom—was founded near Batavia.

Present

Nicknamed "The Bean," the popular "Cloud Gate" was installed in 2004 in Chicago's **Millennium Park,** which welcomes 4.5 million visitors a year.

ON THE MAP

LOCATION, LOCATION

The Land of Lincoln, named for the 16th president, who lived in Springfield, has hills in the north and south shaped by ancient glaciers. Its flat central prairieland fed by hundreds of rivers is ideal for growing corn and soybeans.

GALENA: The home of Civil War Union commander Ulysses S. Grant, who became the 18th president of the United States, has been fully restored to look as it did in the November 14, 1868, issue of *Frank Leslie's Illustrated Newspaper.*

CHICAGO: This largest city of 2,719,000 people boasted the world's first skyscraper in 1885. Today its Willis Tower is the tallest in the Western Hemisphere. At the University of Chicago, in 1942, physicist Enrico Fermi directed the first controlled atomic chain reaction.

TAMPICO: This is the birthplace of the 40th president, Ronald Reagan, who was then raised in Dixon.

LA SALLE: On the Illinois River, nearby Starved Rock State Park has breathtaking canyons, and waterfalls are favorites for hikers. The park is named for the Illini Indians left by their enemies to starve to death on one of the rocks.

SPRINGFIELD: The state capital was home to lawyer Abraham Lincoln and his family before he became president in 1860. He is buried nearby at Lincoln Tomb State Historic Site.

CAHOKIA MOUNDS STATE HISTORIC SITE: Centuries before Columbus reached America, this mysterious prehistoric culture thrived in a city the size of medieval London.

METROPOLIS: This official home of Superman boasts a museum devoted to the Man of Steel.

Map labels

WISCONSIN

Highest point in Illinois

Galena • + Charles Mound 1,235 ft 376 m

UPPER MISSISSIPPI RIVER NATIONAL WILDLIFE AND FISH REFUGE

Freeport · Rockford · Harvard · Belvidere · Schaumburg · Arlington Heights · Waukegan · HACKMATACK N.W.R. · Evanston · Park Ridge

Savanna · Grand Detour · Sycamore · Elgin · Cicero · Chicago

Dixon · DeKalb · Naperville · Aurora · PULLMAN NAT. MON.

Sterling · Tampico · Mendota · Sandwich · Joliet · Morris

Rock Island · Moline · Geneseo · La Salle · Ottawa

Kewanee · Peru · Oglesby · STARVED ROCK S.P. · Streator · Kankakee

MARK TWAIN N.W.R. · Galesburg · Chillicothe · Pontiac · Watseka

Monmouth · Peoria · Pekin · Morton · Normal · Rantoul · Hoopeston

Nauvoo · Macomb · Canton · CHAUTAUQUA N.W.R. · EMIQUON N.W.R. · Bloomington · Clinton · Champaign · Urbana · Danville

Carthage · Beardstown · LINCOLN'S NEW SALEM S.H.S. · VERMILION NATIONAL WILD & SCENIC RIVERS

MARK TWAIN N.W.R. · Quincy · MEREDOSIA N.W.R. · LINCOLN HOME N.H.S. · Tuscola

Jacksonville · Springfield · Decatur · Paris

Pittsfield · Taylorville · Mattoon · Charleston

White Hall · Carlinville · Pana · Lake Shelbyville

Jerseyville · Litchfield · Effingham · Robinson

MARK TWAIN N.W.R. · Alton · Vandalia

Edwardsville · Granite City · CAHOKIA MOUNDS S.H.S. · Flora · Olney

East St. Louis · Salem · Lawrenceville

Belleville · Centralia · Mt. Carmel

Red Bud · Nashville · Fairfield · Mt. Vernon

Du Quoin · Carmi

Kaskaskia Island · Chester · Benton · West Frankfort

Murphysboro · CRAB ORCHARD N.W.R. · Harrisburg

Carbondale · Marion · Shawneetown

SHAWNEE NATIONAL FOREST

Anna · Metropolis

CYPRESS CREEK N.W.R. · Cairo

IOWA · MISSOURI · ILLINOIS · INDIANA · KENTUCKY · LAKE MICHIGAN

Rivers: Mississippi · Rock · Green · Fox · Illinois · Spoon · La Moine · Sangamon · Salt Creek · Mackinaw · Vermilion · Embarras · Wabash · Kaskaskia · Big Muddy · Ohio · Macoupin Creek · McKee Creek · Hennepin Canal · Pecatonica · Mississippi

Lakes: Carlyle Lake · Rend Lake · Lake Shelbyville

0   40   80 miles
0   40   80 kilometers
Albers Conic Equal-Area Projection

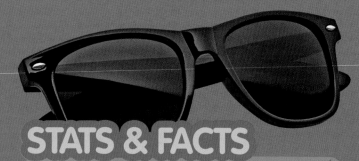

STATS & FACTS

STATEHOOD: December 3, 1818; 21st state

CAPITAL: Springfield

TOTAL AREA: 57,914 sq mi; 149,998 sq km

LAND AREA: 55,584 sq mi; 143,961 sq km

POPULATION: 12,880,580

POPULATION DENSITY: 232 people per sq mi

MAJOR RACIAL/ETHNIC GROUPS: 71.5% white, 14.5% African American, 4.6% Asian, 0.3% Native American, Hispanic (any race) 15.8%

INDUSTRY: financial services, biotechnology, automotive, tourism, machinery and metals, chemicals, printing and publishing

AGRICULTURE: corn, soybeans, hogs, cattle, dairy products, eggs, wheat

PEOPLE/CULTURE: Hillary Rodham Clinton, among the first women to run for president of the United States, was born in Chicago in 1947. She was first lady from 1992 to 2000, when her husband Bill Clinton was president, and then secretary of state under President Barack Obama, from 2009 to 2013.

NATURAL FORCES: Chicago does experience gusts from Lake Michigan, but that isn't why it's called **the Windy City.** The nickname was chosen for the city's long-winded politicians, not its weather.

NATURAL FEATURES: A **fossilized rain forest** was discovered in an eastern Illinois coal mine near the town of Danville in 2004. Scientists think an earthquake buried the forest 300 million years ago.

ANIMALS: Though rarely seen, the **southeastern shrew** is common in Illinois, where it burrows in tunnels and eats insects.

HISTORY: Illinois was the first state to ratify **the 13th Amendment** to the U.S. Constitution, which made slavery illegal.

INDIANA

THE HOOSIER STATE

Hoosier?" If someone knocked on the door of an early Indiana cabin, the pioneer inside might have called out "Who's here?" So goes one idea about how the state's nickname originated. Another is that a hardworking group of Indiana canal laborers were called Hoosier's Men, after their foreman. No one is certain, but Indiana's friendly, reliable people have been known by the name since the 1830s.

Indiana wears the results of ancient continental ice sheets across five-sixths of its land. Kettle lakes and huge piles of glacial gravel lie sprinkled across northern sections. A mixture of clay, sand, rocks, and other sediments called glacial till provides central Indiana's gentle landscape with fertile prairie soils. The state's southern reaches escaped these giant icy bulldozers and are more ruggedly landscaped with tree-covered hills and lowlands. Most of the state slopes gently to the southwest—draining to the Wabash River and from there to the Ohio River, which forms the southern border.

Early mound-building peoples left traces of their presence, but Algonquian peoples lived here when the French arrived in the 1670s. To protect their water route between the Great Lakes and the Mississippi River, the French constructed forts along Indiana rivers, including Vincennes on the lower Wabash. The earliest European settlement in the region, this became British property with the end of the French and Indian War in 1763. But in 1779, during the American Revolution, rebels from Kentucky seized Vincennes. Settlers poured in via this southern connection in the years that followed, leading to conflicts with Native Americans. The Battle of Tippecanoe in 1811 signaled the end of Native American control of the region. Most were

STATE FLOWER
Peony

STATE BIRD
Cardinal

forced to leave the land that the U.S. Congress named for them. The Indiana Territory was separated from the larger Northwest Territory at the turn of the 19th century, and statehood was welcomed in 1816.

Abundant rains and warm summers made the state a farming leader. Indiana industry sprouted with the arrival of the railroads at mid-century. Manufactured goods were joined by a giant steel-making effort at the beginning of the 20th century. Labor movements got an early start in Indiana. By 1920 the state had almost three million people. Indiana's economy "bottomed out" during the Great Depression but boomed both during and after World War II, producing automobile parts, electrical goods, and communications equipment.

Indiana's central location gave rise to the nickname "crossroads of America." Indianapolis became an early hub of farm product shipping and processing. An early automaking center that lost its lead to Detroit, the city celebrates each Memorial Day weekend with the famous Indianapolis 500 race. From bike racing to basketball, other sports also draw attention to the Hoosier State. College and university athletes from across the country are honored in the new NCAA Hall of Champions in Indianapolis.

Indiana's economy, like that of others in the region, is shifting from an emphasis on heavy industry to a more technology-oriented job market. As factories close, workers who were accustomed to high union wages often have to settle for lower paying jobs. But there are bright spots. The opening and expansion of automobile assembly plants has brought thousands of new jobs to Indiana over the past several decades. Indiana continues to be a top-ranking agricultural state, and jobs in service industries, such as tourism and pharmaceuticals, are increasing. Overall the future looks promising for the Hoosier State's 6.6 million residents.

IT'S A FACT:
The Indiana city of Santa Claus receives more than half a million "Dear Santa" letters at Christmas time every year.

A TIME LINE OF THE HOOSIER STATE

1779

George Rogers Clark's capture of Vincennes from the British helped Americans gain control of the Northwest Territory.

1850s

The **Underground Railroad,** a network of escape routes that helped slaves find freedom, was very active in Indiana.

Early 1900s

Enormous mills built by U.S. Steel in Gary attracted migrant workers and laid the foundation for Indiana's steel industry.

1915

Johnny Gruelle, who got his start as a newspaper cartoonist in Indianapolis, created the **Raggedy Ann doll.**

1950s–1960s

Indiana began building more miles of **interstate highway** for each square mile of territory than any other state. Today more major interstate highways intersect in Indiana than anywhere else in the country.

Present

The **Indianapolis 500 auto race,** held each Memorial Day weekend, attracts huge crowds and celebrates Indiana's auto heritage.

ON THE MAP

LOCATION, LOCATION

In this state called the "crossroads of America," highways from all directions converge at Indianapolis. The same ancient glacier that shaped Illinois also carved Indiana, leaving kettle lakes and huge piles of glacial gravel across the landscape, as well as rich soil for crops.

INDIANA DUNES NATIONAL LAKESHORE: Along the shore of Lake Michigan, massive Mount Baldy and other dunes are sandy habitats supporting unique lichens, mosses, and more than 20 kinds of orchids.

NAPPANEE: At the 80-acre (32.5-ha) Old Order Amish Farm, established by the first Amish settlers to Indiana in 1893, visitors can enjoy Amish cooking, take a carriage ride, and more.

PERU: Home of famous composer Cole Porter, it is also home of the International Circus Hall of Fame. Every July, kids and volunteers put on a three-ring circus to sellout crowds.

FORT WAYNE: Named after the Revolutionary War general "Mad" Anthony Wayne, this early fort at the intersection of three rivers became a crossroads for river— and later railroad— travel and trade.

INDIANAPOLIS: During the Civil War, it was a center for the Union Army's campaign in the West. Today the capital has 852,860 people and is the state's business, sports, and cultural hub. Its Fountain Square features European architecture and awesome art galleries.

VINCENNES: This earliest fort built by the French on the Wabash River was later won by the British, and then by the Americans during the Revolution.

GREENSBURG: Since the 1870s trees have sprouted out of the courthouse tower some 110 feet (33.5 m) above the ground. One grew to 15 feet (4.5 m). Today two remain.

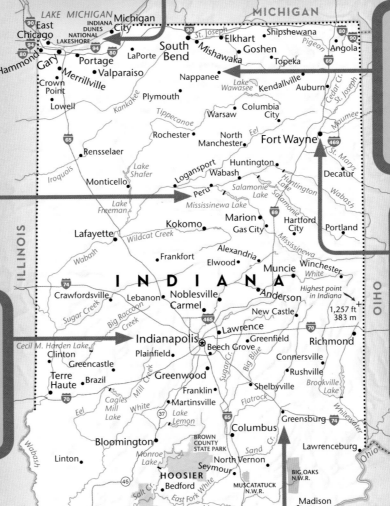

STATS & FACTS

STATEHOOD: December 11, 1816; 19th state

CAPITAL: Indianapolis

TOTAL AREA: 36,418 sq mi; 94,321 sq km

LAND AREA: 35,867 sq mi; 92,895 sq km

POPULATION: 6,596,855

POPULATION DENSITY: 184 people per sq mi

MAJOR RACIAL/ETHNIC GROUPS: 84.3% white, 9.1% African American, 1.6% Asian, 0.3% Native American, Hispanic (any race) 6.0%

INDUSTRY: manufacturing, coal production, automotive, machinery, chemicals, metals, biotechnology

AGRICULTURE: corn, soybeans, hogs, dairy products, eggs, hay, wheat

NATURAL FEATURES: At **Hanging Rock and Wabash Reef,** the limestone containing 400-million-year-old fossilized coral reef rises 75 feet (23 m) above the river and is being undercut by it, giving the site its "hanging" appearance.

ANIMALS: **Great blue herons** have developed a rookery of 100 nests at Indiana Dunes National Lakeshore.

HISTORY: In 1880 Wabash became the first city in the country to be illuminated by **electric lights.**

PEOPLE/CULTURE: John Chapman, better known as **Johnny Appleseed,** is buried in Archer Park in Fort Wayne. Every year the city hosts a festival to celebrate the man who planted apple orchards from Pennsylvania to Illinois.

NATURAL FORCES: The **Tri-State Tornado,** which ripped through Indiana, Illinois, and Missouri in 1925, traveled 219 miles (352 km) and had up to a mile (1.6-km)-wide path. It is the deadliest tornado in U.S. history.

IOWA

THE HAWKEYE STATE

owa is rich from the ground up. Its soils are legendary—some layered hundreds of feet deep. About nine of every ten acres of the state are used for agriculture. Long, warm summer days, plenty of rainfall, and winters that preserve plant nutrients combine to make Iowa croplands the envy of other farm states. The state produces more corn, soybeans, hogs, and eggs than any other. Iowa's treasure lies not in silver or gold but in abundant and fertile soil.

Thousands of years ago massive sheets of ice from the north formed most of Iowa's gently rolling landscape. Iowa is held in the arms of two great rivers, the Mississippi to the east and the Missouri to the west. The state's other streams flow in southerly paths to meet up with one of the two river giants. In some years spring snowmelt or summer downpours cause flooding and damage along some or all of Iowa's rivers.

In the summer of 1673 French explorers Jacques Marquette and Louis Joliet canoed down the Mississippi, meeting natives on its western shore who called themselves "the people." That word, translated and changed by French and later English speakers, is "Iowa." The region was not settled by large numbers of whites until the 1830s. Its prairie soils, which supported grasses as high as riders on horseback, were difficult to plow until the invention of the steel plow. The federal government fought the Sauk and Fox peoples for Iowa and Illinois lands in the Black Hawk War in 1832. Within 20 years, most of the Native American groups were forced out to the west.

At first part of the Michigan and then the Wisconsin Territory, Iowa became the 29th state in late 1846. The state's population grew as immigrants from northern Europe arrived. Steamboats

STATE FLAG

Designed because Iowan National Guardsmen wanted a state emblem, the flag has three stripes: blue for loyalty, justice, and truth; white for purity; and red for courage.

STATE FLOWER
Wild Rose

STATE BIRD
American Goldfinch

moved settlers in and goods out. The completion of a bridge over the Mississippi River at Davenport paved the way for the railroad. When men boarded trains to fight in the Civil War, women kept the farms going.

The completion of a railroad across the state after the war helped bring growth and prosperity. But good times were mixed with hard times in the late 1800s. Organizations like the Grange were formed to help ensure that farmers received fair prices for their crops. With the development of cars and trucks in the early 20th century, Iowans built better roads to bring their crops to market, and in the 1930s rural electric cooperatives made power available to every house and farm. The Great Depression hit Iowa farmers hard, but World War II helped restore prosperity by boosting demand for farm products. Tough times returned in the 1980s, forcing thousands of farmers to go out of business. The state population fell by nearly 140,000 between 1980 and 1990.

Efforts to diversify the economy helped the population rebound to a slow-growing 3.1 million. But Iowa is still tied to its soil. Recent years have seen bigger farms but fewer farmers, who use huge machinery and satellite technology to precisely plant, weed, and harvest their sprawling fields. On average, each Iowa farmer produces enough food to feed roughly 155 people worldwide. Agriculture has long fed the state's chief industry—food processing—which includes cereal milling, meatpacking, and even popcorn bagging. The manufacture of farm machinery, the sale of ethanol for fuel, and the use of wind farms to generate electricity are all sources of income for Iowa's farmers. Its cities are known for insurance, banking, and printing and publishing. To ensure the future health of its agriculture and its citizens, Iowa is committed to land stewardship with efforts to preserve the state's rich soil, fight erosion, and protect waterways.

IT'S A FACT:
The first brand-name popcorn, Jolly Time, started in Cloid H. Smith's Sioux City home.

A TIME LINE OF THE HAWKEYE STATE

1832

The defeat of the Sauk Indians at the **Battle of Bad Axe** along the Mississippi River helped open Iowa to white settlers.

1867

The arrival of the railroad at Council Bluffs opened a new and faster way to get goods to market. It also brought more settlers.

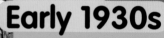

Early 1930s

During the Depression, farmers seeking more money for their products tried to decrease supply by **blocking roads to market.**

2008

Heavy rains in June 2008 led to **one of the worst floods in Iowa's history** and caused billions of dollars in property damages.

Present

Immigration is changing the makeup of the state. One out of every 14 Iowans is Asian American or Latino. Many own businesses that contribute more than $1 billion to the state income.

ON THE MAP

LOCATION, LOCATION

Snug between America's great rivers, the Mississippi and the Missouri, Iowa is a prairie state whose warm summer days, abundant rainfall, and winters that protect plant nutrients put her farmlands at the top of the list. Spring snowmelt and summer downpours can cause epic floods.

EFFIGY MOUNDS NATIONAL MONUMENT:
Here, more than a thousand years ago, ancient Native Americans began building 191 sacred mounds in the shape of birds, mammals, reptiles, and more.

HOLY CROSS:
Outside this city, farmers feed much of the grain they produce to livestock. Besides feeding animals and people, Iowa's corn is also converted to ethanol. Blended with gasoline, it fuels cars.

SIOUX CITY:
While exploring the Louisiana Purchase, Meriwether Lewis and William Clark lost the only casualty on their expedition here, to appendicitis. Nearby Floyd's Bluff was named for Sgt. Charles Floyd.

ATLANTIC:
Not far from here, in Adair, Jesse James and his gang made off with $3,000 in July 1873 after they made a legendary train robbery—the first moving train robbery in the world. Adair celebrates Jesse James Days every year.

DES MOINES:
Iowa's capital and largest city has 203,433 residents—some 80,000 people come to work downtown each day. At Capital Square, the atrium is so tall that the Statue of Liberty, from foot to torch, would fit in it!

BLOOMFIELD:
Just northeast of this city, on the Des Moines River, you'll find the famous house that artist Grant Wood used as a backdrop for his painting "American Gothic." His models for the stern-faced wife and pitchfork-holding farmer were his sister and his dentist!

STATS & FACTS

STATEHOOD: December 28, 1846; 29th state

CAPITAL: Des Moines

TOTAL AREA: 56,272 sq mi; 145,743 sq km

LAND AREA: 55,869 sq mi; 144,701 sq km

POPULATION: 3,107,126

POPULATION DENSITY: 56 people per sq mi

MAJOR RACIAL/ETHNIC GROUPS: 91.3% white, 2.9% African American, 1.7% Asian, 0.4% Native American, Hispanic (any race) 5.0%

INDUSTRY: manufacturing, food processing, machinery, electronic equipment, chemicals, communications, finance, insurance

AGRICULTURE: corn, soybeans, hogs, cattle, eggs, dairy products, hay, wheat, oats

PEOPLE/CULTURE: **The Amana Colonies,** established in 1855 by people of German heritage, strive to achieve an ideal society.

ANIMALS: **Hogs** outnumber people more than six to one in Iowa.

NATURAL FORCES: More than a quarter of the electricity generated in Iowa comes from **wind energy.**

HISTORY: Iowa's nickname comes from **Black Hawk,** a Sauk Indian chief who started the Black Hawk War in 1832.

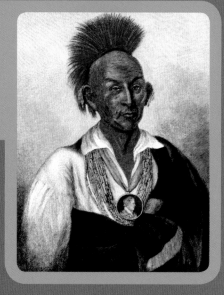

NATURAL FEATURES: Iowa ranks as the **nation's second largest agricultural producer** after California; its black soil is the most fertile in the country.

KANSAS

THE SUNFLOWER STATE

"Home on the Range." A Kansas doctor, Brewster Higley, wrote the famous lyrics that describe an ideal 19th-century farming life of happy homesteads where "the skies are not cloudy all day." Most Kansans would probably still agree with him about their prairie state.

The landscape of Kansas is mostly low, rolling hills, with wooded river valleys in its eastern half. Its surface slopes gently upward from Missouri to Colorado. In the east, the rocky Flint Hills preserve a 50-mile (80-km)-long swath of prairie. The iron-colored Red Hills in the southwest and the fossil-rich Smoky Hills in the state's north-central section reveal that much of Kansas was the bottom of a vast shallow sea millions of years ago.

The state takes its name from the Kansa—"people of the south wind"—but winds are not always kind to Kansas. Storms produce hail that can ruin crops and property. Tornadoes twist across the Sunflower State, and blizzards howl in winter. Precipitation levels are higher in the east.

In 1541 Spanish explorer Francisco Vásquez Coronado searched here in vain for a city of gold. Wichita, Cheyenne, Osage, and Kiowa peoples—among others—called the region home. U.S. control came in 1803 with the Louisiana Purchase, and the Santa Fe Trail brought settlers and traders in the 1820s. But most considered the land here unfit to settle, so eastern Kansas was set up to be used as land for the relocation of Native Americans in the 1830s. But within two decades, Congress decided that the land was needed for white settlement after all.

The Kansas-Nebraska Act of 1854 brought waves of immigrant settlers and allowed them to vote whether they wanted slavery. Newcomers began pushing Native Americans out, and groups for and against slavery battled each other. Proslavery border ruffians attacked

STATE FLAG

KANSAS

Many people thought the sunflower was too weedlike to be on the flag. But it was featured when the flag became official in 1923.

STATE FLOWER
Sunflower

STATE BIRD
Western Meadowlark

Lawrence and other cities in 1856, and antislavery fighter John Brown led a raid in return. Kansas finally joined the Union as a free state in 1861, just before the Civil War.

Kansas boomed after the war. Within a few decades, huge herds of bison that once roamed free were wiped out, and beef cattle took their place. Cowboys drove longhorns north from Texas to the railroad at Dodge City and Abilene. While cattle were bought, gunfights were fought. Lawmen like Bat Masterson, Wild Bill Hickok, and Wyatt Earp really did battle outlaws here in the Wild West. Another Kansas battler, Carry Nation, helped lead the temperance movement to control alcohol in the late 19th and early 20th centuries.

World War I sparked food demand, and Kansas reaped farming benefits. Then came the Dust Bowl of the 1930s. Thousands left the state, but Kansas fought back with groundwater irrigation in the west and better conservation methods. When World War II arrived, Kansas was a main food supplier. It has become known as the breadbasket of America, and it is still the nation's leading wheat producer.

The state's industrial economy soared in the 20th century with airplane manufacturing based in Wichita. Meatpacking facilities have long prepared state beef for market. Huge military bases add thousands of jobs to the economy. Oil and natural gas wells dot the Kansas plains, and the state is one of the few sources of helium, a gas used to float balloons.

Today most of Kansas' 2.9 million live in its eastern cities. Hispanics make up the largest minority, followed by African Americans and Asians. It has been 60 years since the *Brown v. Board of Education of Topeka* court case that helped integrate the nation's schools. Looking forward, the state seeks to improve its bioscience and other medical research facilities while keeping its industry, military bases, and agriculture intact. Yes, most Kansans would seldom say a "discouraging word" about their "Home on the Range."

IT'S A FACT:
Pizza Hut, the world's largest pizza company, opened its first restaurant in Wichita in 1958.

A TIME LINE OF THE SUNFLOWER STATE

1856

The violence caused when **border ruffians** from Missouri tried to get Kansas to vote for slavery led to the nickname "Bleeding Kansas."

1870s

Railroad expansion and a movement to drive Native Americans out of Kansas led to **the slaughter of millions of bison.**

1890s–1911

Carry A. Nation, who smashed saloons with her hatchet, was part of a reform movement that was given voice by the Populist Party.

1938–39

MGM studios filmed *The Wizard of Oz,* about Dorothy's adventures after she was blown to a magical world by a tornado. The film was made in Hollywood but is considered to be Kansas lore.

1956

An 8-mile (13-km) stretch of I-70 opened near Topeka, **the first section of an interstate system built with funds from the 1956 Federal-Aid Highway Act.** It would grow into a 40,000-mile (64,370-km) system.

Present

The **aviation industry,** which developed in Wichita after World War II, has lost thousands of jobs since 2008 because of an economic downturn.

ON THE MAP

LOCATION, LOCATION

Some 82 million years ago Kansas was an ancient sea holding the fossils of marine reptiles. Today Kansas is a mix of rolling hills, wooded river valleys, and prairies. Its name, meaning "people of the south wind," seems to represent the tornadoes that roll through each summer.

WASHINGTON: To the east of Washington stands the Hollenberg Station. Starting in 1860, the Hollenberg family welcomed Pony Express riders along the Oregon-California Trail at this station, until the Pony Express was replaced by the telegraph in 1861.

FORT SCOTT NATIONAL HISTORIC SITE: Kansas seems far west for the Civil War, but a decisive battle was won here in 1864 by 2,500 Union troops against 7,000 Confederates.

LUCAS: Samuel Perry Dinsmoor used 113 tons (102.5 metric T) of concrete to create the Garden of Eden here. Visitors can see Dinsmoor, who died in 1932. He lies in a concrete tomb with a glass top!

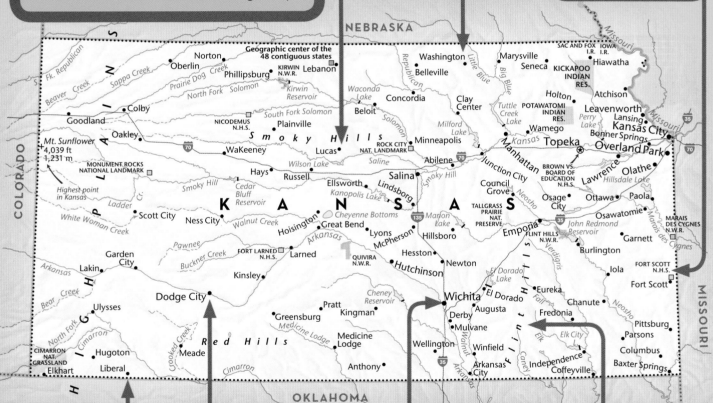

LIBERAL: Follow the yellow brick road to a replica of Dorothy's early 20th-century farmhouse. Guided tours and a museum show how *The Wizard of Oz* was filmed, and what Dorothy's life was like in 1930s Kansas.

DODGE CITY: This rail town was once a destination for cattle drives from Texas. Kansas is still cattle country and ranks third in the nation for beef production, with 5.85 million cattle and calves in 2013.

WICHITA: This largest city has a population of 386,552 and is home to the Sedgwick County Zoo, which features grizzly bears, bison, wolves, and other prairie creatures.

FLINT HILLS: The Tallgrass Prairie National Preserve here is the nation's last great expanse of tallgrass prairie, which once covered 140 million acres (56.6 million ha) across North America.

0   50   100 miles
0   50   100 kilometers
Albers Conic Equal-Area Projection

STATS & FACTS

STATEHOOD: January 29, 1861; 34th state

CAPITAL: Topeka

TOTAL AREA: 56,272 sq mi; 145,743 sq km

LAND AREA: 81,815 sq mi; 211,900 sq km

POPULATION: 2,904,021

POPULATION DENSITY: 35 people per sq mi

MAJOR RACIAL/ETHNIC GROUPS: 91.3% white, 2.9% African American, 1.7% Asian, 0.4% Native American, Hispanic (any race) 5.0%

INDUSTRY: manufacturing, food processing, machinery, electronic equipment, chemicals, communications, finance, insurance

AGRICULTURE: corn, soybeans, hogs, cattle, eggs, dairy products, hay, wheat, oats

ANIMALS: Black-tailed prairie dogs live in large communities called "towns."

HISTORY: In the late 1800s paleontologists found so many fossils in Kansas that they started the **"Kansas Fossil Wars"** and competed to get the best specimens. Some resorted to bribes and trickery.

NATURAL FEATURES: Dry air and a constant temperature of 68.5°F (20.3°C) make the underground chambers of **an old salt mine** near Hutchinson ideal for storing valuables, including thousands of original Hollywood movies.

NATURAL FORCES: On Sunday, April 14, 1935, strong winds blowing across the Kansas Dust Bowl swirled clouds of black dust hundreds of feet high. The day is known as **Black Sunday.**

PEOPLE/CULTURE: Barton County is named after famed Civil War nurse and founder of the American Red Cross, **Clara Barton.**

MICHIGAN

THE GREAT LAKE STATE

Great Lake State is the perfect nickname for Michigan, with its two huge peninsulas surrounded by the country's four largest lakes: Superior, Huron, Michigan, and Erie. The state's real name is from the Chippewa word *mici-gama,* meaning "great lake."

Michigan's Upper Peninsula extends east from Wisconsin, and its Lower Peninsula juts north from Ohio and Indiana. The "Big Mac" bridge links the two at the five-mile (8-km)-wide Straits of Mackinac. The lakes provided easy transport routes for the French in the 17th century, when they met and traded furs with Ojibwa, Ottawa, and Potawatomi peoples. Father Jacques Marquette established the first European settlement at Sault Sainte Marie in 1668.

The British defeated the French here during the French and Indian War and then abandoned the region to the United States by 1796. The Michigan Territory was formed in 1805, and New Englanders moved in, farming and building towns. By 1837 Michigan had gained the resource-rich Upper Peninsula and statehood.

For decades Upper Peninsula mines led the U.S. in iron and copper output. Michigan also produced salt, gypsum, and oil. Loggers cut white pines on both peninsulas. Railroads and steamships hauled cargo to market, a task made easier by the completion of locks on the Soo Canals that linked Lakes Superior and Huron.

By the late 1800s the iron and steel industry had grown strong here, ignited by several "horseless carriage" pioneers, including Henry Ford. He built an assembly line in 1913 and began mass-producing cars. Assembly-line jobs gave rise to labor unions and attracted immigrants—huge numbers of African Americans from the

STATE FLAG

Michigan's first flag flew in 1837, with a picture of the first governor. Today it has state animals and the national bird, the bald eagle.

STATE FLOWER
Apple Blossom

STATE BIRD
Robin

U.S. South plus Germans, Hungarians, Poles, Irish, Ukrainians, and Italians. During World War II, auto factories were converted to military uses, and the state earned the name Arsenal of Democracy.

The state's automaking methods spread abroad, and by the 1970s, foreign competition had slowed Detroit's momentum. The city declined along with its top industry. It has lost jobs and more than half its population in the past four decades. Racial tensions, which had flared violently during the 1940s, erupted again into riots in 1967. The city has worked hard since to address racial concerns and to restart its economy.

Low, rolling hills spread across the Lower Peninsula's southern half, while a higher plateau of birches, aspens, and oaks covers the northern half. Towering along Lake Michigan's shore are rows of sand dunes, which are a popular tourist attraction. The climate here is also perfect for fruit, and Michigan ranks as a top producer of cherries and cultivated blueberries. Pine forests dominate the wild Upper Peninsula. Black bears and white-tailed deer abound, while moose and wolves still live on Isle Royale in Lake Superior. Winter brings snow-sports enthusiasts to ski resorts, and summer vacationers enjoy water activities on the state's more than 10,000 lakes.

Today the vast majority of the state's 9.9 million people live south of a line stretching from Muskegon to Bay City. This ethnically diverse state has one of the largest group of Arab peoples in the nation, which is among the fastest growing Arab populations in the United States. Detroit (often called Motown) is a national hub of African-American entertainment and culture.

Michigan still ranks as a leader in motor vehicle manufacturing, but it is also known for a variety of other products, ranging from chemicals to breakfast food. Michigan is working hard to diversify its economy, focusing on service and high-technology businesses.

IT'S A FACT:
The world's largest herd of registered Holstein cows lives in Elsie, Michigan. These dairy cows are among the country's major milk producers.

A TIME LINE OF THE GREAT LAKE STATE

1763–66

Chief Pontiac's efforts to drive the British from the region ended in defeat for the Ottawa, who were forced to sign a peace treaty.

1855

The completion of the **Soo Canal** provided a means of shipping iron ore mined on the Upper Peninsula to steel centers on the Great Lakes.

1906

Businessman W. K. Kellogg started his **Toasted Corn Flake Company** in Battle Creek, today called "Cereal City."

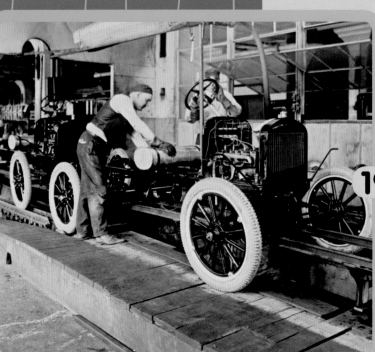

1913

The introduction of the **auto assembly line** at the Highland Park Ford Plant revolutionized mass production in industry.

Present

Private firms and philanthropic organizations have provided money and support for **Detroit's revitalization** efforts since the city declared bankruptcy—the largest municipal bankruptcy in the country.

ON THE MAP

LOCATION, LOCATION

Michigan's two huge peninsulas are surrounded by the country's four largest lakes—Superior, Huron, Michigan, and Erie. The Lower Peninsula is the state's business center and home of three big auto industries. The Upper Peninsula is rich with forests and wildlife—a vacationers' paradise.

ISLE ROYALE: In this isolated national park with more than 150 miles (240 km) of hiking trails, wolves living in packs hunt for moose.

KEWEENAW PENINSULA: This adventurer's paradise boasts a 100-mile (160-km) water trail for canoers and kayakers as well as underwater shipwrecks for divers.

SENEY: At the Seney National Wildlife Refuge, researchers discovered that loons change their call when they move to a new territory. It's a mystery why.

MACKINAC ISLAND: To protect the environment, cars aren't allowed on this island developed in the late 1800s by wealthy railroad families. Instead, you can ride bikes or horse-drawn carriages to see Victorian-style summer homes along the shore.

TRAVERSE CITY: At the annual National Cherry Festival, some 160 pounds (73 kg) of ice cream and 300 pounds (136 kg) of fresh cherries might go into making a 320-foot (98-m)-long cherry sundae that feeds 3,000 people.

DETROIT: This largest city with a population of 688,701 is America's car capital. The "Big Three" U.S. auto manufacturers—Chrysler, Ford, and General Motors—are all based here.

LANSING: This capital city mixes business with access to the outdoors. The 13-mile (21-km) paved Lansing River Trail passes through parks, natural areas, and into the heart of Lansing's Old Town.

ANN ARBOR: It's the home of the University of Michigan and its football team, the Wolverines. The university has some 19 schools and colleges and teaches more than 65 foreign languages!

Albers Conic Equal-Area Projection

STATS & FACTS

STATEHOOD: January 29, 1861; 34th state

CAPITAL: Lansing

TOTAL AREA: 96,716 sq mi; 250,494 sq km

LAND AREA: 56,804 sq mi; 147,121 sq km

POPULATION: 9,909,877

POPULATION DENSITY: 174 people per sq mi

MAJOR RACIAL/ETHNIC GROUPS: 78.9% white, 14.2% African American, 2.4% Asian, 0.6% Native American, Hispanic (any race) 4.4%

INDUSTRY: manufacturing, transportation equipment and automotive, machinery, metals, chemicals, pharmaceuticals, minerals

AGRICULTURE: dairy products, corn, soybeans, cattle, greenhouse, wheat, hay

ANIMALS: Although Michigan is sometimes known as the **Wolverine State** because of the many wolverine pelts traded by early trappers, none of these animals are left in the state.

PEOPLE/CULTURE: **Harriet Quimby,** who became the first female pilot to fly solo over the English Channel in 1912, was born in Branch County.

NATURAL FORCES: Michigan's **1994 cold snap—** coldest of the 20th century with temperatures as low as minus 55°F (−48°C)—caused schools to close for several days.

NATURAL FEATURES: Isle Royale was designated an **international biosphere reserve** in 1980. The wolf/moose predator/prey study conducted there is the longest continuous study of this kind in the world.

HISTORY: In the 1960s Detroit's **Motown** record label revolutionized pop music with talented artists like Stevie Wonder (left) and Marvin Gaye (right).

MINNESOTA

THE GOPHER STATE

Awash in water—falling, flowing, still, and marshy—that's Minnesota. The state borders the greatest of the Great Lakes—Superior—and is the source of the country's mightiest river—the Mississippi. State license plates reference its "10,000 Lakes." Minnesotans might mention that there are actually twice that many or more. "Minnesota" comes from a Dakota term meaning "cloudy water," describing the light-colored clay suspended in the Minnesota River.

Thick woods and lakes cover Minnesota's gravelly northern third, but its central and southwest areas are nearly treeless plains with soils perfect for farming. The Mississippi River drains south to the Gulf of Mexico. Northern rivers flow east to Lake Superior or north into Canada.

When French fur traders scouted Minnesota lands and waters in the late 17th century, they met eastern Dakota peoples. Within decades, rival Ojibwa armed with French guns pushed the Dakota southwest into the prairies. The territory came under American control by 1818. The U.S. Army established Fort Snelling as a key frontier outpost in the 1820s. Most of the Minnesota Territory was opened for settlement by 1851, and the 32nd state joined the Union in 1858. Fierce conflict soon arose between the settlers and the Dakota, and the Indians were largely driven north to Canada and west to the Dakota Territory. For the next half century, Minnesota's tall timber, fertile soils, and mineral resources attracted waves of newcomers, especially from Norway, Sweden, and Germany.

Over several decades, Minnesota's vast pine forests were largely clear-cut for lumber. Eventually, many cut-over areas were reforested and are today national, state, and private forests. The use of smaller trees for pulpwood and paper has helped keep timber an important Minnesota business. While wheat had grown to be the top crop by 1870, other grains and dairy farming gained importance later on. It is still a bountiful farm state, where farmers grow oats, corn, and soybeans; raise pigs and cows; and produce milk and cheese.

In 1865 rich deposits of iron ore were found in northeastern Minnesota's Mesabi Range. Mining boomed, with more than a hundred open pits by 1900. Transported to Duluth and then shipped to blast furnaces along Lakes Erie and Michigan, Minnesota iron ore became U.S. steel. The state has led the nation in iron ore production ever since.

Minneapolis grew up around the Falls of St. Anthony, where the Mississippi's power was used to grind acres of wheat and cut miles of timber. Just ten miles (16 km) downstream, St. Paul became Minnesota's capital. Water highways and railroad empires helped make the Twin Cities a premier trading and market center, serving areas all the way to the Pacific. Innovative manufacturing of plastics and other products followed. A majority of the state's people now live in cities big and small, producing processed foods, machinery, paper, printed materials, and chemical products.

Minnesota today is an exciting mix of "cold and new." Rather than letting chilly winters keep them indoors, Minnesotans celebrate the frigid season with snowy sports such as ice fishing, hockey, and snowmobiling. Summers bring great north woods swimming, fishing, and canoeing.

The state's 5.4 million residents are protecting their water resources while they plunge into new industries. A pioneer in computers and other high-tech manufacturing, Minnesota is working to build a successful biotechnology industry. In these and other ways, Minnesota's future seems—like its sky-blue waters—limitless!

STATE FLAG

The Minnesota state seal is encircled by a wreath of lady's slipper with the date 1858, when Minnesota became a state.

STATE FLOWER
Lady's Slipper

STATE BIRD
Common Loon

IT'S A FACT:
Minnesota has one recreational boat per every six people, more than any other state.

A TIME LINE OF THE GOPHER STATE

1680

Father Louis Hennepin, while held captive by the Dakota, was the first white person to see the site that is now Minneapolis.

1862

Outrage over **the Dakota Indian attack on New Ulm** ended in 38 executions of the attackers and the Dakota being forced out of Minnesota.

1880s–1950s

Workers like this man mined hematite iron ore from rich deposits in the **Mesabi Range.** Today lower grade taconite iron ore is mined.

1932

The **first cellophane tape** was developed by the Minnesota Mining and Manufacturing (3M) Company.

1996

The **record low** for the state was minus 60°F (–51°C), set on February 2, at Tower, in the state's northeast.

Present

Each year 40 million people visit **Bloomington's Mall of America,** the largest enclosed retail/family entertainment complex in the United States.

ON THE MAP

LOCATION, LOCATION

Bordered by the great Lake Superior and the mighty Mississippi River to the east, it's a land of water, often called Land of 10,000 Lakes. The rich soil of its central land grows corn, soybeans, and wheat, while its northern woods and lakes welcome canoers, hikers, and campers.

GRAND RAPIDS: Just outside this city, beautiful Lake Winnibigoshish, called Lake Winnie by locals, is just one of Minnesota's lakes that offers great scenery and great fishing.

SUPERIOR NATIONAL FOREST: Snow, ice, and frigid temperatures are part of the fun in northeast Minnesota. Cross-country skiers, snowboarders, and ice fishers all make the most of its long winters.

MESABI RANGE: With iron-rich ore first discovered here in 1890, the range became a booming center for mining.

DULUTH: As a major port and railway center for shipping lumber, wheat, and ore, Duluth in the early 1900s was home to more millionaires per capita than any other U.S. city.

ST. PAUL: This capital city shares the nickname Twin Cities with Minneapolis. St. Paul's original name was Pig's Eye Landing, for the French-Canadian tavern owner, Pierre (Pig's Eye) Parrant, who first brought settlers here.

MINNEAPOLIS: This largest city has a population of 400,070. Its skyway system links 8 miles (that's 13 km, or 80 blocks) of restaurants, shops, businesses, and hotels, so you can spend a busy day there and never go outside!

ROCHESTER: It's home to the trendsetting Mayo Clinic, founded by pioneer doctor William Worrall Mayo in 1863. Today the clinic has 55,000 doctors, nurses, and other staff.

The "Northwest Angle" is the northernmost point in the 48 contiguous states.

Highest point in Minnesota — Eagle Mt. 2,301 ft 701 m

Source of the Mississippi River

MANITOBA · CANADA · U.S. · ONTARIO · LAKE SUPERIOR · NORTH DAKOTA · SOUTH DAKOTA · WISCONSIN · IOWA

MINNESOTA

0 — 50 — 100 miles
0 — 50 — 100 kilometers
Albers Conic Equal-Area Projection

164

STATS & FACTS

STATEHOOD: May 11, 1858; 32nd state

CAPITAL: St. Paul

TOTAL AREA: 86,939 sq mi; 225,171 sq km

LAND AREA: 79,610 sq mi; 206,189 sq km

POPULATION: 5,457,173

POPULATION DENSITY: 69 people per sq mi

MAJOR RACIAL/ETHNIC GROUPS: 85.3% white, 5.2% African American, 4.0% Asian, 1.1% Native American, Hispanic (any race) 4.7%

INDUSTRY: food processing, machinery, chemicals, paper products/timber, biotechnology, minerals

AGRICULTURE: corn, soybeans, hogs, dairy products, cattle, turkeys, oats, rice, vegetables

ANIMALS: Look up in a tree in the Minnesota forest and **a fisher** may be staring back at you. Better climbers than the local red squirrels, this cousin of the weasel with a black rump is quick and agile as it scrambles up a trunk. Despite its name, it doesn't catch fish for food.

HISTORY: In 1952 the **world's first open-heart operation** was performed at the University of Minnesota in Minneapolis.

NATURAL FORCES: The northeast part of the state averages nearly **6 feet (1.8 m) of snow a year.**

PEOPLE/CULTURE: Modern **in-line skates** were invented in 1980 by two Minnesota students who wanted a way to practice ice hockey in the summer.

NATURAL FEATURES: The **Boundary Waters Canoe Area Wilderness,** which borders Canada, was the first wilderness to be set aside for canoeing.

MISSOURI

THE SHOW ME STATE

Gateway to the West." With its mid-continent location and the country's two longest rivers embracing the state, it was natural that Missouri would be described this way. The broad and swift Missouri River sweeps across the state from the west to join the mighty Mississippi on its eastern edge—linking its two biggest cities.

Missouri's name comes from a native group whose name meant "wooden canoe people," or the "town of large canoes." When French settlers arrived in 1700, they found Osage and Illini peoples—and valuable deposits of lead. Trappers and traders peacefully paddled the region's rivers, at least until the United States bought the vast Louisiana Territory from France in 1803. Lewis and Clark set out the next year up the muddy Missouri to open the American West.

Missouri was made a territory in 1812. Broken treaties with Native Americans caused violence until a pact was signed with most native groups in 1815. Settlement was stoked by the arrival of the first bellowing riverboats, which reached Missouri in 1819. The fur trading center of St. Louis soon grew to be a major transport hub. The Missouri Compromise of 1820 allowed Missouri to join the Union as a slave state in 1821. Tent cities sprang up around the state as pioneers headed west from Independence—the jumping-off point for the Santa Fe and Oregon Trails. Pony Express riders high-tailed it west with their mailbags from St. Joseph for fast-and-furious ten-day rides to California.

But tensions grew between residents who were for slavery and those who were against it. While Missouri officially sided with the Union during the Civil War, thousands of its soldiers fought for the Confederacy. Postwar Missouri healed slowly but was prospering in both agriculture and industry by the end of the century. It celebrated its success in 1904 with two events: the Olympics and the World's Fair, both in St. Louis.

The rugged Ozark Plateau, covered with oak, hickory, and pine forests shared with Arkansas and Oklahoma, extends across much of Missouri's south. North of the Missouri River lie hills, valleys, and glacially formed fertile croplands of corn and soybeans. Cotton and rice carpet the Mississippi River bottomlands.

Missouri's economy is amazingly diverse. Some 100,000 farms, more than in any other state but Texas, make Missouri a major producer of soybeans, corn, cattle, and hogs. More than three centuries after lead was first mined, Missouri still leads the nation in lead production, and barge traffic makes St. Louis one of the busiest inland ports in the nation.

Giant stockyards in Kansas City closed in the 1990s, but the urban area is still a sizable farm supplier and a leader in Missouri's reenergized auto industry. Springfield is home to a thriving health care industry and manufacturing sector. The scenic Ozarks boast reservoirs lined with vacation cabins and boat docks. At Branson, dozens of theaters host famous country-western singers for national crowds.

As Missouri strengthens its traditional economic bases, it also strives to be included in a "bio belt" of life-science research by encouraging the growth of high-tech industries. The spectacular Gateway Arch is a symbol of the state's historic role in the nation's settlement as well as the symbol of an open doorway to Missouri's future success.

STATE FLAG

A Missouri town is the United States' geographical center of population, represented by Missouri's coat of arms centered on the U.S. colors.

STATE FLOWER
Hawthorn

STATE BIRD
Eastern Bluebird

IT'S A FACT:
The Gateway Arch in St. Louis is the tallest of all monuments in the United States.

A TIME LINE OF THE SHOW ME STATE

1735

French settlers established Missouri's first permanent white settlement along the Mississippi at **Ste. Genevieve.**

1860–61

The **Pony Express** delivered mail between Missouri and California in just ten days, using a central route later adopted by the railroad.

1904

The **St. Louis World's Fair** marked the centennial of the Louisiana Purchase and showcased electricity and early automobiles.

1915

In Kansas City the Hall brothers began producing high-quality valentines and Christmas cards. Their company grew into today's **Hallmark.**

Present

Branson has become a major country music center, helping to make tourism a multibillion-dollar industry for Missouri.

167

ON THE MAP

LOCATION, LOCATION

With its central location and fed by the two longest U.S. rivers—the Missouri from the west and the Mississippi to the east, Missouri is a crossroads for travelers from each coast. From here Lewis and Clark started their journey to explore the West in 1804.

JEFFERSON CITY: The capital city, named for President Thomas Jefferson, was the site of a mound-building culture some 10,000 years ago. In the 1800s Daniel Boone established Boone's Lick trail here; the city was designed by his son Daniel Morgan Boone.

ST. JOSEPH: From this outpost, Pony Express riders carried letters to California. Their speed was lightning fast for the day, but it was overtaken by the arrival of the telegraph.

HANNIBAL: Samuel Clemens (Mark Twain) used his hometown as the model for settings in his novels *Adventures of Tom Sawyer* and *Adventures of Huckleberry Finn*.

ST. LOUIS: It is home to the Gateway Arch, the tallest monument in the United States. Trams carry one million tourists to the top of the arch each year.

KANSAS CITY: Missouri's largest city has 467,007 people. Local history says that artistic genius Walt Disney created Mickey Mouse while working at an ad agency here, based on a mouse that lived in his desk drawer!

SPRINGFIELD: To the northwest of this city is Ash Grove, where Father Moses Berry turned his family history into a unique museum for slavery education. His family stayed here while many others left after three falsely accused black men were lynched in 1906.

OZARK PLATEAU: The folk music here traces its origins to Scotch-Irish settlers who migrated from Appalachian highlands to this similarly rugged area. Fiddlers play at annual folk festivals.

Map labels

IOWA
NEBRASKA
KANSAS
ILLINOIS
KENTUCKY
TENNESSEE
ARKANSAS
OKLAHOMA

MISSOURI

Maryville, Bethany, Kirksville, Trenton, Chillicothe, Brookfield, Macon, Savannah, St. Joseph, Gallatin, Cameron, SQUAW CREEK N.W.R., Liberty, Richmond, Moberly, Kansas City, HARRY S. TRUMAN N.H.S., Independence, Blue Springs, Marshall, Columbia, Boonville, Centralia, Mexico, Hannibal, Louisiana, Lees Summit, Belton, Warrensburg, Sedalia, California, Jefferson City, Fulton, Hermann, Washington, St. Charles, St. Peters, Florissant, Ferguson, University City, St. Louis, Kirkwood, Union, ULYSSES S. GRANT N.H.S., Harrisonville, Clinton, Eldon, Stanton, Sullivan, Meramec Caverns, Festus, Butler, Lake of the Ozarks, St. James, De Soto, Sainte Genevieve, Park Hills, Farmington, Nevada, Bolivar, Lebanon, Waynesville, Rolla, Salem, Taum Sauk Mt. 1,772 ft +540 m, Highest point in Missouri, Perryville, Fredericktown, Jackson, Ash Grove, Springfield, Seymour, Mountain Grove, Cape Girardeau, Joplin, Webb City, Carthage, Republic, WILSON'S CREEK N.B., Aurora, Ava, GEORGE WASHINGTON CARVER N.M., Monett, Neosho, Pineville, Table Rock Lake, Branson, West Plains, ELEVEN POINT N.W.&S.R., Poplar Bluff, Dexter, MINGO N.W.R., Charleston, Sikeston, New Madrid, Malden, Caruthersville, Kennett, SWAN LAKE N.W.R., BIG MUDDY N.W.R., MARK TWAIN NAT. FOR., CLARENCE CANNON N.W.R., MARAIS DES CYGNES N.W.R., Harry S. Truman Reservoir, Stockton Lake, Bull Shoals Lake, MARK TWAIN NATIONAL FOREST, OZARK NATIONAL SCENIC RIVERWAYS, OZARK PLATEAU, Mark Twain Lake

Rivers: Missouri, Mississippi, Platte, Grand, Thompson, Weldon, Locust Creek, Chariton, Middle Fabius, South Fabius, Wyaconda, Des Moines, Salt, Blackwater, Osage, Gasconade, Niangua, Little Sac, Osage Fork, Sac, Big Piney, Current, Jacks Fork, Eleven Point, Bryant Creek, White, St. Francis, Block, Ohio, Marais des Cygnes, South Grand

0 50 100 miles
0 50 100 kilometers
Albers Conic Equal-Area Projection

STATS & FACTS

STATEHOOD: August 10, 1821; 24th state

CAPITAL: Jefferson City

TOTAL AREA: 69,704 sq mi; 180,533 sq mi

LAND AREA: 68,886 sq mi; 178,414 sq km

POPULATION: 6,063,589

POPULATION DENSITY: 88 people per sq mi

MAJOR RACIAL/ETHNIC GROUPS: 82.8% white, 11.6% African American, 1.6% Asian, 0.5% Native American, Hispanic (any race) 3.5%

INDUSTRY: transportation equipment and automotive, aerospace, food products, chemicals, machinery, printing and publishing, metals, electrical equipment, minerals

AGRICULTURE: soybeans, corn, cattle, hogs, turkeys, rice, hay, cotton, wheat, sorghum grain

ANIMALS: Missouri once raised more **mules—** for westbound wagon trains—than any other state.

NATURAL FEATURES: Old limestone mines near Kansas City have come to house some 5 million square feet (464,515 sq m) of **underground office space** complete with underground roads.

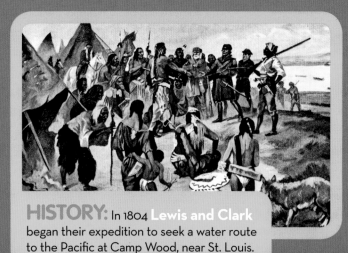

HISTORY: In 1804 **Lewis and Clark** began their expedition to seek a water route to the Pacific at Camp Wood, near St. Louis.

PEOPLE/ CULTURE:
Old West legend Martha "Calamity Jane" Cannary was born in Princeton, Missouri, in 1852. The horseback-riding, gunslinging frontierswoman settled in Deadwood, South Dakota, during the 1876 gold rush.

NATURAL FORCES: In late 1811 and early 1812 **three of the strongest earthquakes in U.S. history** rocked Missouri near New Madrid. The quakes, which scientists believe measured 8 on the Richter scale, caused the Mississippi River to flow backward temporarily!

NEBRASKA

THE CORNHUSKER STATE

"The Great American Desert." So wrote Maj. Stephen Long after he mapped the Nebraska plains for the U.S. government in 1820. Seeing the rolling and mostly tree-free prairies during a bad drought, his expedition found it "almost wholly unfit for cultivation." Nebraskans might chuckle today if they could show the explorer a map showing more than 90 percent of their state covered with farms and ranches.

Based on Long's report, the area that included Nebraska was set up as Indian Territory—but not for long. In the 1840s Omaha, with its fine location along the Missouri and near the Platte River, was the starting point for the long journey west for many Oregon and Mormon Trail trekkers. A natural east-west travel corridor, the broad and shallow Platte gave Nebraska its name, from an Oto Indian term meaning "flat water." Thousands of wagon trains rumbled west alongside the Platte. Some people put down roots in the area, especially in the tallgrass eastern prairies.

Both precipitation and population decline as one travels west in Nebraska. Corn and soybeans thrive in the usually well-watered eastern sections along the Missouri River border, where corn-fed pigs and poultry are raised, too. "Dry farming" is practiced in the west, where dry edible beans grow well in the arid climate and make Nebraska a top producer. Water from reservoirs on the Platte and other streams provides irrigation for agriculture. Catching rainfall like a sponge, the grass-covered Sand Hills help refresh the Ogallala Aquifer, a source of groundwater tapped by thousands of wells.

Two acts of the U.S. Congress had great impacts on Nebraska in the mid-19th century. The Kansas-Nebraska Act in 1854 made the two neighbor territories part of the United States. The Homestead Act of 1862 allowed white settlers to claim—and keep—a "section" of 160 acres (65 ha) of land if they worked for five years to develop it. As immigrants swarmed to Nebraska to obtain their land, the Sioux and Cheyenne of Nebraska lost more and more of theirs. Nebraska became the 37th state in 1867. The tiny town of Lancaster was renamed Lincoln—after the 16th president—and was made the state capital.

In 1869 the Union Pacific Railroad steamed its way across the new state, bringing more immigrants both through and to Nebraska. Families fought the loneliness of a hard life on their scattered homesteads by sometimes meeting with neighbors. In most areas wood was scarce, so many farm families built homes using prairie sod. Cut into blocks held together by strong root systems, this "Nebraska marble" proved to be a durable building material. A Nebraska newspaperman started Arbor Day in 1872—planting trees to help hold soil in place. Nebraska was known as the Tree Planter's State until 1945. It has the only national forest that was planted by people.

Nebraska's population has not grown much since 1900. The state's farmers have ridden an economic "roller coaster" of good followed by bad times over the past century. As elsewhere in the country, the size of farms has increased while the number of farmers has decreased. Some rural counties struggle to keep their people from leaving. Overall, irrigation has expanded, causing concern that overuse of groundwater may leave little for the future. Other activities are helping the state to prosper—meatpacking, insurance, banking, telecommunications, health care, and the U.S. military. Nebraska's slow-growing population will continue to have its roots in the prairies and its eyes on the future.

STATE FLAG

The state seal features the Rocky Mountains, steamboat and rail transportation, agriculture, and the mechanical arts of a smith with a hammer and anvil.

STATE FLOWER
Goldenrod

STATE BIRD
Meadowlark

IT'S A FACT:
It's estimated that as many as ten mammoth fossils are buried under an average square mile (2.6 sq km) of land in Nebraska.

A TIME LINE OF THE CORNHUSKER STATE

1800s

Native Americans lost their lands in eastern Nebraska to the United States by 1854, but tribes in Nebraska's west did not surrender theirs until 1877.

1862

The **Homestead Act** brought a rush of settlers, many building homes of sod because so few trees grew on the Nebraska prairie.

1896

Farmers seeking relief from low prices and overuse of credit supported Democratic candidate **William Jennings Bryan,** backed by the Populists.

1954

Frozen TV dinners were sold by Omaha's Swanson food company, packaged inside a box designed to look like a television set.

Present

Self-made multibillionaire **Warren Buffett**—known as the "oracle of Omaha"—has used a commonsense investment strategy to amass his fortune. Many admire his frugality and philanthropy.

ON THE MAP

LOCATION, LOCATION

In the 1800s thousands of wagon trains made their way west alongside the Platte River. Those who settled on the rich prairie land usually became farmers of corn, soybeans, and wheat, or ranchers of beef cattle. Today farms and ranches cover nearly all of this state.

SAND HILLS: The largest expanse of original native prairie in the United States—with grass-carpeted sand dunes—is in this region. Migrating sandhill cranes fly over it on their way to a stop at the Platte River.

OMAHA: Nebraska's largest city has a population of 434,353. Home to the "oracle of Omaha," Warren Buffett, it is also home to the Henry Doorly Zoo, which features gorillas, lemurs, and also nocturnal creatures.

GERING: Visitors can hike to the 800-foot (244-m) summit of Scott's Bluff, which marked the trail for pioneers traveling west and for Pony Express riders. Wagon-wheel ruts are still visible after 150 years!

CHIMNEY ROCK: This 300-foot (91.5-m) sandstone spire was the most famous landmark along the Oregon Trail. Pioneers often drew it in their journals.

KIMBALL: Running north from this town, along a stretch of highway called the Fossil Freeway, visitors can see the fossils of ancient rhinos, mammoths, and dinosaurs at six stops.

BURWELL: The annual rodeo in this tiny town draws crowds from around the state. It is sometimes called "the place where the Wild West meets the 21st century."

LINCOLN: In the state capital, the University of Nebraska State Museum displays the bones of the largest mammoth (a prehistoric relative of the elephant) discovered in the state. Mammoth bones have been found in all 93 state counties.

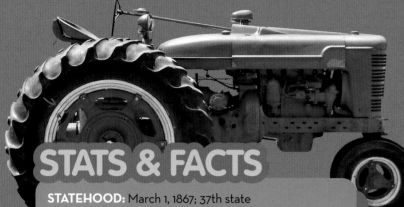

STATS & FACTS

STATEHOOD: March 1, 1867; 37th state

CAPITAL: Lincoln

TOTAL AREA: 77,354 sq mi; 200,345 sq km

LAND AREA: 76,872 sq mi; 199,099 sq km

POPULATION: 1,881,503

POPULATION DENSITY: 24 people per sq mi

MAJOR RACIAL/ETHNIC GROUPS: 86.1% white, 4.5% African American, 1.8% Asian, 1.0% Native American, Hispanic (any race) 9.2%

INDUSTRY: crude oil production, food processing, machinery, metals, transportation equipment, insurance, telecommunications

AGRICULTURE: cattle, corn, soybeans, hogs, sorghum grain, wheat, dairy products

NATURAL FEATURES: Nebraska has more **miles of rivers** within its borders than any other state.

HISTORY: The system of **center pivot irrigation**, which opens dry land to crop production, originated in Nebraska. The state is the largest irrigator in the United States and the largest producer of center pivots in the world.

PEOPLE/CULTURE: Many of Nebraska's early settlers were called **sod-busters** because they used chunks of the grassy prairie (sod) to build their houses.

NATURAL FORCES: Watch out! In 2003 **a hailstone that was 7 inches (18 cm) across**—longer than your hand—fell in Aurora, Nebraska.

ANIMALS: Half a million migrating **sandhill cranes** descend on the Platte River every spring.

NORTH DAKOTA

THE FLICKERTAIL STATE

Look at the flickertails!" North Dakota's energetic little ground squirrels emerge from their burrows to watch the prairies as they flick their tails in expectation. The lives and livelihoods of people in the Flickertail State are also rooted in these rolling lands.

Huge Ice Age glaciers scoured the eastern two-thirds of the land, changing and blocking river courses. Several streams combined to form today's mighty Missouri River, which cuts its channel across the state from west to south. West of the river, lands not smoothed by ice sheets have been eroded into rugged hills and "badlands." North and east of the Missouri Valley, thousands of pan-shaped lakes and ponds left by glaciers dot the state's Drift Prairie. These kettle holes make temporary homes for migrating waterfowl. The terrain slopes gradually downward to the state's eastern border, which is marked by the Red River of the North. This flat valley, once the bottom of a vast glacial lake, contains some of the world's best farmland—and is often subject to flooding.

Although French explorers moved through in the 1730s, it was the Corps of Discovery led by Lewis and Clark that put the area on the map. Staying with Mandan people along the Missouri River in what is now central North Dakota, they met a Shoshone woman named Sacagawea (sometimes spelled Sakakawea) during the winter of 1804-05. As a guide and interpreter, she was indispensable to the expedition. Lake Sakakawea, formed by a dam on the Missouri River, is named in her honor.

Permanent settlement was slow, even after the Dakota Territory was formed in 1861—in part because of later conflicts with Native Americans. It took the coming of the railroad in the 1870s for farmers and ranchers to arrive in greater numbers. North Dakota entered the Union as the 39th state in 1889.

Farming became and is still the major economic activity in the state, even though it has not always been easy. North Dakota farmers have endured drought, dust storms, invasions of grasshoppers, terrible economic times, and, of course, the cold. Blizzards can reduce visibility from miles to feet in minutes. But North Dakota's summer days are long, warm—even hot. Many hours of sunshine at the state's high latitude allow the short growing season to produce fine crops.

Wheat is the top crop here, and North Dakota farms produce lots of it. The 2012 harvest was 339 million bushels, more than enough to provide a bushel for every person in the country. The state leads the country in producing sunflowers, oats, barley, canola, flaxseed, and dry edible beans.

North Dakotans look both below and above their rolling prairies for future vitality—and energy. Since the 1970s oil and natural gas reserves have been tapped in the western half of the state. Closer to the surface lie huge deposits of a kind of coal called lignite, which is burned in nearby power plants to produce electricity. Aboveground, strong winds turn towering wind turbines that generate electricity. This rich variety of energy resources makes North Dakota an exporter of energy to neighboring states and holds continued promise for its economic future.

There is concern over the recent decline in the state's population. Only two states have fewer people than the approximately 739,500 who call North Dakota home. Building on North Dakota's fine education system, state officials work to keep young people from leaving the state to find jobs in other places. Keeping homegrown talent in the state will help ensure a future full of energy and hope.

STATE FLAG

The national bird, the bald eagle, carries a ribbon in its beak with the words "E Pluribus Unum," referring to one nation made of many states.

STATE FLOWER
Prairie Rose

STATE BIRD
Western Meadowlark

GEOGRAPHICAL CENTER OF NORTH AMERICA
RUGBY, ND

IT'S A FACT:
The exact geographic middle of North America is in Rugby, North Dakota.

A TIME LINE OF THE FLICKERTAIL STATE

1804

At Fort Mandan, Lewis and Clark met **Sacagawea,** who guided them across plains and mountains to the Pacific Ocean.

1874–1890

Wheat farms as large as 65,000 acres (26,000 ha) earned such huge profits that they became known as "bonanza farms."

1890

The Hunkpapa Sioux leader **Sitting Bull** was killed at Fort Yates after a Ghost Dance—a spiritual ritual through which Native Americans hoped to end white expansion and regain prosperity.

1951

Oil discovered near Tioga became the state's most valuable mineral. The area currently supplies much of North Dakota's propane gas.

2010s

Tapping oil and natural gas deposits in the **Bakken formation** has made North Dakota the country's second largest oil-producing state and spurred employment.

Present

Garrison Dam provides electricity, flood control, irrigation, and, by creating Lake Sakakawea, support to a rising recreation industry.

ON THE MAP

LOCATION, LOCATION

Located in the upper middle of the continent, North Dakota chills deeply in winter. Norwegian and other European immigrants in the 1800s found summers too short for some crops to mature, so they grew quick-ripening grains like oats, barley, and wheat.

DEVILS LAKE: It got its name when explorers incorrectly translated the Native American name, Miniwaukan. Since then, legends of evil spirits grew, including stories of sea monsters and drowned warriors.

RED RIVER VALLEY: Rich soils, long days of summer sunshine, and plentiful rainfall grow head-high sunflowers here. North Dakota leads the nation in the production of sunflowers, which are used for cooking oil, birdseed, and snacks.

THEODORE ROOSEVELT NATIONAL PARK: It's the only national park named for a U.S. president. Visitors can explore the Painted Canyon, part of the rugged region that enticed the young adventurer on his visit in 1886.

DICKINSON: Travel the roadway east of town to find a 32-mile (51.5-km) stretch of scrap-metal sculptures of bugs, birds, and fanciful beasts by artist Gary Greff.

BISMARCK: In this capital city a bronze statue of Sacagawea—who guided Meriwether Lewis and William Clark west—and her baby son Jean Baptiste stands at the entrance to the North Dakota Heritage Center on the state capitol grounds.

JAMESTOWN: This town's "Buffalo City" features a 26-foot (8-m)-tall statue of a magnificent buffalo, representing the millions that once roamed the plains of North Dakota and other states.

FARGO: North Dakota's largest city has a population of 113,658. Founded in 1871, it takes its name from William Fargo, who started the Wells Fargo Express Company. West Fargo is home to Bonanzaville—an authentic pioneer village.

STATS & FACTS

STATEHOOD: November 2, 1889; 39th state

CAPITAL: Bismarck

TOTAL AREA: 70,700 sq mi; 183,112 sq km

LAND AREA: 68,976 sq mi; 178,647 sq km

POPULATION: 739,482

POPULATION DENSITY: 11 people per sq mi

MAJOR RACIAL/ETHNIC GROUP: 90.0% white, 5.4% Native American, 1.2% African American, 1.0% Asian, Hispanic (any race) 2.0%

INDUSTRY: crude oil production, coal production, manufacturing, tourism, services, government

AGRICULTURE: wheat, sunflower, canola, flaxseed, barley, cattle, dry edible beans, corn, potatoes, soybeans

NATURAL FEATURES: North Dakota has long been the nation's top producer of **sunflowers**—about half the crop. The flowers can grow as tall as 13 feet (4 m).

HISTORY: Meriwether Lewis and William Clark waited out the brutal winter of 1804 at **Fort Mandan.** Visitors can see the reconstructed shelter at Washburn.

NATURAL FORCES: For thousands of years lightning strikes on the prairies of the Great Plains have caused grass fires, keeping the plains healthy by removing dead vegetation, introducing nutrients into the soil, and reducing invader plants. Today **carefully controlled fires** are set by experts to keep the prairies healthy, following rules set by the U.S. Geological Survey.

PEOPLE/CULTURE: When three outlaws stole future president **Theodore Roosevelt's** boat near the Elkhorn Ranch on the Little Missouri River in 1886, he built a new one and chased down the thieves.

ANIMALS: More **waterfowl** hatch in the prairie kettle holes and sloughs of North Dakota than in any other state.

177

OHIO

THE BUCKEYE STATE

hree big C's—and so much more! Shaped a bit like a deep bowl on the map, Ohio brims with natural resources, rich farmlands, lots of people, and three big C cities: Cleveland lies in the north on the shore of Lake Erie; Columbus anchors the middle; and in the southwest stands Cincinnati—alongside the great river that gives Ohio its name.

Long before the Iroquois named the big west-flowing river, the Adena, Hopewell, and Mississippian cultures built huge burial mounds on southern Ohio hilltops. While the French and British struggled to control the Ohio Country in the mid-1700s, the first permanent white settlement was established at Marietta—on the banks of the Ohio—in 1788. The first of many successful Ohio River ports, it was soon surpassed in importance by downriver Cincinnati. The Battle of Fallen Timbers, a total victory for the U.S. Army in 1794, forced the Indians of the Northwest Territory to sign a treaty that opened much of the Ohio Valley to settlers. In 1796 New Englanders arrived on Lake Erie's shores and founded Cleveland. Ohio became the 17th state in 1803, with its capital first at Chillicothe and then Zanesville. In 1816 Ohio established Columbus as its seat of government.

Ohio prospered with its key waterways linking regions east and west. Its Lake Erie rim bustled with business, especially after the Erie Canal was finished in 1825. This provided a route for East Coast water traffic to reach the frontier. Flatboats and then steamboats navigated the Ohio River. The state grew quickly. The growing of corn, wheat, oats, and potatoes—plus the raising of cattle and hogs—made it an agricultural powerhouse

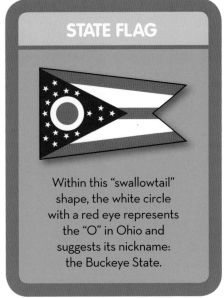

STATE FLAG

Within this "swallowtail" shape, the white circle with a red eye represents the "O" in Ohio and suggests its nickname: the Buckeye State.

STATE FLOWER
Scarlet Carnation

STATE BIRD
Cardinal

by 1850. Industry soon followed, led by meat-packing. By that time, rails connected most major state cities. The so-called Underground Railroad—a loose network of people who helped escaped slaves move north to freedom—maintained many "stations," or safehouses, in Ohio. After the Civil War, the iron and steel industry fired the state's economy. Rich deposits of coal and oil from outside and inside the state fueled this growth.

European immigrants arrived in huge numbers through the second half of the 19th century, finding work in thriving factories. Organized labor groups were formed to promote workers' rights.

Ohio suffered huge job losses during the Great Depression, but its economy rebounded during and after World War II. Ohio became a major manufacturer of rubber and plastics. Lake Erie ports handled bulk mineral cargoes as well as finished products. The Ohio River carried huge volumes of oil and steel in multi-barge tows. By the 1960s pollution problems darkened Ohio's skies and discolored its waterways, especially Lake Erie. Decades of cleanup efforts have paid off, and the state's environment has rebounded well.

Today, the Buckeye State is prospering. With more than 11.5 million people, Ohio is the seventh most populous state and still a top agriculture state. Ohio agriculture supports more than a thousand food-processing operations, making everything from jellies to sausages. Auto assembly and parts plants make the state a national leader in car manufacturing. The state seeks to attract information technology and other emerging industries, while striving to make its cities and towns more livable for residents. Boding well for Ohio's future is the state's continued emphasis on education. Through statewide initiatives, the Ohio Board of Regents wants to increase the number of its citizens with degrees.

IT'S A FACT:
The Cincinnati Reds were the first professional baseball team in the United States, founded in 1869 as the Red Stockings.

A TIME LINE OF THE BUCKEYE STATE

1794

Gen. "Mad" Anthony Wayne's defeat of Native Americans at the Battle of Fallen Timbers helped open the Ohio Valley to settlers.

1871–73

The **Giants of Seville,** Anna and Martin—both at least 7 feet 8 inches (2.3 m) tall—met in a carnival, married, and built a house perfect for their proportions.

1915

Akron's first rubber products were made in the 1870s, and by 1915 it had become known as the "rubber capital of the world."

1969

When the Cuyahoga River caught fire in 1969, it became a symbol of a polluted America and led to environmental legislation.

Present

The **Rock and Roll Hall of Fame,** a centerpiece of Cleveland's waterfront, attracts hundreds of thousands of tourists to the city each year.

ON THE MAP

LOCATION, LOCATION

With its large waterways, Ohio has long been a crossroads between East and West. Lake Erie and the Erie Canal provided huge business after the canal opened in 1825, and flatboats and steamboats plied the Ohio River bringing goods to towns along its banks.

CLEVELAND: This commercial center on the shore of Lake Erie is the home of the comic artists Joe Shuster and Jerry Siegel who created the famous comic hero Superman. Oil slicks from city's factories—now cleaned up—likely caused the Cuyahoga River fire in 1969.

TWINSBURG: It's been hosting the Twins Days Festival every August since 1976. The world's largest annual gathering of twins welcomed more than 2,000 sets of registered multiples in 2012.

DAYTON: Visit nearby Wright Field, the center of aeronautical research and development built on the ground where the Wright brothers tested their early airplanes in 1904-05.

NEW PHILADELPHIA: The Amish and Mennonite Heritage Center is located in nearby Berlin.

SERPENT MOUND STATE MEMORIAL: Visitors can hike around the best preserved of the prehistoric effigy mounds—earthworks in the shape of animals found in parts of the Midwest. This one is 450 yards (411 m) long, and about 4 feet (1.2 m) high.

COLUMBUS: The capital city has a population of 822,553. Its zoo and aquarium feature the world's wildlife, from spider monkeys to manatees.

Map labels

0 25 50 miles
0 25 50 kilometers
Albers Conic Equal-Area Projection

MICHIGAN
CANADA
U.S.
LAKE ERIE
Maumee Bay
CEDAR POINT N.W.R.
S. Bass I.
PERRY'S VICTORY & INTL. PEACE MEMORIAL
JAMES A. GARFIELD N.H.S.
Conneaut
Ashtabula
Geneva
Painesville
Grand
Pymatuning Reservoir
Mosquito Creek L.

Sylvania
Oregon
Maumee
Wauseon
Toledo
OTTAWA N.W.R.
Kelleys Island
Euclid
Cleveland
Mentor
Bryan
Perrysburg
Port Clinton
Sandusky Bay
Lorain
Shaker Heights
Napoleon
Fremont
Sandusky
North Olmsted
Parma
Twinsburg
Warren
Austintown
Niles
Bowling Green
Fostoria
Bellevue
Norwalk
Elyria
Strongsville
CUYAHOGA VALLEY N.P.
Defiance
Tiffin
Brunswick
Kent
Findlay
Willard
Medina
Cuyahoga Falls
Akron
Lake Milton
Youngstown
Van Wert
Blanchard
Bucyrus
Shelby
Ashland
Wooster
Barberton
Orrville
Alliance
North Canton
Salem
Delphos
Lima
Upper Sandusky
Galion
Mansfield
Massillon
Canton
LITTLE BEAVER CREEK N.W.& S.R.
Celina
Kenton
Marion
Blooming Grove
Loudonville
FIRST LADIES N.H.S.
East Liverpool
Wapakoneta
Scioto
Mt. Vernon
Dover
Atwood Lake
Toronto
St. Marys
Indian Lake
Delaware Lake
New Philadelphia
Leesville Lake
Grand Lake (St. Marys)
Highest point in Ohio
Coshocton
Uhrichsville
Steubenville
Bellefontaine
Campbell Hill 1,550 ft 472 m
Delaware
Piedmont L.
Sidney
Marysville
Powell
Westerville
Newark
Frazeysburg
Salt Fork L.
Martins Ferry
Piqua
Urbana
Dublin
Upper Arlington
Licking
Wills Creek
Cambridge
Bellaire
Greenville
Troy
Springfield
Gahanna
Reynoldsburg
Zanesville
Senecaville Lake
Huber Heights
BIG DARBY CREEK
Columbus
Buckeye Lake
Englewood
Trotwood
Fairborn
NATIONAL SCENIC
Lancaster
Dayton
Wright-Patterson A.F.B.
New Lexington
DAYTON AVIATION HERITAGE N.H.P.
Xenia
WAYNE NATIONAL FOREST
Lowell
Marietta
Kettering
Washington Court House
Circleville
Logan
Nelsonville
Middletown
Centerville
Caesar Creek Lake
Deer Creek Lake
Belpre
Oxford
Wilmington
HOPEWELL CULTURE N.H.P.
Athens
Hocking
Hamilton
Lebanon
LITTLE MIAMI NATIONAL SCENIC RIVER
Greenfield
Paint Creek
Fairfield
Mason
Chillicothe
Wellston
Bridgetown
Norwood
Hillsboro
Waverly
Jackson
Cincinnati
SERPENT MOUND STATE MEMORIAL
Peebles
Gallipolis
Point Pleasant
East Fork Lake
Scioto
Georgetown
Wheelersburg
WAYNE NATIONAL FOREST
WEST VIRGINIA
Manchester
Portsmouth
Ironton
South Point
KENTUCKY
INDIANA
PENNSYLVANIA
OHIO

St. Joseph
Maumee
Auglaize
Sandusky
Olentangy
Mohican
Tuscarawas
Muskingum
Ohio
Big Miami
Little Miami
Stillwater
Great Miami
Whitewater
Scioto
Darby Cr.
Deer Cr.
Raccoon Cr.
E. Fk. Little Miami

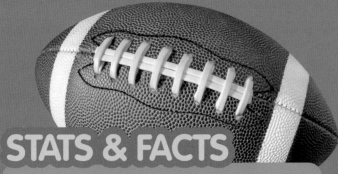

STATS & FACTS

STATEHOOD: March 1, 1803; 17th state

CAPITAL: Columbus

TOTAL AREA: 44,825 sq mi; 116,096 sq km

LAND AREA: 40,948 sq mi; 106,056 sq km

POPULATION: 11,594,163

POPULATION DENSITY: 283 people per sq mi

MAJOR RACIAL/ETHNIC GROUPS: 82.7% white, 12.2% African American, 1.7% Asian, 0.2% Native American, Hispanic (any race) 3.1%

INDUSTRY: coal production, manufacturing, transportation equipment and automotive, ceramic and glass, metals, machinery

AGRICULTURE: corn, soybeans, dairy products, eggs, hogs, hay, wheat, oats, greenhouse

PEOPLE/CULTURE: Ohio is the birthplace of 24 astronauts, including **John Glenn,** the first American to orbit Earth (in 1962), and Neil Armstrong, the first man to walk on the moon (in 1969).

NATURAL FEATURES: Ice Age glaciers gouged grooves in the limestone rocks on **Kelleys Island,** in Lake Erie.

NATURAL FORCES: Ohio gets most of its **precipitation** during the growing season: spring and summer.

HISTORY:
Marietta, Ohio's first permanent European settlement, was named for the French queen Marie Antoinette.

ANIMALS: Wild turkeys were introduced back into Ohio in the 1950s after they had been widely hunted and were nearly gone by 1904.

SOUTH DAKOTA

THE MOUNT RUSHMORE STATE

What's in a word? *Dakota* means "allies" or "friends" to people of the Sioux nations. When French explorers moved through the area in the 1740s, they met people of the Sioux federation who treated them well, and in 1804 Lewis and Clark were allowed to pass through Indian territory as they moved up the Missouri River. But fur traders and settlers who followed in the decades after had clashes with these Native Americans.

In 1868 the Dakota Territory included both North and South Dakota. Soon immigrants, especially from Central Europe and Scandinavia, began arriving by rail. Most settled in the eastern half of the state, where they found rich prairie-grass soils and enough precipitation to grow wheat and other crops. West of the Missouri were drier conditions, better suited for grazing cattle and sheep. The Dakota Territory was halved when both North and South Dakota were admitted to the Union on the same day in 1889. Pierre (pronounced PEER) was made the capital of the southern state.

South Dakota has only one large area of forest, the Black Hills. Named for the dark color of their stately ponderosa pines, the Black Hills are the highest peaks east of the Rocky Mountains. More important, they are sacred to the Lakota people, who see them as "the heart of everything that is." An 1868 treaty had promised to let the Lakota keep their rich hunting grounds forever, but all this changed when the U.S. Army, led by George Armstrong Custer, reported gold in the Black Hills. Although the Lakota, led by Sitting Bull and Crazy Horse, wiped out Custer's troops in neighboring Montana in 1876, they could not win against the bitter campaign launched by the Army. The last conflict in the Indian Wars took place along Wounded Knee Creek on the Pine Ridge Reservation. There, U.S. troops massacred 300 Native American men, women, and children.

Today, one in twelve of South Dakota's people is American Indian. Many live on the nine reservations scattered across the state and battle poverty on these lands. Some fight through the courts for lands that were once theirs. In the Black Hills the Lakota are honoring Chief Crazy Horse with a gigantic memorial, carved out of solid granite.

Another monumental structure in the Black Hills—Mount Rushmore—attracts some three million people each year, making the region a major source of income for the state. Vacationers find a bit of the past in herds of bison and in the Wild West town of Deadwood, where Wild Bill Hickok and Calamity Jane lived.

Farming and ranching still form key parts of the state's economy. South Dakota is a top producer of millet, soybeans, sunflowers, rye, sheep, and cattle. Special facilities convert corn to a motor fuel called ethanol. Meatpacking and other food processing also add value to state farm products. The manufacture of computers and the processing of credit card information have brought jobs to many workers. And the first task of the South Dakota Science and Technology Authority, created in 2004 to foster scientific and technological advancements in the state, was to reopen the former Homestake gold mine (closed in 2002) for scientific research. It is now home to a dedicated underground laboratory undertaking major physics experiments. As they look ahead, the people of South Dakota know that the past is with them as they scout the future.

STATE FLAG

The 1909 flag featured the state's then nickname, the Sunshine State—which became Florida's nickname, too. In 1992 the state adopted a new nickname: the Mount Rushmore State.

STATE FLOWER
Pasqueflower

STATE BIRD
Ring-Necked Pheasant

IT'S A FACT:
The world's largest, most complete fossil of *T. rex* discovered to date was found in 1990 on the Cheyenne River Indian Reservation. It's named Sue, after the fossil hunter who found it.

A TIME LINE OF THE MOUNT RUSHMORE STATE

1830

The arrival of **steamboats** on the upper Missouri River stimulated the fur trade and helped open the region to development.

1874–2002

The discovery of gold in the Black Hills led to the opening of the **Homestake Mine,** the richest and longest-producing mine in the U.S.

1876

Lakota hero Crazy Horse defeated Lt. Col. George Armstrong Custer at the **Battle of the Little Bighorn,** killing 263 white soldiers in defense of Native American territory.

1930s

Dust storms called **black blizzards and plagues of grasshoppers** accompanied a ten-year drought, worst in the state's history.

Present

The completion of a **monument in the Black Hills to Lakota chief Crazy Horse**—which will be taller than the Washington Monument—is part of a drive to build tourism.

ON THE MAP

LOCATION, LOCATION

The Dakota Territory started out with both North and South Dakota, but it was split in half when both were admitted to the Union on the same day in 1889. The Black Hills, forested mountains named for their dark-colored ponderosa pines, have long been sacred to the Lakota people.

LEMMON: Discover Petrified Wood Park, the largest park of its kind in the world. Fossils and petrified wood are arranged in unusual shapes, including a castle and pyramids.

CLARK: This "potato capital of South Dakota" features an annual Mashed Potato Wrestling Contest!

BELLE FOURCHE: Just outside the city is the geographic center of the United States. When Alaska and Hawaii were added to the Union in 1959, the center point moved there from Lebanon, Kansas.

0   25   50 miles
0   25   50 kilometers
Albers Conic Equal-Area Projection

BLACK HILLS: In 1927 Gutzon Borglum began sculpting four key presidents into Mount Rushmore: George Washington, Thomas Jefferson, Theodore Roosevelt, and Abraham Lincoln. Nearby, the Lakota hero Crazy Horse is joining the 60-foot (18-m) figures.

BADLANDS NATIONAL PARK: Here, strange shapes etched into layers of volcanic ash and soft sediments frustrated early white settlers. Today they enchant visitors to the park.

PIERRE: The capital is one of five U.S. state capitals that don't have a major interstate running through them. Its South Dakota Cultural Heritage Center has some 1,300 Native American, mainly Sioux, artifacts.

SIOUX FALLS: South Dakota's largest city has some 164,676 residents. It got its start in the 1800s after land developers came looking for the Big Sioux River waterfalls to provide water power.

Map labels

MONTANA

NORTH DAKOTA

WYOMING

MINNESOTA

IOWA

NEBRASKA

SOUTH DAKOTA

GREAT PLAINS

CUSTER NATIONAL FOREST
Buffalo
Bison
GRAND RIVER NATIONAL GRASSLAND
S. Fork Grand
Little Missouri
Thunder Butte Creek
Moreau
Sulphur Creek
Cherry Creek
Lemmon
McIntosh
STANDING ROCK INDIAN RESERVATION
POCASSE N.W.R.
Eureka
Leola
Mobridge
Selby
Ipswich
Aberdeen
Timber Lake
CHEYENNE RIVER INDIAN RESERVATION
Dupree
Gettysburg
Faulkton
Redfield
Groton
SAND LAKE N.W.R.
James
LAKE
Lake Traverse
Britton
TRAVERSE (SISSETON)
Sisseton
WAUBAY N.W.R.
Waubay Lake
Webster
Coteau des Prairies
INDIAN RES.
Milbank
Big Stone Lake
Geographic center of the U.S. (50 states)
Geographic center of the U.S. monument
Belle Fourche
Spearfish
Deadwood
Lead
Sturgis
Black Hawk
Rapid City
BLACK HILLS
Highest mountains east of the Rockies
Belle Fourche
Cheyenne
Crazy Horse Memorial
MT. RUSHMORE NAT. MEM.
Custer
Harney Peak 7,242 ft 2,207 m
Highest point in South Dakota
JEWEL CAVE N.M.
CUSTER S.P.
BUFFALO GAP NAT. GRASSLAND
WIND CAVE N.P.
Hot Springs
GAP
Edgemont
FOREST
GRASSLAND
PINE RIDGE INDIAN RESERVATION
Pine Ridge
Martin
LACREEK N.W.R.
White
Little White
BADLANDS NATIONAL PARK
Wall
MINUTEMAN MISSILE N.H.S.
Philip
Kadoka
Murdo
Kennebec
Bad
White River
Winner
ROSEBUD INDIAN RESERVATION
Rosebud
Keya Paha
Onida
Highmore
Miller
Fort Pierre
Pierre
FORT PIERRE NATIONAL GRASSLAND
LOWER BRULE INDIAN RES.
CROW CREEK INDIAN RESERVATION
Fort Thompson
Lake Sharpe
Crow Creek
Chamberlain
Plankinton
Wessington Springs
Woonsocket
Howard
Lake Francis Case
Platte
Parkston
Armour
Gregory
Burke
YANKTON
LAKE ANDES N.W.R.
Lake Andes
IND. RES.
Wagner
Tyndall
Lewis & Clark Lake
MISSOURI NATIONAL RECREATIONAL RIVER
Yankton
De Smet
Huron
Sand Creek
Volga
Brookings
FLANDREAU IND. RES.
Madison
Flandreau
Mitchell
Salem
Alexandria
Sioux Falls
Parker
Lennox
Freeman
Beresford
Vermillion
Elk Point
N. Sioux City
Canton
Clear Lake
Watertown
Lake Poinsett
Big Sioux
James
Missouri
Moreau
Lake Oahe
Okobojo Creek
Foster Creek
Grand

184

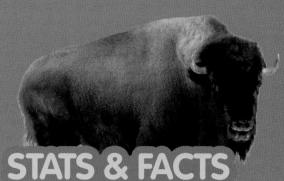

STATS & FACTS

STATEHOOD: November 2, 1889; 40th state

CAPITAL: Pierre

TOTAL AREA: 77,117 sq mi; 199,731 sq km

LAND AREA: 75,885 sq mi; 196,540 sq km

POPULATION: 853,175

POPULATION DENSITY: 11 people per sq mi

MAJOR RACIAL/ETHNIC GROUPS: 85.9% white, 8.8% Native American, 1.3% African American, 0.9% Asian, Hispanic (any race) 2.7%

INDUSTRY: food processing, electronics manufacturing, mining, tourism, services

AGRICULTURE: wheat, cattle, soybeans, corn, hogs, sunflower, sorghum grain, flaxseed, dry edible beans, hay, barley, oats

HISTORY: **Mount Rushmore** is named after New York City attorney Charles Rushmore, who traveled out West to check out the legal title to properties in the area.

PEOPLE/CULTURE: South Dakota is home to the Dakota, Lakota, and Nakota tribes, which together make up the **Sioux Nation.**

NATURAL FORCES: South Dakota is divided into **two main climates:** humid, continental climate in the east and semiarid steppe in the west.

ANIMALS: More than **175 different butterfly species** live in South Dakota.

NATURAL FEATURES: Major erosion of **the Badlands** began half a million years ago, and the land today resembles the surface of the moon.

WISCONSIN

THE BADGER STATE

Badger State, a name that refers to lead miners who lived like burrowing animals in caves during the 1820s, is one state nickname. Another—America's Dairyland—comes from the state's cheesemaking and milk-producing traditions. Wisconsinites would say that while both of these names refer to particular resources, neither captures the state's wide-ranging landscapes and activities.

Jean Nicolet, a Frenchman searching for a Northwest Passage to Asia, stepped ashore from "La Baye" (Green Bay) to meet not Chinese but Winnebago natives in 1634. Jacques Marquette and Louis Joliet found Ojibwa and Menominee peoples as they paddled and portaged their way across the territory in 1673 to reach the Mississippi River. The explorers found waterways everywhere—lakes, streams, and wetlands of all sizes in this region the Ojibwa called "gathering of the waters," and the French called "Ouisconsin."

Gigantic fingers of continental glaciers formed much of Wisconsin's present landscape, gouging out Lakes Superior and Michigan. As they retreated, the glaciers left rocks in looping mounds called moraines across northern uplands and eastern lowlands. Central wetlands that produce the nation's top cranberry crop were once a glacial lake bed. Ridges blocked the ice's path into southwestern Wisconsin, leaving tall bluffs and steep-sided valleys untouched.

The British took control of all French lands east of the Mississippi in 1763. Green Bay became Wisconsin's first permanent European settlement the next year. The region passed to American control after the Revolutionary War,

STATE FLAG

Below the state motto, "Forward," sits the state animal, the badger. In 1979 "Wisconsin" and its date of statehood were added for easy recognition.

STATE FLOWER
Wood Violet

STATE BIRD
Robin

becoming part of the sprawling Northwest Territory. Native American resistance ended with the Black Hawk War in 1832, and the Wisconsin Territory was formed in 1836. Wisconsin joined the Union in 1848 as the 30th state, with Madison as its capital. German immigrants arrived in great numbers and settled in Milwaukee. The city became a center of German culture, with its meatpacking and beer brewing.

Rural settlers found soils across southern Wisconsin fertile enough to grow wheat and other crops. Loggers cut down immense stands of white pines across the northern half of the state. Wisconsin owes its trademark dairy farming to Swiss settlers. For most of the 20th century, Wisconsin was the country's largest producer of dairy products.

The 20th century also saw industrial Wisconsin reach high gear. Cities large and small built factories, turning out everything from bathroom fixtures to cooking pots. "Machine shop of the world," Milwaukee rumbled with the manufacture of railroad cars, heavy machinery, and then small engines; large numbers of Polish and African-American laborers arrived to fill factory jobs. Wisconsin grew to be one of the world's top papermaking centers as sawmills and pulp mills harnessed hydropower. Wisconsin's water resources also made it a haven for fishers and sport enthusiasts.

Today Wisconsin is facing the decline of manufacturing and family-owned farms as well as an urgent need to protect natural resources. The state works to keep existing factories successful and has sponsored research to expand biotechnology and other new businesses. The state has endeavored to make industrial polluters pay for the cleanup of areas such as Fox River, which is contaminated by chemicals called polychlorinated biphenyls, or PCBs. Farmers are looking to new markets as they grow both profitable and earth-friendly organic crops.

IT'S A FACT:

The Ringling Bros. Barnum and Bailey Circus got its start in Baraboo. The Ringling brothers started traveling with their first circus in 1884, using a rented horse.

A TIME LINE OF THE BADGER STATE

1634

Frenchman **Jean Nicolet,** who was seeking a water route to China, was one of the first Europeans to set foot on Wisconsin soil.

1820s

The **mining of lead** for use in paint and in shot for guns rose sharply, causing miners to pour into southwestern Wisconsin. They were nicknamed "badgers."

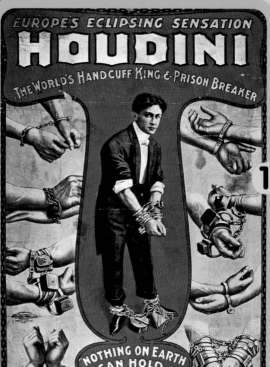

EUROPE'S ECLIPSING SENSATION
HOUDINI
THE WORLD'S HANDCUFF KING & PRISON BREAKER
"NOTHING ON EARTH CAN HOLD HOUDINI A PRISONER"

1882

Harry Houdini, the famous magician who could escape any chain or locked box underwater, arrived in Milwaukee from Hungary at the age of eight, and appeared a year later as "Ehrich, Prince of the Air."

1890–1925

Wisconsin's Progressive Movement, led by **"Fighting Bob" La Follette,** initiated key political, social, and economic reforms.

2012

Wisconsin produced 26 percent of the country's total **cheese** output. Hundreds of kinds, from cheddar to Gruyère, are made in the state

Present

Founded in 1903, **Harley-Davidson Motor Company** is a symbol of the state's tradition as a center of small-engine manufacturing.

ON THE MAP

LOCATION, LOCATION

The nation's highest producer of dairy products in the 20th century, Wisconsin owes its famous dairy techniques to Swiss settlers. On the fertile soil fed by the state's rivers, farmers also grow wheat, potatoes, soybeans, and corn. Its lakes make it a prime vacation spot, too!

OSHKOSH: This home to the world's wildest annual airshow also features a museum for experimental aircraft. Visitors can climb into cockpits of stomach-flipping simulators and build their own airplanes!

LAKE SUPERIOR: The world's largest freshwater lake in surface area has a large bay called Chequamegon. Some kids learn to pronounce it with this joke: What did the boy say when his sister put on her sweater? "She-wom-agun!"

APPLETON: The first hydroelectric plant in the country was built on the Fox River here in 1882.

WISCONSIN DELLS: At Noah's Ark—the world's largest waterpark—prepare to spend days in your swimsuit. It's overflowing with snaking slides, lazy rivers, and churning wave pools.

MADISON: The capital was home to the legendary architect Frank Lloyd Wright. In nearby Middleton the American Girl Company started in 1986 to celebrate girls and their potential, through books, dolls, and other products.

WATERTOWN: In 1856 a German immigrant named Margarethe Schurz opened the first kindergarten in the United States in Watertown. Her concept of teaching young children through play quickly spread across the nation.

MILWAUKEE: The name of this largest city (population 599,164) comes from the Native American word *milliocki*, meaning "gathering place by the water." Its 11-day Summerfest features 11 themed stages and a 23,000-seat amphitheater.

Map labels

LAKE SUPERIOR
APOSTLE ISLANDS NAT. LAKESHORE
Apostle Islands
RED CLIFF I.R.
BAD RIVER INDIAN RES.
Bayfield
Madeline I.
Washburn
Chequamegon Bay
Superior
CHEQUAMEGON-
Ashland
BAD RIVER INDIAN RES.
Hurley
MICHIGAN
Bois Brule
St. Croix
NICOLET
Turtle Flambeau Flowage
Land O' Lakes
Brule
Hayward
L. Chippewa
LAC DU FLAMBEAU IND. RES.
Pine
Popple
CHEQUAMEGON-
Namekagon
Spooner
Park Falls
Eagle River
NICOLET
Niagara
ST. CROIX
LAC COURTE OREILLES IND. RES.
NATIONAL
Menominee
NATIONAL
ST. CROIX INDIAN RES.
Rhinelander
SOKAOGON CHIPPEWA I.R.
Washington Island
GREEN BAY N.W.R.
SCENIC
Rice Lake
Ladysmith
Highest point in Wisconsin
Timms Hill +1,951 ft 595 m
FOREST COUNTY POTAWATOMI I.R.
FOREST
St. Croix Falls
Jump
FOREST
Peshtigo
RIVERWAY
Flambeau
Yellow
Tomahawk
Antigo
Wolf
Marinette
Apple
New Richmond
Red Cedar
Medford
Merrill
MENOMINEE
WOLF N.W.&S.R.
Oconto
Hudson
Chippewa Falls
Lake Wissota
51
INDIAN RES.
Door Peninsula
Sturgeon Bay
River Falls
Eau Claire
Wausau
STOCKBRIDGE I.R.
Shawano
Oconto
Green Bay
Algoma
ST. CROIX N.W.&S.R.
Menomonie
Altoona
Big Eau Pleine Res.
39
Lake Du Bay
Ashwaubenon
ONEIDA INDIAN RES.
De Pere
Mississippi
Marshfield
WISCONSIN
 Pine
New London
Two Rivers
Lake Pepin
Chippewa
Stevens Point
Plover
Waupaca
Appleton
Kaukauna
Manitowoc
Pepin
Black River Falls
Wisconsin Rapids
Wisconsin
Menasha
43
MINNESOTA
WISCONSIN WINNEBAGO I.R.
Neenah
Lake Winnebago
TREMPEALEAU N.W.R.
NECEDAH N.W.R.
Petenwell Lake
Lake Poygan
Oshkosh
Sheboygan
Black
Tomah
Castle Rock Lake
Ripon
Fond du Lac
LAKE MICHIGAN
Onalaska
Sparta
FOX RIVER N.W.R.
Rock
La Crosse
Wisconsin Dells
Waupun
HORICON N.W.R.
UPPER MISSISSIPPI RIVER NATIONAL
Viroqua
Reedsburg
Portage
Beaver Dam
West Bend
Port Washington
Kickapoo
Baraboo
Sun Prairie
Watertown
Menomonee Falls
Richland Center
Lake Wisconsin
Mequon
WILDLIFE AND FISH REFUGE
Prairie du Chien
Spring Green
Middleton
Mendota L.
Monona
Brookfield
Wauwatosa
Dodgeville
Madison
90
94
Milwaukee
Lancaster
Stoughton
Fort Atkinson
Waukesha
West Allis
S. Milwaukee
Platteville
Whitewater
Racine
Janesville
Burlington
Fox
94
Monroe
Rock
Sugar
Beloit
Pleasant Prairie
Kenosha
90
ILLINOIS
IOWA
Pecatonica
Mississippi

0   50   100 miles
0   50   100 kilometers
Albers Conic Equal-Area Projection

STATS & FACTS

STATEHOOD: May 29, 1848; 30th state

CAPITAL: Madison

TOTAL AREA: 65,498 sq mi; 169,639 sq km

LAND AREA: 54,310 sq mi; 140,663 sq km

POPULATION: 5,757,564

POPULATION DENSITY: 106 people per sq mi

MAJOR RACIAL/ETHNIC GROUPS: 86.2% white, 6.3% African American, 2.3% Asian, 1.0% Native American, Hispanic (any race) 5.9%

INDUSTRY: manufacturing, lumber and paper products, food processing, minerals, transportation equipment, metals, machinery

AGRICULTURE: dairy products, corn, cattle/calves, soybeans, potatoes, oats, vegetables, hay, wheat, dry edible beans, oats, barley

NATURAL FEATURES: **Door County** has more than 250 miles (400 km) of shoreline, which is longer than any other county in the United States.

PEOPLE/CULTURE: **Laura Ingalls Wilder,** who wrote the *Little House on the Prairie* books based on her life in the Midwest forests and prairies, was born in Pepin in 1867.

HISTORY: In the 1600s **Madeline Island in Lake Superior** was visited by French traders and Jesuit priests who lived with the native Ojibwa. A log museum features the story of Madeline, the chief's daughter, who married a French fur trader.

NATURAL FORCES: **Ice covers most of the streams** in the state from late November to late March.

ANIMALS: The largest population of **Brown Swiss cows** lives in Wisconsin.

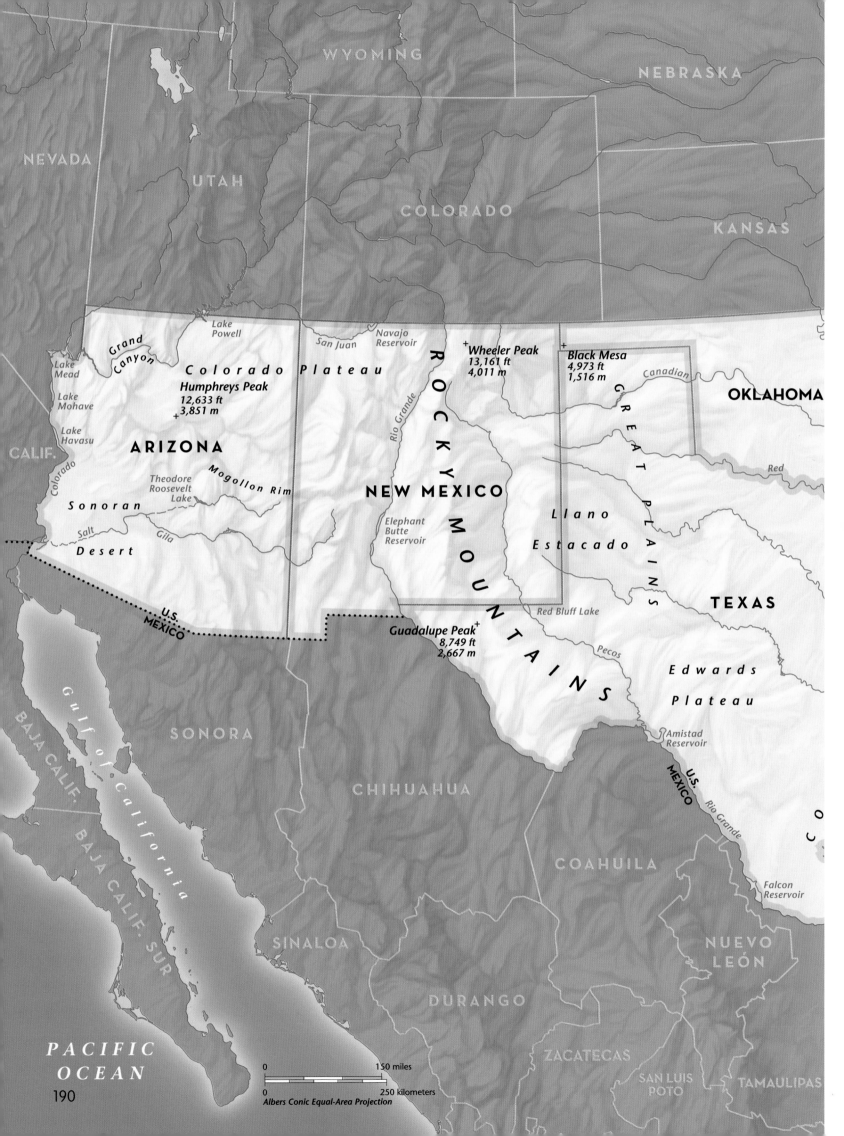

NEVADA

UTAH

WYOMING

COLORADO

NEBRASKA

KANSAS

CALIF.

Grand Canyon

Lake Mead

Lake Mohave

Lake Havasu

Colorado

Salt

Lake Powell

San Juan

Navajo Reservoir

Colorado Plateau

Humphreys Peak
12,633 ft
+ 3,851 m

ARIZONA

Theodore Roosevelt Lake

Mogollon Rim

Gila

Sonoran

Desert

+ Wheeler Peak
13,161 ft
4,011 m

Rio Grande

R O C K Y   M O U N T A I N S

NEW MEXICO

Elephant Butte Reservoir

+ Black Mesa
4,973 ft
1,516 m

Canadian

G R E A T   P L A I N S

OKLAHOMA

Red

Llano

Estacado

Red Bluff Lake

TEXAS

U.S.
MEXICO

Guadalupe Peak +
8,749 ft
2,667 m

Pecos

Edwards

Plateau

Amistad Reservoir

SONORA

CHIHUAHUA

COAHUILA

U.S.
MEXICO

Rio Grande

Falcon Reservoir

NUEVO LEÓN

BAJA CALIF.

Gulf of California

BAJA CALIF. SUR

SINALOA

DURANGO

ZACATECAS

SAN LUIS POTO

TAMAULIPAS

PACIFIC OCEAN

190

0   150 miles
0   250 kilometers
Albers Conic Equal-Area Projection

IOWA

ILLINOIS

INDIANA

OHIO

MISSOURI

KENTUCKY

TENNESSEE

ARKANSAS

GEORGIA

Lake O' The Cherokees

Arkansas

Eufaula Lake

ALABAMA

Lake Texoma

MISSISSIPPI

LA.

Sabine

Trinity

Toledo Bend Reservoir

Sam Rayburn Reservoir

Lake Livingston

Brazos

Colorado

Sabine Lake

Galveston Bay

COASTAL PLAIN

Matagorda Bay

Matagorda I.

Corpus Christi Bay

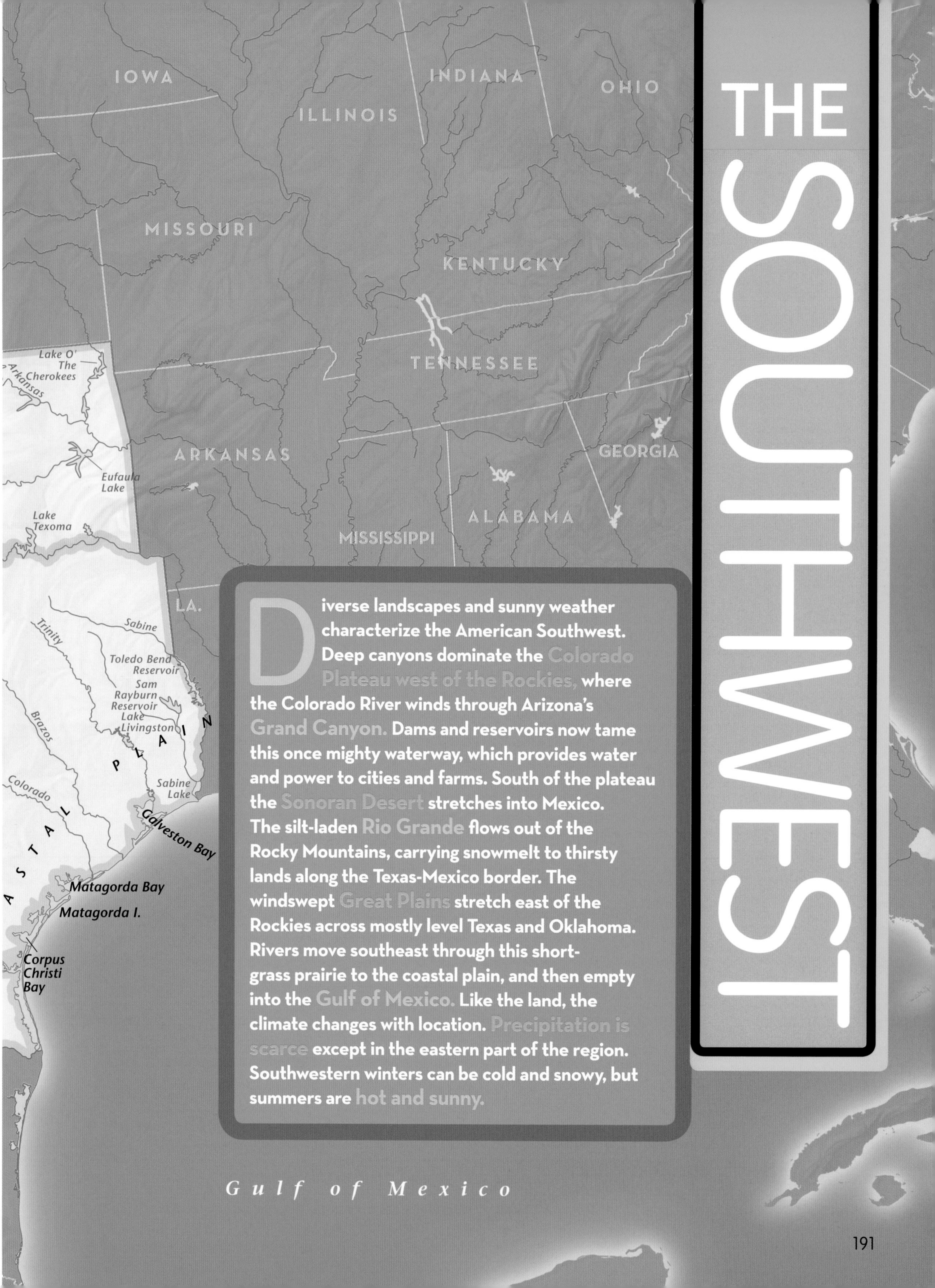

Diverse landscapes and sunny weather characterize the American Southwest. Deep canyons dominate the Colorado Plateau west of the Rockies, where the Colorado River winds through Arizona's Grand Canyon. Dams and reservoirs now tame this once mighty waterway, which provides water and power to cities and farms. South of the plateau the Sonoran Desert stretches into Mexico. The silt-laden Rio Grande flows out of the Rocky Mountains, carrying snowmelt to thirsty lands along the Texas-Mexico border. The windswept Great Plains stretch east of the Rockies across mostly level Texas and Oklahoma. Rivers move southeast through this short-grass prairie to the coastal plain, and then empty into the Gulf of Mexico. Like the land, the climate changes with location. Precipitation is scarce except in the eastern part of the region. Southwestern winters can be cold and snowy, but summers are hot and sunny.

Gulf of Mexico

THE
SOUTHWEST

ENCHANTED PLACES AND MULTICULTURAL FACES

Long before Christopher Columbus reached the New World, resourceful Indians farmed the landscapes of the Southwest. Near rivers and springs, ancestral Puebloan, Zuni, and Hopi peoples planted fields of corn, beans, squash, and chili peppers. The ancestral Puebloan first built their villages with sunbaked adobe bricks high atop mesas. Later they wedged their homes and granaries within the vertical walls of sheltered canyons. East of the Rocky Mountains, the Comanche and Apache adapted to life on the southern Great Plains by hunting bison and gathering plants.

In 1540 the Spanish conquistador Francisco Vásquez de Coronado rode north from Mexico to claim this "Kingdom of New Mexico." By 1610, just ten years before *Mayflower* pilgrims settled Massachusetts, Spain's cluster of buildings near Santa Fe became America's first capital. During the next century, European guns and diseases overwhelmed the Indians.

In 1821 the Santa Fe Trail broadened American trade and settlement. The next year Stephen F. Austin led the first band of American farmers into the Hill Country of central Texas. By 1824 Mexico had gained control of the Southwest from Spain, but Los Americanos were now firmly established here. In 1835 rebellious Americans revolted against Mexican rule. Ten years later Texas joined the Union. In 1848, after war with Mexico, Arizona and New Mexico became part of the United States.

Oil discoveries in the early 1900s attracted new settlers to Texas and Oklahoma. Around this same time, water and electricity provided by dams built on the Rio Grande and the Colorado River, as well as dozens of smaller water projects, led to the growth of modern cities and huge farming operations.

In recent decades new industries have emerged. The cities of Dallas, Oklahoma City, Phoenix, and Albuquerque are important centers of technology and business. New Mexico is a key player in solar energy and weapons research, while Texas hosts the command post for U.S. astronauts. Since 1914 the Houston Ship Channel has linked the city's oil refineries with the Gulf Coast and the rest of the world. Abundant sunshine and a slower lifestyle attract newcomers. While growth fuels the economy, it depletes groundwater in huge aquifers that lie beneath much of the region.

The Southwest is a fast-growing region with a dynamic modern economy that retains much of its Native American, Hispanic, and Wild West heritage. Each year millions of tourists explore its canyons, mountains, and deserts. These landscapes, combined with the region's unique settlement history, contribute to its reputation as an enchanted and multicultural place.

ARIZONA
NEW MEXICO
OKLAHOMA
TEXAS

"WILDNESS SO GODFUL, COSMIC, PRIMEVAL, BESTOWS
A NEW SENSE OF EARTH'S BEAUTY AND SIZE."
—CONSERVATIONIST AND AUTHOR JOHN MUIR,
FROM *STEEP TRAILS*

ARIZONA

THE GRAND CANYON STATE

ittle spring"—that's the meaning of the Native American term for Arizona. Knowing this, you'd expect water to be a big deal here, and you'd be right. Very little rain falls on much of the state, and most rivers and streams flow for only part of the year. Conserving water is key to Arizona's future success.

Millions of years of tug-of-war between uplift in the Earth's crust and erosion by rivers has created the spectacular scenery of the Colorado Plateau in the north. The mile (1.6-km)-deep Grand Canyon is the plateau's crown jewel, but Monument Valley and the Painted Desert are among its other treasures. Forests of ponderosa pine grow on the Mogollon Rim, a long line of steep cliffs that provide a 2,000-foot (600-m) step-down to the Basin and Range region. Major dams have been built to harness rivers here. To the south and west, ranges are lower and basins are broader—and bone dry. The Sonoran Desert stretches across more than 25,000 square miles (65,000 sq km) of the state into Mexico. Some areas of the desert average 5 to 6 inches (13–15 cm) of rain per year. Summer sun bakes the saguaro and other cacti, with daily summer temperatures averaging above 100°F (38°C).

Native peoples have succeeded in this challenging land for more than 2,500 years. The ancestral Puebloan inhabited cliff dwellings in Canyon de Chelly, and the Hohokam built dams and dug ditches to bring water from the Gila and Salt Rivers to fields of corn, beans, and squash. The Hopi were living in Oraibi when the Navajo and Apache peoples arrived more than 500 years ago. First Spain then Mexico ruled the region, and settlers fought the Indians for control of the land. Arizona became a U.S. territory after the Mexican-American War in 1848. Silver and copper

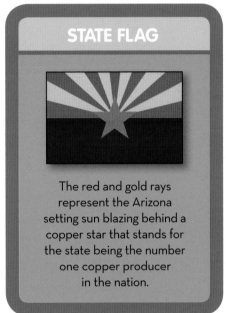

STATE FLAG

The red and gold rays represent the Arizona setting sun blazing behind a copper star that stands for the state being the number one copper producer in the nation.

STATE FLOWER
Saguaro Cactus Flower

STATE BIRD
Cactus Wren

attracted settlers from the East, as did cheap land for sheep and cattle ranching. But settlement didn't really begin to grow until after the fighting with the Apache ended in 1886. By the time statehood was granted in 1912, huge irrigation projects were under way. Farming of cotton and citrus fruits boomed. Year-round water meant opportunities for industries, too.

Arizona is now home to 6.7 million people, with most of this growth occurring after World War II. Before the war the population was mainly rural, but now most people live in and around Phoenix and Tucson. The state's climate and scenic beauties have attracted residents, tourists, and businesses alike. People come just to breathe the state's clean, dry air. The introduction of air-conditioning brought even more people. Cloud-free skies and wide-open spaces attracted the military, especially for air bases and desert warfare research. Related industries, such as aircraft and weapons manufacture, followed. Recently, electronics and other high-tech businesses have thrived.

All this growth brings challenges. For decades, Arizona's five C's—copper, cattle, cotton, citrus, and climate—were the basis for the state's prosperity. Arizona still produces more copper than all other states combined, but its importance has declined. The three agricultural C's are still farmed but face problems with markets and the state's water supply, which must accommodate not just agriculture but the demands of a sizable urban population. Arizona has made great strides in water conservation, but there's more to be done. With more than 50 percent of the state's water supply going to outdoor use, municipalities are encouraging citizens to use less. The city of Tempe offers its residents a financial incentive to convert their front lawn to a low-water-use desert landscape, and Phoenix closely monitors its citizens' water consumption.

IT'S A FACT:
Unlike most of the United States, Arizona doesn't observe daylight saving time.

A TIME LINE OF THE GRAND CANYON STATE

1692–1821

Spanish missions like San Xavier del Bac, rebuilt in 1783, were founded to teach Arizona's Native Americans Christianity.

1886

Arizona's Indian wars ended when a lack of food forced Apache chief **Geronimo** to surrender to the U.S. Army.

1911

The **Theodore Roosevelt Dam,** first of several in the Salt River Project, began bringing water and electricity to fast-growing Phoenix.

1960s

Migration from inside the U.S. began changing the face of the Phoenix metro area. From 2005 to 2010 it was the most popular destination for settlement for people ages 55 to 65.

1968

London Bridge, which once spanned England's River Thames, was purchased for Lake Havasu City. The bridge was shipped to Arizona and reconstructed in the desert.

Present

The **Kitt Peak National Observatory** in southern Arizona offers 20-some telescopes for scientific use, providing diverse observatories for both nighttime astronomy and study of the sun.

ON THE MAP

LOCATION, LOCATION

In this state of cliffs and canyons bordering five other states and Mexico, the breathtaking Grand Canyon, Monument Valley, and Painted Desert were shaped over millions of years by uplift in the Earth's crust and erosion by the Colorado and other rivers.

MONUMENT VALLEY: The flattop buttes and mesas here have been the backdrops for countless Westerns. Today visitors can take trail rides through the stunning scenery.

PAGE: At Antelope Canyon visitors can explore this unique and colorful rock formation—one of the most photographed areas for representing the Southwest.

NAVAJO NATION RESERVATION: Of the 21 American Indian tribes in Arizona, the Navajo Nation is the largest. At more than 27,000 square miles (70,000 sq km), the reservation is the largest in the United States.

LAKE POWELL: The nation's second largest reservoir is named for John Wesley Powell, the first white person to navigate and map the Grand Canyon.

GRAND CANYON: Visitors who stand on a glass-bottomed sidewalk 4,000 feet (1,219 m) above this canyon can see how the Colorado River has been carving this natural wonder of the world for millions of years. Some five million people visit each year.

PHOENIX: With a population of 1,513,367, it's the state's largest city—and also its capital. It was the site of an ancient cliff-dwelling people who occupied the Pueblo Grande between A.D. 700 and A.D. 1400.

TOMBSTONE: Daily reenactments of the Wild West's most famous shootout—featuring the legendary Doc Holliday and the Earp brothers—take place at the O.K. Corral. The bullets are phony!

Albers Conic Equal-Area Projection

STATS & FACTS

STATEHOOD: February 14, 1912; 48th state

CAPITAL: Phoenix

TOTAL AREA: 113,998 sq mi; 295,254 sq km

LAND AREA: 113,635 sq mi; 294,312 sq km

POPULATION: 6,731,484

POPULATION DENSITY: 59 people per sq mi

MAJOR RACIAL/ETHNIC GROUPS: 73.0% white, 4.6% Native American, 4.1% African American, 2.8% Asian, Hispanic (any race) 29.6%

INDUSTRY: electronics, high-tech research and development, aerospace, food processing, transportation, communications, services, printing and publishing, minerals

AGRICULTURE: dairy products, cattle, greenhouse, lettuce, hay, cotton, wheat, vegetables

PEOPLE/CULTURE: **John Wesley Powell,** a Civil War veteran who had lost an arm during the war, was the first white person to successfully navigate the Grand Canyon.

WILDLIFE: Arizona's largest lizard, **the Gila monster,** is the only wild poisonous lizard in the United States.

WEATHER/CLIMATE: During **a heat wave in 1981,** the temperature shot higher than 95°F (35°C) for 115 days.

NATURAL FEATURES: At **Sedona,** massive red sandstone towers and spires called Cathedral Rock, Coffeepot, and Thunder Mountain were once part of an ancient seafloor, later sculpted into formations by wind and rain.

HISTORY: People have been carving pictures called **petroglyphs** into rock cliffs in Verde Valley near Flagstaff for thousands of years.

NEW MEXICO

THE LAND OF ENCHANTMENT

The year was 1610. Ten years before the *Mayflower* landed on Cape Cod, Santa Fe became the capital of New Mexico, a province of New Spain. Nearly four centuries later, the handsome Palace of the Governors still stands in what is now the state capital. Spanish, Mexican, and Native American influences blend across rugged and scenic New Mexico.

The state's landscape was shaped by forces much older—the uplift of ancient seafloors, massive volcanic eruptions, and millions of years of erosion. The northwest corner contains the Colorado Plateau's deeply cut valleys and mesas. Ship Rock, the hardened neck of an eroded volcano, stands there as a lonely reminder of a fiery past. Rolling lands of the Great Plains cover the eastern third of the state, while the rugged spine of the Rockies reaches into central New Mexico. The Rio Grande flows through its middle from Colorado south to Texas and Mexico, and deserts cover much of the southern portion.

Immigrants have long ventured to New Mexico. The first may have been Ice Age hunters 12,000 years ago. Evidence of their presence has been found near the town of Clovis, and tips from their spears are known worldwide as Clovis points. When the Spanish first explored here in the 1500s, they found Zuni, Hopi, and Tewa peoples living in clusters of apartment-like structures. They named these stone and adobe (mud-brick) buildings pueblos after the Spanish word for towns. Some of these centuries-old dwellings are still occupied. The newcomers settled across the region, building missions, setting up ranches, and trading with the native people.

After Mexico gained independence from Spain in 1821, it began trading with the United States. As the Santa Fe Trail brought

STATE FLAG

Around the sun are four sets of four rays: the local Zia people believed that gifts were given by a higher power in groups of four.

STATE FLOWER
Yucca

STATE BIRD
Roadrunner

more and more Americans, conflicts arose that sparked the Mexican-American War. New Mexico became a U.S. territory in 1850, soon after the war ended. More migrants arrived from the East, first by wagon train and then rail. They mined silver and gold, raised cattle and sheep, and irrigated crops in river valleys. Statehood came late, with New Mexico becoming the 47th state in 1912.

New kinds of immigrants arrived in the 20th century. Artists were lured by the state's colorful landscapes and dramatic skies. Historic Taos Pueblo and Sante Fe became world-famous art centers. Another group arrived—quietly—in 1943. Government scientists came to isolated Los Alamos to build a top-secret weapon. Their success was marked by the explosion of the first atomic bomb in the New Mexico desert in July 1945.

Today New Mexico is still home to many specialists in military, nuclear, and space program research. Much high-tech work is concentrated around Albuquerque. Mines produce uranium, potash, and lead. Oil and natural gas wells dot the southeast, northwest, and northeast of the state, and mountain forests grow ponderosa pines for lumber. Cattle ranches can be upward of a hundred square miles (259 sq km) in area. A farming speciality is chili peppers, with New Mexico being second only to California in production. Tourists in increasing numbers visit historic sites, enjoy desert vistas, and hike wild landscapes.

New Mexico takes pride in its ethnic diversity. More than 46 percent of its population claims Hispanic heritage, the highest level in the nation, and there are 22 native Indian tribes. But poverty is a problem—especially among native peoples—and an overall population increase has created water-use issues that New Mexico's people must solve if their state is to remain the Land of Enchantment.

IT'S A FACT:
At Four Corners, in the northwest corner of the state, you can stand in four states at once: New Mexico, Arizona, Utah, and Colorado.

A TIME LINE OF THE LAND OF ENCHANTMENT

1610

Santa Fe, the oldest capital city in the nation, has been the seat of government in New Mexico since Spanish territorial days.

1863–68

Thousands of Navajo were rounded up by the U.S. Army and forced to march to a reservation called **Bosque Redondo.**

1945

The first test of a **U.S.-made atomic bomb** was at Trinity Site in the desert near Alamogordo on July 16, 1945.

1947

Many believe that an alien spaceship crashed in Roswell—the U.S. government denies it. Today, the city's **International UFO Museum and Research Center** lets visitors investigate the incident.

2003

Forest fires are a yearly spring-summer threat. In 2003 a task force was created to help prevent damage to high-risk communities.

Present

Spaceport America, owned by the state of New Mexico, houses aerospace facilities. Here, Virgin Galactic prepares to launch tourists on suborbital spaceflights.

ON THE MAP

LOCATION, LOCATION

From painted deserts to snowy peaks to suburban adobe houses built in the spirit of the ancient Pueblo people, New Mexico is truly a Land of Enchantment. Nestled among five other states and Mexico, its landscape features valleys, plains, mesas, and mountains.

ESPANOLA: Some 1,500 ancient Pueblo people carved a mile-long (1.6-km) village into the cliffs at Puye Cliff Dwellings starting in the A.D. 900s.

TAOS PUEBLO: Native Americans have lived in an adobe house here for more than a thousand years, making it the country's oldest continuously inhabited building.

SHIP ROCK: The hardened neck of an eroded volcano rises 1,583 feet (482 m) above the Four Corners high-desert plain of the Navajo Nation. It last erupted 40 million years ago.

LOS ALAMOS: At the Los Alamos National Laboratory, the scientific site where the first atomic bomb was made, visitors can learn about the event at the Bradbury Science Museum.

ALBUQUERQUE: The largest city with 556,495 people, it features a tramway at Sandia Peak where visitors climb 4,000 feet (1,219 m) in just 15 minutes in suspended tramcars for a view of New Mexico's rugged landscape.

WHITE SANDS NATIONAL MONUMENT: The world's largest white gypsum desert has massive, wave-like dunes covering 275 square miles (442 sq km). The dunes and its plants and animals are protected here.

CARLSBAD CAVERNS: In this massive cave system, including the deepest limestone cave in the U.S., hundreds of thousands of Mexican free-tailed bats hang out during the day; at night they leave to search for insects.

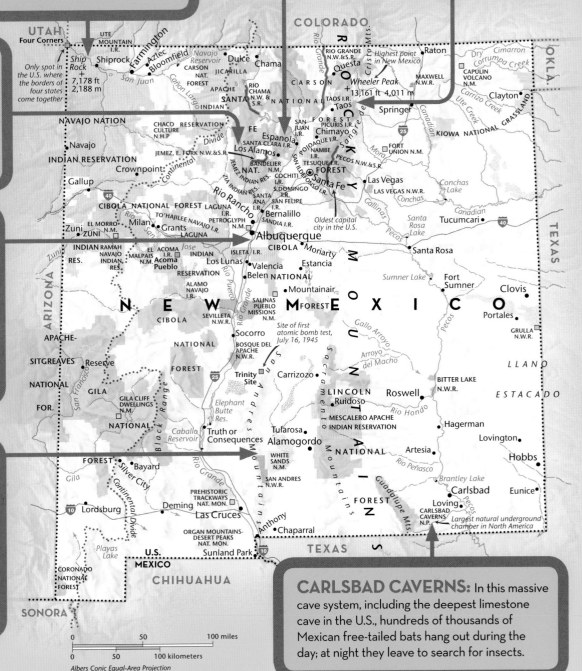

STATS & FACTS

STATEHOOD: January 6, 1912; 47th state

CAPITAL: Santa Fe

TOTAL AREA: 121,590 sq mi; 314,915 sq km

LAND AREA: 121,356 sq mi; 314,309 sq km

POPULATION: 2,085,572

POPULATION DENSITY: 17 people per sq mi

MAJOR RACIAL/ETHNIC GROUPS: 68.4% white, 9.4% Native American, 2.1% African American, 1.4% Asian, Hispanic (any race) 46.3%

INDUSTRY: crude oil production, natural gas production, minerals, government, food processing, chemicals, electronic equipment

AGRICULTURE: dairy products, cattle, hay, peanuts, pecans, cotton, dry edible beans, wheat, sorghum grain, greenhouse

ANIMALS: New Mexico's state bird, **the roadrunner,** can reach ground speeds of 15 miles an hour (24 km/h)!

HISTORY: Built around 1610 and still standing, the **Palace of Governors** in Santa Fe housed governors during the Spanish colonial and Mexican periods, and the American governor until 1909.

NATURAL FORCES: Most of the rains in the summer happen during intense (but brief) **thunderstorms.**

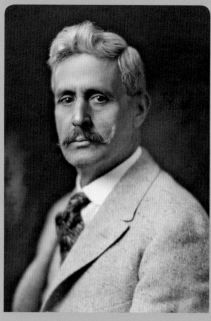

PEOPLE/CULTURE: In 1928 **Octaviano Ambrosio Larrazolo** became the first Latino senator. Today New Mexico has the highest percentage of citizens of Latino and American Indian heritage of any state.

NATURAL FEATURES: The **Big Room,** an underground feature in Carlsbad Caverns National Park, is big enough to hold six football fields.

OKLAHOMA

THE SOONER STATE

They just couldn't wait to get there. Eager 1880s homesteaders who couldn't stand the wait for Oklahoma Territory to open were called "Sooners." Later, as many as 50,000 immigrants made wild "land runs," claiming lands to settle. The most famous land run, on April 22, 1889, saw a patch of prairie turn into a city of 10,000 newcomers in just a few hours. The place? Oklahoma City.

More than half a century earlier, a much different and sadder migration had begun to create the Oklahoma of today. Federal troops pushed Cherokee, Choctaw, Chickasaw, Creek, and Seminole people from their homes in the Southeast to lands west of the Mississippi River. Fifteen thousand Cherokee people endured the most tragic of these journeys during the winter of 1838–39. As many as 4,000 died along the trek, which became known as the Trail of Tears. The journey ended in what became known as Indian Territory, then much larger than present-day Oklahoma. These immigrants joined other groups already there, including the Osage, Pawnee, and Comanche. Not surprisingly, when a Choctaw chief was asked to name the redivided territory in 1866, he chose *okla* (people) and *homa* (red). The state kept the name when it entered the Union in 1907. Today, members of nearly 40 tribes live here, making up more than 8 percent of the total population.

One of the easiest state shapes to recognize, Oklahoma resembles a cooking pan, complete with handle. Landforms range from mountains to flatlands, and habitats from deep woods to sparse grasslands. The Ozark Plateau, shared with Missouri and Arkansas, covers the state's northeast corner. This rugged region is eroded by fast-flowing streams, many of which have been dammed for hydropower, flood control, and recreation. Other highlands include the forested Ouachita Mountains in the southeast and the Wichita Mountains in the southwest. Much of the rest of the pan is filled with a mixture of hills and plains, rolling out to the panhandle. There, the drier High Plains are topped by Black Mesa, Oklahoma's highest point, at 4,973 feet (1,516 m).

Oklahoma's resources lie both below and aboveground. Oil is found all across the varied landscape, with "black gold" pumped even on the state capitol grounds in Oklahoma City. Oil refining is a major industry, as is manufacturing of aviation components, auto parts, and electronics. Many of the state's fastest-growing occupations are related to health care. Top agricultural activities include cattle ranching and wheat growing. Pork, poultry, dairy products, and peanuts are also leading commodities.

In the 1930s Oklahoma farmers fell victim to drought and to farming practices that had stripped the soil of its natural protection. Wind eroded their plowed fields, sending thousands of Okies on the road, some to as far as California. Better care of the fragile soil has allowed much of the farmland to recover, but the wind can still be a problem. Cold fronts clash with warm and humid air each spring, often producing destructive tornadoes. A 2013 EF5 twister that struck west of Oklahoma City was the widest tornado ever recorded: 2.6 miles (4.2 km) wide at its maximum, carving a 16.2-mile (26-km) path across the land.

Oklahoma today has great promise, but problems as well. Average income is among the lowest in the nation, with many Native Americans living in poverty. Farms and ranches are struggling to survive. But with its diversity and a wealth of natural resources, Oklahoma is bound to prosper "sooner" rather than later.

STATE FLAG

Oklahoma's flag—its 14th!—honors its Native American population with an Osage battle shield, an olive branch, and a peace pipe.

STATE FLOWER
Mistletoe

STATE BIRD
Scissor-Tailed Flycatcher

IT'S A FACT:
The first parking meters in the country were installed in Oklahoma City in 1935.

A TIME LINE OF THE SOONER STATE

1830–1842

The forced march of the Cherokee from their homes in the Southeast to Indian Territory became known as the **Trail of Tears.**

1889

When the government **opened former Indian land to settlement,** thousands rushed in to stake their claims. Each settler got 160 acres (65 ha).

1930s

Drought and poor conservation practices **stripped farms of topsoil,** forcing thousands of farmers to abandon their land.

1995

A memorial and museum in Oklahoma City marks the site where antigovernment militants destroyed the **Murrah Federal Building** in 1995, in an act of domestic terrorism.

2013

Eighty-two tornadoes hit Oklahoma, including 15 on just one day: May 20.

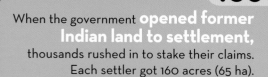

ON THE MAP

LOCATION, LOCATION

Cooking-pan shaped Oklahoma, a state of mountains, woods, and plains, shares borders with Arkansas, Missouri, Kansas, Colorado, New Mexico, and Texas. Its rugged northeastern Ozark Plateau has fast-flowing streams that provide hydropower. Its underground oil, or "black gold," has supplied the nation since the 1800s.

BARTLESVILLE: It's the site of the nation's first commercial oil well in 1897. Today Oklahoma is fifth among states in crude oil production.

TULSA: Once the "oil capital of the world," this city is still the oil center for the state. A gold-painted oil worker looms above Tulsa as a monument to its boomtown days.

FAIRFAX: This is the home of famous ballerina Maria Tallchief, of the Osage tribe. Her talent is honored in a mural in the rotunda of the state capitol.

OKLAHOMA CITY: The state's largest city, with a population of 610,613, is also the capital. The capitol building has a working oil well on its grounds.

CLINTON: Its Oklahoma Route 66 Museum tells about the two-lane "main street of America" that once linked New York and Los Angeles. Some 400 miles (644 km) of the route still cross the state.

TORNADO ALLEY: In this twister-heavy region, scientists carry out critical research in an attempt to predict tornadoes and their destructive paths.

TAHLEQUAH: Six miles (9.5 km) south of this Cherokee Nation tribal capital, the Cherokee Heritage Museum features traditions of its people, who were forced to relocate to Oklahoma from the Southeast in the 1800s.

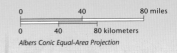

0   40   80 miles
0   40   80 kilometers
Albers Conic Equal-Area Projection

COLORADO

NEW MEXICO

Black Mesa 4,973 ft 1,516 m   *Highest point in Oklahoma*

Kenton   • Boise City   Guymon

H I G H   Beaver

RITA BLANCA NATIONAL GRASSLANDS

P L A I N S

OPTIMA N.W.R.   *Optima Lake*

• Buffalo

Alva

SALT PLAINS N.W.R.

Great Salt Plains Lake

• Woodward

• Shattuck

• Fairview

Enid

KANSAS

Blackwell   Ponca City

Salt Fork

Rock Creek

Fairfax

OSAGE

NATION

Pawhuska   RESERVATION

Skiatook Lake

Sooner Lake   Sand Springs

Perry   *Keystone Lake*

Stillwater

Claremore

Owasso

Catoosa

Pryor

Lake Hudson

MISSOURI

Miami   • Quapaw

Bartlesville   Vinita   Grove

Vinita

Oologah Lake

"O" The Cherokees

• Watonga   Kingfisher

BLACK KETTLE NATIONAL GRASSLAND

WASHITA N.W.R.

WASHITA BATTLEFIELD N.H.S.

• Clinton

Sayre

• Elk City

• Texola

• Hobart

• Mangum

Hollis

Altus

Lake Altus

Salt Fork

Elm Fork Red

North Fork Red

Frederick

Prairie Dog Town Fork

Red

O K L A H O M A

Guthrie

Edmond

El Reno

Weatherford

Yukon

Bethany

Moore

Norman

⊛ Oklahoma City

Tecumseh

Shawnee

Seminole

Wewoka

Cushing

Sapulpa

Bristow

Jenks

Bixby

Tulsa   • Broken Arrow

Wagoner

Muskogee

Ft. Gibson Lake

O Z A R K

Tahlequah

Illinois

P L A T E A U

OZARK PLATEAU N.W.R.

Tenkiller Lake

Sallisaw

SEQUOYAH N.W.R.

DEEP FORK N.W.R.

Deep Fork

Okmulgee

Henryetta

Checotah

Canadian

Holdenville

Little

McAlester

Eufaula Lake

Wilburton

Poteau

Heavener

OUACHITA

Robert S. Kerr Lake

A R K A N S A S

Anadarko

Chickasha

Purcell

Ada

McGee Cr. Lake

Atoka

ARKANSAS

WICHITA MTS. WILDLIFE REFUGE

WICHITA MTS. N.R.A.

Wichita Mts.

Lawton

Walters

• Marlow

Duncan

Waurika Lake

Pauls Valley

Sulphur

CHICKASAW N.R.A.

Coleman

Tishomingo

Arbuckle Mts.

Ouachita Mountains

Kiamichi

Sardis Lake

Little

Antlers

Mountain Fork

NATIONAL

Hugo Lake

Broken Bow Lake

LITTLE RIVER N.W.R.

Broken Bow

FOREST

Idabel

Lone Grove

• Ardmore

Madill

TISHOMINGO N.W.R.

Blue

Durant

Lake Texoma

Muddy Boggy Cr.

Hugo

Red

TEXAS

204

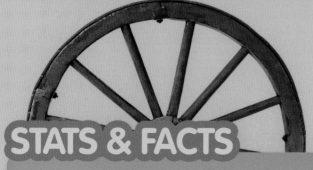

STATS & FACTS

STATEHOOD: November 16, 1907; 46th state

CAPITAL: Oklahoma City

TOTAL AREA: 69,898 sq mi; 181,036 sq km

LAND AREA: 68,667 sq mi; 177,847 sq km

POPULATION: 3,878,051

POPULATION DENSITY 56 people per sq mi

MAJOR RACIAL/ETHNIC GROUPS: 72.2% white, 8.6% Native American, 7.4% African American, 1.7% Asian, Hispanic (any race) 8.9%

INDUSTRY: natural gas production, crude oil production, minerals, food production, machinery, metals, government

AGRICULTURE: cattle, wheat, hogs, broiler chickens, dairy products, hay, eggs, corn, soybeans

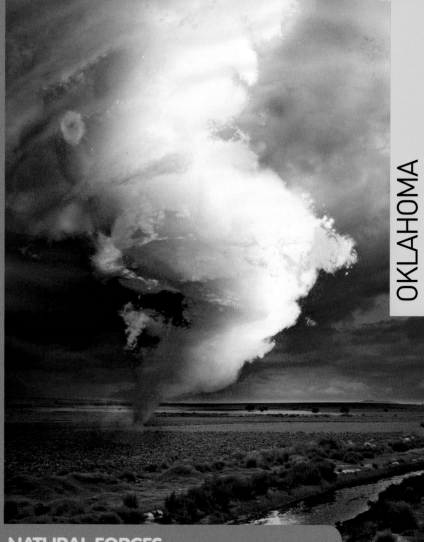

NATURAL FORCES: Oklahoma is in the middle of **Tornado Alley,** a region of the Great Plains where more observable twisters strike than any place else on Earth.

ANIMALS: The first national preserve for bison was founded in 1907; it became the **Wichita Mountains Wildlife Refuge.**

HISTORY: In 1930 an oil gusher called **Wild Mary Sudik** put so much gas in the air that people in Oklahoma City couldn't light matches for fear of causing an explosion.

PEOPLE/CULTURE: Oklahoma City's airport is named after **Will Rogers,** a famous humorist and actor who performed in Wild West shows and on Broadway. He was born in Oologah in 1879.

NATURAL FEATURES: Oklahoma has more **artificial lakes** than any other state, with more than 1 million surface acres (404,686 ha) of water.

TEXAS

THE LONE STAR STATE

Texas is bigger than most countries— and it once was one! In 1836 Texans fought Mexico for independence. The best known battle took place in San Antonio at a mission called the Alamo: A band of volunteers fought for days against Gen. Antonio López de Santa Anna's Mexican Army— and died. But six weeks later, on April 21, other Texans defeated Santa Anna near San Jacinto. Their famous battle cry? "Remember the Alamo!"

When it entered the Union in 1845 as the 28th state, Texas was considered so large that Congress gave it the chance to split into five separate states. It never did divide itself, so it's not surprising that sprawling Texas has an amazing mix of environments. Sunbaked deserts and cold peaks in the west contrast with warm, swampy bayous along the Louisiana border. Ranchers in the Texas Panhandle may endure bitter winter winds on the same day that grapefruit is picked in the Rio Grande Valley 800 miles (1,280 km) to the south.

The Spanish first arrived on Texas's Gulf shores in 1519, and the area became part of New Spain. For nearly two centuries France struggled with Spain for control of the region. Then New Spain won its independence in 1821 and became Mexico. Texas became an independent republic in 1836, and nine years later, it joined the United States.

Within a dozen years, cattle was king in Texas. Cowboys on horseback let their longhorns graze freely across the range. Huge herds were driven to market along the Chisholm Trail all the way to Kansas. Such cattle drives ended as the open range was fenced. Angus, Hereford, and other cattle breeds now join longhorns on Texas ranches large and small. Cattle ranching is still big business, and the rugged individualism of "cowboy culture" lives on.

The panhandle has some of the state's best farmlands, where wheat, sorghum, and soybeans are grown. Year-round warmth allows winter vegetables and citrus fruits to be produced in the far south. Irrigated cotton is grown on the dry plains. Scenic rivers run from the higher lands of west and central Texas southeast to the Gulf of Mexico. Shrimp, crabs, and oysters are caught in Gulf waters.

The discovery of East Texas oil in 1901 brought wealth and propelled the state into the modern era. World War II fueled state manufacturing. San Antonio became a major military hub and biotechnology research center. In recent decades Texas cities have become leaders in banking, electronics, and many high-tech industries.

Today Texas is second only to Alaska in area and second only to California in population (about 27 million). In 2001 another "second" was achieved when George W. Bush became the second Texas Bush to become president. The state ranks first among states in number of counties (254), number of farms and amount of farmland, cattle production, and oil and gas output. Texas ranks high in the influence of Hispanic, mostly Mexican, culture. More than a third of its people are Hispanic; it is projected that Hispanic Texans will form a plurality of the state's population by 2020.

Texans face problems, too. A long border and massive immigration sometimes bring trouble. The U.S. Border Patrol works to keep out illegal migrants and drugs. The Texas economy rides unsteady oil prices. Pollution comes from oil industries and millions of Texas cars and trucks. State population has increased by approximately five million since 2000. But the promise of the Lone Star State shines for newcomers and old hands alike.

STATE FLAG

The single star reflects the state nickname: Lone Star. It's the only state flag that was also the flag of an independent republic.

STATE FLOWER
Bluebonnet

STATE BIRD
Mockingbird

IT'S A FACT:
People in Mission Control at the Johnson Space Center in Houston were the first people to talk to astronauts on the moon.

A TIME LINE OF THE LONE STAR STATE

1718

San Antonio de Valero, later known as **the Alamo,** was one of several missions built throughout Texas by the Spanish.

1836

Sam Houston defeated Santa Anna in the Battle of San Jacinto, winning Texas independence from Mexico.

1901

The discovery of oil at Spindletop near Beaumont led to the building of refineries that support the state's oil and gas industry.

1950

George H. W. Bush, who would become the 41st U.S. president, moved his family, including future president George W. Bush, to Midland, Texas.

1999

The **Texas Bigfoot Research Center** got its start looking for the mysterious Texas Bigfoot of Indian lore—called Woolly Booger by locals. Researchers collect hair samples, footprint casts, and eyewitness reports.

Present

The **Lyndon B. Johnson Space Center,** site of a mission simulator, is the foundation of the space technology industry in Houston.

BIGFOOT CROSSING

ON THE MAP

LOCATION, LOCATION

The enormous Lone Star State, once an independent republic, boasts landscapes ranging from western peaks and deserts to southeastern bayous. Its legendary Rio Grande forms the border between Texas and Mexico. Real-life cowboys—some on horseback—still herd cattle on ranches across open ranges.

FOSSIL RIM WILDLIFE RESEARCH CENTER: An hour southwest of Arlington, visitors can see black rhinos and other endangered African animals roaming in the Texas countryside. Their offspring will be reintroduced to their native environment.

FORT WORTH: Visitors can browse the city's National Cowgirl Museum and Hall of Fame, which celebrates legendary women of the West, or watch a rodeo in the Stockyards historic neighborhood.

IRAAN: Combining the names of Ira and Ann Yates who struck oil on their farm in 1926, it's just one of the colorful town names that pop up across Texas. Others are: Goodnight, Cut and Shoot, Wink, Muleshoe, North Zulch, Birthright, Turkey, and Noodle.

RIO GRANDE: This 1,250-mile (2,011-km) border between Texas and Mexico has been a river of commerce and conflict. Many Mexicans cross it at legal checkpoints each day to work in Texas. Others risk their lives to enter the United States illegally, outside the checkpoints.

PECOS RIVER: The land along this Rio Grande tributary is known for its blend of Latino and cowboy cultures. It's the home of the folklore cowboy character Pecos Bill—no bronco could throw him!

HOUSTON: The state's largest city, with a population of 2,195,914, is home to the Johnson Space Center. Its high-tech visitor facility shows what it's like to live in space.

AUSTIN: Famed for its rebellious spirit and innovation in art, music, and politics, the capital is home to Texas' last true dance hall, the Broken Spoke, and to the University of Texas at Austin.

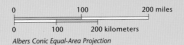

0   100   200 miles
0   100   200 kilometers
Albers Conic Equal-Area Projection

STATS & FACTS

STATEHOOD: December 29, 1845; 28th state

CAPITAL: Austin

TOTAL AREA: 268,581 sq mi; 695,621 sq km

LAND AREA: 261,797 sq mi; 678,051 sq km

POPULATION: 26,956,958

POPULATION DENSITY: 103 people per sq mi

MAJOR RACIAL/ETHNIC GROUPS: 70.4% white, 11.8% African American, 3.8% Asian, 0.7% Native American, Hispanic (any race) 37.6%

INDUSTRY: crude oil production, natural gas production, electronic equipment (computers), chemicals, transportation equipment and automotive, tourism, machinery, metals

AGRICULTURE: cattle, cotton, dairy products, sheep, greenhouse, wheat, hay, pecans, corn

ANIMALS: The official state small mammal, the **nine-banded armadillo,** "little armored one" in Spanish, has a leathery, armorlike shell for protection. When surprised, it jumps straight up—as high as 4 feet (1.2 m)!

HISTORY: Six **national flags** have flown over Texas: Spanish, French, Mexican, Texan, Confederate, and American.

NATURAL FORCES: In 1900 **a massive hurricane and storm surge** killed thousands of people in Galveston.

NATURAL FEATURES: Called PINS by the locals, **Padre Island National Seashore** is the world's longest undeveloped barrier island beach. Its dunes, water, and sky shelter coyotes, sea turtles, ghost crabs, jellyfish, and some 380 species of birds.

PEOPLE/CULTURE: The annual **Fiesta San Antonio** in April honors the heroes of the Alamo and Battle of San Jacinto, notable battles in Texas' fight for independence from Mexico in 1836. Parades, exhibits, shows, and a Miss San Antonio pageant celebrate the heritage, culture, and spirit of this legendary Texas city.

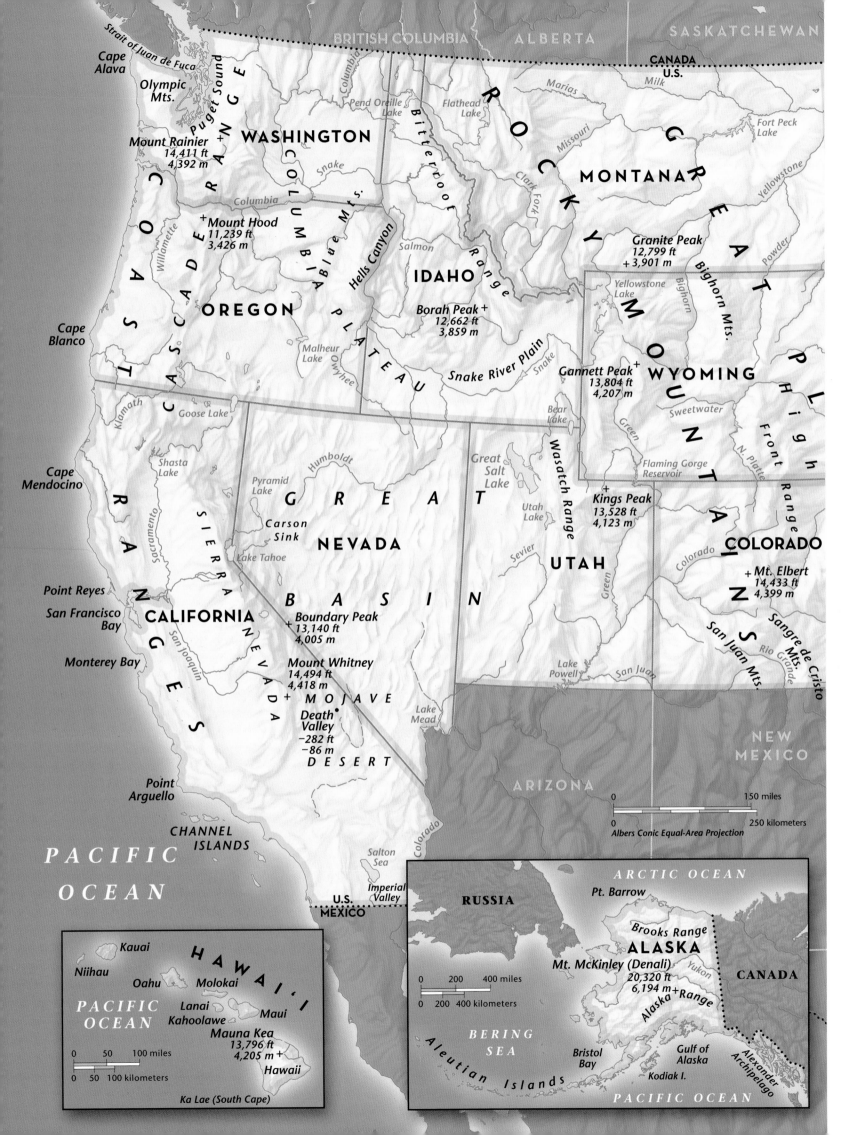

Strait of Juan de Fuca

Cape Alava

Olympic Mts.

BRITISH COLUMBIA   ALBERTA   SASKATCHEWAN

CANADA
U.S.

Columbia

Marias

Milk

Fort Peck Lake

Puget Sound

Pend Oreille Lake

Flathead Lake

WASHINGTON

Mount Rainier
14,411 ft
4,392 m

Snake

Columbia

Bitterroot

Missouri

MONTANA

Yellowstone

R O C K Y

G R E A T

+Mount Hood
11,239 ft
3,426 m

Blue Mts.

Hells Canyon

Salmon

Bitterroot Range

Clark Fork

Granite Peak
12,799 ft
+3,901 m

Powder

OREGON

COLUMBIA PLATEAU

IDAHO

Borah Peak +
12,662 ft
3,859 m

Yellowstone Lake

Bighorn

Bighorn Mts.

M O U N T

Cape Blanco

Willamette

Malheur Lake

Owyhee

Snake River Plain

Snake

Gannett Peak +
13,804 ft
4,207 m

WYOMING

Sweetwater

Front Range

High

P L A

Bear Lake

Green

N. Platte

Goose Lake

Klamath

Shasta Lake

Humboldt

Great Salt Lake

Wasatch Range

Flaming Gorge Reservoir

Cape Mendocino

Sacramento

Pyramid Lake

G R E A T

Utah Lake

+ Kings Peak
13,528 ft
4,123 m

I N S

COLORADO

+ Mt. Elbert
14,433 ft
4,399 m

Carson Sink

NEVADA

Colorado

SIERRA

Lake Tahoe

B A S I N

Sevier

UTAH

Green

Sangre de Cristo Mts.

Point Reyes

San Francisco Bay

CALIFORNIA

NEVADA

Boundary Peak
+ 13,140 ft
4,005 m

San Juan Mts.

Rio Grande

Monterey Bay

R A N G E S

San Joaquin

Mount Whitney
14,494 ft
4,418 m
+

Lake Powell

San Juan

Death Valley
−282 ft
−86 m

M O J A V E

Lake Mead

NEW MEXICO

D E S E R T

Lake Mead

ARIZONA

Point Arguello

CHANNEL ISLANDS

Salton Sea

Colorado

0   150 miles

0   250 kilometers

Albers Conic Equal-Area Projection

Imperial Valley

U.S.
MEXICO

PACIFIC

OCEAN

ARCTIC OCEAN

Pt. Barrow

RUSSIA

Brooks Range

ALASKA

Kauai

Niihau

Oahu

Molokai

H A W A I ' I

PACIFIC OCEAN

Lanai

Kahoolawe

Maui

Mt. McKinley (Denali)
20,320 ft
6,194 m + Range

CANADA

Yukon

Alaska Range

0   200   400 miles

0   200   400 kilometers

Mauna Kea
13,796 ft
4,205 m +

Hawaii

BERING SEA

Bristol Bay

Gulf of Alaska

Alexander Archipelago

0   50   100 miles

0   50   100 kilometers

Ka Lae (South Cape)

Aleutian Islands

Kodiak I.

PACIFIC OCEAN

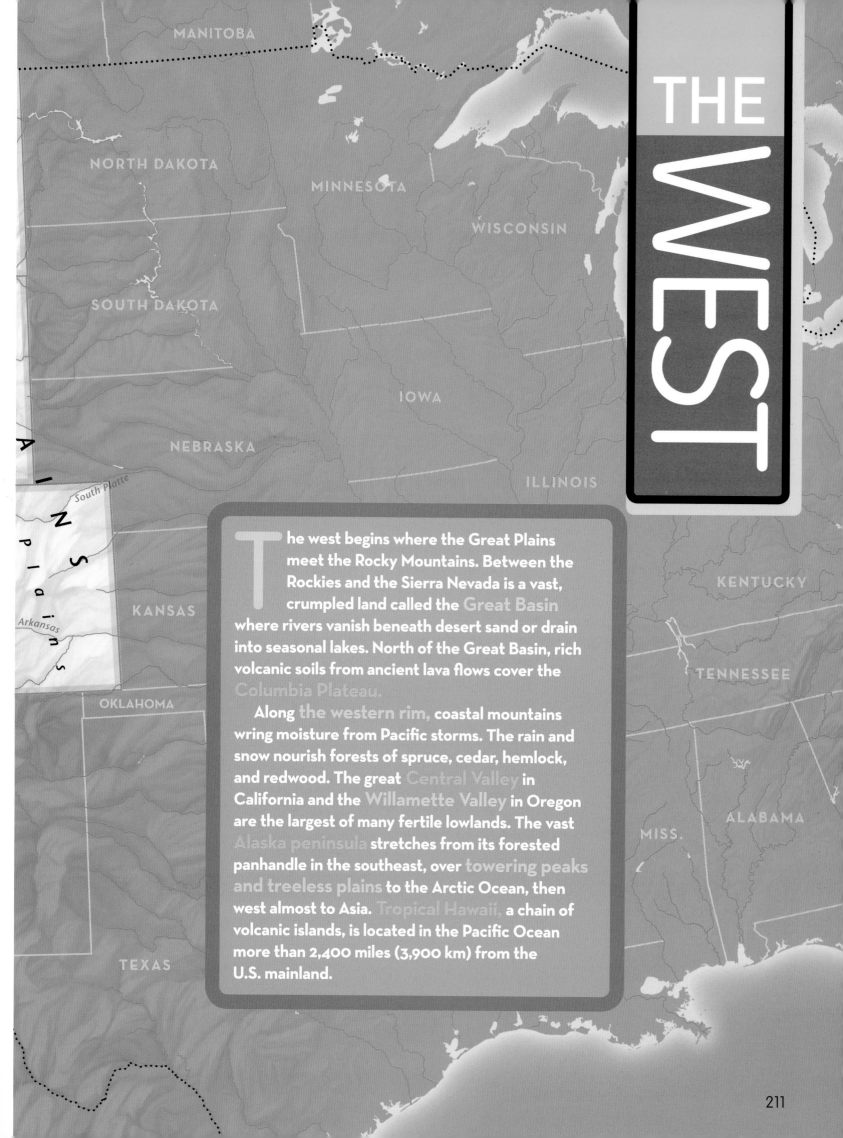

THE WEST

The west begins where the Great Plains meet the Rocky Mountains. Between the Rockies and the Sierra Nevada is a vast, crumpled land called the Great Basin where rivers vanish beneath desert sand or drain into seasonal lakes. North of the Great Basin, rich volcanic soils from ancient lava flows cover the Columbia Plateau.

Along the western rim, coastal mountains wring moisture from Pacific storms. The rain and snow nourish forests of spruce, cedar, hemlock, and redwood. The great Central Valley in California and the Willamette Valley in Oregon are the largest of many fertile lowlands. The vast Alaska peninsula stretches from its forested panhandle in the southeast, over towering peaks and treeless plains to the Arctic Ocean, then west almost to Asia. Tropical Hawaii, a chain of volcanic islands, is located in the Pacific Ocean more than 2,400 miles (3,900 km) from the U.S. mainland.

THE WEST

A RESTLESS LANDSCAPE AND ENDURING FRONTIER

Geographic extremes rule in the West. The nation's highest, lowest, wettest, and driest places are here, along with volcanoes, earthquakes, flash floods, mudslides, and wildfires. For thousands of years the Nez Perce thrived in the Northwest by spearing salmon and collecting berries. Paiute irrigated fields of corn and squash in the Great Basin, and Blackfeet hunted game in the Rockies.

Europeans did not reach this region of the New World until 1542, when Juan Cabrillo sailed up the coast. Vitus Bering navigated the Alaska Panhandle during 1741, and in 1778 Captain James Cook reached Hawaii. The Spanish built a string of missions along the California coast beginning in 1769. But the rest of the region remained largely unsettled until the 1840s, when thousands of people followed the Oregon and California Trails across the West. Other groups, such as Brigham Young's Mormon pioneers, settled Utah's Salt Lake Valley. With the discovery of gold in California in 1848, the world literally rushed in.

By 1869 the transcontinental railroad linked the eastern and western halves of the country. New arrivals from every corner of the globe fanned out across the West to take advantage of America's untapped riches. By the early 1900s—50 years after the California gold rush—Americans had largely displaced Mexicans in California, Native Hawaiians in Hawaii, and Native Americans throughout the West. At the same time, the American conservation movement emerged when the U.S. Congress created the world's first national park: Yellowstone (1872).

Today mining, logging, ranching, and fishing remain important in rural areas. Every western state depends upon farming, especially California, where huge corporate operations employ migrant field workers. However, providing water both to farms and growing cities in this mostly arid land is an enormous challenge that will require creative leadership to solve.

Since the 1920s many new industries have emerged to energize the economies and cultures of this vast region, from entertainment to aerospace. Hawaii tops the nation in macadamia nuts and some tropical fruits. Alaska's North Slope is a leading source of crude oil. For mountain states, ski resorts and vacation/retirement homes now make up an increasingly important part of their economies.

Although the West clings to its frontier image, most people live in rapidly growing and ethnically diverse cities such as Seattle, Los Angeles, and Denver. The continuing challenge will be to provide a decent standard of living for the millions who live here while preserving the scenic beauty and natural resources that led them to the region.

ALASKA
CALIFORNIA
COLORADO
HAWAII
IDAHO
MONTANA
NEVADA
OREGON
UTAH
WASHINGTON
WYOMING

"OUT WHERE THE HAND CLASP'S A LITTLE STRONGER,
OUT WHERE THE SMILE DWELLS A LITTLE LONGER,
THAT'S WHERE THE WEST BEGINS."
—POET AND NEWSPAPER COLUMNIST ARTHUR CHAPMAN,
FROM "OUT WHERE THE WEST BEGINS"

ALASKA

THE LAST FRONTIER

Seward's Icebox." That's what critics called the continent's vast, mostly unexplored northwestern peninsula when William Seward arranged for its purchase from Russia in 1867. But few complained when Joe Juneau discovered gold in 1880. By the end of the century, people were pouring through the Chilkoot Pass en route to the Klondike goldfields.

The newcomers found more than gold. There were huge catches of salmon and impressive timber harvests. Today the state is still a leading source for salmon, crab, halibut, and herring. Although Alaska ranks first in acres of forested land, the state's forest industry has been in decline over the past 20 years.

Alaska's strategic importance to the United States became critical when the Japanese invaded the Aleutian Islands during World War II. The 1,522-mile (2,450-km) Alaska-Canada (Alcan) Highway was completed in just eight months. Originally built as a military supply road, it is still the only land route to Alaska. Population in the territory grew steadily after the war, and the Last Frontier became the 49th state in 1959.

More than twice as large as Texas, the state totals a sixth of the country's entire area. Mountains abound, topped by massive Mount McKinley (Denali), North America's highest peak. Snow-fed rivers rush to the sea while tens of thousands of blue-ice glaciers inch their way across the land. Cold northern treeless plains called tundra contrast with the dense evergreen trees of the Tongass National Forest 1,000 miles (1,600 km) to the milder southeast. Alaska's position on the Arctic Circle brings long and sometimes warm "midnight sun" summer days, while winters can be brutally cold with long hours of darkness.

STATE FLAG

Designed by a 13-year-old seventh grader from an orphanage in Seward, it features the North Star, symbolizing the future of the northernmost state.

STATE FLOWER
Forget-Me-Not

STATE BIRD
Willow Ptarmigan

Powerful forces are at work far below the land. The 1912 volcanic eruption of Mount Katmai was the largest in North America in the last century, and the 1964 earthquake that rocked Anchorage was among the most powerful ever recorded.

The discovery of huge oil reserves on the North Slope in 1968 spurred the state's most recent growth. Workers by the thousands moved from other states to help build an 800-mile (1,280-km)-long pipeline from Prudhoe Bay to the ice-free port of Valdez. Hundreds of thousands of barrels of crude oil move through the pipeline every day, making Alaska a top oil producer.

Thanks to wise legislation, every Alaskan shares in these oil earnings. But costs to the environment can be high. In 1989 one of the biggest oil spills in U.S. history dumped 11 million gallons (41.6 million L) of crude oil in Alaska's Prince William Sound. Coastal ecosystems and fishing towns still feel the effects. A debate over plans to drill for oil in the Arctic National Wildlife Refuge pits those who want to preserve the wilderness against those who want to exploit its energy reserves. The issue is far from being resolved.

Alaskans today are still pioneers in many ways. Their state is a mix of wild and tamed that is unlike any other. Huge moose and brown bears sometimes stroll right into cities. Legislators must travel to the state capital by water or air because no road connects Juneau to the rest of the world. Where schools are few and far between, children attend school over the Internet, and doctors often travel by bush plane to see patients. Alaska's native peoples make up a higher percentage of the population than in any other state, and many follow their traditional lifestyles. Alaskans face amazing opportunities and tough challenges—especially concerning the state's rich natural resources and fragile environments. But it's easy for them to see that Seward got a great bargain in buying this great land.

IT'S A FACT:
Barrow, the northernmost city in the United States, has two months of continuous darkness in winter and three months of continuous sunlight in the summer.

A TIME LINE OF THE LAST FRONTIER

1867

The **agreement to purchase Alaska** from Russia was a bold and controversial move to expand U.S. territory.

1896–1900

Gold rushes, first in Canada's Klondike region and then in Alaska, focused U.S. attention on the territory's vast resources.

1942

The Japanese invasion of the Aleutians in World War II led to the building of a military supply route called the **Alcan Highway.**

1976

Alaska native students won a court case to **open public high schools** in 126 native villages, which had only elementary schools.

1980

Designated a national park in 1917 by President Woodrow Wilson, Mount McKinley's 2 million acres (809,371 ha) were renamed **Denali National Park and Preserve.**

1968–Present

The **trans-Alaska pipeline** can transport more than 2 million barrels of crude oil per day from the North Slope to the Port of Valdez.

ON THE MAP

LOCATION, LOCATION

Alaska, from the Eskimo word *alakshak*, meaning "great lands," is a massive state of northern rivers, glaciers, and tundra, and southern evergreen forests. A third of the land is above the Arctic Circle, so summers boast long days of light while winters are cold and dark.

PRUDHOE BAY: It is America's largest oil field and the starting point for the trans-Alaska pipeline, which moves some 16 billion gallons (60.5 billion L) a year on its 800-mile (1,287-km) journey to Valdez.

DENALI: From the Indian name meaning "great one," it's also called Mount McKinley, after the 25th president. At 20,320 feet (6,194 m) above sea level, it's the highest point in North America.

LITTLE DIOMEDE ISLAND:
Little Diomede Island is only 2.5 miles (4 km) from Russian territory.

HUBBARD GLACIER: One of some 600 named glaciers in Alaska, it flows from the St. Elias Mountains to the sea near Alaska's southeast panhandle. When a chunk of ice breaks off through a process called calving, the noise is thunderous.

WILLOW: Just outside Anchorage, it's the official starting point for the Iditarod dogsled race each March. Called the "Last Great Race on Earth," it runs some 1,000 miles (1,600 km) north to Nome, on the Bering Sea.

ALEUTIANS: The distance from southeast Alaska to the tip of the Aleutian chain roughly equals the distance from Miami to Los Angeles.

ANCHORAGE: Alaska's biggest city has a population of 300,950. It's not uncommon to see a bull moose as tall as 7 feet (2 m) and weighing as much as 1,200 pounds (540 kg) wandering the downtown streets.

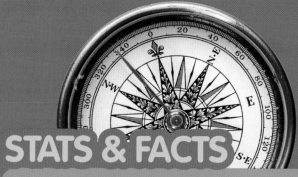

STATS & FACTS

STATEHOOD: January 3, 1959; 49th state

CAPITAL: Juneau

TOTAL AREA: 663,267 sq mi; 1,717,854 sq km

LAND AREA: 571,951 sq mi; 1,481,347 sq km

POPULATION: 736,732

POPULATION DENSITY: 1 person per sq mi

MAJOR RACIAL/ETHNIC GROUPS: 66.7% white, 14.8% Native American, 5.4% Asian, 3.3% African American, Hispanic (any race) 5.5%

INDUSTRY: crude oil production, natural gas production, food processing, lumber, government, minerals

AGRICULTURE: greenhouse, seafood, cattle, dairy products, hay, barley, potatoes

PEOPLE/CULTURE: **Susan Butcher** won the Iditarod sled race three years in a row: 1986, 1987, and 1988.

HISTORY: **William Seward,** who arranged for the purchase of the future Alaska—once called Seward's Folly—was secretary of state under President Abraham Lincoln.

NATURAL FEATURES: Alaska is the only state with land in the Eastern Hemisphere. It also has the **westernmost and northernmost points** in the United States.

NATURAL FORCES: The **most powerful earthquake** ever recorded in North America struck Prince William Sound in 1964. Anchorage, about 75 miles (120 km) northwest of the epicenter, suffered the most property damage.

ANIMALS: **Kodiak bears** only live on the islands of the Kodiak archipelago. They are the largest bears in the world.

CALIFORNIA

THE GOLDEN STATE

"Just add water." Californians have followed this simple recipe for more than a century to grow their state. Snowmelt from Sierra Nevada slopes and Colorado River water make distant deserts produce and temperate croplands produce more. Water sharing also helped propel the state into the modern era by allowing industries to sprout and cities to bloom.

California's fields and factories make it the nation's leading producer of food and manufactured goods. In terms of money earned, milk, almonds (shelled), and grapes are the state's leading farm products. It also produces more than 99 percent of the nation's total of more than a dozen specialty crops, including artichokes, raisins, walnuts, and kiwifruit. California is also home to manufacturing, biotechnology, and information technology. The state continues to be a major center for the entertainment industry, including motion-picture and television production. Sites such as Disneyland and Sea World, as well as large cities including Los Angeles and San Francisco, draw millions of tourists each year.

The Golden State has a stunning array of natural resources and environments. There are abundant minerals, vast forests of gigantic pines and redwoods, and unrivaled fisheries along its nearly 1,000-mile (1,600-km) coast. In the north stand the majestic peaks of the Cascade Range. Deep within Death Valley, the driest and hottest place on the continent, lies Badwater. At 282 feet (86 m) below sea level, it is North America's lowest point. Eighty-plus miles (130 km) west stands 14,494-foot (4,418-m) Mount Whitney in the Sierra Nevada. The Coast Ranges rise along the Pacific Ocean. In between lies the fertile Central Valley, source of most of California's agricultural wealth.

Explorer Juan Rodríguez Cabrillo claimed California for Spain in 1542. But it was not until 1769 that colonization began. Father Junípero Serra established the first of a string of missions. There, priests worked to convert the native people to Christianity. With the missions came presidios (forts) and pueblos (towns). Some of these, such as San Francisco, San Jose, and San Diego, now rank among the nation's largest urban areas. In 1821 control passed to Mexico and then in 1848 to the United States after the Mexican-American War. That same year gold was discovered on the American River. In 1849 thousands of "forty-niners" headed for California to strike it rich. By the time statehood was achieved in 1850, the population had grown to almost 100,000.

Today about one out of eight Americans lives in California, making it by far the most populous state. More than 90 percent of the people live in urban areas. More than one in three Californians is Hispanic, and more than 13 percent are of Asian descent.

Such a diverse land is not without problems. There are frequent earthquakes, forest fires, and other natural disasters. Problems with freeway congestion, air pollution, and water supply recur. The state experiences dry years, spurring growers and water managers to prioritize water supply improvements. Without a reliable water supply, the state's agriculture industry—and the jobs that go with it—will suffer. A rebounding economy and a tax hike approved by state voters have given California a sizable budget surplus, the first in more than a decade. The question of how to allocate that money, much of which will go into paying off the state's debts, will be debated among the state's lawmakers.

STATE FLAG

American settlers revolting against Mexican rule raised the historic Bear Flag at Sonoma on June 14, 1846. Some mistook the first flag's image for a pig.

STATE FLOWER
Golden Poppy

STATE BIRD
California Quail

IT'S A FACT:

California's farms produce nearly half of all U.S.-grown fruits, nuts, and vegetables, and the state produces more milk than the state of Wisconsin.

A TIME LINE OF THE GOLDEN STATE

1769

Mission San Diego de Alcalá was the first of 21 missions built by the Spanish in an effort to convert native people to Christianity.

1848

A **gold rush** brought fortune seekers from around the world and sparked the westward movement across the country.

1906

The **San Francisco earthquake** led to the first government-sponsored study of the cause of earthquakes in the United States.

1923

The **Hollywood sign** was put up across the city's hilltop. It started as a real estate sign, but today it's the symbol for the world-famous entertainment capital.

2003

In a special **recall election,** California voted to remove its governor from office, the first state ever to take such action.

Present

California's **Central Valley** is the nation's agricultural heartland, but persistent drought and the state's arid lands offer challenges for the future.

219

ON THE MAP

LOCATION, LOCATION

Spanning the West Coast from Oregon to Mexico, California is a land of contrasts. From Death Valley at 282 feet (86 m) below sea level, you can travel to 14,494-foot (4,418-m) Mount Whitney in less than a day. Its industries range from agriculture to filmmaking.

SACRAMENTO: The capital city features the historic site Old Sacramento, where visitors experience what this booming city was like during the gold rush and the opening of the transcontinental railroad in the 1800s.

SAN FRANCISCO: This center for artists and poets is famous for its Victorian architecture, cable cars, and the 1.7-mile (2.7-km) Golden Gate Bridge, which spans San Francisco Bay with 746-foot (227-m)-high towers.

COLOMA: Gold was first detected here in 1848, at the sawmill of Capt. John Sutter. The gold rush of 1849 followed, with some 80,000 people pouring into California.

YOSEMITE NATIONAL PARK: First protected in 1864, this national park is known for its High Sierra, glaciers, and ancient giant sequoias. Here, in 1918 Clare Marie Hodges became the first female park ranger in the National Park Service.

SILICON VALLEY: Between Palo Alto and San Jose, this is America's high-tech center. It's the site of hundreds of tech start-ups, and home to the giants Apple, Facebook, and Google.

LOS ANGELES: With its population of 3,884,307, it's the largest city and home to Hollywood, America's movie capital. At Universal Studios amusement park, visitors can ride roller coasters based on blockbuster films.

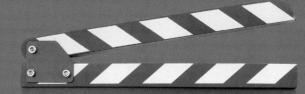

STATS & FACTS

STATEHOOD: September 9, 1850; 31st state

CAPITAL: Sacramento

TOTAL AREA: 163,696 sq mi; 423,970 sq km

LAND AREA: 155,959 sq mi; 403,933 sq km

POPULATION: 38,802,500

POPULATION DENSITY: 249 people per sq mi

MAJOR RACIAL/ETHNIC GROUPS: 57.6% white, 13.0% Asian, 6.2% African American, 1.0% Native American, Hispanic (any race) 37.6%

INDUSTRY: information technology, computers, entertainment, tourism, crude oil production, food processing, machinery

AGRICULTURE: dairy products, grapes, cattle, rice, eggs, vegetables, greenhouse, wheat, sweet potatoes, dry edible beans, fruit

ANIMALS: Every year hundreds of **northern elephant seals** converge on the beaches of Año Nuevo State Reserve, located south of San Francisco, to mate and give birth.

PEOPLE/CULTURE: Comedian and actor **Jack Black** was born in Santa Monica, California, in 1969. His parents were both rocket scientists. Besides acting in many movies, he is the voice for the animated character Kung Fu Panda.

NATURAL FORCES: Due to its sunny climate, California produces more **solar energy** than any other state.

HISTORY: The largest plane of its day, the wooden **Spruce Goose** made only one flight, off Long Beach in 1947. It was built to carry World War II troops, but was finished too late.

NATURAL FEATURES: California has the highest and lowest points in the lower 48 states: Mount Whitney and **Death Valley.**

COLORADO

THE CENTENNIAL STATE

Reach for the sky! Colorado is known around the world for its lofty mountains and its Mile-High City, Denver. The state has more than 50 peaks higher than 14,000 feet (4,200 m), and averages an elevation of 6,800 feet (2,070 m). No other state measures up to that.

Yet Colorado is more than snowcapped peaks. The flatter, drier High Plains cover its eastern third. Here, cattle are ranched where buffalo once roamed. In a broad southern valley that was once the bed of an ancient sea lies Great Sand Dunes National Park and Preserve, with dunes topping 700 feet (210 m). The state's western third is rugged plateau, cut by rivers into deep valleys and flat-topped mesas.

Colorado's snowcapped peaks provide water for wildlife, farms, and cities far from the state. Life-giving rivers flow from high peaks to drier lands around. The state takes its name from its most famous river. Spanish explorers, who saw the rusty-colored waters cutting through red stone canyons far downstream from its source in what is now Rocky Mountain National Park, named it Colorado, meaning "colored red." The Rio Grande runs south and east all the way to the Gulf of Mexico. To the northeast flows the South Platte; to the southeast, the Arkansas.

Along a creek flowing from the Front Range, prospectors found another Colorado treasure in 1858—gold. Thousands of fortune seekers moved in, and the city of Denver was founded. The Cheyenne and Arapaho fought to hold onto their lands, but the settlers won out. By 1870 railroads linked the territory with the rest of the country, bringing more people. Some settlers ranched cattle on the High Plains, while others farmed crops in irrigated fields. Towns sprang up in mountain valleys across the territory with the

STATE FLAG

The flag's colors represent the state's environment: blue for its skies, white for snowcapped mountains, red for the soil, and gold for abundant sunshine.

STATE FLOWER
Rocky Mountain Columbine

STATE BIRD
Lark Bunting

discovery of silver, other minerals, and more gold. In 1876, on the nation's 100th birthday, the Centennial State entered the Union.

Colorado grew rapidly through the 20th century. Oil and natural gas deposits were tapped in both the eastern plains and western plateaus. Coal and iron helped Pueblo become a steel center. Denver, located where the plains meet the mountains, grew into the trade, transportation, and financial center for the entire Rocky Mountain region. Today the Mile-High City enjoys diverse industry that includes aviation and aerospace, software, telecommunications, and tourism, as well as varied manufacturing such as electronics, computer equipment, and pharmaceuticals. As the population has grown, so has the demand for water. Most of the runoff from rain and snow flows into rivers on the western side of the Rockies, but most of the people live and work on the eastern side. To solve this problem, rivers have been dammed and tunnels built to carry water through the mountains for homes, industry, and irrigation.

Colorado's fresh, powdery snow attracts millions of skiers and snowboarders to its slopes each year. Reborn mining towns, such as Aspen and Telluride, boom each winter, and Vail is one of the country's largest ski resorts. Some people even move to Colorado just for the snow!

Colorado's treasures can be the source of problems, too. Industrial pollution and development put the state's wetlands and its nearly 75,000 miles (120,000 km) of streams at risk. Toxic minerals from abandoned mines pollute water supplies. Since 2000 the population has increased from 4.3 million to more than 5.3 million. The heavy volume of traffic and industry creates smog that hangs like a huge brown cloud over the Denver region. Although progress has been made in cleaning up the air, there is pressure to weaken some of the controls.

IT'S A FACT:
The U.S. Mint in Denver produces millions of coins a year. Almost six billion of the coins are in circulation today.

A TIME LINE OF THE CENTENNIAL STATE

1833

Bent's Fort, a prominent landmark and trading center on the Santa Fe Trail, was Colorado's first permanent settlement.

1858

With the discovery of gold in the Front Range north of Pikes Peak, thousands of **fortune seekers headed to Colorado** in covered wagons.

1954

President Dwight D. Eisenhower toured reclamation projects, including **reservoirs and irrigation lines** that carried water to dry farmlands.

1976

Colorado became the only state in history **to turn down the Winter Olympics,** partly because of the cost, pollution, and tourist invasion the games would bring.

Present

The **North American Aerospace Defense Command (NORAD)** keeps watch for air attacks directed at the U.S. or Canada.

ON THE MAP

Albers Conic Equal-Area Projection

LOCATION, LOCATION

The only state with more than 50 peaks topping 14,000 feet (4,200 m), Colorado also boasts plains where herds of buffalo once roamed. The state's name comes from the river that Spanish explorers called "colored red," or Colorado, as it cut through the land's red rock.

DENVER: The capital and largest city has a population of 649,495. Called the Mile-High City for its elevation (the capitol's 13th step is exactly a mile above sea level!) many of its settlers came west for gold mining and the railroad business.

PIKES PEAK: Outside Colorado Springs, you can drive up this 14,115-foot (4,302-m) mountain, one of the most visited in North America. Katharine L. Bates wrote "America the Beautiful" after seeing the scenery from its peak.

ASPEN SKI RESORT: In the Colorado Rockies, millions of snow enthusiasts bring their skis and boards—plus billions of dollars—to the state each year. In 2012 a record 60 million visitors spent $17 billion in the state.

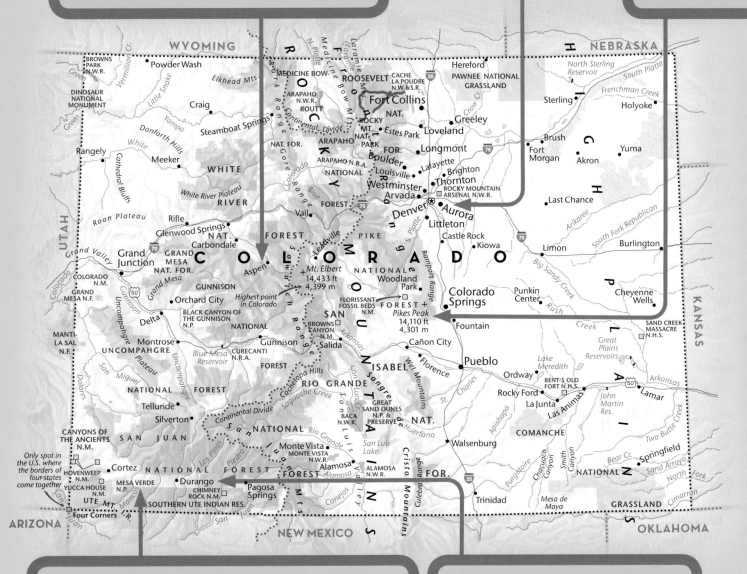

MESA VERDE NATIONAL PARK: The ancestral Puebloan built spectacular villages into the sandstone canyon walls here. One, Cliff Palace, housed 100 to 125 people in its 140-plus rooms. It was mysteriously abandoned more than 700 years ago.

DURANGO: From this Old West town, you can board an 1880s locomotive that travels a steep rail through the San Juan Mountains to the mining town of Silverton.

STATS & FACTS

STATEHOOD: August 1, 1876; 38th state

CAPITAL: Denver

TOTAL AREA: 104,094 sq mi; 269,601 sq km

LAND AREA: 103,718 sq mi; 268,627 sq km

POPULATION: 5,355,866

POPULATION DENSITY: 52 people per sq mi

MAJOR RACIAL/ETHNIC GROUPS: 81.3% white, 4.0% African American, 2.8% Asian, 1.1% Native American, Hispanic (any race) 20.7%

INDUSTRY: natural gas production, crude oil production, food processing, computer equipment, transportation equipment, metals

AGRICULTURE: cattle, dairy products, potatoes, onions, wheat, hay, corn, dry edible beans

ANIMALS: In Rocky Mountain National Park and other mountain wildlands, watch for the zigzagging scamper of the **snowshoe hare.** Named for its big, furry hind feet, the hare is a fast mover. Look for its small, black-tipped tail and long ears. In summer, its coat turns brown and gray, for camouflage; in winter, it's pure white.

NATURAL FEATURES: More than one million years ago an ancient sea occupied the area that today is **Great Sand Dunes National Park and Preserve,** with 700-foot (210-m)-high, wind-shaped sand dunes.

HISTORY: The U.S. gained the territory in what would be western Colorado with the 1848 **Treaty of Guadalupe Hidalgo,** which ended the Mexican-American War.

NATURAL FORCES: The **Colorado Avalanche Information Center** in Boulder informs skiers and snowmobilers of avalanche conditions after big snowstorms. Snow masses can roar down mountains at 30 miles an hour (48 km/h).

PEOPLE/CULTURE:

Margaret Tobin Brown's husband struck it rich by finding gold in Leadville in 1893. But she is hailed as **"Unsinkable Molly"** because she helped women and children leave the *Titanic* ocean liner before it sank in 1912.

HAWAII

THE ALOHA STATE

Mark Twain called them "the loveliest fleet of islands that lies anchored in any ocean." Though they look like green jewels in an ocean-blue setting, these islands were formed by a red-glowing force of nature. As the Pacific plate grinds slowly to the northwest, molten rock pushes up through a "hot spot" to form the islands. The oldest, worn down by millions of years of weather and waves, lie near Russia's Kamchatka Peninsula, far to the northwest of today's main islands. The newest is the "Big Island" of Hawaii where eruptions from Kilauea and gigantic Mauna Loa continue to build new land. Thousands of years from now there will be a new island. Molten material is slowing pushing a seamount called Loihi toward the surface.

The first settlers were Polynesians who paddled double-hulled canoes from islands farther west, perhaps 1,500 years ago. They established thriving communities on each of the eight major islands. Captain James Cook claimed the islands for the British Empire in 1778, naming them the Sandwich Islands for the Earl of Sandwich. But the name didn't last long. By 1810 a native chieftain, King Kamehameha I, had succeeded in unifying the islands, and the entire island group became known as Hawaii.

Change came rapidly. Hawaii became a center of the Pacific whaling industry. Imported Christianity took root among many native Hawaiians; imported diseases took the lives of many more. A special trade agreement allowed American businesses to export sugar tax-free. This led to a boom in sugarcane production. Workers were brought in mostly from Asia to work the plantations. Eventually this resulted in greater ethnic diversity and fewer pure Hawaiians. In 1893 the sugar barons helped overthrow Queen Lili'uokalani, the last monarch. Hawaii became a U.S.

STATE FLAG

In 1845 King Kamehameha III of the independent nation of Hawaii dedicated this flag, which remained when Hawaii became a state.

STATE FLOWER
Hibiscus

STATE BIRD
Hawaiian Goose
(Nene)

territory in 1900. By the following year the naval station at Pearl Harbor was under construction.

The Japanese attack on Pearl Harbor brought the nation into World War II and Hawaii into the modern era. Thousands of people from the U.S. mainland moved in to work for the war effort, and many stayed on after peace was restored. More people immigrated in the postwar years. In 1959 Hawaii entered the Union as the 50th state.

The introduction of jet airline service to Hawaii opened the doors to tourism. By 1970 this industry had replaced agriculture as the state's chief economic activity. These days the islands are a peaceful getaway for vacationers, especially from Japan and the U.S. mainland. Millions each year enjoy the state's scenic delights and tropical climate. Tourists hike in lush Kauai rain forests, view volcanoes on the Big Island and whales off Maui, or shop in the famous Waikiki district of Oahu. Many enjoy surfing or sunning on the beautiful beaches—some of volcanic black sand.

Hawaii has the greatest ethnic diversity of any U.S. state. Fewer than one in four residents are white, and roughly four in ten are of primarily Asian descent. Though few "pure" Hawaiians remain, it is estimated that a majority of people here are part Hawaiian. There is a movement among Hawaiian natives for some form of self-government that ranges from leaving the Union to reclaiming land taken from them when the monarchy was overthrown.

Other issues affect daily lives. A heavy reliance on tourism means that a drop in the number of visitors can cause difficulty for residents who live in a state where the high cost of importing goods makes everyday items expensive. Habitat loss, which places more and more native flora and fauna on the endangered species list, is also linked to this industry. The state has its problems. But it also has what Hawaiians call a "spirit of aloha" that places value on working together for the betterment of their home.

IT'S A FACT:
There are only 13 letters in the Hawaiian alphabet: A, E, I, O, U, H, K, L, M, N, P, W, and a glottal stop—a consonant sound like the one you make in the middle of the word "uh-oh."

A TIME LINE OF THE ALOHA STATE

1782–1810

King Kamehameha gained control of the islands from local chiefs and became the first king of a unified Hawaii.

1848

Profits from sugarcane led U.S. businessmen to pressure the government to make Hawaii part of the U.S.

1941

Japan's attack on the naval base at **Pearl Harbor** on December 7 caused the United States to officially enter World War II.

1983

Kilauea—the world's most active volcano—began its current eruption cycle. Since then, its lava has extended the coastline of the Big Island, adding 500 acres (202 ha).

Present

Resort areas like **Waikiki,** in the shadow of Diamond Head, have made tourism Hawaii's most important industry.

ON THE MAP

LOCATION, LOCATION

Hawaii's location made it a stopping point for early Polynesian navigators, who settled here some 1,500 years before the first white explorers came. Today there are no racial or ethnic majorities because the mix of settlers over time has put everyone in the minority.

OAHU: At Oahu visitors experience what many think is the world's best surfing. Waves as high as 12 feet (4 m) or more usually crash against North Shore beaches during winter, generated by North Pacific storms.

MOUNT WAIALEALE: On the island of Kauai, it's the wettest place in the United States, with 460 inches (1,168 cm) of rainfall per year.

LAHAINA: From this town on Maui's west coast you can watch 40-ton (36,300-kg) humpback whales create incredible splashes.

MOLOKINI ISLAND: On a snorkel journey off this small island between Maui and Kahoolawe, you'll find an undersea world teeming with sea turtles, tropical fish, and maybe a shark or two.

HONOLULU: The capital and largest county has a population of 953,207. At the Honolulu Surfing Museum, which honors the "sport of kings," visitors find folklore and surfboards of every era—even the planks of ancient Hawaiians.

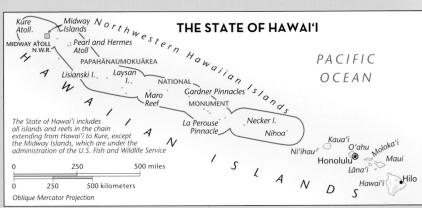

HAWAII: While snorkeling offshore near the Big Island, you can likely see Hawaii's state fish, the *humuhumunukunukuapua'a*, a type of triggerfish, pronounced "who-moo-who-moo-noo-koo-noo-koo-ah-pooah-ah."

HAWAII VOLCANOES NATIONAL PARK: You can witness Kilauea volcano spewing molten lava into the sea, forming new land.

STATS & FACTS

STATEHOOD: August 21, 1959; 50th state

CAPITAL: Honolulu

TOTAL AREA: 10,931 sq mi; 28,311 sq km

LAND AREA: 6,423 sq mi; 16,635 sq km

POPULATION: 1,419,561

POPULATION DENSITY: 221 people per sq mi

MAJOR RACIAL/ETHNIC GROUPS: 38.6% Asian, 24.7% white, 10.0% Hawaiian/Pacific Islander; 1.6% African American, Hispanic (any race) 8.9%

INDUSTRY: tourism, food processing, defense installations

AGRICULTURE: greenhouse, cane for sugar, macadamia nuts, coffee, cattle

HISTORY: Before she was queen, **Queen Lili'uokalani** wrote the second of Hawaii's national anthems: "He Mele Lāhui Hawaii" ("The Song of the Hawaiian Nation"), in use 1866–1876.

ANIMALS: More than 25 percent of **species found on the U.S. endangered species list** are native to Hawaii, sometimes known as the "endangered species capital of the world."

NATURAL FORCES: In 1956 **38 inches (96 cm) of rain fell over 24 hours** at the Kilauea Sugar Co. Plantation at Kauai.

PEOPLE/ CULTURE: President Barack Obama played basketball in high school at the Punahou School. In 1979, when he was a senior, his team won the state championship.

NATURAL FEATURES: Papahanaumokuakea National Marine Monument is larger than all the U.S. national parks combined. Its waters feature 7,000 sea creatures, ancient volcanoes, and **miles of coral reef** hiding lost shipwrecks.

IDAHO

THE GEM STATE

Gem of the Mountains, another nickname for Idaho, fits the state in several ways. Among the rich variety of minerals found here, the deep purple Idaho star garnet is treasured by gem collectors. The state's snow-topped peaks sparkle jewel-like in the sun. And cold, clear streams, like the Clearwater and Salmon Rivers, flow like sparkling necklaces through the state's mountain valleys. The state's official name comes from the *Idaho*, a Columbia River steamship. With the discovery of gold in 1860 along the Clearwater River, the diggings came to be called the Idaho mines. When a state name was needed, Idaho won the prize.

Prospectors traveled up the Columbia and Snake Rivers, staking claims to gold, silver, and other minerals in the valleys north of present-day Boise. Ranchers and others followed the miners, and by 1890 the population reached 90,000. That year, with "leftover" lands from neighboring Wyoming and Montana, Idaho was admitted to the Union as the 43rd state with Boise as its capital.

Today most residents live south and east of Boise on the Snake River Plain. This broad valley, though poor in rainfall, is rich with both hydropower and water for fields thanks to a series of dams built across the river. Fertile volcanic soils combine with mild temperatures to support the state's famous potato crop.

Forested mountains cover most of sparsely populated central Idaho and the northern panhandle. Lewis and Clark crossed the Bitterroot Range in 1805, opening the region to trappers who supplied beaver pelts for markets in the East. Until the 1830s, these mountain men would gather to trade furs, supplies, and tall tales. One popular spot for these rendezvous was near Bear Lake on the Idaho-Utah border.

The natural resources that first brought people to the state still provide Idahoans with work. Mining remains a key industry, with the state supplying a broad array of industrial minerals, including lead, zinc, and copper. Phosphate, used as a fertilizer and even in soft drinks, is mined in the arid far southeast. Processing of the huge potato crop into various frozen styles also provides work for residents. Many are employed in the harvesting and processing of spruce, fir, and pine trees from the state's vast forests. Indeed, national forests cover more than a third of the state, an area exceeded only by the forests in Alaska.

Among the most rugged and remote in the United States, Idaho's wild lands attract tourists who want to "get away from it all." Thrill seekers come to raft roaring rivers, hike rocky trails, and fish icy streams in the Salmon River, Sawtooth, and Bitterroot ranges. Winter sports are popular, too, such as skiing at one of the country's biggest resorts—Sun Valley.

Idaho faces challenges, too. The Boise region has been one of the fastest growing in this state of approximately 1.6 million people. Population growth has generated environmental issues, including air pollution from traffic congestion. Forests are being cut down as demands for housing increase. As mining and logging operations downsize, computer and other high-technology businesses provide new employment opportunities. The rise of dairy farms has led to complaints about waste management. Adventure tourism provides an ever growing economic boost to the state, but increasing visitor numbers may threaten the wilderness experience they seek. It is crystal clear that Idaho's people must seek a balance between the use and the protection of plentiful natural resources for their state to continue as a gem of the mountains.

STATE FLAG

The state seal—the only seal designed by a woman, Emma Edwards Green—shows a woman with scales of justice, to honor women's equality.

STATE FLOWER
Syringa (Mock Orange)

STATE BIRD
Mountain Bluebird

IT'S A FACT:

In 1802 President Thomas Jefferson hosted a dinner where potatoes, a key Idaho product, were served in the "French style," now known as French fries.

A TIME LINE OF THE GEM STATE

1805
With the help of Indian guides, Lewis and Clark crossed the **Bitterroot Range** on their quest to reach the Pacific Ocean.

1860
Gold miners quickly snapped up the **potatoes farmed by Mormon colonists** from Salt Lake City—the first to plant a sizable potato crop.

1877
The Army's arrest of a **Nez Perce** chief led to a war that ended with the Native Americans being forced to move to reservations.

1907
President Theodore Roosevelt established **Caribou National Forest.** Now merged with Targhee National Forest, the Caribou-Targhee covers more than 3 million acres (1,214,057 ha).

1976
The Teton Dam collapse increased inspections of existing dams, canceled some projects, and promoted the use of concrete in future dams.

Present
Idaho's **mountains, lakes, rivers, and wildlife** have made tourism, including snow sports, an important year-round industry.

ON THE MAP

LOCATION, LOCATION

The Gem State's northern mountains hold some 240 minerals, including the rare star garnet—a gem found in abundance only in Idaho and India. Idaho's legendary potatoes are grown in the fertile volcanic soil fed by the Snake River in the southeast.

BOISE: Idaho's capital and biggest city, with a population 214,237, is a mix of urban companies and outdoor recreation. Pronounced boy-see (Not boy-zee), the name comes from *bois*, the French word for trees, from French-Canadian trappers.

HELLS CANYON NATIONAL RECREATION AREA: North America's deepest river gorge has walls that tower a mile (1.6 km) high. You can take a wild boat ride down the Snake River here.

CRATERS OF THE MOON: Part of the training for NASA's Apollo astronauts was to learn the volcanic rocks at Craters of the Moon National Monument and Preserve. The jagged, lunar-like landscape formed thousands of years ago when molten lava bubbled to the surface.

CALDWELL: Drive slowly along Highway 55 through this town and you'll wonder at this unusual crossroad: Chicken Dinner Road. Guess what might have happened here!

BLACKFOOT: Visitors to the Idaho Potato Museum can learn all about Idaho's famous crop and its many uses—from potato salad to French fries.

SHOSHONE ICE CAVES: Residents from the nearby town once chipped ice chunks from this lava tube to cool their summer drinks. Today locals and travelers alike may duck inside to escape the summer heat.

TWIN FALLS: The Snake River plunges 212 feet (64 m) over a series of craggy cliffs at this breathtaking "Niagara of the West."

Albers Conic Equal-Area Projection

STATS & FACTS

STATEHOOD: July 3, 1890; 43rd state

CAPITAL: Boise

TOTAL AREA: 83,570 sq mi; 216,446 sq km

LAND AREA: 82,747 sq mi; 214,314 sq km

POPULATION: 1,634,464

POPULATION DENSITY: 20 people per sq mi

MAJOR RACIAL/ETHNIC GROUPS: 89.1% white, 1.4% Native American, 1.2% Asian, 0.6% African American, Hispanic (any race) 11.2%

INDUSTRY: manufacturing, electronic and computer equipment, food processing, forest products, chemicals, mining, tourism

AGRICULTURE: dairy products, cattle, potatoes, wheat, barley, corn, dry edible beans, hay

ANIMALS: **Wood duck chicks** have to jump as much as 60 feet (18 m) from the tree-hole nest where they hatch to the water below, where their mom waits for them.

NATURAL FEATURES: The **Big Wood River,** sometimes called the Upside Down River, has the curious feature of changing from 100 feet (30 m) wide and 4 feet (1.2 m) deep to 4 feet wide by 100 feet deep just a short distance away.

NATURAL FORCES: Even when the outside temperature climbs to 95°F (35°C), inside **Crystal Caves** it's a constant 32°F (0°C). There's a year-round frozen river and waterfall, too.

PEOPLE/ CULTURE: Olympic gold medal skier **Picabo (peek-a-boo) Street** was born in 1971 in Triumph, Idaho. When she was born she was just called "baby girl." The name Picabo comes from a nearby town.

HISTORY: Famous bank and train robber Butch Cassidy and his partner, the Sundance Kid, made headlines with their gang, **the Wild Bunch,** by robbing a bank in Montpelier in 1896. After that, the exploits of the partners—who were charming and likable—spread across the West.

MONTANA

BIG SKY COUNTRY

Recipe for Montana: Take three parts shortgrass prairie and two parts mountain. Lace with small streams and large rivers. Sprinkle with gold, silver, copper, lots of animals, and a few people. Freeze in winter and warm in summer under a Big Sky.

Fourth largest state, sprawling Montana—a Spanish word meaning "mountainous"—has dozens of ranges in its west and flat to gently rolling prairies in its east. The western Continental Divide winds along Rocky Mountain ridges that form its border with Idaho, splitting waterways along the way. To the west, rivers flow to the Pacific; to the east, the mighty Missouri River runs through grassy plains to the Mississippi then south to the Gulf of Mexico. Montana's climate divides there as well. The west is comparatively wet and mild year-round. Extremes are typical in the east, with very cold winters and hot, dry summers.

In a pattern typical of western settlement, mineral riches brought fortune seekers to Montana. Many cities trace their beginnings to mining in the 1860s. Prospectors found gold in Last Chance Gulch along what is now state-capital Helena's main street. A massive copper deposit called "the richest hill on earth" put Butte on the map. Virginia City, once rich with gold, is now a ghost town. Mineral wealth propelled Montana to territorial status in 1864 and statehood in 1889.

Livestock grazing on open range in eastern Montana was followed by fenced cattle and sheep ranches and wheat farms. Miners were joined by loggers and sawmill workers, who turned spruce, fir, pine, and cedar trees into lumber and other wood products for the rest of the country.

STATE FLAG

MONTANA

The flag was first carried as a banner by Montana volunteers during the Spanish American War in 1898. The Spanish words mean "Gold and Silver."

STATE FLOWER
Bitterroot

STATE BIRD
Western Meadowlark

Gold, silver, and even sapphires are still mined in Montana's mountain west. But these days minerals even more vital for the nation—oil and coal—come from the state's Great Plains. The nonresident travel industry is a top employer in the state and is thriving, as more tourists came to Montana in 2012 than in any previous year in state history. People come to fish and canoe the state's plentiful rivers, and to hike and hunt the state's vast wild lands. Glacier National Park features snowcapped peaks, deep glacier-carved valleys, and spectacular lakes. The scenic Beartooth Highway passes through two of Montana's many national forests on its way to Yellowstone National Park.

There's lots of history to see in Montana, too. Lewis and Clark traveled more miles in Montana than in any other present-day state. They met mostly friendly and helpful native people as they followed the Missouri. On June 25, 1876, near another Montana river—the Little Big Horn—a meeting between whites and Indians was anything but friendly. Crazy Horse led 2,000 Lakota and Cheyenne warriors against George Armstrong Custer and about 215 U.S. Army troops. It was the last major victory by Native Americans in the Indian Wars. Blackfeet, Crow, Northern Cheyenne, Sioux, and other native peoples still live in Montana, making up more than 6 percent of the state's population. Most live on one of seven reservations across the state.

As celebrities and billionaires have bought homes and ranches in Montana, some residents do not welcome the increased land prices and other changes this trend has brought. There is also a struggle over logging and mining decisions that impact the natural environment. Although Montana's population has increased by approximately 90,000 in the past decade alone, great expanses of the state remain largely untouched by people.

IT'S A FACT:
At 200 feet (61 m) long, the Roe River in Montana is the world's shortest river.

A TIME LINE OF BIG SKY COUNTRY

1860s

The arrival of steamboats at **Fort Benton,** a key trading post on the Missouri River, made it the world's most remote inland port.

1863

The rip-roaring Old West town of **Virginia City** was founded. Today it's a ghost town and the most complete original western town in the U.S. Visitors can even pan for gold here! Other ghost towns include Comet, Pony, and Combination.

1876

The Plains Indian victory at the **Battle of the Little Bighorn** was short-lived. Within a year they were forced onto reservations.

1886–87

The **bitter winter of 1886–87,** coupled with too many cattle grazing on too little land, almost destroyed the cattle industry.

1982

Berkeley Pit copper mine closed. Efforts to treat unsafe water seeping into the pit have turned it into an environmental laboratory.

Present

Montana's wide-open spaces appeal to second-home buyers, including media mogul **Ted Turner,** who was the fifth largest landowner in the state in 2013.

ON THE MAP

LOCATION, LOCATION

Named for the Spanish word for "mountainous," Montana is defined by the Rockies: The western Continental Divide sends rivers on its western side to the west and rivers on its eastern side south and east. The climate to the west is wet and mild, while eastern winters are cold and summers hot.

CROW RESERVATION: Montana has a tribally controlled college on each of its Indian reservations. Tribes include the Crow, Northern Cheyenne, and Blackfeet.

CHOTEAU: The fossil of a turkey-size dinosaur—possibly the link between Asian and American horned dinosaurs—was found here.

CHINESE WALL: The Chinese Wall is a natural feature running along the Continental Divide in western Montana. It was created by mountain-building forces that lifted the limestone reef of an ancient seabed 1,000 feet (304 m).

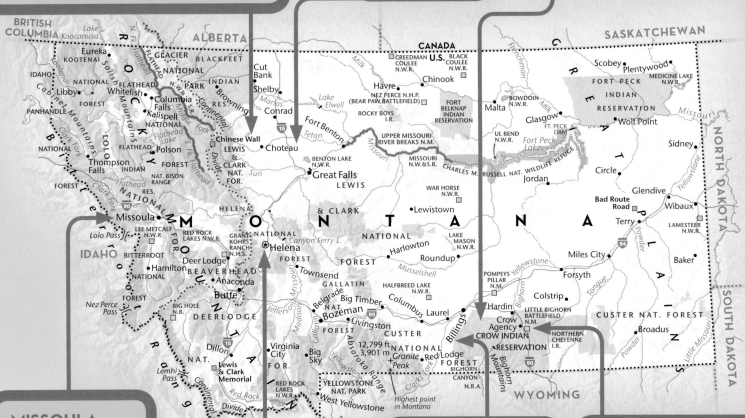

MISSOULA: The country's largest base for training smoke jumpers—firefighters who parachute into the wilderness to fight wildfires—is in Missoula.

HELENA: Atop the capitol stands a statue that arrived mysteriously by train in the 1890s, without records or the sculptor's name. In 2006 the sculptor's granddaughter came forward and confirmed that the statue was named "Montana."

BILLINGS: This largest city has a population of 109,059 and was called the "magic city" because it grew so quickly from the time it was founded in the late 1800s and named for the former Northern Pacific Railroad president Frederick H. Billings.

LITTLE BIGHORN BATTLEFIELD: In 1876, in an area called Greasy Grass by the Native Americans, Lt. Col. George Armstrong Custer made his famous last stand against Plains Indian warriors.

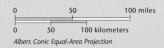

Albers Conic Equal-Area Projection

STATS & FACTS

STATEHOOD: November 8, 1889; 41st state

CAPITAL: Helena

TOTAL AREA: 147,042 sq mi; 380,838 sq km

LAND AREA: 145,552 sq mi; 376,979 sq km

POPULATION: 1,023,579

POPULATION DENSITY: 7 people per sq mi

MAJOR RACIAL/ETHNIC GROUPS: 89.4% white, 6.3% Native American, 0.6% Asian, 0.4% African American, Hispanic (any race) 2.9%

INDUSTRY: mining, forest products, processed foods, tourism, coal production

AGRICULTURE: wheat, cattle, barley, hay, dairy products, dry edible peas, canola, lentils, sheep

NATURAL FEATURES: Montana is the only state with **river systems** that empty into the Hudson Bay, Pacific Ocean, and the Gulf of Mexico. They're playgrounds for fishers across the nation.

NATURAL FORCES: Montana holds the record for **rapid temperature changes.** On January 11, 1980, in Great Falls, the temperature rose from minus 32°F (-36°C) to 15°F (-9°C) in seven minutes.

HISTORY: On September 8, 1883, the last spike on the **Northern Pacific Railroad** was driven at Gold Creek, Montana. The railroad opened up the territory to new people who settled in towns and on farms, leading to economic growth and loss of the frontier.

ANIMALS: Its black ear tufts will give away the **Canada lynx** every time. Spreading south from Canada, this cat thrives in the Montana wilderness. It has a thick coat and uses its big, furry feet like snowshoes.

PEOPLE/ CULTURE: Paleontologist **Jack Horner,** who served as a model for the character Alan Grant in the movie *Jurassic Park,* found fossils of dinosaur nests with eggs and juveniles and concluded that dinosaurs exhibited family behavior.

NEVADA

THE SILVER STATE

Like a big slice of pie, Nevada angles between California, Utah, and Arizona. The Sierra Nevada, the mountains that give the state its name, rise along the long border with California and block rain and snow moving in from the Pacific Ocean. This helps make Nevada, which averages only about 9 inches (23 cm) of precipitation each year, the driest of the 50 states.

Nevada's dry landscape looks like wrinkled paper. Parallel rows of more than 150 north-south mountain ranges rise between at least 90 broad valleys in this Great Basin region. Most rivers flowing into these basins dry up in the summer heat. The Paiute, Shoshone, and Washoe peoples and their ancestors roamed this basin-and-range landscape for thousands of years before Europeans and their descendants came to this remote region. In the 1770s the Spanish blazed a trail across the southeast corner to connect their settlements in New Mexico with their missions in California. After the Mexican-American War in 1848, Nevada and much of the Southwest came under U.S. control. Mormons from Utah followed the Spanish Trail in the 1850s to settle in a mountain-ringed valley named Las Vegas ("the meadows"). Here and in other settlements they irrigated crops and raised livestock. Then came mining riches.

Prospectors struck silver and gold in Virginia City, northeast of Lake Tahoe, in 1859. The so-called Comstock Lode turned out to be one of the richest silver deposits ever found. This mineral wealth helped Nevada become a U.S. territory in 1861 and the 36th state in 1864, as hordes of hopeful settlers arrived. Carson City, a nearby mining camp, was made the capital. Though great wealth came from many mines over the next half century, mining created a "boom or bust" economy.

STATE FLAG

Sagebrush, the state flower, wreathes the motto, "Battle Born." The words reflect the state's entry into the Union in 1864, during the Civil War.

STATE FLOWER
Sagebrush

STATE BIRD
Mountain Bluebird

Prosperity would be replaced by hard times after each mineral deposit was "played out." Nevada was hit hard by the Great Depression in the 1930s. The state needed to find a more stable base for its economy. Making gambling legal was one answer to the up-and-down mining activity. Water was needed to irrigate desert valleys and provide light to homes, hotels, and gaming tables. Federal money and thousands of imported workers built the spectacular 726-foot (221-m)-high Hoover Dam. The project, which spans the Colorado River, supplies water and power to cities and farms across several states and, by forming Lake Mead, provides water recreation in the middle of a desert, too.

Las Vegas, Reno, and Lake Tahoe attract tens of millions of tourists each year. People come to live, too. Beyond the cities are cattle and sheep ranches, farms, and mines. Nevada is still the country's top gold producer and, in 2012, produced more than $11 billion worth of nonfuel mineral commodities—the largest value of any state.

While Nevada now bets on its gaming wealth, future good luck is not a sure thing. Tourists visit less often when the nation's economy is weak or when the cost of transportation is high, creating a big problem in a state where many wages depend on these visitors. Nevada's population has grown, too, by more than 700,000 in the past decade alone. Despite an unemployment rate higher than the national average and a recovering but still unstable housing market, Nevada continues to be one of the nation's fastest-growing states. This growth puts stress on already limited water supplies. Nevada must share Colorado River water with neighbor states as well as with Mexico. There is concern, too, about the long-term effects of past nuclear testing on federal land and the plan to bury nuclear wastes from around the country in Yucca Mountain.

IT'S A FACT:
Las Vegas, Nevada, is the brightest spot on Earth; it is often called the "neon capital of the world" and even has a Neon Museum!

A TIME LINE OF THE SILVER STATE

1843–45

Lt. John C. Frémont, during his exploration of the Great Basin, named **Pyramid Lake** for this rock formation.

1859

The **discovery of silver and gold** led to a rush in settlement, the opening of many mines, and statehood in 1864.

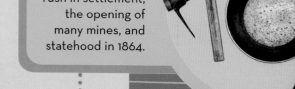

1931

After lawmakers legalized gambling, **casinos** began to attract tourists, laying the foundation for Nevada's largest industry.

2000s

More than 6,000 people a month moved to Nevada in the early 2000s, fueling a **construction boom** that was hard hit during the housing crisis that began in 2007. Nevada had the highest home foreclosure rate of any state.

Present

A decades-old controversy continues about whether **Yucca Mountain** can provide safe, long-term storage for U.S. nuclear waste.

ON THE MAP

LOCATION, LOCATION

Nevada is a region of mountains and desert, with dazzling Lake Tahoe as a jewel at Nevada's elbow border with California. Named for the Sierra Nevada it shares with California, Nevada is the driest state because the mountains block precipitation from the Pacific Ocean.

BLACK ROCK DESERT:
Some 60,000 years ago it was a sparkling lake. Today this salt-and-sand desert is a race course. The world's land speed record of 763 miles an hour (1,228 km/h) was set here by a jet-powered car in 1997.

VIRGINIA CITY:
The Wild West boomtown looks just like it did 150 years ago, when prospectors struck silver nearby.

GREAT BASIN NATIONAL PARK:
It's the nation's darkest stargazing destination. On a ranger-led astronomy tour you can see a glowing patch of the Milky Way—brighter here than anywhere in the United States.

LAKE TAHOE NEVADA STATE PARK:
Visitors can take a boat ride on one of America's largest, deepest, and bluest bodies of water. Ringed by mountains, Lake Tahoe is a favorite for summer water sports and winter skiing on the nearby slopes.

OVERTON:
At nearby Valley of Fire State Park you can see prehistoric graffiti called petroglyphs, chiseled by ancestral Puebloan people into fascinating red-rock formations.

CARSON CITY:
The capital was named for the frontiersman and scout Christopher "Kit" Carson. Mail was once delivered to Carson City and residents of the surrounding valley by a Norwegian mailman on homemade skis.

HOOVER DAM:
Named for President Herbert Hoover, this massive dam spans the Colorado River between Nevada and Arizona. Built in the 1930s to provide water and hydroelectric power, it was one of the largest man-made structures in the world.

LAS VEGAS:
This largest city with a population of 603,488 earned the nickname Sin City for its gambling and partying ways. The main street, "the Strip," features an Egyptian pyramid, battling pirate ships, and other fun sights.

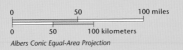

0   50   100 miles

0   50   100 kilometers

Albers Conic Equal-Area Projection

Map Labels

OREGON

IDAHO

CALIFORNIA

UTAH

ARIZONA

DUCK VALLEY INDIAN RES.

SHELDON NATIONAL WILDLIFE REFUGE

FORT McDERMITT

Jackpot

SUMMIT LAKE I.R.

Summit L.

Kings

Quinn

Santa Rosa Range

Desert Valley

N. Fork Owyhee

Bruneau

Marys

Thousand Springs Cr.

Falls Cr.

HUMBOLDT- TOIYABE

Humboldt

Osgood Mts.

Rock Creek

Little Humboldt

Tuscarora Mts.

Independence Mts.

N. Fk. Humboldt

Bishop Creek Res.

Wells

Pequop Range

Toano Range

G R E A T

Black Rock Range

Winnemucca

Black Rock Desert

Smoke Creek Desert

Black Rock Desert

Rye Patch Res.

East Range

Humboldt

Battle Mountain

Carlin

Elko

Spring Creek

SOUTH FORK I.R.

FOREST

West Wendover

Goshute Mts.

Oreana

Reese

Shoshone Range

Cortez Mts.

Pine Creek

Ruby Mts.

RUBY LAKE N.W.R.

Cherry Creek Ra.

GOSHUTE I.R.

PYRAMID LAKE I.R.

Winnemucca Lake

Lovelock

Humboldt Lake

Carson Sink

Stillwater Range

Clan Alpine Mts.

Desatoya Mts.

B A S I N

Eureka

McGill

Schell Creek Range

Pyramid Lake

Sparks

Reno

Fernley

Silver Springs

STILLWATER N.W.R.

Ely

Egan Range

Wilson Creek Range

Virginia City

LAKE TAHOE STATE PARK

Dayton

Carson City

Fallon

Carson

N E V A D A

GREAT BASIN N.P.

Lake Tahoe

WASHOE I.R.

Yerington

WALKER RIVER I.R.

Gabbs Valley

Gabbs

Toiyabe Range

Shoshone Mts.

Pancake Range

Grant Range

Stateline

Gardnerville

H U M B O L D T - T O I Y A B E   N A T I O N A L   F O R E S T

Walker Lake

West Walker

Wassuk Range

Hawthorne

Big Smoky Valley

Toquima Range

Monitor Range

Hot Creek Range

Seaman Range

Pioche

Excelsior Mts.

Columbus Salt Marsh

Tonopah

Boundary Peak 13,143 ft 4,006 m

Goldfield

INYO NAT. FOR.

Highest point in Nevada

Cactus Range

Kawich Range

Rachel

Belted Range

Caliente

Pahute Mesa

Pahranagat Range

PAHRANAGAT N.W.R.

DEATH VALLEY NATIONAL PARK

Beatty

DESERT NATIONAL WILDLIFE RANGE

M O J A V E

Sheep Range

Meadow Valley Wash

Mesquite

ASH MEADOWS N.W.R.

Indian Springs

MOAPA RIVER I.R.

Virgin

Overton

HUMBOLDT- TOIYABE N.F.

TULE SPRINGS FOSSIL BEDS

VALLEY OF FIRE STATE PARK

Pahrump

N.M.

LAKE MEAD

Lake Mead

Las Vegas

N. Las Vegas

Henderson

Boulder City

Hoover Dam

NATIONAL

Colorado

RECREATION

D E S E R T

Lake Mohave

AREA

Laughlin

FORT MOJAVE I.R.

CALIFORNIA

STATS & FACTS

STATEHOOD: October 31, 1864; 36th state

CAPITAL: Carson City

TOTAL AREA: 110,561 sq mi; 286,351 sq km

LAND AREA: 109,826 sq mi; 284,448 sq km

POPULATION: 2,839,099

POPULATION DENSITY: 26 people per sq mi

MAJOR RACIAL/ETHNIC GROUPS: 66.2% white, 8.1% African American, 7.2% Asian, 1.2% Native American, Hispanic (any race) 26.5%

INDUSTRY: tourism and gaming, mining/minerals, aerospace, warehousing, trucking, government

AGRICULTURE: cattle, hay, dairy products, onions, potatoes, wheat

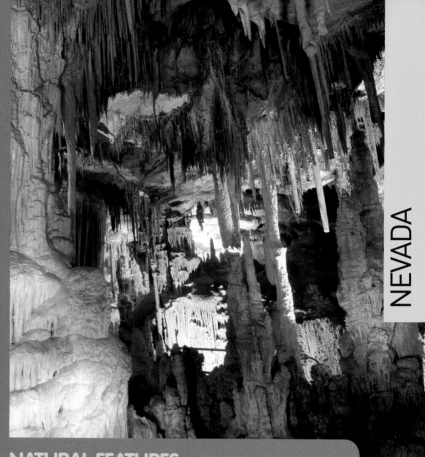

NATURAL FEATURES: **Lehman Caves** (a single cave, name aside), in Great Basin National Park, contains the best examples of shield formations in the country.

ANIMALS: Male **bighorn sheep** in the Nevada mountains compete for females by butting their horns in battles that can last 24 hours.

NATURAL FORCES: Nevada is the **driest state** in the country. It receives on average less than 10 inches (25 cm) of precipitation a year.

WARNING
Restricted Area

WARNING!
NO TRESPASSING

WARNING
MILITARY INSTALLATION

PHOTOGRAPHY OF THIS AREA IS PROHIBITED

HISTORY: About 100 miles (160 km) northwest of Las Vegas is the top secret Air Force base known as **Area 51.** Some people think that alien spacecraft are hidden underground there.

PEOPLE/CULTURE: Nevada's capital is named for explorer **Christopher "Kit" Carson,** who helped map the Oregon Trail through Nevada. He couldn't read or write, but he knew French, English, Spanish, and several Indian languages, and was a favorite guide.

OREGON

THE BEAVER STATE

"If you poke a broomstick in the ground, it will grow!" To an 1840s farm family looking for a new life in the American West, such words about the rich soils of Oregon's Willamette Valley pulled like a magnet. Tens of thousands of hopeful settlers came by wagon train across the Oregon Trail, generating enough population for Oregon to become a state in 1859. Most Oregonians still call this broad and beautiful valley home.

East of the Willamette loom the giant, snow-crowned volcanoes of the Cascade Range—Hood, Jefferson, and the Three Sisters. To the west, the Coast Ranges stand shrouded in fog and covered in mossy forest. A string of picturesque fishing towns, jewel-like state parks, and lonely lighthouses stretch along the rocky coast. Howling winds blast the shore in winter, whipping up huge waves that crash against it, chipping away the land. Rocky sea stacks stand as remnants of a long-ago shoreline.

The mountains split the state into two main climate regions. They force Pacific moisture out on the western slopes but block most precipitation from reaching the Columbia Plateau and Great Basin lands to the east. Here, semiarid lands favor cattle ranching and farming of wheat, hay, sugar beets, and other specialty crops with water from the Snake and other rivers. Oregon's diverse agriculture yields more than 200 different farm products. The state ranks first in the production of a number of products, including Christmas trees, hazelnuts, blackberries, prunes and plums, and several varieties of grass seed. That's right, the green grass on a lawn near you may have had its beginnings on an Oregon seed farm.

Trees—big trees!—also love Oregon's climate. They cover nearly half the state. Forests of towering Douglas fir and western hemlock carpet the slopes of the Coast and Cascade Ranges, while ponderosa pines thrive in the eastern highlands. Logging has been one of Oregon's leading economic activities for decades. Although significant areas of forest have been set aside for conservation and for the protection of wildlife, Oregon is still the country's timber leader.

However, Oregon is more than forests and fields. Where the Willamette River flows into the Columbia, a trading center bloomed into Portland, the City of Roses. Its docks receive imported cars from Asia, and its factories process wood products and computer components. Portland is recognized as a model city for its success in keeping its downtown healthy and active.

Oregon faces challenges in managing its rich natural resources and sources of scenic beauty in a way that will maintain the quality of life that its people long have enjoyed. The Columbia River provides water to run massive hydroelectric plants that generate most of Oregon's electricity. While a boon to industry, the dams have disrupted river flow and contributed to the decline of the state's once rich salmon fishery. Opportunities in computer and other high-tech jobs have encouraged people to emigrate to the "Silicon Forest" from California and other states. There has also been an increase in the number of Hispanic and Asian residents. With the population increasing at a rate of more than 40,000 people each year, there is major concern over the loss of agricultural land and the competition for water. Logging of old-growth forests that have been standing for centuries—long before there ever was an Oregon—stirs controversy. While the struggle to balance economic growth and preserve the environment will be ongoing, a fine Pacific coast position and plentiful natural assets hold great promise for Oregon's future.

STATE FLOWER
Oregon Grape

STATE BIRD
Western Meadowlark

STATE FLAG

The flag's front displays the state seal with the eagle, symbol of the United States. The back features the state animal, the beaver.

STATE OF OREGON
1859

IT'S A FACT:
A giant fungus in Oregon spreads out over an area the size of 20,000 basketball courts.

A TIME LINE OF THE BEAVER STATE

Early 1800s

John McLoughlin and his fur trading company helped newcomers settle in the region. He is known as the "father of Oregon."

1850s

Development boomed with the Donation Land Law of 1850, which gave 320 acres (130 ha) to settlers who farmed land for four years.

Late 1800s

Logging of vast stands of trees began at the end of the century, providing the basis for the state's forest-products industry.

1990

The **northern spotted owl** was first protected after it faced habitat loss as a result of timber harvesting and displacement by barred owls.

Present

Portland's cool, urban vibe and outdoorsy appeal attracts millions of visitors a year.

243

ON THE MAP

LOCATION, LOCATION

Oregon's terrain ranges from deserts, forests, and mountains to a jagged Pacific coastline. Through the fertile Willamette Valley runs the Columbia River, which explorers Lewis and Clark followed to the Pacific Ocean in 1805. To the valley's east towers the volcanic Cascade Range.

PORTLAND:
The largest city with a population of 609,456, Portland is home to the Bonneville Power Administration, which provides some 30 percent of the electricity used in the Pacific Northwest.

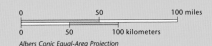

SALEM:
The capital city and cultural center boasts summer art fairs and festivals. Its Gilbert House Children's Museum is a huge interactive museum with a gigantic Erector set, a miniature village, and a woolly mammoth dig site.

COLUMBIA RIVER:
This river feeds the Willamette Valley soil, making it a place rich with vineyards and farmlands.

NEWPORT:
The Oregon Coast Aquarium here features transparent tunnels through underwater exhibits that re-create the shipwreck "graveyard" along Oregon's rocky and treacherous coast.

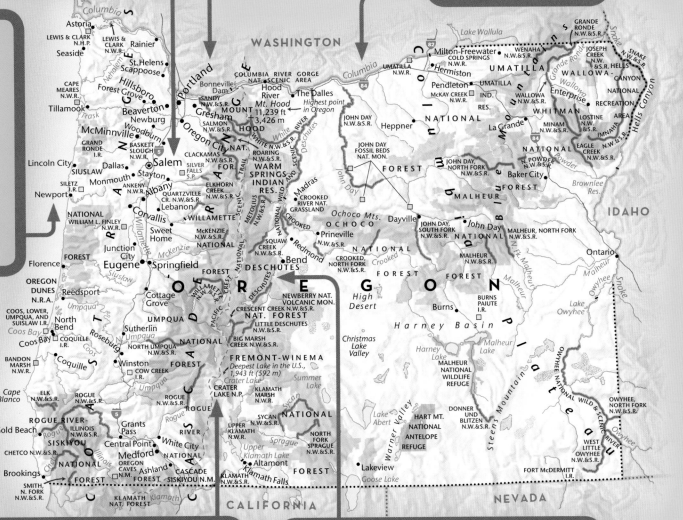

CRATER LAKE NATIONAL PARK:
The nation's deepest lake nestles in the crater of a volcano that erupted and collapsed 8,000 years ago.

DESCHUTES RIVER:
Net fishing for salmon, lamprey eels, and more has been a way of life here for generations of Native Americans. Logging, farming, and pollution have hurt fish populations and traditions.

STATS & FACTS

STATEHOOD: February 14, 1859; 33rd state

CAPITAL: Salem

TOTAL AREA: 98,381 sq mi; 254,805 sq km

LAND AREA: 95,997 sq mi; 248,631 sq km

POPULATION: 3,970,239

POPULATION DENSITY: 41 people per sq mi

MAJOR RACIAL/ETHNIC GROUPS: 83.6% white, 3.7% Asian, 1.8% African American, 1.4% Native American, Hispanic (any race) 11.7%

INDUSTRY: manufacturing, forest products, computers and electronics, printing and publishing, machinery, metals

AGRICULTURE: greenhouse, cattle, dairy products, wheat, canola, vegetables, potatoes

NATURAL FEATURES: Snaking 80 miles (129 km) through the Cascade Range between Oregon and Washington, the **Columbia River Gorge** is a windsurfer's paradise. The mountains create a wind tunnel effect, sending 35-mile-an-hour (56 km/h) winds through the gorge.

ANIMALS: Oregon takes its nickname from the **abundant beavers** that gave rise to a thriving fur trade in the early 1800s.

HISTORY: In order to escape discrimination, between 1870 and 1930 Chinese laborers built **underground tunnels** in Pendleton, Oregon, to live and work in.

NATURAL FORCES: While Oregon's yearly snowfall on the western coast and eastern plateau can range from 0 to 60 inches, in the mountains it's another story: **Crater Lake National Park,** in the Cascade Range, measured 252 inches (640 cm) on the ground in April 1983.

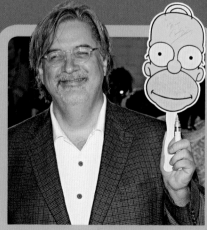

PEOPLE/CULTURE: The creator of *The Simpsons* television show, **Matt Groening,** was born in Portland, Oregon, in 1954.

UTAH

THE BEEHIVE STATE

This is the right place." So said Brigham Young, as he looked out over the Great Salt Lake Valley from the Wasatch Mountains on July 24, 1847. Young had just led a hardy group of Mormon pioneers to find freedom in the west to practice their religion. From the 1847 group of some 1,500 immigrants, Mormon communities grew quickly to 40,000 by 1860. Irrigation helped communities thrive on the thin strip of fertile soil along the Wasatch Front. Today, approximately six in ten Utah residents are Mormons, and the region between Brigham City and Provo is still the most populated.

Utah brims with scenic landforms. The north-south running Wasatch join the Uinta Mountains, which reach east along the Wyoming border. Topped by Kings Peak at 13,528 feet (4,123 m), the Uintas are the only major range in the Rockies that runs east-west. The dry valleys and rugged ranges of the Great Basin stretch west and southwest of the Wasatch. Here, rivers may flow into low areas during spring, but none flow out. Salts carried from the surrounding mountains are left behind as the water evaporates. When mountain man Jim Bridger first tasted the water of the Great Salt Lake in 1824, he thought he had reached the Pacific Ocean! In Utah's southern section stands the Colorado Plateau, a huge raised tableland shared with Colorado, New Mexico, and Arizona. Here, the Colorado and other rivers slice down through layers of colored rocks, forming scenic canyon lands.

For thousands of years the Ute, Paiute, and Shoshone peoples

STATE FLAG

A beehive and sego lilies form the state emblem. In 1847 Brigham Young's Mormons settled in Salt Lake Valley. In 1896 Utah joined the Union.

STATE FLOWER
Sego Lily

STATE BIRD
California Gull

lived in this remote region. But it was the Mormons who settled in great numbers. They dug ditches to channel water from streams to their fields. With hard work and cooperation they turned the desert into farmland. In 1869 the Golden Spike that completed the first transcontinental railroad was driven into the ground near Promontory, north of the Great Salt Lake. Mining of copper and other minerals brought more people and wealth to Utah in the 20th century.

Mormons wanted Utah to enter the Union with the name Deseret, meaning "honeybee," in recognition of all their hard work. Congress thought that sounded too much like "desert," so the state was named Utah after the native Ute people. But its nickname, Beehive State, honors its Mormon settlers.

Nearly two-thirds of the state's land area is controlled by the federal government. Government building of weapons parts and rockets has been important to the economy since World War II. The vast western flatlands make perfect testing grounds for fast cars and missiles. But the government has also helped make tourism a huge industry for the state. Some of the best skiing, rock climbing, mountain biking, hiking, and boating are on government land. Manufacturing, especially of computer and other high-tech equipment, is another key industry.

Mormons sometimes argue with non-Mormons over land use, civil versus religious rights, and other issues. Decades of military weapons testing and unregulated mining damaged some land areas and negatively affected the health of citizens. Struggles continue over further mining and building on Utah's fragile natural areas. Movement along a fault near Salt Lake City could trigger an earthquake, and drought and water shortages are always a concern.

IT'S A FACT:
The Hole N" The Rock house was carved out of massive sandstone rock near Moab. It includes a stone bathtub.

A TIME LINE OF THE BEEHIVE STATE

1776

After this first recorded expedition by Spanish friars, **Bryce Canyon** had many visitors, including Ebenezer Bryce, who settled near the otherworldly rock spires in the 1870s.

1847

Brigham Young, with an advance group of 148 followers, arrived in Salt Lake Valley and established Utah's first Mormon settlement.

1869

The completion of the **first transcontinental railroad** brought settlers and opened new markets for Utah's farm and mining products.

1952

Uranium deposits near Moab provided a basis for weapons development industries that now raise environmental concerns.

2002

Salt Lake City hosted the **2002 Winter Olympics** and its mascots, Coal, Powder, and Copper, paid homage to the state's natural resources.

Present

Desert expanses make excellent testing grounds and have helped make Utah a leader in **defense systems and aerospace technology.**

ON THE MAP

LOCATION, LOCATION

Utah's scenic national parks, such as Arches and Zion, were formed as the Colorado and other rivers sliced through layers of colored rock, sculpting their unique landforms. Utah has long been a sacred land, for groups from the first Native Americans to the Mormon pioneers.

SALT LAKE CITY: The capital and largest city has a population of 191,180. Brigham Young brought his followers from the Church of Jesus Christ of Latter-day Saints, or Mormons, here in the 1800s. Some 14 million Mormons live worldwide.

DINOSAUR NATIONAL MONUMENT: In this park shared by Utah and Colorado (there are no fossils on the Colorado side!), find 1,500 fossils at the Utah Quarry Visitor Center, including parts of *Stegosaurus* and *Diplodocus*. They were covered by river sand 150 million years ago.

THE GREAT SALT LAKE: Three to five times saltier than the ocean and the largest lake west of the Mississippi River, it's the remnant of the ancient inland sea called Lake Bonneville.

GREAT SALT LAKE DESERT: It holds the Bonneville Salt Flats, a 30,000-acre (12,140-ha) remnant of ancient Lake Bonneville. Today they're a hot spot for race drivers who join contests without speed limits.

ZION NATIONAL PARK: You can hike through the deep canyons of swirled sandstone in the state's most visited park. The unique shape of the Zion Narrows makes the passage popular with photographers.

ARCHES NATIONAL PARK: Here, eroding forces over millions of years have carved some 2,000 sandstone bridges, balanced boulders, and more. The largest arch stretches 306 feet (93 m) end to end.

TRAIL OF THE ANCIENTS: Visitors can follow this route, which runs through Monument Valley and Natural Bridges National Monument. It goes backward in time through the spectacular sandstone scenery dotted with ancestral Puebloan sites.

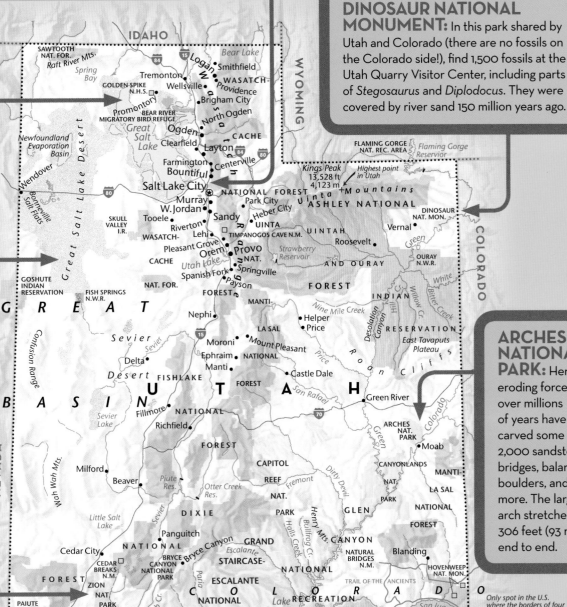

0   30   60 miles
0   30   60 kilometers
Albers Conic Equal-Area Projection

STATS & FACTS

STATEHOOD: January 4, 1896; 45th state

CAPITAL: Salt Lake City

TOTAL AREA: 84,899 sq mi; 219,887 sq km

LAND AREA: 82,144 sq mi; 212,751 sq km

POPULATION: 2,942,902

POPULATION DENSITY: 36 people per sq mi

MAJOR RACIAL/ETHNIC GROUPS: 86.1% white, 2.0% Asian, 1.2% Native American, 1.1% African American, Hispanic (any race) 13.0%

INDUSTRY: natural gas production, mining, aerospace, computer hardware and software, electronic systems, machinery

AGRICULTURE: dairy products, cattle, hay, hogs, wheat, barley, turkeys, sheep, greenhouse, corn

ANIMALS: The endangered **Utah prairie dog** lives in three areas in southwest Utah: Awapa Plateau, Paunsaugunt Plateau, and the west desert. Before the West was settled, some five billion prairie dogs may have thrived on the Great Plains.

PEOPLE/CULTURE: **Philo T. Farnsworth,** who invented the technology used in the television, and Butch Cassidy, the famous western outlaw, were both born in Beaver, Utah.

NATURAL FORCES: **Annual precipitation** varies from less than 5 inches (13 cm) in Utah's arid Great Salt Lake Desert to more than 60 inches (152 cm) in the northern mountain ranges.

HISTORY: During World War II, **paratroopers** from the Tenth Mountain Regiment trained on the slopes of the Alta ski center.

NATURAL FEATURES: **Rainbow Bridge** is the world's largest natural stone bridge. It's 290 feet (88 m) high and 275 feet (84 m) across.

WASHINGTON

THE EVERGREEN STATE

Wet and mild, hip and wild. Washington State is all of these and more. Although the weather, especially in the western third, is known to be foggy and rainy with mild temperatures, it does not dampen the spirit and creativity of the people who live there. The forces of nature that created the state's spectacular landscapes are still at work. Residents enjoy the beauty and deal with the wildness.

Washington forms the northwest corner of the lower 48 states. The Coast Ranges are topped by the towering Olympic Mountains. These slopes are drenched with moisture—an average of 12 to 14 feet (3–4 m) a year. Temperate rain forests of spruce, hemlock, fir, and cedar thrive there. Just east is glacially carved Puget Sound, along which most of the state's residents live. Majestic, snow-clad Mount Rainier, is an active volcano in the nearby Cascade Range. In 1980 Mount St. Helens, in the southern part of the range, literally blew its top—a dramatic reminder that powerful forces are still at work here. These western mountains block most precipitation from moving to the eastern part of the state, where it is dry enough for sagebrush and short grasses to grow.

Zigzagging from northeast to southwest across the state is the massive Columbia. The largest-volume river in the western United States, the Columbia is perhaps the hardest working, too. A huge system of dams, topped by the Grand Coulee, spin turbines to create electricity and form reservoirs to provide water for agriculture.

Sea journeys brought early explorers to the area, and sea otters brought fur traders. But it was Lewis and Clark's overland route to the Pacific and the opening of the Oregon Trail that spurred settlement in the mid-1800s. Native Americans, including the Nez Perce, Yakima, and Spokane, fought to keep their lands but lost. The first railroad reached the territory in the 1880s, and by the end of the decade Washington gained statehood. When gold was discovered in Canada's Yukon Territory in the 1890s, Washington became the shipping gateway to the goldfields. The Evergreen State boomed, growing from 75,000 people in 1889 to 1.25 million by 1920.

Its nickname suits the state, with more than half the land cloaked in forests. Early development centered on logging, along with fishing from coastal waters, cattle and wheat farming in the east, and orchards—especially apple—scattered throughout. Manufacturing "took off" when aircraft builders, aluminum companies, and defense industries set up shop in the Puget Sound area during the two World Wars. The successes of a coffee company and a computer software giant caused Seattle's population to explode in the 1990s.

Over the years, residents have learned lessons about economic growth and state resources. The state's once thriving salmon catch has been greatly reduced, in part through overharvest and dam construction. Concerns about forest preservation have led to less logging, though the forest industry is still huge. Washington's successful aerospace and computer industries face intense global competition. Seattle, regarded as one of the country's most beautiful cities, is jammed with traffic that negatively impacts air quality. The city has taken steps to improve air quality, including an effort to "green" its own fleet of vehicles.

Bright spots in the state's economic forecast include encouraging numbers on job growth in, among other fields, education and health services, as well as a renewed emphasis on preserving resources through wise management to ensure that future generations of Washingtonians will benefit from the state's natural riches.

STATE FLAG

The only state flag that is green is also the only flag with a president's picture, appropriate because it's the only state named after a president.

STATE FLOWER
Coast Rhododendron

STATE BIRD
American Goldfinch

IT'S A FACT:
Billions of apples are handpicked each year from Washington's orchards. (There are no apple-picking machines!)

250

A TIME LINE OF THE EVERGREEN STATE

1775–1792

Spanish explorers were followed by **British and American fur traders and merchants.** At various times, each claimed the region.

1880s

Riots in Seattle between Chinese workers and white newcomers seeking jobs led to the establishment of labor unions.

1940s

The **Boeing Company** began building military aircraft during World War II. Today it is the world's largest aircraft manufacturer.

1980

The cataclysmic volcanic eruption of **Mount St. Helens** caused the largest landslide ever recorded and its ash cloud completely blocked out the sun in Spokane, 250 miles (400 km) northeast.

Present

Amazon, the "Earth's most customer-centric company," was started in Seattle in 1995 by Jeff Bezos to sell books online. Today it's the world's top e-tailer—from electronics to clothes.

ON THE MAP

LOCATION, LOCATION

The northwesternmost of the lower 48 states, Washington is among the wettest and driest: Its Olympic Mountains get an average of 12 to 14 feet (3–4 m) of rain a year; the western Cascade Range blocks moisture from the ocean so that the eastern part of the state has desertlike areas.

SPOKANE: Named for the Spokane Indians, or "Children of the Sun," this is the second largest city in the state. It hosted the 1974 World's Fair in its unique Riverfront Park, a converted rail yard.

CAPE FLATTERY: On the Olympic Peninsula, it's the point farthest northwest in the contiguous United States. Follow the Cape Flattery Trail built by the Makah tribe to see breathtaking views along the Pacific Coast.

OLYMPIC NATIONAL PARK: The stunning landscape here includes towering snowcapped mountains, meadows bursting with wildflowers, waterfalls, lakes, rain forests, and rugged coastline with dashing waves.

SEATTLE: The largest city with some 652,405 people, Seattle overlooks Puget Sound and the state's most populated area. Built in 1851 and named for a friendly Duwamish Indian leader, Sealth, Seattle has grown into a hub for shipping, aircraft building, and technology.

OLYMPIA: In today's capital city Salish Indians once gathered shellfish. In the 1840s a Maine native settled here and laid it out like a New England town. By the 1850s Chinese immigrants had built a Chinatown, too.

MOUNT ST. HELENS NATIONAL VOLCANIC MONUMENT: This still active volcano exploded in 1980, flattening more than 200 square miles (520 sq km) of forest with ash and volcanic debris.

COLUMBIA RIVER VALLEY: Along this river and its tributaries is grown some 60 percent of the nation's total apple crop. Soil, climate, and irrigation also allow growers to produce massive amounts of grapes, cherries, and pears.

STATS & FACTS

STATEHOOD: November 11, 1889; 42nd state

CAPITAL: Olympia

TOTAL AREA: 71,300 sq mi; 184,665 sq km

LAND AREA: 66,544 sq mi; 172,348 sq km

POPULATION: 7,061,530

POPULATION DENSITY: 106 people per sq mi

MAJOR RACIAL/ETHNIC GROUPS: 77.3% white, 7.2% Asian, 3.6% African American, 1.5% Native American, Hispanic (any race) 11.2%

INDUSTRY: aerospace, computer software, electronics, biotechnology, food processing, tourism, lumber and wood products

AGRICULTURE: apples, dairy products, wheat, potatoes, cattle, barley, seafood, vegetables, fruit

NATURAL FEATURES: Washington has more **glaciers** than any other state except Alaska.

HISTORY: Sam Hill built a **replica of England's Stonehenge** on a bluff overlooking the Columbia River to honor the soldiers from Klickitat County who fought and died in World War I.

NATURAL FORCES: The Olympic Peninsula is home to the only **temperate rain forest** in the lower 48 states. Rainfall averages 12–14 feet (3–4 m) a year. Sitka spruce and western hemlock trees abound—some 250 feet (76 m) high and 30 feet (9 m) around.

PEOPLE/CULTURE: **Bill Gates,** a co-founder of the computer company Microsoft, grew up in Seattle. His mother was a schoolteacher and his father an attorney. His company released the first Xbox game system in 2001.

ANIMALS: Making Puget Sound their home, **orcas** (aka killer whales) are the world's largest dolphins, with 6-foot (2-m) dorsal fins.

253

WYOMING

THE EQUALITY STATE

High, wide, and windy—all describe Wyoming. The state is second only to Colorado in mean elevation, averaging 6,700 feet (2,040 m). It stretches 360 miles (580 km) east to west and 280 miles (450 km) north to south. Winds blow hard across rugged mountains and dry basins, making Wyoming the windiest state. In winter, winds can pick up dry snow, creating "ground blizzards" even on clear days. Wyoming could be described as lonely, too. Though ninth largest in area, the state has the lowest population. More people live in the city of Denver, Colorado, than in all of Wyoming!

Wyoming may be short on people, but it is tall on scenery. Mysterious Devils Tower—perhaps more famous for its role in the movie *Close Encounters of the Third Kind* than for being the nation's first national monument—is a reminder of an ancient volcanic past. Three hundred miles (483 km) to the west, heat from Earth's core still reaches the surface. Yellowstone National Park has more geysers than any other place in the world. These and other geothermal features share the park with canyons, waterfalls, forests, and wildlife. In fact, Wyoming's huge variety of wildlife—elk, moose, pronghorn, bison, bears (both black and grizzly), deer, coyotes, mountain lions, and eagles—makes the entire state seem like a big game park.

Just south of Yellowstone are the glacier-carved peaks of the Tetons, the youngest range in the Rockies. The Tetons are still growing—about a foot (30 cm) every four centuries. Near the end of the Wind River Range, ruts from Oregon Trail wagons can still be seen along South Pass. This natural gateway through the Rockies opened the West to settlement beginning in the 1830s.

Oil was discovered in the Wind River Basin in 1833. A year later Fort Laramie, the first real settlement in Wyoming, was founded as a trading post on land where Cheyenne, Arapaho, and other native peoples had long lived. As a military post, it played a key role both in protecting settlers and in the wars and treaties that eventually gave them control of the land.

The Union Pacific Railroad, which reached Wyoming in 1867, brought a boom in settlement and spurred economic activities that are still important to the state. Ranching became a big business. Cattle, at first longhorns from Texas, were fattened on the open range and then shipped by train to the East. Other homesteaders came to ranch sheep and farm crops. Coal deposits were mined along the early rail route. Coal is moved out of the Powder River Basin by rail, with more than 30 states receiving coal from Wyoming.

People came in search of other minerals, too. In 1888 oil was struck near Casper, and the state today is still a top producer. Wyoming also ranks third in natural gas production and second in total energy production. Uranium was found in the 1950s. Wyoming now leads the nation in uranium production.

The opening of Yellowstone National Park in 1872 brought tourists to Wyoming, and this industry is key to Wyoming's future. Visitors come to relive the Wild West, staying at dude ranches and cheering at town rodeos. The U.S. government owns about half the state. Much of this land is used for recreation and tourism, but logging, grazing, and mining are permitted in select areas. Some people are concerned that these activities could hurt the land and the state's future. Careful management can ensure that Wyoming's wild, wide-open spaces will be around for all to enjoy for many years to come.

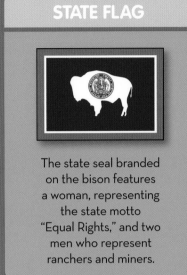

STATE FLAG

The state seal branded on the bison features a woman, representing the state motto "Equal Rights," and two men who represent ranchers and miners.

STATE FLOWER
Indian Paintbrush

STATE BIRD
Western Meadowlark

IT'S A FACT:
The Wind River actually changes its name midstream, becoming the Big Horn River just north of the Wind River Canyon.

A TIME LINE OF THE EQUALITY STATE

1825

The **Green River Rendezvous** was the annual meeting place for trappers who came to trade furs for food and other supplies.

1869

Wyoming's territorial legislature was the first in the U.S. to **allow women to vote** and to hold office on an equal basis with men—hence the state's nickname: the Equality State.

1880s

By 1887 overgrazing and a **series of terrible winters** had caused many ranches to fail, crippling Wyoming's cattle industry.

1910–Present

The development of Salt Creek and other oil fields around Casper made the city the center of **Wyoming's oil industry.**

Present

The geothermal features and abundant wildlife of **Yellowstone National Park** attract more than three million visitors a year.

ON THE MAP

LOCATION, LOCATION

This highest-elevation state after Colorado boasts the Black Hills on the eastern border; the Bighorn and Laramie Mountains mid-state; and the Teton Range—the youngest part of the Rockies—along its western border. Brisk winds across its mountains and basins make Wyoming the windiest state.

CODY: The town and its Buffalo Bill Center of the West are named after Buffalo Bill Cody, the Wild West showman who introduced the world to the sharpshooter Annie Oakley. There's a nightly summer rodeo, too.

PINEDALE: At the Green River Rendezvous, bucking bronco riders compete for prize money and glory. Wyoming's cowboy tradition dates to the 1870s, when horsemen began guiding Texas longhorns north to graze on grassy plains.

GRAND TETON NATIONAL PARK: Visitors hike or horseback ride through the scenic peaks, or raft the Snake River.

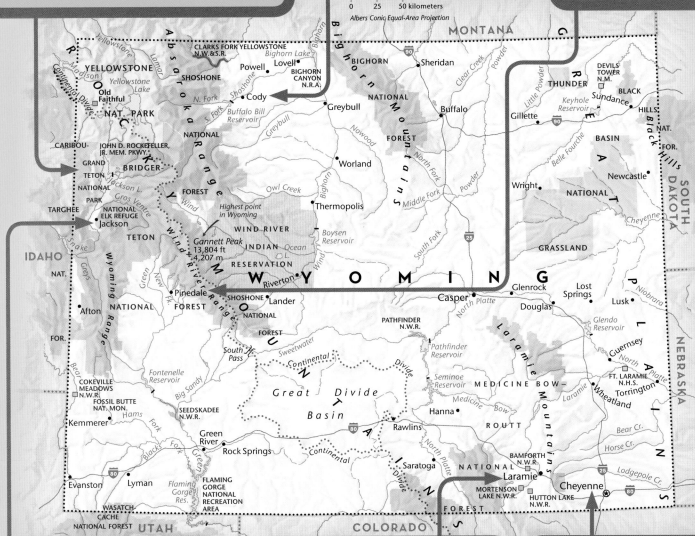

JACKSON: In the shadow of the Tetons, this town is a year-round recreational and winter skiing mecca and is home to one of the largest wintering concentrations of elk.

LARAMIE: This Wyoming settlement was built in 1868 near the railroad line. Today a booming arts and recreation center, it has activities from ice fishing at Sodergreen Lake to sky-watching at the planetarium to taking a ghost tour.

CHEYENNE: The capital and largest city has a population of just 62,448. At the Frontier Days Old West Museum, visitors find hundreds of artifacts, including stagecoaches, saddles, and firearms.

STATS & FACTS

STATEHOOD: July 10, 1890; 44th state

CAPITAL: Cheyenne

TOTAL AREA: 97,814 sq mi; 253,336 sq km

LAND AREA: 97,100 sq mi; 251,489 sq km

POPULATION: 584,153

POPULATION DENSITY: 6 people per sq mi

MAJOR RACIAL/ETHNIC GROUPS: 90.7% white, 2.4% Native American, 0.8% African American, 0.8% Asian, Hispanic (any race) 8.9%

INDUSTRY: coal production, natural gas production, crude oil production, tourism, mining

AGRICULTURE: sheep, hay, hogs, cattle, barley, corn, dry edible beans, wheat, oats

NATURAL FEATURES: President Theodore Roosevelt named **Devils Tower** the country's first national monument in 1906. A Kiowa legend says it rose from the ground to save girls being chased by a bear.

HISTORY: The **Teapot Dome scandal**, which blackened President Harding's administration, concerned oil leases in Wyoming and California. Its name comes from the shape of the rock formation above the oil deposits in Wyoming.

NATURAL FORCES: More than half of the world's **active geysers** are found in Yellowstone National Park.

ANIMALS: Since the mid-1990s, **wolves** continue to be successfully introduced into Yellowstone National Park.

PEOPLE/CULTURE: **Vernon Baker,** a highly decorated African-American soldier and World War II veteran, was raised in Cheyenne, Wyoming. He was awarded the Medal of Honor in 1997.

U.S. TERRITORIES

Far-flung tropical islands. The United States claims 14 island territories scattered across 10 time zones. Of these, only the 5 largest—Puerto Rico and the U.S. Virgin Islands in the Caribbean Sea and the Northern Marianas, Guam, and American Samoa in the Pacific Ocean—have their own governments, cultures, and economies. Each of these territories was acquired from another country as the result of a war or international agreement, and each is a valued part of the United States.

Residents of all but American Samoa are U.S. citizens, and all territories except the Northern Marianas have a nonvoting delegate in the U.S. House of Representatives. Many island people, seeking new opportunities, have moved to the mainland United States. The country's population now includes 4.8 million Hispanics of Puerto Rican origin, and tens of thousands of American Samoans live in Hawaii and other Pacific states. Meanwhile, each year millions of mainlanders are lured by the promise of sun and sand to these distant shores.

AMERICAN SAMOA Pop.: 55,000

FLAG: The eagle grips two Samoan emblems: a fly whisk, or *fue*, that symbolizes the wisdom of its chiefs, and a war club, or *uatogi*, meaning power.

Some 55,000 people, mainly descendants of Polynesian seafarers who arrived here some 4,000 years ago, call American Samoa home. This territory processes huge tuna catches for U.S. markets. Fagatele Bay National Marine Sanctuary serves as a symbol of the concern Samoan people have for the environment.

GUAM Pop.: 160,000

FLAG: The emblem's shape is like the slingshot stones once used by the Chamorro people for hunting. Inside is a beach and a traditional outrigger canoe.

A popular slogan says this westernmost territory, which is home to 160,000 residents, is "Where America's Day Begins." Much of Guam belongs to the U.S. military. Tourism, especially in the form of tropic-seeking Japanese visitors, is the island's most important economic activity. Native Taotao dancers can be seen performing at the local Pacific Arts Festival.

NORTHERN MARIANA ISLANDS Pop.: 52,000

FLAG: The white star is a symbol of the United States. Behind it, a gray stone called latte is traditionally used for the foundation of buildings on the islands.

Most people here live on Saipan, the center for commercial and government activities. The Chamorro, people whose ancestors came from Southeast Asia, make up the indigenous population. Islanders farm, work in the garment industry, or hold government jobs. Tourism is growing thanks to fabulous beaches.

PUERTO RICO Pop.: 3,620,897

FLAG: It is like the Cuban flag, but with the colors reversed. It symbolizes the ties between Cuba and Puerto Rico fighting Spain for freedom in the 1800s.

Spanish-speaking Puerto Rico has more people than 22 U.S. states. Manufacturing, especially of medicines and electronics, has surpassed an agricultural economy based on sugar, coffee, and tobacco. El Yunque rain forest is among the attractions that fuel a thriving tourist industry.

IT'S A FACT:
If Puerto Rico were a state, it would have the 29th largest population. Its area is larger than Rhode Island and Delaware together.

VIRGIN ISLANDS Pop.: 104,000

FLAG: One eagle foot holds three arrows, for the territory's three major islands; the eagle's other foot clutches an olive branch.

The islands of St. Thomas, St. Croix, and St. John—purchased from Denmark in 1917—make up most of the U.S. Virgin Islands. Sugar mills are evidence of a past dominated by plantation farming. Today profits come mainly from tourism, but the territory is making an effort to diversify and grow new industries.

IT'S A FACT:
The U.S. Virgin Islands three main isles have nicknames: St. Croix is Twin City, St. John is Love City, and St. Thomas is Rock City. Combined, their area is only twice the size of Washington, D.C.

LOCATION, LOCATION

Like jewels strung from the Pacific to the Atlantic, these five U.S. territories are tropical islands that have become key to the American economy and tourism. All have military bases, adding to the United States' presence around the world.

ON THE MAP

NORTHERN MARIANAS: Like Guam, the Northern Marianas are home to the native Chamorro people. Portuguese explorer Ferdinand Magellan was the first European to visit, in 1521, and named the land Islas de Los Ladrones ("islands of thieves"), after a misunderstanding with the natives. Spanish Jesuit priests later renamed them the Marianas.

PUERTO RICO: Deep in the Puerto Rican hills of Arecibo lies the world's largest—and most sensitive—single-dish radio telescope. It's 1,000 feet (304 m) in diameter and covers 20 acres (8 ha).

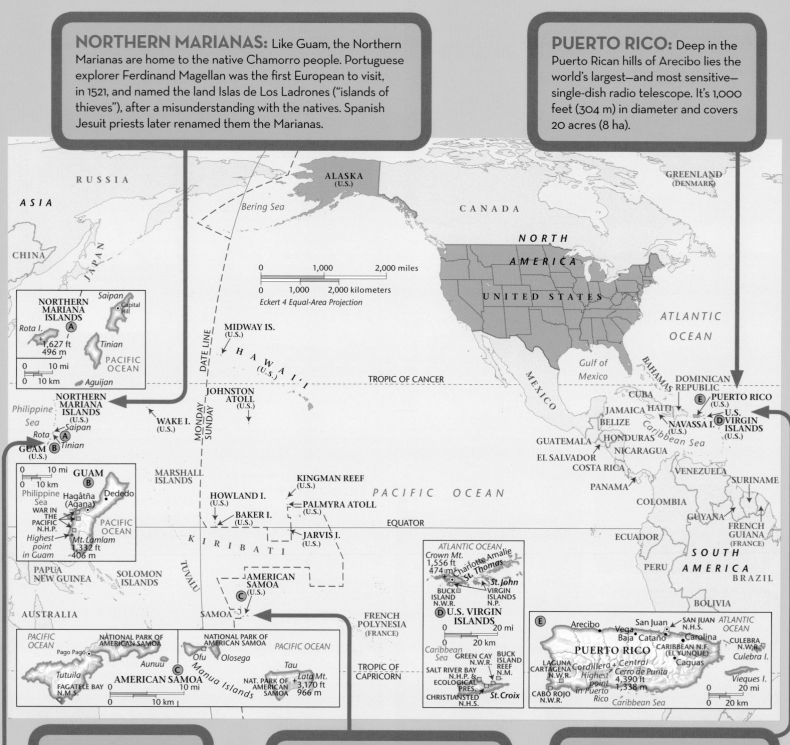

GUAM: Ancient stone pillars around the Guam islands look like mushrooms with very long stems. Experts think that these stones, called latte stones, were used to build the foundations of houses of the upper class.

AMERICAN SAMOA: The name Samoa means "sacred earth," and people take it seriously. Three of the ten volcanic islands are covered by a U.S. national park that protects habitats, plants, and animals, including the endangered flying fox—a fruit bat with a wingspan as long as a barn owl's.

VIRGIN ISLANDS: It's the only U.S. territory to be bordered by the Atlantic Ocean and the Caribbean Sea. It's also the only one where you drive on the left side of the road. This dates back to the islands' days of British rule.

FACTS AND FIGURES

ALL 50 STATES

Capital City: Washington, D.C.

Largest City: New York City, population: 8,175,133

Total Area: 3,794,083 sq mi; 9,826,630 sq km

Land Area: 3,537,439 sq mi; 9,161,923 sq km

Population: 308,745,538

Population Density: 87.4 people per sq mi

Major Racial/Ethnic Groups 72.4% white; 12.6% African American; 4.8% Asian; 0.9% Native American; Hispanic (any race) 16.3%

TOP 10 STATES IN MINERALS

1. Nevada
2. Arizona
3. Minnesota
4. Utah
5. Alaska
6. Florida
7. California
8. Texas
9. Michigan
10. Missouri

TOP 10 STATES IN FARM PRODUCTS

(by net farm income)

1. California
2. Iowa
3. Minnesota
4. Nebraska
5. Texas
6. North Carolina
7. North Dakota
8. Georgia
9. Illinois
10. South Dakota

TOP 5 STATES IN FISHERIES

1. Alaska
2. Massachusetts
3. Maine
4. Louisiana
5. Washington

EXTREMES

Strongest U.S. Surface Wind
231 miles an hour (372 km/h): Mount Washington, New Hampshire, April 12, 1934

Oldest Living U.S. Tree
Methuselah bristlecone pine, in California: **4,789 years old**

World's Tallest Living Tree
"Hyperion," a coast redwood in Redwood National Park, California: **379.1 feet (115.54 m)**

World's Largest Gorge
Grand Canyon, Arizona: **277 miles (446 km) long** along the river; **600 feet to 18 miles (183 m–29 km) wide;** about **1 mile (1.6 km) deep**

Highest World Temperature
134°F (56.6°C): Death Valley, California, July 10, 1913

Lowest U.S. Temperature
Minus 80°F (–62.2°C): Prospect Creek, Alaska, January 23, 1971

Highest U.S. Point
Mount McKinley (Denali), Alaska: **20,320 feet (6,194 m)**

Lowest U.S. Point
Death Valley, California: **282 feet (86 m) below sea level**

Longest U.S. River System
Mississippi-Missouri: **3,710 miles (5,971 km) long**

Rainiest U.S. Spot
Waialeale (mountain), Hawaii: **average annual rainfall 423 inches (1,074 cm)**

U.S. Metropolitan Areas With More Than 5 Million People
(A metropolitan area is a city and its surrounding suburban areas.)

1. **New York,** pop. 18,897,109
2. **Los Angeles,** pop. 12,828,837
3. **Chicago,** pop. 9,461,105
4. **Dallas-Fort Worth,** pop. 6,371,773
5. **Philadelphia,** pop. 5,965,343
6. **Houston,** pop. 5,946,800
7. **Washington, D.C.,** pop. 5,582,170
8. **Miami,** pop. 5,564,635
9. **Atlanta,** pop. 5,268,860

U.S. PRESIDENTS

George Washington
Born: Feb. 22, 1732
Birthplace: Westmoreland Co., VA
Died: Dec. 14, 1799
Dates of terms:
April 30, 1789–March 3, 1793;
March 4, 1793–March 3, 1797
Party: Federalist

John Adams
Born: Oct. 30, 1735
Birthplace: Braintree, MA
Died: July 4, 1826
Dates of term:
March 4, 1797–March 3, 1801
Party: Federalist

Thomas Jefferson
Born: April 13, 1743
Birthplace: Shadwell, VA
Died: July 4, 1826
Dates of terms:
March 4, 1801–March 3, 1805;
March 4, 1805–March 3, 1809
Party: Democratic-Republican

James Madison
Born: March 16, 1751
Birthplace: Port Conway, VA
Died: June 28, 1836
Dates of terms:
March 4, 1809–March 3, 1813;
March 4, 1813–March 3, 1817
Party: Democratic-Republican

James Monroe
Born: April 28, 1758
Birthplace: Westmoreland Co., VA
Died: July 4, 1831
Dates of terms:
March 4, 1817–March 3, 1821;
March 4, 1821–March 3, 1825
Party: Democratic-Republican

John Quincy Adams
Born: July 11, 1767
Birthplace: Braintree, MA
Died: Feb. 23, 1848
Dates of term:
March 4, 1825–March 3, 1829
Party: Democratic-Republican

Andrew Jackson
Born: March 15, 1767
Birthplace: Waxhaw, SC
Died: June 8, 1845
Dates of terms:
March 4, 1829–March 3, 1833;
March 4, 1833–March 3, 1837
Party: Democratic

Martin Van Buren
Born: Dec. 5, 1782
Birthplace: Kinderhook, NY
Died: July 24, 1862
Dates of term:
March 4, 1837–March 3, 1841
Party: Democratic

William Henry Harrison
Born: Feb. 9, 1773
Birthplace: Berkeley, VA
Died: April 4, 1841
Dates of term:
March 4, 1841–April 4, 1841*
Party: Whig

John Tyler
Born: March 29, 1790
Birthplace: Greenway, VA
Died: Jan. 18, 1862
Dates of term:
April 4, 1841–March 3, 1845
Party: Whig

James Knox Polk
Born: Nov. 2, 1795
Birthplace: Mecklenburg Co., NC
Died: June 15, 1849
Dates of term:
March 4, 1845–March 3, 1849
Party: Democratic

Zachary Taylor
Born: Nov. 24, 1784
Birthplace: Orange Co., VA
Died: July 9, 1850
Dates of term:
March 4, 1849–July 9, 1850*
Party: Whig

Millard Fillmore
Born: Jan. 7, 1800
Birthplace: Locke, NY
Died: March 8, 1874
Dates of term:
July 10, 1850–March 3, 1853
Party: Whig

Franklin Pierce
Born: Nov. 23, 1804
Birthplace: Hillsboro, NH
Died: Oct. 8, 1869
Dates of term:
March 4, 1853–March 3, 1857
Party: Democratic

James Buchanan
Born: April 23, 1791
Birthplace: Mercersburg, PA
Died: June 1, 1868
Dates of term:
March 4, 1857–March 3, 1861
Party: Democratic

Abraham Lincoln
Born: Feb. 12, 1809
Birthplace: Hardin Co., KY
Died: April 15, 1865
Dates of terms:
March 4, 1861–March 3, 1865;
March 4, 1865–April 15, 1865*
Party: Republican

Andrew Johnson
Born: Dec. 29, 1808
Birthplace: Raleigh, NC
Died: July 31, 1875
Dates of term:
April 15, 1865–March 3, 1869
Party: Democratic

Ulysses Simpson Grant
Born: April 27, 1822
Birthplace: Point Pleasant, OH
Died: July 23, 1885
Dates of terms:
March 4, 1869–March 3, 1873;
March 4, 1873–March 3, 1877
Party: Republican

Rutherford Birchard Hayes
Born: Oct. 4, 1822
Birthplace: Delaware, OH
Died: Jan. 17, 1893
Dates of term:
March 4, 1877–March 3, 1881
Party: Republican

James Abram Garfield
Born: Nov. 19, 1831
Birthplace: Orange, OH
Died: Sept. 19, 1881
Dates of term:
March 4, 1881–Sept. 19, 1881*
Party: Republican

Chester Alan Arthur
Born: Oct. 5, 1829
Birthplace: Fairfield, VT
Died: Nov. 18, 1886
Dates of term:
Sept. 20, 1881–March 3, 1885
Party: Republican

Grover Cleveland
Born: March 18, 1837
Birthplace: Caldwell, NJ
Died: June 24, 1908
Dates of term:
March 4, 1885–March 3, 1889
Party: Democratic

Benjamin Harrison
Born: Aug. 20, 1833
Birthplace: North Bend, OH
Died: March 13, 1901
Dates of term:
March 4, 1889–March 3, 1893
Party: Republican

Grover Cleveland
Born: March 18, 1837
Birthplace: Caldwell, NJ
Died: June 24, 1908
Dates of term:
March 4, 1893–March 3, 1897**
Party: Democratic

William McKinley
Born: Jan. 29, 1843
Birthplace: Niles, OH
Died: Sept. 14, 1901
Dates of terms:
March 4, 1897–March 3, 1901;
March 4, 1901–Sept. 14, 1901*
Party: Republican

Theodore Roosevelt
Born: Oct. 27, 1858
Birthplace: New York, NY
Died: Jan. 6, 1919
Dates of terms:
Sept. 14, 1901–March 3, 1905;
March 4, 1905–March 3, 1909
Party: Republican

William Howard Taft
Born: Sept. 15, 1857
Birthplace: Cincinnati, OH
Died: March 8, 1930
Dates of term:
March 4, 1909–March 3, 1913
Party: Republican

Woodrow Wilson
Born: Dec. 28, 1856
Birthplace: Staunton, VA
Died: Feb. 3, 1924
Dates of terms:
March 4, 1913–March 3, 1917;
March 4, 1917–March 3, 1921
Party: Democratic

Warren Gamaliel Harding
Born: Nov. 2, 1865
Birthplace: Corsica, OH
Died: Aug. 2, 1923
Dates of term:
March 4, 1921–Aug. 2, 1923*
Party: Republican

Calvin Coolidge
Born: July 4, 1872
Birthplace: Plymouth Notch, VT
Died: Jan. 5, 1933
Dates of terms:
Aug. 3, 1923–March 3, 1925;
March 4, 1925–March 3, 1929
Party: Republican

Herbert Clark Hoover
Born: Aug. 10, 1874
Birthplace: West Branch, IA
Died: Oct. 20, 1964
Dates of term:
March 4, 1929–March 3, 1933
Party: Republican

Franklin Delano Roosevelt
Born: Jan. 30, 1882
Birthplace: Hyde Park, NY
Died: April 12, 1945
Dates of terms:
March 4, 1933–Jan. 20, 1937;
Jan. 20, 1937–Jan. 20, 1941;
Jan. 20, 1941– Jan. 20, 1945;
Jan. 20, 1945–April 12, 1945*
Party: Democratic

Harry S Truman
Born: May 8, 1884
Birthplace: Lamar, MO
Died: Dec. 26, 1972
Dates of terms:
April 12, 1945–Jan. 20, 1949;
Jan. 20, 1949–Jan. 20, 1953
Party: Democratic

Dwight David Eisenhower
Born: Oct. 14, 1890
Birthplace: Denison, TX
Died: March 28, 1969
Dates of terms:
Jan. 20, 1953–Jan. 20, 1957;
Jan. 20, 1957–Jan. 20, 1961
Party: Republican

John Fitzgerald Kennedy
Born: May 29, 1917
Birthplace: Brookline, MA
Died: Nov. 22, 1963
Dates of term:
Jan. 20, 1961–Nov. 22, 1963*
Party: Democratic

Lyndon Baines Johnson
Born: Aug. 27, 1908
Birthplace: Stonewall, TX
Died: Jan. 22, 1973
Dates of terms:
Nov. 22, 1963–Jan. 20, 1965;
Jan. 20, 1965–Jan. 20, 1969
Party: Democratic

Richard Milhous Nixon
Born: Jan. 9, 1913
Birthplace: Yorba Linda, CA
Died: April 22, 1994
Dates of terms:
Jan. 20, 1969–Jan. 20, 1973;
Jan. 20, 1973–Aug. 9, 1974***
Party: Republican

Gerald Rudolph Ford
Born: July 14, 1913
Birthplace: Omaha, NE
Died: Dec. 26, 2006
Dates of term:
Aug. 9, 1974–Jan. 20, 1977
Party: Republican

James Earl Carter, Jr.
Born: Oct. 1, 1924
Birthplace: Plains, GA
Dates of term:
Jan. 20, 1977–Jan. 20, 1981
Party: Democratic

Ronald Wilson Reagan
Born: Feb. 6, 1911
Birthplace: Tampico, IL
Died: June 5, 2004
Dates of terms:
Jan 20, 1981–Jan. 20, 1985;
Jan. 20, 1985–Jan. 20, 1989
Party: Republican

George Herbert Walker Bush
Born: June 12, 1924
Birthplace: Milton, MA
Dates of term:
Jan. 20, 1989–Jan. 20, 1993
Party: Republican

William Jefferson Clinton
Born: Aug. 19, 1946
Birthplace: Hope, AR
Dates of terms:
Jan. 20, 1993–Jan. 20, 1997;
Jan. 20, 1997–Jan. 20, 2001
Party: Democratic

George Walker Bush
Born: July 6, 1946
Birthplace: New Haven, CT
Dates of terms:
Jan. 20, 2001–Jan. 20, 2005;
Jan. 20, 2005–Jan. 20, 2009
Party: Republican

Barack Hussein Obama
Born: Aug. 4, 1961
Birthplace: Honolulu, HI
Dates of terms:
Jan. 20, 2009–Jan. 20, 2013;
Jan. 20, 2013–
Party: Democratic

*Died while in office   **Second term of office   ***Resigned while in office

DECLARATION OF INDEPENDENCE

The Declaration of Independence along with the Constitution on the next pages forms the backbone of our nation. The Declaration, written in 1776, was the brainchild of **Thomas Jefferson,** a young delegate to the Continental Congress. As representatives of the colonists, the Congress wanted to create a document that would declare the colonies' freedom from England. To write it, they chose Jefferson. He was just 35 years old, while most other delegates were older and more experienced. Jefferson filled the document with exciting ideas of the Enlightenment, the 18th-century era when many leaders, scholars, and philosophers believed that they could only achieve personal liberty if they broke away from rule by a king. The Declaration of Independence presents his strong views for a democratic society. Those views—and the document—were quickly accepted by the Congress in the name of all future Americans.

IN CONGRESS, July 4, 1776.
The unanimous Declaration of the thirteen united States of America,

When in the Course of human events, it becomes necessary for one people to dissolve the political bands which have connected them with another, and to assume among the powers of the earth, the separate and equal station to which the Laws of Nature and of Nature's God entitle them, a decent respect to the opinions of mankind requires that they should declare the causes which impel them to the separation.

We hold these truths to be self-evident, that all men are created equal, that they are endowed by their Creator with certain unalienable Rights, that among these are Life, Liberty and the pursuit of Happiness.— That to secure these rights, Governments are instituted among Men, deriving their just powers from the consent of the governed, —That whenever any Form of Government becomes destructive of these ends, it is the Right of the People to alter or to abolish it, and to institute new Government, laying its foundation on such principles and organizing its powers in such form, as to them shall seem most likely to effect their Safety and Happiness. Prudence, indeed, will dictate that Governments long established should not be changed for light and transient causes; and accordingly all experience hath shewn, that mankind are more disposed to suffer, while evils are sufferable, than to right themselves by abolishing the forms to which they are accustomed. But when a long train of abuses and usurpations, pursuing invariably the same Object evinces a design to reduce them under absolute Despotism, it is their right, it is their duty, to throw off such Government, and to provide new Guards for their future security.—Such has been the patient sufferance of these Colonies; and such is now the necessity which constrains them to alter their former Systems of Government. The history of the present King of Great Britain is a history of repeated injuries and usurpations, all having in direct object the establishment of an absolute Tyranny over these States. To prove this, let Facts be submitted to a candid world.

He has refused his Assent to Laws, the most wholesome and necessary for the public good. He has forbidden his Governors to pass Laws of immediate and pressing importance, unless suspended in their operation till his Assent should be obtained; and when so suspended, he has utterly neglected to attend to them. He has refused to pass other Laws for the accommodation of large districts of people, unless those people would relinquish the right of Representation in the Legislature, a right inestimable to them and formidable to tyrants only. He has called together legislative bodies at places unusual, uncomfortable, and distant from the depository of their public Records, for the sole purpose of fatiguing them into compliance with his measures. He has dissolved Representative Houses repeatedly, for opposing with manly firmness his invasions on the rights of the people. He has refused for a long time, after such dissolutions, to cause others to be elected; whereby the Legislative powers, incapable of Annihilation, have returned to the People at large for their exercise; the State remaining in the mean time exposed to all the dangers of invasion from without, and convulsions within. He has endeavoured to prevent the population of these States; for that purpose obstructing the Laws for Naturalization of Foreigners; refusing to pass others to encourage their migrations hither, and raising the conditions of new Appropriations of Lands. He has obstructed the Administration of Justice, by refusing his Assent to Laws for establishing Judiciary powers. He has made Judges dependent on his Will alone, for the tenure of their offices, and the amount and payment of their salaries. He has erected a multitude of New Offices, and sent hither swarms of Officers to harrass our people, and eat out their substance. He has kept among us, in times of peace, Standing Armies without the Consent of our legislatures. He has affected to render the Military independent of and superior to the Civil power. He has combined with others to subject us to a jurisdiction foreign to our constitution, and unacknowledged by our laws; giving his Assent to their Acts of pretended Legislation: For Quartering large bodies of armed troops among us: For protecting them, by a mock Trial, from punishment for any Murders which they should commit on the Inhabitants of these States: For cutting off our Trade with all parts of the world: For imposing Taxes on us without our Consent: For depriving us in many cases, of the benefits of Trial by Jury: For transporting us beyond Seas to be tried for pretended offences For abolishing the free System of English Laws in a neighbouring Province, establishing therein an Arbitrary government, and enlarging its Boundaries so as to render it at once an example and fit instrument for introducing the same absolute rule into these Colonies: For taking away our Charters, abolishing our most valuable Laws, and altering fundamentally the Forms of our Governments: For suspending our own Legislatures, and declaring themselves invested with power to legislate for us in all cases whatsoever. He has abdicated Government here, by declaring us out of his Protection and waging War against us. He has plundered our seas, ravaged our Coasts, burnt our towns, and destroyed the lives of our people. He is at this time transporting large Armies of foreign Mercenaries to compleat the works of death, desolation and tyranny, already begun with circumstances of Cruelty & perfidy scarcely paralleled in the most barbarous ages, and totally unworthy the Head of a civilized nation. He has constrained our fellow Citizens taken Captive on the high Seas to bear Arms against their Country, to become the executioners of their friends and Brethren, or to fall themselves by their Hands. He has excited domestic insurrections amongst us, and has endeavoured to bring on the inhabitants of our frontiers, the merciless Indian Savages, whose known rule of warfare, is an undistinguished destruction of all ages, sexes and conditions.

In every stage of these Oppressions We have Petitioned for Redress in the most humble terms: Our repeated Petitions have been answered only by repeated injury. A Prince whose character is thus marked by every act which may define a Tyrant, is unfit to be the ruler of a free people.

Nor have We been wanting in attentions to our Brittish brethren. We have warned them from time to time of attempts by their legislature to extend an unwarrantable jurisdiction over us. We have reminded them of the circumstances of our emigration and settlement here. We have appealed to their native justice and magnanimity, and we have conjured them by the ties of our common kindred to disavow these usurpations, which, would inevitably interrupt our connections and correspondence. They too have been deaf to the voice of justice and of consanguinity. We must, therefore, acquiesce in the necessity, which denounces our Separation, and hold them, as we hold the rest of mankind, Enemies in War, in Peace Friends.

We, therefore, the Representatives of the united States of America, in General Congress, Assembled, appealing to the Supreme Judge of the world for the rectitude of our intentions, do, in the Name, and by Authority of the good People of these Colonies, solemnly publish and declare, That these United Colonies are, and of Right ought to be Free and Independent States; that they are Absolved from all Allegiance to the British Crown, and that all political connection between them and the State of Great Britain, is and ought to be totally dissolved; and that as Free and Independent States, they have full Power to levy War, conclude Peace, contract Alliances, establish Commerce, and to do all other Acts and Things which Independent States may of right do. And for the support of this Declaration, with a firm reliance on the protection of divine Providence, we mutually pledge to each other our Lives, our Fortunes and our sacred Honor.

U.S. CONSTITUTION AND BILL OF RIGHTS

The U.S. Constitution is the supreme—or highest—law of the United States. It establishes a government that protects the people and their personal rights.

Behind locked and guarded doors, the Constitution was shaped by framers, or composers, in 1787, in the same building in Philadelphia where the Declaration of Independence was signed in 1776—today's Independence Hall. The document wasn't ratified, or accepted, as the law of the land until 1788. Nine out of 13 states had to vote for it.

Check out the Constitution's opening words: "We, the people of the United States, in Order to form a more perfect Union, establish Justice, insure domestic Tranquility, provide for the common defence, promote the general Welfare, and secure the Blessings of Liberty . . ." They echo Thomas Jefferson's words in the Declaration of Independence written 11 years earlier, that everyone has the right to "Life, Liberty and the pursuit of Happiness."

THE BILL OF RIGHTS
These amendments were ratified December 15, 1791, and form what is known as the "Bill of Rights."

Amendment I
Congress shall make no law respecting an establishment of religion, or prohibiting the free exercise thereof; or abridging the freedom of speech, or of the press; or the right of the people peaceably to assemble, and to petition the Government for a redress of grievances.

Amendment II
A well regulated Militia, being necessary to the security of a free State, the right of the people to keep and bear Arms, shall not be infringed.

Amendment III
No Soldier shall, in time of peace be quartered in any house, without the consent of the Owner, nor in time of war, but in a manner to be prescribed by law.

Amendment IV
The right of the people to be secure in their persons, houses, papers, and effects, against unreasonable searches and seizures, shall not be violated, and no Warrants shall issue, but upon probable cause, supported by Oath or affirmation, and particularly describing the place to be searched, and the persons or things to be seized.

Amendment V
No person shall be held to answer for a capital, or otherwise infamous crime, unless on a presentment or indictment of a Grand Jury, except in cases arising in the land or naval forces, or in the Militia, when in actual service in time of War or public danger; nor shall any person be subject for the same offence to be twice put in jeopardy of life or limb; nor shall be compelled in any criminal case to be a witness against himself, nor be deprived of life, liberty, or property, without due process of law; nor shall private property be taken for public use, without just compensation.

WHAT'S THE CONSTITUTION ALL ABOUT?

Need a quick guide to the U.S. Constitution? These ten facts should do the trick. For a deeper look, check out the official website of the U.S. Archives, in Washington, D.C., where the original copy is kept: http://www.archives.gov/exhibits/charters/constitution_transcript.html.

THE CONSTITUTION:

1 Is a total of **five pages,** shorter than any other constitution used in the world today.

2 Starts with a **preamble,** or opening statement, that says fairness and liberty make a stronger society.

3 Has **seven articles,** or rules, that form the framework for the U.S. government.

4 Creates a government that's **a republic,** meaning that power is in the hands of the people and is carried out by representatives whom the people elect.

5 **Creates three branches of government:** The legislative branch, which includes the senators and congressmen who make the laws; the executive branch—made up of only the president—which carries out the laws; and the judicial branch, headed by the Supreme Court, which determines how the laws are carried out.

6 Establishes a system of **checks and balances,** so that no single branch becomes too strong. For instance, Congress can make a law, but the president can veto it if he feels it isn't good for the country. The president can appoint a judge to the Supreme Court, but the Senate can reject the judge if he or she seems to be unqualified.

7 Spells out the **rights and responsibilities** of the state governments and how they relate to the federal government.

8 Has had **27 amendments**—or changes—since 1789.

9 Has ten amendments that were added in 1791. Together they're called the **Bill of Rights.** They protect each person—and the government can't break them. The right to speak freely and the right to practice your own religion are just two of the amendments. Check out all ten rights above.

10 Includes **17 amendments** that came later. Some give people civil rights—such as freedom from slavery. Others make government processes clearer; still others restrict government power that might not be good for the people, such as making voters pay a tax at the polls. Among the most well known amendments are the 13th, which abolished slavery (passed in 1865), and the 19th, which gave women the right to vote (passed in 1919).

Amendment VI

In all criminal prosecutions, the accused shall enjoy the right to a speedy and public trial, by an impartial jury of the State and district wherein the crime shall have been committed, which district shall have been previously ascertained by law, and to be informed of the nature and cause of the accusation; to be confronted with the witnesses against him; to have compulsory process for obtaining witnesses in his favor, and to have the Assistance of Counsel for his defence.

Amendment VII

In Suits at common law, where the value in controversy shall exceed twenty dollars, the right of trial by jury shall be preserved, and no fact tried by a jury, shall be otherwise re-examined in any Court of the United States, than according to the rules of the common law.

Amendment VIII Excessive bail shall not be required, nor excessive fines imposed, nor cruel and unusual punishments inflicted.

Amendment IX The enumeration in the Constitution, of certain rights, shall not be construed to deny or disparage others retained by the people.

Amendment X

The powers not delegated to the United States by the Constitution, nor prohibited by it to the States, are reserved to the States respectively, or to the people.

THE CONSTITUTION

On this parchment in 1787, Jacob Shallus, a Pennsylvania State Assembly clerk, inscribed the Constitution text. It was the work of ten committee members from across the new United States, with the greatest contribution from Virginia's James Madison, who is often called the father of the Constitution.

RESOURCES

Barber, Nathan. *Get Wise! Mastering U.S. History.* Peterson's, 2004.

Ciovacco, Justine. *A Kid's Guide to the People and Places of America: State-by-State Atlas.* DK Publishing, 2003.

Garrington, Sally. *United States. Facts on File.* New York: 2003.

Hakim, Joy. *A History of US,* 11 vols., 2nd rev. ed. Oxford University Press, 1999.

Hintz, Martin. *United States of America,* 2nd series. Scholastic, Inc., 2004.

Johnston, Robert D. *The Making of America.* National Geographic Society, 2002.

Lyon, James, and Andrew Dean Nystrom. *Lonely Planet USA,* 2nd ed. Lonely Planet Publications, 2002.

National Geographic Society. *Atlas of North America.* National Geographic Society, 1985.

National Geographic Society. *Historical Atlas of the United States.* National Geographic Society, 1988.

National Geographic Society. *National Geographic United States Atlas for Young Explorers,* updated ed. National Geographic Society, 2004.

Pogany, Don. *Our Flag Was Still There: 50 States in 100 Days.* Barnes and Noble, 2002.

Reader's Digest. *Discover America: A Comprehensive Travel Guide to Our Country's Greatest Destinations.* Reader's Digest, 2004.

Rogers, Mary M., ed. *United States—in Pictures.* Lerner Publications, 1995.

Sedeen, Margaret, ed. *National Geographic Picture Atlas of Our Fifty States.* National Geographic Society, 1991.

Stewart, George R. *Names on the Land: A Historical Account of Place-Naming in the United States,* 3rd ed. Houghton Mifflin, 1967.

Webster's New Geographical Dictionary, 3rd ed. G. & C. Merriam Co., 1997.

World Almanac. *The World Almanac and Book of Facts 2004.* World Almanac Books, 2004.

More advanced texts include:

Boyer, Paul S., ed. *The Oxford Companion to United States History.* Oxford University Press, 2001.

Conzen, Michael P., ed. *The Making of the American Landscape.* Unwin Hyman, 1990.

Davis, Kenneth C. *Don't Know Much About History: Everything You Need to Know About American History but Never Learned.* Harper Collins, 2003.

Faragher, John Mack, Mari Jo Buhle, Daniel Czitrom, and Susan H. Armitage, eds. *Out of Many: A History of the American People,* 4th ed. Prentice Hall, 2002.

Halberstam, David. *Defining a Nation: Our America and the Sources of Its Strength.* National Geographic Society, 2003.

Hine, Robert V., and John Mack Faragher. *The American West: A New Interpretive History.* Yale University Press, 2000.

Hudson, John C. *Across This Land: A Regional Geography of the United States and Canada.* Johns Hopkins University Press, 2002.

Thematic map spread sources:

"Battles of the Civil War." *National Geographic,* April 2005 (supplement).

Grove, Noel. *Atlas of World History.* National Geographic Society, 1997.

Historical Atlas of the United States. National Geographic Society, 1988, 1997.

Kostyal, K. M. *Founding Fathers: The Fight for Freedom and the Birth of American Liberty.* National Geographic Society, 2014.

National Park Service. www.nps.gov.

National World War II Museum. www.nationalww2museum.org.

Nicolson, Adam. "25 Years After the Wall Cracked Open, a New Berlin Is Emerging." news.nationalgeographic.com/news/2014/11/141107-berlin-wall-25th-anniversary-germany-history/.

Population Reference Bureau. *2014 World Population Data Sheet.* www.prb.org.

Space Launch Report. www.spacelaunchreport.com/logdec.html.

Thomas, William G. *Railroads and the Making of Modern America.* railroads.unl.edu/resources.

Trowbridge, David. *United States History.* Vol. 2. Flat World Knowledge, 2012.

United States Census Bureau. *2013 American Community Survey.* www.census.gov/acs/www/data_documentation/2013_release/.

United States Geological Survey. "Federal Lands of the United States," in National Atlas of the United States (database). nationalmap.gov.

United States Geological Survey. *The National Atlas of the United States.* Washington, D.C, 1970.

Ward, Adolphus William et al., eds. *The Cambridge Modern History Atlas.* Map 78. Macmillan, 1912.

White, Matthew. *The Cold War.* users.erols.com/mwhite28/coldwar1.htm.

USEFUL WEBSITES

State facts:
http://www.census.gov/schools/facts/
http://www.ipl.org/div/stateknow/
http://www.infoplease.com/states
http://www.50states.com/

State websites:
http://www.state.[state postal abbreviation].us
(for example, Alabama's website is http://www.state.al.us)

State of the State addresses:
http://www.nga.org/cms/stateofthestates

National Park Service:
http://www.nps.gov

U.S. Census Bureau:
http://www.census.gov

The United States Mint—America the Beautiful Quarters® Program:
http://www.usmint.gov/mint_programs/50sq_program/?action=quarter_history

Agricultural information: USDA crop data is housed in the Mann Library at Cornell University. For listings of Crop Production Annual Summaries:
http://usda.mannlib.cornell.edu/

For USDA Economic Research Service:
http://www.ers.usda.gov/

For mineral resource information, go to the U.S. Geological Survey:
http://minerals.usgs.gov/minerals/pubs/state/

GLOSSARY

Acadians: French Canadians who settled in Canada.

al Qaeda: A broad-based Islamic military organization founded in Afghanistan.

antimonopoly: Against exclusive control of a commodity or service in a particular market.

aquifer: Underground reservoir of water.

armistice: Temporarily stopping warfare by reaching an agreement before the signing of a peace treaty.

assassinate: To murder, usually a politically important or prominent person, in a surprise attack.

Bering land bridge: Land that provided a path for people and animals to travel from what today is Russia into Alaska.

boomtown: A town that sprang up suddenly when miners went West to look for gold and other precious resources.

boycott: When people refuse to buy or participate in something as a way of protesting.

Census: The official government count of the population.

civil rights: The rights that every person should have, such as to not be discriminated against because of your skin color.

Cold War: The rivalry between the United States and the Soviet Union after World War II.

colonist: A person who lives in a colony; for instance, British colonists living in the American colonies.

Communism: A belief that the community (not individuals) should own the natural resources and means of production (such as mines and factories).

Confederacy: The government of 11 southern states that seceded from the Union during the Civil War.

conquistador: Soldiers, usually Spanish or Portuguese, who explored the South and Southwest, aiming to claim lands for their nations.

Continental Congress: A body of delegates during the American Revolution who spoke for the people of the colonies that became the U.S.A.

crude oil: Petroleum that hasn't been refined.

delta: The triangular area of land at the mouth of a river. Its soil is very rich.

depression: A period when the economy isn't working and many people are not making money. American had a Great Depression in the 1930s.

drought: A long period without rain, which often causes rivers and land to dry up and destroys crops.

eastern seaboard: A region of the United States along the Atlantic Ocean, extending from Florida to Maine.

economy: A financial system.

erosion: A gradual wearing away of rock or earth.

extinction: When there are no more of a species left living.

fracking: The injection of fluids into rock beds at high pressure to free up oil or natural gas resources.

freedom riders: Black and white people who rode buses together through the South in 1961 to protest segregation.

fugitive: Someone who runs away to avoid being captured.

gigabyte: A unit of computer storage information, which is roughly 1 billion bytes.

gin: A machine invented by Eli Whitney to clean raw cotton.

glaciers: Massive sheets of ice that move slowly and have carved out valleys and other landforms in the U.S.

GPS: Stands for Global Positioning System; a radio system that uses satellite signals to show you where you are.

greenhouse gas: Gases that trap heat in Earth's atmosphere.

hard tack: A hard biscuit, bread, or cracker.

immigrant: A person who comes to live permanently in a foreign country.

imperial power: Extending a nation's power by acquiring territories or establishing economic and political dominance.

indentured servant: A person who works for another person in return for payment of travel expenses and food and housing.

internment: To confine or impound, especially during a war.

medieval: From the period of the Middle Ages, around the 1500s.

melting pot: A society composed of many different cultures.

mesa: Elevated landforms, usually steep cliffs, found in the Southwest.

munitions: Guns and other weapons, like cannon.

NAACP: The National Association for the Advancement of Colored People; an American organization working to end discrimination.

natural resources: Natural elements, such as freshwater, clean air, and rich soil, that help people thrive. Minerals like gold and silver are also resources.

oil rig: A structure for drilling oil, either on land or deep in the ocean floor.

old growth: A forest that has very old, very large trees with great biodiversity.

pact: An agreement between people, groups, or nations.

panhandle: A strip of land extending from the main land of a state.

patent: The exclusive right, granted by the government, to sell an invention.

prairie: Flat and fertile lands of tall, waving grass, also good for farmlands, dominant in the Midwest.

predominantly: Mainly—often used in population, such as predominantly Caucasian.

prospector: A person who explores or searches for valuable ores, oil, etc.

prototype: A first model or first example of something from which others will be developed.

pueblo: An apartment-like structure of clay built by early Southwest Indians.

Puritan: A member of a Protestant religious group in the 16th and 17th centuries that opposed many customs of the Church of England.

R&B: Rhythm and blues music, which grew from African music.

ratify: To approve something, such as a law. The U.S. Constitution was ratified, or approved, in 1788.

Reconstruction: The period (1865–1877) following the Civil War intended to help newly free slaves and the states that were returning to the U.S.A.

safe house: A safe place where slaves escaping from slavery took refuge.

segregation: Keeping people of different races separated.

silt: Grainy particles of rock and clay often carried along with a river.

sit-in: A protest in which people sit or stay in a place and don't leave until their demands are answered.

sprawl: Outgrowth of cities, often into suburbs of family housing that surround the city.

strife: Trouble or bitter rivalry. Examples include disputes between workers and bosses, between political parties, or between early settlers and native peoples.

suborbital: Not going into a full orbit of the Earth.

tax: Money people are required to pay to the government.

temperate rain forest: A forest with many types of trees in the temperate zone (as opposed to tropical zone) that receives heavy rainfall.

truck farm: A farm that is dedicated to growing fresh fruits and vegetables for markets.

Tennessee Valley Authority (TVA): A government organization started in 1933 to produce electricity and help grow the economy in the Tennessee Valley.

tycoon: A wealthy and powerful industrialist.

urban: A city, or like a city.

INDEX

Boldface indicates illustrations.

INDEX

INDEX

ILLUSTRATIONS CREDITS

GI: Getty Images SS: Shutterstock

Front cover (UP), FloridaStock/SS; (LO LE), Digital Stock; (LO CTR), Mike Flippo/SS; (LO RT), holbox/SS **Spine** (UP), Mike Flippo/SS; (CTR), aaltair/SS; (LO), Can Balcioglu/SS **Back cover** (UP), EyeWire Images; (CTR LE), Anita Erdmann/Alamy; (CTR RT), Can Balcioglu/SS; (LO), Pat & Chuck Blackley/Alamy

Front Matter 1, American Spirit/SS; 2-3, Gary Blakeley/SS; 4 (UP), NASA; 4 (LO), Pat & Chuck Blackley/Alamy; 5 (UP), Library of Congress; 5 (LO), SS/Garsya; 6, SurangaSL/SS; 10-11, Rawpixel/SS; 12 (UPR), North Wind Picture Archives/Alamy; 12 (MIDR), North Wind Picture Archives/Alamy; 14 (LE), Roel Smart/iStockphoto; 14 (UP), The Granger Collection, NYC—All rights reserved; 14 (CTR UP), Pictorial Press Ltd/Alamy; 14 (CTR LO), Wikimedia Commons; 14 (LO RT), The Granger Collection, NYC—All rights reserved; 16 (LOL), Ivan Collins/Oregon Historical Society; 18 (UPR), Wikimedia Commons; 18 (UPL), Alexander Gardner/Library of Congress; 18 (MID1), The Print Collector/Alamy; 18 (MID2), Matthew Brady/Library of Congress; 18 (LOL), Julian Vannerson/Library of Congress; 20 (UPL), Lewis Hine/Library of Congress; 20 (MIDL), Archive Pics/Alamy; 20 (LOL), Pictorial Press Ltd/Alamy; 22 (UPR), Military Images/Alamy; 22 (MIDR), Kriss Russell, GI; 22 (MIDL), Niday Picture Library/Alamy; 24 (UPL), Everett Collection Inc./Alamy; 24 (MID1), Everett Collection Inc./Alamy; 24 (MID2), AF Archive/Alamy; 24 (LOL), Everett Collection Inc./Alamy; 26 (UPR), Underwood Archives/Bridgeman Images; 26 (LOL), Universal Images Group Limited/Alamy; 28, David Handschuh/Corbis; 30, ilozavr/SS; 31, Ruth Black/SS; 32 (MIDL), RGB Ventures/Alamy; 32 (LOL), Holly Kuchera/SS; 33, Jan Wachala/Alamy; 34 (LOL), Wiskerke/Alamy; 35 (UPL), North Wind Picture Archives/Alamy; 35 (MIDR), North Wind Picture Archives/Alamy; 35 (MIDL), Everett Historical/SS; 35 (LOR), Jon Bilous/SS; 37 (UPL), Avprophoto/SS; 37 (UPR), Odegov/SS

The Northeast 40-41, Robert Harding Picture Library Ltd./Alamy; 42 (LOL), Margo Harrison/SS; 43 (UPL),Wikipedia; 43 (MIDR), North Wind Picture Archives/Alamy; 43 (MIDL), North Wind Picture Archives/Alamy; 43 (LOR), Navy Media Content Service; 45 (UPL) Rich Koele/SS; 45 (UPR), Kim Reinick/SS; 45 (MIDL), ClassicStock/Alamy; 45 (LOL), Library of Congress; 45 (LOR), Brandon Cole Marine Photography/Alamy; 46 (LOL), AptTone/SS; 47 (UPL), Visions of America, LLC/Alamy; 47 (MIDR), Zee/Alamy; 47 (MIDL), Dreamstime; 47 (LOR), Steve Bower/SS; 49 (UPL), browndogstudios/iStockphoto, 49 (UPR), Bridgeman Art; 49 (LOL), Eric Carr/Alamy; 49 (LOR), The Miss America Organization; 50 (LOL), Debra Millet/SS; 51 (UPR), Bridgeman Art; 51 (MIDL), Mathew Brady/Library of Congress; 51 (MIDR), Everett Collection Inc./Alamy; 51 (LOL), Alex Staroseltsev/SS; 53 (UPL), Stephen Coburn/SS; 53 (UPR), Design Pics Inc./Alamy; 53 (MIDR), Jerry and Marcy Monkman/Alamy; 53 (LOL), Bridgeman Art; 54 (LOL), TopSeller/SS; 55 (UPL), North Wind Picture Archives/Alamy; 55 (MIDR), Peter Newark American Pictures/Bridgeman Art; 55 (MIDL), Archive Images/Alamy; 55 (LOR), Bill Cobb/Superstock; 57 (UPL), SS; 57 (UPR), David Dohnal/SS; 57 (LOL), Library of Congress; 57 (LOR), Aurora Photos/Alamy; 58 (LOL), Laura Bartlett/SS; 59 (UPL), Library of Congress; 59 (MIDR), North Wind Picture Archives/Alamy; 59 (MIDL), Alexius Sutandio/SS; 59 (LOR), Marcio Jose Bastos Silva/SS; 61 (UPL),Victor Maffe/iStockphoto; 61 (UPR), Jorge Salcedo/SS; 61 (LOL), Flip Nicklin/Corbis; 61 (LOR), Lordprice Collection/Alamy; 62 (LOL), Nattika/SS; 63 (UPL), North Wind Picture Archives/Alamy; 63 (MIDR), Lewis Hine/Library of Congress; 63 (MIDL), NASA; 63 (LOR), Everett Collection Inc./Alamy; 65 (UPL), Bomshtein/SS, 65 (UPR), Garry Black/Alamy; 65 (MIDL), Jose Azel/GI; 65 (LOR), Ken Catania/GI; 66 (LOL), SS; 67 (UPR), INTERFOTO/Alamy; 67 (MIDL), Niday Picture Library/Alamy; 67 (LOR), Bill Massey/John Giannotti; 69 (UPL), Dmitry Kosterev/SS; 69 (UPR), Cosmo Condina North America/Alamy; 69 (LOL), Library of Congress; 69 (LOR), SS; 70 (LOL), IM photo/SS; 71 (UPR), North Wind Picture Archives/Alamy; 71 (MIDL), Marc Venema/GI; 71 (LOR), Spencer Platty/GI; 73 (UPL), Nikada/SS; 73 (UPR), Mihai Andritoiu/Alamy; 73 (LOL), Pietro Scozzari/TIPS Images/ZUMAPRESS.com/Newscom; 73 (LOR), REDAV/SS; 74 (LOL), Edwin Verin/SS; 75 (UPL), Classic Image/Alamy; 75 (MIDR), Niday Picture Library/Alamy; 75 (LOL), Delmas Lehman/SS; 77 (UPL), Christopher S. Howeth/SS; 77 (UPR), David Maxwell/Alamy; 77 (MIDL), Creative Commons/Flickr; 77 (LOL), Courtesy Heritage Auctions; 77 (LOR), Old Paper Studios/Alamy; 78 (LOL), Newport Historical Society; 79 (UPL), North Wind Picture Archives/Alamy; 79 (MIDR), Jessica Rinaldi/Corbis; 79 (LOL), JeffG/Alamy; 81 (UPL), Tobik/SS; 81 (UPR), Kenneth C. Zirkel/Corbis; 81 (MIDL), Sean Pavone/SS; 81 (LOL), Rachel Torres/Alamy; 81 (LOR), Marilyn Barbone/SS; 82, Jiri Hera/SS; 83 (UPR), INTERFOTO/Alamy; 83 (MIDL), North Wind Picture Archives/Alamy; 83 (LOL), Designsstock/SS; 83 (LOR), Ipatov/SS; 85 (UPL), Morgan Lane Photography/SS; 85 (UPR), Edward Fielding/SS; 85 (MIDL), Tierfotoagentur/Alamy; 85 (LOL), Wikimedia Commons; 85 (LOR), Aurora Photos/Alamy

The Southeast 88-89, Dave Allen Photography/SS; 90 (LOL), Courtesy Tennessee Tombigbee Waterway;91 (UPL), SOTK2011/Alamy; 91 (MIDR), Glasshouse Images/Alamy; 91 (LOL), Michael Doolittle/Alamy; 93 (UPL),Violet Kaipa/SS; 93 (UPR), Holly Kuchera/SS; 93 (LOL), Library of Congress; 93 (LOR), Jason Ross/Alamy; 94 (LOL), pagadesign/iStockphoto; 95 (UPR), Arkansas History Commission; 95 (MIDL), Everett Collection Historical/Alamy; 95 (LOR), snyferok/iStockphoto; 97 (UPL), Stefano Cavoretto/SS; 97 (UPR), Bill Grant/Alamy; 97 (LOL), Daniel Dempster Photography/Alamy; 97 (LOR), Library of Congress; 98 (LOL), Scott Prokop/SS; 99 (UPR), North Wind Picture Archives/Alamy; 99 (MIDL),Valentyn Volkov/SS; 99 (LOR), Songquan Deng/SS; 101 (UPL), Good Shoots/SS; 101 (UPR), Liquid Productions, LLC/SS; 101 (LOL), MaszaS/SS; 101 (LOR), Library of Congress; 102 (LOL), Lars Christensen/SS; 103 (UPR), North Wind Picture Archives/Alamy; 103 (MIDL), North Wind Picture Archives/Alamy; 103 (LOL), ravl/SS; 103 (LOR), Rob Hainer/SS; 105 (UPL), RedHelga/iStockphoto; 105 (UPR), Dick DeMarsico/Library of Congress; 105 (MIDL), Alamy; 105 (LOL), SS; 105 (LOR), Marvin Dembinsky Photo Associates/Alamy; 106, SS; 107 (UPL), Chiyact/iStockphoto; 107 (UPR), Mary Evans Picture Library/Alamy; 107 (LOL), Gary Warnimont/Alamy; 107 (LOR), Pictorial Press Ltd/Alamy; 109 (UPL), Materio/iStockphoto; 109 (UPR), Sharron Schiefelbein/Alamy; 109 (LOL), North Wind Picture Archives/Alamy; 109 (LOR), David J. Phillip/AP Photo; 110 (LOL), SS; 111 (UPL), North Wind Picture Archives/Alamy; 111 (UPR), World History Archive/Alamy; 111 (MIDL), Harris & Ewing Collection/Library of Congress; 111 (LOR), Chuck Wagner/SS; 113 (UPL), Ann Quigley/SS; 113 (UPR), Rob Hainer/SS; 113 (MIDL), Michael Patrick O'Neill/Alamy; 113 (LOR), Mira/Alamy; 114 (LOL), Garsya/SS; 115 (UPL), North Wind Picture Archives/Alamy; 115 (MIDR), Niday Picture Library/Alamy; 115 (LOL), Photos 12/Alamy; 115 (LOR), Premium UIG/GI; 117 (UPL), Quang Ho/SS; 117 (UPR), Spondylolithesis/iStockphoto; 117 (MIDL), Norfolk Southern Railway; 117 (LOR), John A. Tupy/USAD; 118 (LOL), Cvandyke/SS; 119 (UPR), North Wind Picture Archives/Alamy; 119 (MIDL), GL Archive/Alamy; 119 (MIDR), Jack Moebes/Corbis; 119 (LOL), US Army Photo/Alamy; 121 (UPL), Brad Whitsitt/SS; 121 (UPR), SS; 121 (MIDL), Paris Pierce/Alamy; 121 (LOL), Steve Bloom Images/Alamy; 121 (LOR), Archive Pics/Alamy; 122 (LOL), iStockphoto; 123 (UPR), North Wind Picture Archives/Alamy; 123 (MIDL), Bridgeman Art; 123 (LOR), Cassiede Alain/SS; 125 (UPL), Andrea Hill/iStockphoto; 125 (UPR), Polly Dawson/SS; 125 (LOL), ClassicStock/Alamy; 125 (LOR), Jamie McCarthy/iStockphoto; 126 (LOL), AF Archive/Alamy; 127 (UPL), Bridgeman Art; 127 (MIDR), Ian Dagnall/Alamy; 127 (LOL), f11photo, SS; 129 (UPL), Markus Gann/SS; 129 (UPR), North Wind Picture Archives/Alamy; 129 (MIDL), Betty Shelton/SS; 129 (LOR), John Wollwerth/SS; 130 (LOL), David B. Gleason/Wikimedia Commons; 131 (UPL), North Wind Picture Archives/Alamy; 131 (MIDR), North Wind Picture Archives/Alamy; 131 (MIDL), North Wind Picture Archives/Alamy; 131 (LOL), Wikipedia; 133 (UPL), skodonnell/iStockphoto; 133 (UPR), Design Pics Inc./Alamy; 133 (MIDL),Trigger Image/Alamy; 133 (LOL), Library of Congress; 133 (LOR), North Wind Picture Archives/Alamy; 134 (LOL), Andrey Burmakin/SS; 135 (UPL), North Wind Picture Archive/Alamy; 135 (MIDL), Jim West/Alamy; 135 (MIDR), Wikimedia Commons; 135 (LOR), Pat & Chuck Blackley/Alamy; 137 (UPL), iStockphoto; 137 (UPR), Radoslaw Lecyk/ SS; 137 (MIDL), National Postal Museum/Smithsonian; 137 (LOL), Library of Congress; 137 (LOR), Orhan Cam/SS

The Midwest 140-141, Bruce Leighty/GI; 142 (LOL), Thomas Barrat/SS; 143 (UPL), North Wind Picture Archives/Alamy; 143 (MIDR), Mary Evans Picture Library/Alamy; 143 (MIDL), Dan McCoy/Corbis; 143 (LOR), Tupungato/SS; 145 (UPL), Mega Pixel, SS; 145 (UPR), Everett Collection/SS; 145 (MIDL), Chris Mellor/GI; 145 (LOL), Robert Lubeck/Animals Animals/Earth Scenes; 145 (LOR), Niday Picture Library/Alamy; 146 (LOL), Carolyn Franks/SS; 147 (UPL), North Wind Picture Archives/Alamy; 147 (LOL), carroteater/SS; 147 (MIDR), Maryann Preisinger/Dreamstime; 149 (UPL), TOSP Photo/SS; 149 (UPR), Eric Shoening/visitindiana.com; 149 (MIDL), Wahed Mohammed/SS; 149 (LOL), North Wind Picture Archives/Alamy; 149 (LOR), Bettmann/Corbis; 150 (LOL), Jolly Time; 151 (UPL), North Wind Picture Archives/Alamy; 151 (MIDL), CSU Archives/Everett Collection; 151 (MIDR), Archive Images/Alamy; 151 (LOR), David K. Purdy/Corbis; 153 (UPL), Vaclav Volrab/SS; 153 (UPR), Granger Collection; 153 (MIDL), Scott Sinklier/Alamy; 153 (MIDR), Scott Sinklier/Alamy; 153 (LOL), North Wind Picture Archives/Alamy; 154 (LOL), Alaettin Yildirim/SS; 155 (UPL), North Wind Picture Archives/Alamy; 155 (MIDR), Heritage Image Partnership Ltd./Alamy; 155 (LOL), Christie's Images/Corbis; 157 (UPL), Olaf Simon/iStockphoto; 157 (UPR), Dennis Jacobsen/Can Stock Photo Inc.; 157 (MIDL), Diana Staresinic-Deane; 157 (LOL), Library of Congress; 157 (LOR), Everett Collection Historical/Alamy; 158 (LOL), Eric Isselee/SS; 159 (UPL), North Wind Picture Archives/Alamy; 159 (MIDL), Everett Collection Historical/Alamy; 159 (MIDR), goldnetz, SS; 159 (LOR), Rolf Hicker, GI; 161 (UPL), SS; 161 (UPR), Michal Ninger/SS; 161 (MIDL), Library of Congress; 161 (LOL), Mark Baldwin, SS; 161 (LOR), Gilles Pétard Collection/GI; 162 (LOL), komkrich ratchusiri/SS; 163 (UPR), Ivy Close Images/Alamy; 163 (MIDL), Everett Collection Historical/Alamy; 163 (MIDR), Courtesy 3M; 163 (LOR), Jeffrey J Coleman/SS; 165 (UPL), Dmitrij Skorobogatov/SS; 165 (UPR), Reimar 5/Alamy; 165 (MIDL), Sergiy Zavgorodny/IStockphoto; 165 (LOR), Wildnerdpix/SS; 166 (LOL), Planet5D LLC/SS; 167 (UPL), Legends of America; 167 (MIDR), North Wind Picture Archives/Alamy; 167 (MIDL), Library of Congress; 167 (LOR), Danita Delimont/Alamy; 169 (UPL), SS; 169 (UPR), Can Stock Photo Inc; 169 (MIDL), North Wind Picture Archives/Alamy; 169 (LOL), State Historical Society of Missouri; 169 (LOR), Library of Congress; 170 (LOL), Nature Picture Library; 171 (UPL), Karl Bodmer, Bridgeman Art; 171 (MIDR), Library of Congress; 171 (MIDL), Library of Congress; 171 (LOR), KRT/Newscom; 173 (UPL), Todd Harrison/iStockphoto; 173 (UPR), Grant Heilman Photography/Alamy; 173 (MIDL), Cecilia Lim H M/SS; 173 (LOL), NOAA; 173 (LOR), Ann Cantelow/SS; 174 (LOL), Peter Rimar/Wikimedia; 175 (UPL), Everett Collection Historical/Alamy; 175 (MIDR), illustrart/SS; 175 (MIDL), Pictorial Press Ltd./Alamy; 175 (LOR), beaucroft/iStockphoto; 177 (UPL), SeDmi/SS; 177 (UPR), Bill Bachmann/Alamy; 177 (LOL), George Grantham Bain/Library of Congress; 177 (LOR), FLPA/Alamy; 178 (LOLE), Meng Luen/SS; 179 (UPL), ClassicStock/Alamy; 179 (MIDR), Courtesy Village of Seville; 179 (MIDL), Worytko Pawel/SS; 179 (LOR), Philip Scalia/Alamy; 181 (UPL), Craig Barhorst/SS; 181 (UPR), NASA; 181 (MIDL), Stan Rohrer/Alamy; 181 (LOL), Heritage Image Partnership Ltd./Alamy; 181 (LOR), Can Stock Photo Inc.; 182 (LOL), Gino's Premium Images/Alamy; 183 (UPR), Library of Congress; 183 (MIDL), Library of Congress; 183 (LOL), Prisma Bildagentur/Alamy; 183 (LOR), Eric Isselee/SS; 185 (UPL), Eric Isselee/SS; 185 (UPR), Critterbiz/SS; 185 (MIDL), Heritage Image Partnership Ltd./Alamy; 185 (LOL), Jo Crebbin/SS; 185 (LOR), tedpagel/Can Stock Photo Inc; 186 (LOL), Niday Picture Library/Alamy; 187 (UPR), The Mining Museum and Rollo Jamison Museum; 187 (MIDL) Peter Newark American Pictures/Bridgeman Art; 187 (LOL), Harley Davidson Press; 187 (LOR), Burke Triolo/PhotoLibrary; 189 (UPL), azure1/SS; 189 (UPR), Door County Visitor Bureau; 189 (MIDL), Bettmann/Corbis; 189 (LOL), Nancy Bauer/SS; 189 (LOR) R. Fassbind/SS

The Southwest 192-193, Gert Hochmuth/SS; 194, SS; 195 (UPL), Spring Images/Alamy; 195 (MIDR), Everett Collection Inc./Alamy; 195 (MIDL), Library of Congress; 195 (LOR), Bill Florence, SS; 197 (UPL), Vitaly Raduntsev/SS; 197 (UPR), North Wind Picture Archives/Alamy; 197 (MIDL), Krzysztof Wiktor/SS; 197 (LOL), Dennis W. Donohue/SS; 197 (LOR), ImageBroker/Alamy; 198 (LOL), Legacy Images/SS; 199 (UPL), North Wind Picture Archives/Alamy; 199 (MIDR), curraheeshutter/iStockphoto; 199 (LOL), julos/iStockphoto; 199 (LOR), Courtesy Virgin Galactic; 201 (UPL), SS; 201 (UPR), C. Emory Moody/Alamy; 201 (MIDL), Library of Congress; 201 (LOR), Doug Meek/SS; 202 (LOL), Danny E Hooks/SS; 203 (UPL), The Granger Collection; 203 (MIDR), Peter Newark American Pictures/Bridgeman Art; 203 (MIDL), Dorothea Lange/Library of Congress; 203 (LOR), age footstock/Alamy; 205 (UPL), SS; 205 (UPR), Fer Gregory/iStockphoto; 205 (MIDL), JudiLen/iStockphoto; 205 (LOL), Betty LaRue/Alamy; 205 (LOR), Hulton Archive/GI; 206 (LOLE), NASA; 207 (UPL), f11photo/SS; 207 (MIDR), Sam Houston Memorial Museum Images Collection; 207 (MIDL), ClassicStock/Alamy; 207 (LOR), canstockphoto; 209 (UPL), J. Helgason/SS; 209 (UPR), Rolf Nussbaumer Photography/Alamy; 209 (MIDL), M. Timothy O'Keefe/Alamy; 209 (LOL), Thomas Barrat/SS; 209 (LOR), Victor Martins/Fiesta@San Antonio Commission; 210 (UPL), Ivaschenko Roman/SS

The West 212-213, Solent News/Corbis; 214 (LOL), Theeradech Sanin/SS; 215 (UPL), Everett Collection Historical/Alamy; 215 (MIDR), North Wind Picture Archives/Alamy; 215 (MIDL), Jacob W. Frank/Flickr RM/GI; 215 (LOR), Design Pics Inc./Alamy; 217 (UPL), Alex Staroseltsev/SS; 217 (UPR), Design Pics Inc./Alamy; 217 (MIDL), GeorgiosArt/Can Stock Photo Inc.; 217 (LOR), Jeff Mondragon/Alamy; 218 (LOL), Evgeny Karandaev/SS; 219 (UPL), John Elk III/Alamy; 219 (MIDR), Eli Maier/SS; 219 (MIDL), Juan Camilo Bernal/SS; 219 (LOR), iStockphoto; 221 (UPL), Alex Staroseltsev/SS; 221 (UPR), Eduardo Rivero/SS; 221 (MIDL), DFree/SS; 221 (LOL), AP Photo; 221 (LOR), Paul D. Lemke/iStockphoto; 222, Melinda Fawver/SS; 223 (UPL), Dan Leeth/Alamy; 223 (MIDR), ClassicStock/Alamy; 223 (MIDL), Everett Collection Inc./Alamy; 223 (LOR), George Steinmetz/Corbis; 225 (UPL), Skip Odonnell/iStockphoto; 225 (UPR), Howard Sandler/SS; 225 (MIDL), Serinus/SS; 225 (LOL), World History Archive/Alamy; 225 (LOR), auddmin/SS; 226 (LOL), Mega Pixel/SS; 227 (UPR), Wikimedia Commons; 227 (UPL), Nuttapong/SS; 227 (MIDL), Jim Sugar/GI; 227 (LOR), tomas del amo/SS; 229 (UPL), Nick Andros/SS; 229 (UPR), Photo Resource Hawaii/Alamy; 229 (MIDL), incamerastock/Alamy; 229 (LOL), Laura S. L. Kong/GI; 229 (LOR), Andre Seale/Alamy; 230 (LOL), M. Unal Ozmen,SS; 231 (UPL), The Granger Collection; 231 (MIDR), SS; 231 (MIDL), Royal Ontario Museum 2010; 231 (LOR), Silvrshootr/iStockphoto; 233 (UPL), Danny E Hooks/SS; 233 (UPR), Steve Bloom Images/Alamy; 233 (MIDL), Lee O'Dell/SS; 233 (LOL), Wally McNamee/Corbis; 233 (LOR), Universal History Archive/GI; 234 (LOL), Patti McConville/Alamy; 235 (UPL), North Wind Picture Archives/Alamy; 235 (MIDR), Library of Congress; 235 (MIDL), North Wind Picture Archives/Alamy; 235 (LOR), Ted Thai/GI; 237 (UPL), Michael Balderas/iStockphoto; 237 (UPR), Kent Sorensen/SS; 237 (MIDR), North Wind Picture Archives/Alamy; 237 (LOL), jimkruger/iStockphoto; 237 (LOR), EPA/Alamy; 238 (LOL), Alex Helin/SS; 239 (UPL), North Wind Picture Archives/Alamy; 239 (MIDR), Richard Cummins/GI; 239 (MIDL), Kobby Dagan/SS; 239 (LOL), Jim West/Alamy; 241 (UPL), Perttu Sironen/iStockphoto; 241 (UPR), Aurora Photos/Alamy; 241 (MIDL), Robert McGouey/Alamy; 241 (LOL), SipaPhoto/SS; 241 (LOR), Library of Congress; 242 (LOL), Premium Stock Photography/Alamy; 243 (UPR), The Granger Collection; 243 (MIDL), North Wind Picture Archives/Alamy; 243 (MIDR), Joel Sartore/GI; 243 (LOL), Jack Sullivany/Alamy; 245 (UPL), Tatiana Popova/SS; 245 (UPR), Russ Bishop/Alamy; 245 (MIDL), Jody Ann/SS; 245 (LOL), S. Bukley/SS; 245 (LOR), Pierre Leclerc/SS; 246 (LOL), Courtesy Hole N' the Rock; 247 (UPL), Doug Meek/SS; 247 (MIDR), Lebrecht Music and Arts Photo Library/Alamy; 247 (MIDL), Wikimedia Commons; 247 (LOR), Matthew Stockman/GI; 249 (UPR), blickwinkel/Alamy; 249 (MIDL), Bettmann/Corbis; 249 (LOL), Dick Durrance 1941, All Rights Reserved; 249 (LOR), Cephas Picture Library/Alamy; 249 (UPL), LilKar/SS; 250 (LOL), Valentina R./SS; 251 (UPL), North Wind Picture Archives/Alamy; 251 (MIDR), Joe Mabel/Wikimedia Commons; 251 (MIDL), Popperfoto/GI; 251 (LOR), Joe Ravi/SS; 253 (UPL), Valentyn Volkov/SS; 253 (UPR), Gunter Marx/Alamy; 253 (MIDL), whojiggy/SS; 253 (LOL), JStone/SS; 253 (LOR), Yan Ke/SS; 254 (LOL), ImageBroker/Alamy; 255 (UPL), Everett D. Graff Collection, American Heritage Center/University of Wyoming; 255 (MIDR), Bridgeman Art; 255 (MIDL), Jonathan Blair/Corbis; 255 (LOR), Alexey Kamenskiy/Can Stock Photo Inc.; 257 (UPL), Irina Orel/SS; 257 (UPR), Mike Norton/SS; 257 (MIDL), The Granger Collection; 257 (LOL), Ruth Fremson/AP Photo; 257 (LOR), Anita Erdmann/Alamy

Back Matter
260 (UPR), Chones/SS; 260 (MID), Tsekhmister/SS; 260 (LOL), Alexander Raths/SS; 262, WikiMedia Commons; 265, Wikipedia

STAFF FOR THIS BOOK

Priyanka Sherman and Amy Briggs, *Senior Editors*
Eva Absher-Schantz, *Art Director*
Lori Epstein, *Senior Photo Editor*
Carl Mehler, *Director of Maps*
Sven M. Dolling, Michael McNey, and XNR Productions,
    Map Research and Production
Paige Towler, *Editorial Assistant*
Sanjida Rashid and Rachel Kenny, *Design Production Assistants*
Michael Cassady, *Rights Clearance Specialist*
Grace Hill, *Managing Editor*
Mike O'Connor, *Production Editor*
Lewis R. Bassford, *Production Manager*
George Bounelis, *Manager, Production Services*
Susan Borke, *Legal and Business Affairs*

PRODUCED BY POTOMAC GLOBAL MEDIA, LLC

Project Team:
Kevin Mulroy, *Publisher*
Barbara Brownell Grogan, *Editor in Chief*
Carol Farrar Norton, *Art Director*
David Hicks, *Picture Editor*
Jane Sunderland, *Consulting Editor*
Julie Beer, Michelle R. Harris, *Contributing Writers*
Robert Johnston, Brendan McConville, *History Consultants*
Martha Sharma, *Geography Consultant*

PUBLISHED BY THE NATIONAL GEOGRAPHIC SOCIETY

Gary E. Knell, *President and CEO*
John M. Fahey, *Chairman of the Board*
Melina Gerosa Bellows, *Chief Education Officer*
Declan Moore, *Chief Media Officer*
Hector Sierra, *Senior Vice President and General Manager, Book Division*

SENIOR MANAGEMENT TEAM, KIDS PUBLISHING AND MEDIA

Nancy Laties Feresten, *Senior Vice President*
Jennifer Emmett, *Vice President, Editorial Director, Kids Books*
Julie Vosburgh Agnone, *Vice President, Editorial Operations*
Rachel Buchholz, *Editor and Vice President,* NG Kids *magazine*
Michelle Sullivan, *Vice President, Kids Digital*
Eva Absher-Schantz, *Design Director*
Jay Sumner, *Photo Director*
Hannah August, *Marketing Director*
R. Gary Colbert, *Production Director*

DIGITAL

Anne McCormack, *Director*
Laura Goertzel, Sara Zeglin, *Producers*
Emma Rigney, *Creative Producer*
Bianca Bowman, *Assistant Producer*
Natalie Jones, *Senior Product Manager*

MAP KEY

Symbol	Description
•Aspen	Town of under 25,000 residents
•Frankfort	Town of 25,000 to 99,999
• San Jose	City of 100,000 to 999,999
• Chicago	City of 1,000,000 and over
⊛	State capital
⊗	National capital
▫	Point of interest
-282 ft -86 m	Low point with elevation below sea level (in feet and meters)
+ 2,301 ft 701 m	Mountain peak with elevation above sea level
)(4,725 ft 1,440 m	Mountain pass with elevation above sea level
95 1	Interstate / federal highway number
	Interstate or selected other highway
- - - -	Trail
••••••••	Subject state or national boundary
••••••••	Neighboring state or provincial boundary
••••••••	Continental divide

Symbol	Description
	River
- - -	Intermittent river
	National Wild & Scenic River, N.W.&S.R
	Canal
	Lake and dam
	Intermittent lake
	Dry lake
	Swamp
	Glacier
	Area below sea level
	Sand
	Lava
	Indian Reservation, I.R.
	State Park, S.P.
	State Historical Park, S.H.P.
	State Historic Site, S.H.S.
	National Marine Sanctuary, N.M.S.
	National Forest, N.F.

Symbol	Description
	National Grassland, N.G.
	National Wildlife Refuge, N.W.R.
	National Battlefield, N.B.
	National Battlefield Park, N.B.P.
	National Battlefield Site, N.B.S.
	National Historic Site, N.H.S.
	National Historical Area, N.H.A.
	National Historical Park, N.H.P.
	National Lakeshore
	National Military Park, N.M.P.
	National Memorial, NAT. MEM.
	National Monument, NAT. MON.
	National Park, N.P.
	National Parkway
	National Preserve, NAT. PRES.
	National Recreation Area, N.R.A.
	National River
	National Riverway
	National Scenic Area
	National Seashore
	National Volcanic Monument

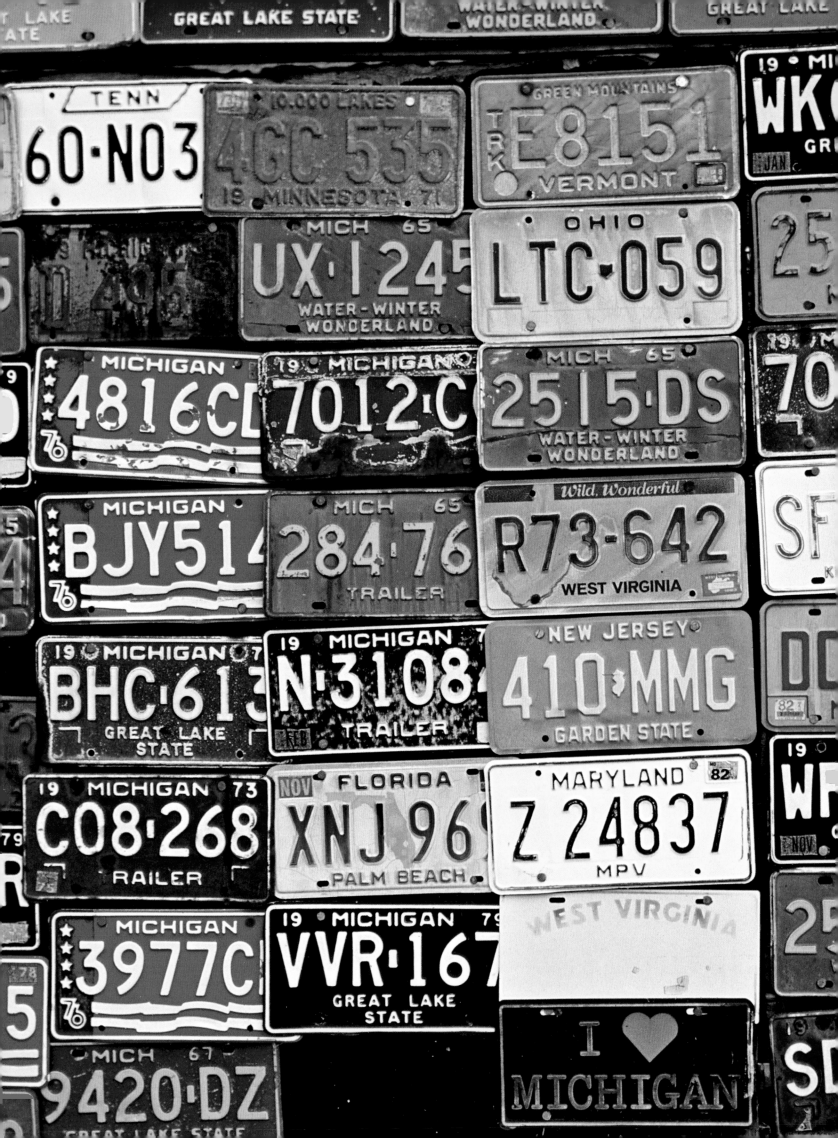